A Commentary on

THE COMPLETE

GREEK TRAGEDIES

Aeschylus

A Commentary on

THE
COMPLETE
GREEK
TRAGEDIES

Aeschylus

James C. Hogan

THE UNIVERSITY OF CHICAGO PRESS

Chicago and London

The University of Chicago Press, Chicago 60637
The University of Chicago Press, Ltd., London

© 1984 by The University of Chicago
All rights reserved. Published 1984
Printed in the United States of America

93 92 91 90 89 88 87 86 85 84   54321

Quotations from *The Complete Greek Tragedies*
© 1942, 1953, 1956 by The University of Chicago.
Quotations from *Agamemnon* © 1947 by Richmond Lattimore.

Library of Congress Cataloging in Publication Data

Hogan, James C.
A commentary on the Complete Greek tragedies—
Aeschylus.

Bibliography: p.
Includes indexes.
1. Aeschylus—History and criticism.   I. Aeschylus.
Plays. English. 1953.   II. Title.
PA3829.H62   1984   882′.01   84-2688
ISBN 0-226-34842-3
ISBN 0-226-34843-1 (pbk.)

James C. Hogan is the Frank T. McClure Professor of
Classics at Allegheny College.

for Norman Rabkin

CONTENTS

ACKNOWLEDGMENTS

I WISH TO THANK several friends and colleagues who have helped me during the writing of this commentary. Provost Andrew Ford, President David Baily Harned, and the Faculty Development Committee of Allegheny College granted sabbatical leave and financial assistance for travel and research. Don Vrabel of Allegheny's Pelletier Library was constantly useful in providing interlibrary loans. Janet Bean was generous of her time in typing the manuscript. John Hanners read the manuscript and asked numerous stimulating questions. Noel Robertson read a draft on the *Oresteia* and saved me from several errors in matters of religion and history. Bill Scott's notes encouraged me to persevere. An anonymous reader for the University of Chicago Press deserves particular credit for prompting me to revise several passages. My colleague and friend Sam Edwards has endured much commentary over coffee. The impulse for this commentary came from a National Endowment for the Humanities seminar directed by Norman Rabkin. I hope he will find this book useful.

THE THEATER OF AESCHYLUS

WE ARE ACCUSTOMED to fragments of the Greek experience, for painting, sculpture, and architecture have frequently survived only in bits and pieces. Much of our understanding of ancient history depends on reconstructing inscriptions and interpreting allusions. Even when a statue or temple survives more or less intact, we have lost the painted decoration the Greeks enjoyed. With Aeschylus we are in some respects more fortunate, though perhaps not even 10 percent of his total work is extant. For the most part the seven surviving tragedies are complete and present intelligible texts. In the broader context of theatrical experience, however, we are also faced with fragments here, for we have the text but not the music, the dance, or the staging. The Greeks were not trying to save their theater or records of it, and, as a result, in the course of several centuries of theater in Athens, there was constant renovation, remodeling, and new construction at the site we know as the Theater of Dionysus. Thus it is much easier to discuss the themes of these plays than to describe their production. This introduction to the plays includes a description of the theatrical context, but the interested reader will want to consult the studies of Pickard-Cambridge, Flickinger, Taplin, Arnott, Baldry, and others who have contributed more detailed and comprehensive accounts.

Most of the surviving plays were first staged at the religious festival of the god Dionysus, called the City Dionysia, in the early spring. In a day of preliminary celebration the statue of the god was taken from his temple in the precinct below the theater and carried into the country, from which he then returned in a triumphant procession. There followed four days of drama: three for tragedies, one for comedy. Each of the three dramatists selected for production offered in a single day three tragedies and a satyr play (a kind of farcical burlesque, often derived from the same legend treated in the tragedies). These plays began in the morning and must have taken the better part of a full day for performance. Because this annual holiday in behalf of the god of the vine and ecstatic religious experience was public and occurred at the beginning of the sailing season, men and women came not only from Athens and its environs but also from other cities of the Greek world. For the Athenians the festival was an occasion for civic pride and display. The image of Dionysus occupied a seat of honor in the front row; public officials and priests of the god had choice seats; and the general public, perhaps seated by tribes, filled the south slope of the Acropolis. Estimates of attendance vary greatly, from five to fifteen thousand, and for a modern parallel we should probably look to outdoor passion plays or to regional historical pageants of the kind that Paul Green has made popular.

Some seats were reserved for priests of Dionysus and for other dignitaries, but the average man wanted to arrive early to avoid having to sit two hundred feet or more up the slope. On three sides the theater encloses the orchestra (which means "a place for dancing"), a flat, unpaved, circular area perhaps sixty or seventy feet in diameter. Here the chorus, probably twelve men in these plays, took its place and remained throughout the play (an exception to this rule occurs in the *Eumenides*, where the chorus of Furies leaves in pursuit of Orestes). As for the area behind the orchestra, all is controversy. Some scholars assume both a stage, perhaps raised only three or four feet, and a stage building for all the plays; yet none of the plays before the *Oresteia* requires the palace or temple that became the typical backdrop, and there is only meager evidence for a raised stage at any time in the fifth century. The usefulness of a stage building is obvious: the actors need a place to change, and a background would probably improve acoustics and define the area of action. A stage building, however, does not require a stage, i.e., a raised platform physically separating the actors from the chorus. The later theater undoubtedly had a stage, and with it came a decreasing role for the chorus; but it is hard to imagine the final lament of the *Persians* played with Xerxes anywhere but in the midst of the Persian nobles who form the chorus, and it is still more difficult to imagine the Furies of the *Eumenides* claiming less than a fully integrated dramatic presence. So while I have used the term "stage" throughout these notes, I hope the reader will think rather of the more awkward "staging area," by which I mean the ground beyond the orchestra where scenes between actors might be played. In such scenes the chorus does not enter the action but serves as a witness of it. If the reader fears some blurring of distinction between actor and chorus, it should be remembered that costume and mask would be a great help. We should think, I believe, of flexibility and dynamic interaction between actors and chorus, not least because the formal elements of poetry, music, and dance insure the geometry and symmetry associated with Archaic Greek style. On either side of the lower flanks of the theater two entrances (the *parodoi*, singular *parodos*) provide access for the spectators and later for the actors and chorus (hence the chorus's entrance song is known as the *parodos*). At least for the *Oresteia*, if not earlier, the stage building also provided for exits and entrances. Looking beyond the theater, the spectator would see, lower down on the hill, the temple and precinct of Dionysus.

What did the Greeks see and hear in their theater? What kind of experience was it? Here we know more about specific matters than about the total effect. The drama is poetic; actors and chorus wear masks and in some cases elaborate costumes (Aeschylus liked grand costumes); the chorus, accompanied by a flute-player, chants its lines in anapestic meter but sings, while dancing, the lyrics. Choral song and dance divide the scenes or episodes, when, for the most part, the actors have retired from the stage. Given the use of masks, full costume, and the size of the theater, we may assume that gesture and speech take a stylized, slower tempo than in our more realistic drama. The religious occasion, the masks and song, the subject matter (almost invariably from familiar legends concerning the families and events of Greek myth), all imply a drama that is both ritualistic and lyric. Analogies to modern opera come to mind, but the differences are equally significant.

If we look more closely at production of the play, we should perhaps begin by noting that the poet, especially in Aeschylus' time, had a very commanding role. He composed the music as well as the text, and both Aeschylus and Sophocles acted in some of their plays. While the state appointed a *choregos*, perhaps closest to our producer, to provide the funds needed for training the chorus, the poet directed his work and so must have come reasonably close to the kind of total control over production that Wagner aspired to at Bayreuth. But he also worked within conventions, some of which seem to us a little odd. For example, we do not know why the Greek theater adopted the mask. Such representations as we have from fifth- and fourth-century vases are fairly realistic; they are not, that is, the grotesque faces familiar from the Japanese Noh. In large theaters, masks, like full costume, serve to enhance the size of the actor and make him more clearly visible to the distant spectators. Yet we are told that Thespis introduced the mask in the sixth century, at the beginnings of Attic tragedy, which means that its origin is rooted in the style and substance of Greek tragedy, not in practical consideration for the spectator. So while the actor might change a mask while offstage (the blinded Oedipus is a familiar example), through most of his part significant gesture was limited to his body and to vocal inflection. Given the size of the theater, nuance in facial expression was hardly feasible in any case, but the mask's rigid formality and implicit assertion of a simple, unitary ethos greatly intensified the sense of ritual. Again, whatever the origins of tragedy, the chorus became in time (but not in the time of Aeschylus) something less than an integral component of the play. Debate over the style and function of the tragic chorus continues, not least of all because we know next to nothing about the dance, the music, and the disposition of the chorus during dialogue. It should be noted here, parenthetically, that most of the single lines and short passages of nonlyric verse assigned in these translations to the chorus were in fact spoken only by the leader of the chorus (the *coryphaeus*). Yet another "rule," the one that limited tragedy to three actors, is unexplained. Aristotle tells us that tragedy originated in the dithyrambic chorus (contests between these choruses of fifty, both for men and boys, continued through the fifth century); that Aeschylus added the second actor; that Sophocles added the third. Since six to eight roles are not uncommon, the individual actor changed masks and costumes to play a series of parts. Because we can find no intrinsic reason for such a limit, the most plausible inference may be that such demanding parts found but few actors competent to perform them. The three-actor "rule," then, which Aeschylus perhaps violated in the *Libation Bearers* (see on *LB* 889), was nothing more than a recognition that exceptional talent was rare and ought to be used to full advantage.

A variety of other practical matters will be discussed in the notes. Some scholars believe, for example, that Aeschylus made use of the crane, a favorite device of Euripides for moving people on and off the stage. For us this machine figures only in the *Prometheus Bound*. More likely to have been present for tableaux is a trolley or low cart known as the *eccyclema*. Having no revolving stage or any practical way of distinguishing interior from exterior scenes, the dramatists required some means of making visible to the audience the grisly business that usually takes place offstage. Twice in the *Oresteia*, in very similar scenes, bodies are produced from out of the stage building. How did they get out? In the most primitive era of Greek drama they were no doubt carried out by scene-shifters. Whenever the dramatists started using stage buildings and backdrops—and Aeschylus could surely have had some sort of frame building if he had wanted one—the central door opened and a low cart or trolley, carrying the tableau, was pushed out onto the stage. The idea is simple, the means practical, and Aeschylus may have used the eccyclema at the beginning of the *Eumenides* to display Orestes surrounded by Furies. As in so many matters of staging, preference for this trolley seems ultimately based on more general assumptions about the shape, rhythm, and realism of Aeschylean theater.

Such assumptions are properly based on the texts, but the texts that have survived, like the external evidence, leave much to be desired by those who would recover Aeschylean practice. In the first place, a tradition of hand-copied manuscripts over a period of two thousand years inevitably produced a raft of errors of omission as well as commission. For example, the first page of the *Libation Bearers* was lost in transmission, so the opening lines must be pieced together, incompletely, from quotations in other ancient texts. Second, so far as we know, until the second half of the fourth century no official authorized text existed; any subsequent production (not, apparently, a very common habit in the fifth century) was likely to be "brought up to date" or otherwise improved, just as Shakespeare's plays have been adapted, improved, and modernized in later productions. Unhappily for Aeschylus, such tampering can seldom be corrected. We may be fairly confident that the last scene of the *Seven* belongs, at least in part, to a staging subsequent to Sophocles' *Antigone*, but we have no quarto or folio text to compare to the extant version. Our texts do come with marginal notes appended (the "scholia," written by "scholiasts," as the ancient commentators are called), but these mostly date from the Alexandrian period or later and are seldom of value for problems of staging.

Given the paucity of authentic contemporary evidence for the Greek theater, the reader may wonder if praise for these tragedies is not another aspect of our infatuation with Hellenism. Skepticism will surely be justified, too, for readers of English translations who must endure scholarly raptures over the poetry of Greek tragedy. It is, I think, legitimate to ask about the merits of these lyrics, and the choral lyrics are the crux of the translator's problem. Our only response can be to describe them, for English and Greek are such disparate languages that in many respects no version will ever be more than the roughest approximation.

Today no one speaks classical Greek, and if, by some time machine, we could, Aeschylus might sound very odd indeed. In contrast to the stress accent of English, Greek had a musical or pitch accent. Yet, for reasons no one seems to understand, from the earliest poetry of Homer until the Byzantine period Greek poetry was regulated by a quantitative metrical scansion in which the rhythm was marked by patterns of long and short syllables. Thus the most common meter of speech in these plays is the iambic trimeter, i.e., three units of the form $\times - \cup -$ (where $-$ is a long syllable, $\cup$ a short, and $\times$ is common, either long or short). Now this pattern may be the closest to ordinary speech, as Aristotle says, and we may compare it to blank verse, but it is not based on normal word accent. The rhythmic interplay between the quantitative syllabic pattern (the meter) and the tonal inflection of the normal Greek (the pitch) must have produced remarkable variety and nuance, particularly in the more complex lyric meters. Several other metrical units may be named, though most of them will be found only rarely, and usually quaintly, in English. The iambic meter mentioned above is found in speech and dialogue. The anapestic (an anapest is ⌣⌣ –, and the anapestic metron is a pair of these feet, with substitution of a spondee, – –, permitted) occurs in transitional passages, i.e., in choral chant as the chorus enters or exits, in the introduction of new characters, and in choral passages where it contrasts with the lyric meters, which are sung. The chanting is said to have been a kind of recitative, somewhere between speech and song. In the commentary I have used the embracing category "lyric" to mark passages that are sung, whether by the chorus or by an actor. The choral lyrics (called the *parodos* and *stasima*) are large responsive systems built up from a variety of shorter units, e.g., the dactylic (– ⌣͡⌣ – ⌣͡⌣), the cretic (– ⌣ –), the choriamb (– ⌣ ⌣ –), and longer units, such as the glyconic (× × – ⌣⌣ – ⌣ –). Such systems may be six or eight lines in length, and each one has a metrically responsive system. These two systems are called the strophe and the antistrophe, literally "turning" and "counterturning," terms derived from the dance movement accompanying the choral song. Occasionally an independent unit, known variously as epode, ephymnion, or mesode, will occur within or concluding such a series. All the choral lyrics were sung and were accompanied by a flute.

While we have little hope of reclaiming in English the song and poetry of Greek tragedy, we can perhaps find its analogue in modern musical dramas in which spoken and musical speech are mingled. This would enable us to perceive at least the elements of artifice, formality, symmetry, and lyric intensity that separate this mode of tragedy from Ibsen, Chekhov, and O'Casey. These characteristics may be seen in the uniform structure of the plays (prologue, choral parodos, three to five scenes, divided by the stasima or choral lyrics, and, finally, the exodos). Though it exhibits great variety from play to play, this simple structure provides a unifying formal experience. Just as the choral lyrics insist on a fundamental symmetry in the responsive strophe/antistrophe structure (aa, bb, cc), yet achieve variety and flexibility through the addition of astrophic elements, so scenes often aim at a quantitative and rhythmic balance seldom sought in later theater. In the great *kommos* (lament) of the *Libation Bearers* almost one hundred fifty lines are organized metrically into two long patterns: aba A cbc A ded A fef; a b c c a b. In this scheme A is an anapestic stanza chanted by the chorus, and each of the lyric triads is sung by Orestes, chorus, and Electra (aba) in turn; the first and third stanzas in each triad are responsive, while the middle element of the first and third triads responds metrically to that of the middle elements of the second and fourth. As often happens, the last section manages a variation, here both in the responsive order and in the distribution of parts (Ch/El/Or/Ch/El/Ch)—as it were, a bit of Dionysiac caprice in a monumental Apolline symmetry.

This enthusiasm for stylized order is found on every hand. Aeschylus' *stichomythia* (lines of dialogue spoken alternately by two characters) and epirrhematic scenes (mixed lyric and spoken passages) may reflect certain primitive and ritualistic origins of tragedy, but they also almost invariably reveal an artful order that curbs and channels the passions of characters bent on murder and violent grief. For the reader of the Greek text this tension between the disorder of passion and the order of poetic form also appears in the arrangement of word and phrase. Because Greek is an inflected language, great economy and precision can be realized:

> for hateful word, hateful word
> (*LB* 309 f.)

> for bloody stroke, stroke bloody
> (*LB* 312)

Interlocking patterns such as these (ABAB, ABBA) are relatively easy in a language in which prefix and suffix determine syntax, and they could have resulted in an affected mannerism had not Aeschylus so often endowed them with multiple meaning and ironic ambiguity. At *LB* 649–51, for example, this sentence occurs:

> Delayed in glory, pensive from
> the murk, Vengeance brings home at last
> a child, to wipe out the stain of blood shed long ago.

The Greek speaks of the child (Orestes) brought home by a Fury (= "Vengeance") to avenge his father's death, and "child" is the first word, "Vengeance" the last, in the sentence. The lines achieve balance as well as a periodic effect, but the separation at either end of the sentence latently expresses an antithesis, for the Fury, or spirit of Vengeance, who brings him home will subsequently attack him for murdering his mother. When Clytaemestra prays

> Zeus, Zeus accomplisher, accomplish these my prayers.
> Let your mind bring these things to pass. It is your will.
>
> (*Ag* 973–74)

she offers a triple use of the Greek stem *tel-* ("accomplish"), with end rhyme (*telei/telein*). The variations in form take their substance from ambiguities, involving the accomplishment of marriage and of sacrifice, and from the ironic identification of Zeus and the lord of the house.

Such a passage invites discussion on moral and theological issues (the role of Zeus, the culpability of Agamemnon), on matters of staging (Has Agamemnon already entered the palace? Is this an aside?), and the relation of language to the dramatic event. Of course the reader who is limited to English is in a much better position to judge dramatic issues than poetic quality, but because of Aeschlyus' obvious love of language and linguistic play I have included notes on rhetoric, image, and metaphor. Again and again Aeschylus reminds us of the magical and musical qualities of speech, and he is not so somber as some critics may imply. He may be playful even at moments of intense dramatic crisis, as when a servant tells Clytaemestra:

> I tell you he is alive and killing the dead

which, because of natural syntactical ambiguity, might also be

> I tell you the dead are killing the living.

And the queen delays her call for an ax to compliment the verbal play:

> Ah, so. You speak in riddles, but I read the rhyme.
>
> (*LB* 886 f.)

Riddles, puns, *double entendre*, and etymological fantasies abound. When the chorus, unable to comprehend the simple statement that Agamemnon will die, responds "peace," Cassandra, the Trojan captive, responds with wordplay at two removes:

> Useless; there is no god of healing in this story.
>
> (*Ag* 1248)

Their "peace" suggests singing the triumphant *paean* (song of victory), on which she puns with *paiōn* (of Apollo, the god of healing). This is a bitter jest for her, whose prophetic gifts have been so notoriously abused by Apollo. Her punning, however, also looks ahead to the large and dubious part Apollo will yet play in the trilogy, when he will draw blood to heal.

Although singling out any particular area of Aeschylus' linguistic art may be risky, his elaborate interweaving of image and metaphor must be given special attention. Already in antiquity he was noted for bold, even outrageous, metaphor, and on occasion we must admit that excess fathers bombast. Yet if we examine a single chain of figurative language, such as the net imagery in the *Oresteia*, we find a poet not only bold but equally succinct and allusive, able not only to weave into that net metaphors from the hunt, from sacrifice, and from abstract genealogies, but also to find dramatic symbols to fulfill on the stage the wealth of his language. Agamemnon has hunted down Troy (*Ag* 127), Zeus throws a net over the city (*Ag* 357 f.), Clytaemestra entangles her husband in circling nets (*Ag* 1382), which Orestes displays after avenging his father:

> And this thing: what shall I call it and be right, in all
> eloquence? Trap for an animal or winding sheet
> for dead man? Or bath curtain? Since it is a net,
> robe you could call it, to entangle a man's feet.
>
> (*LB* 997–1000)

His uncertainty about naming the net depends no more on moral repugnance than on the fact that all these names are true. All echo earlier images and descriptions in the *Agamemnon*, so that the cloth displayed, the bloody symbol of Clytaemestra's treachery, is literally saturated with metaphorical connotation as well as with the king's blood. Later these crimson colors occur in the final scene of the *Eumenides*, where they are incorporated into the imagery and dramatic symbolism of reconciliation.

Just as the net metaphor has a dramatic correlative in Aga-memnon's winding sheets, so the metaphors associated with Justice (*dikē*) eventually are realized in the trial scene in the *Eumenides*. In these two major metaphorical systems in the *Oresteia* we see the poet's habit of weaving and expanding imagery through the plays. This allusive quality endows language with a dynamic intensity that pulls against the slower tempo of decision and event. Sometimes a single cluster of words, strung along in apposition, gathers so many strands of thought and metaphor that we may wonder how even the well-trained Greek listener could comprehend the whole:

> forcing a second sacrifice unholy, untasted,
> working bitterness in the blood
> and faith lost.
>
> (*Ag* 151–53)

Lattimore almost manages the concision of the Greek (eleven words), but after the first line the Aeschylean metaphor expands as no comparably concise English can. "Working bitterness in the blood" translates three words: "bitterness" alludes to the strife that has filled the house with murder since Pelops and Atreus and that now emerges again in the revenge of Clytaemestra; "working" translates a word meaning "carpenter" or "builder," as if the sacrifice, like a good joiner, fits snugly in place the rafters of the bitter quarrel; and "carpenter" also alludes to the house as agent and focus of the action. "In the blood" implies that such sacrifice is innate and thus suggests an inevitable or fated quality in the murderous cycle. "Faith lost" more literally means "fearing no man" (a single compound in the Greek), and grammatically it modifies "sacrifice," though conceptually it is transferred from Clytaemestra, who in the name of revenge will fear no one. Thus the imagery becomes dramatic through devices we rather lamely term "apposition" and "transferred epithet"; but if we look for modern parallels, we shall more readily find them in Rimbaud than in our dramatists.

More than a little of Aeschylus' imagery is derived from the poetic tradition, and the same is true of the proverbs, myths, and moral arguments. Homer and Hesiod are his primary sources, but Solon and the elegiac tradition also contribute much. Harder to assess, but obviously present, is the non-literary element (saws, proverbs, colloquialisms, words and phrases from ritual, etc.). In any case, we should remember that what for us is literature was for Aeschylus' contemporaries an oral tradition that most of the audience knew from informal recitations in cafés and after dinner, from their own singing, and from poetry competitions at festivals. For his audience, then, Aeschylus' allusions to Hesiodic genealogies and didacticism was not heavy learning to challenge their wits but the natural raw material any poet would incorporate into new poems. They expected oblique references to myth, and they were accustomed to think of myth as providing moral examples. Some Greek poets, like Solon, took poetry as a means of teaching, and all were accepted as teachers, even Homer, who did not intend to teach. Unlike ourselves, the Greeks looked to their poets for moral and religious teaching. Since they had no sacred texts, the poets were free to spin out new versions of myth, new variations on old doctrine, and new characters from old stories.

By the fifth century a great body of myth was available to the dramatists in what we may call authorized versions, which often meant the Homeric versions. But even Homer varied his material to suit the situation (the differing characterizations of Odysseus in the *Iliad* and *Odyssey* are a prime example). All the dramatists saw the ironic possibilities they might achieve by manipulating the traditional stories. As with poetic allusion, the Greek audience derived satisfaction from recognizing and comparing similar and dissimilar objects, as, for example, in the complex comparison of the Homeric Agamemnon and his Aeschylean counterpart. The irony that derives from the intersection of texts is most complex and, for us, very difficult to assess, because we have so few texts from archaic literature. Easier to perceive is the irony of ambiguity, which is never more variously set round its victim than in Clytaemestra's welcome to Agamemnon. When she dreams of the wounds he has taken (*Ag* 891 ff.), he hears only a woman "straining at too great length"; but the audience knows well that she has dreamed the dream of seeing those wounds at her sacrifice of the king. Irony always victimizes: in this scene Agamemnon, soon to be slain, is prepared for that role as he turns helplessly in the net of his wife's verbal cunning. The audience already knows these stories, sometimes in several versions, and it has no doubt of the king's fate as he squirms to escape her toils. By the same token, however, the audience also knows that, when Clytaemestra says,

> By my child's Justice driven to fulfilment, by
> her Wrath and Fury, to whom I sacrificed this man,
> (*Ag* 1432 f.)

she must reckon with the Justice, Wrath, and Fury of Orestes' revenge. Now the queen is not unaware that her son is a threat, but she does not know, as the audience does from all versions, that she is just as surely doomed as the man she has murdered. The Greek audience, then, witnesses a new version of the old story. Despite great liberties for invention, the playwright is not so much revealing a story as offering a re-enactment. This is not to say that there is no suspense or surprise in Aeschylean theater. His audience does not know how Agamemnon will be characterized, whether Aegisthus or Clytaemestra will be the protagonist in the revenge, or that Cassandra will figure in the action (or, when she appears, whether she will speak or have a mute part).

We should also note that, unlike Sophocles and Euripides, Aeschylus favored a series of connected plays, the trilogy. The trilogy dramatizes a single story through the course of three plays. It presents a single chronological sequence, a set of characters belonging to the same family, and interrelated themes and motifs. Our only surviving example, the *Oresteia*, dramatizes universal moral, social, and theological problems which, were they compressed into a single play, would run the risk of stultifying turgidity. The size of his canvas gives the poet a dramatically credible opportunity to depict evolving moral law, whereas the brevity of the single tragedy is more naturally suited to depicting character at the moment of crisis. While there is no absence of realistic detail in characterization, it is perhaps not unfair to say that Aeschylus was more interested in ideas and passions than in fidelity to nature. Consequently, his characters, while neither cartoons nor heavy with allegory, walk in the shadow of larger concerns. The *Oresteia* moves from the purely human action of the *Agamem-*

non, where there is much talk of god but no specific presence, to the divinely instructed retribution of Orestes in the *Libation Bearers*, and, finally, to the conflict among Apollo, Athena, and the Furies in the *Eumenides*. For all the talk of justice (*dikē*) in the first play, the murder of a king preempts the focus. Orestes, however, becomes the very battleground for contending claims of justice, though once again much abstract argument is shelved when the supposedly dead son confronts his mother and victim. As if to compensate for some diminution in the human drama, the third play offers a spectacularly hideous chorus of Furies, some rather nasty legalistic sparring, and a finale full of pageantry and festivity. In strictly dramatic terms the pace of the trilogy sometimes slows, and there will be those who wish Orestes' fate were more his own and less a matter of cosmic jurisdiction. As compensation we have in the *Oresteia* a truly monumental dramatic poem, full of intense passion, with a poetic coherence and integrity rarely achieved.

One last word about staging: my talk of "pageantry" in the preceding paragraph is the product of my interpretation of the text. Oliver Taplin, to whose work I am much indebted, has argued forcefully *against* the view of a "spectacular" Aeschylus. Taplin would have us believe that the text itself tells us all we need to know and, further, that the text reveals an austere playwright, much less given to parades, torchlight, a cast of thousands, and other delights of Disney and De Mille than many commentators ancient and modern describe. While trying to present both sides of this issue, I should add that to me the truth lies somewhere between Taplin's archeological purity and the more sensational productions sometimes imagined. Since the poet was active in the production of his play and so could instruct actors, carpenters, dancers, and designers, we should not expect from the poetry indications of every gesture, entrance, inflection, scenic contrivance, and nuance of dramatic vitality. The poet was not burdened, so far as we can tell, with instructing posterity on the proper historical production of his plays. So far as we know, Aeschylus expected only a single production of the *Oresteia*. He died two years after it first played, probably never having seen it a second time himself. All of which is not to say that we should not carefully weigh the evidence of our texts, only that they are the major fragment of our knowledge but not a necessary limit on our understanding.

I imagine that the manner of acting was somewhat stylized but not what we might call declamatory. The old nurse Cilissa of the *Libation Bearers*, like the priestess of the *Eumenides* crawling from her temple in fear, presents for a moment an unexpected slice of life (though the level of poetic diction hardly descends). On the other hand, the credibility of Clytaemestra's claim, that not she but

> the old stark avenger
> of Atreus for his revel of hate
> struck down this man,
> *(Ag* 1501–3)

depends on her and our perception that a titanic daimonic force has worked this sacrifice. So, too, the elements of ritual and religion ought to inspire constantly a sense of the holy and suprahuman. If such is the tone in a general way, then we cannot direct Agamemnon to play his part like a sheep led to the bath by a cunning adulteress. On stage his vanity should be tempered by a sense of the dignity natural to a king. Her malevolence is inspired by a diabolic, even blasphemous, revenge. Her power and passion are fixed on a single goal, from which she never deviates until, forced by circumstance, she appeals to her son for a mother's mercy. Even then she invokes the daimonic Furies, who will avenge her murder. Such instructions as these are based on a general view of the plays and their meaning. I assume that Aeschylus instructed his actors not only in the particulars of each scene but in these larger conceptions of character and event. Every reader will want to reimagine these plays, and it is for this purpose that my notes are offered.

Tragic chorus, invoking a ghost by its grave. Antikenmuseum, Basel. (This and the other pictures of actors and chorus members are from ancient Greek vase paintings.)

Flute player and maenad from a tragic chorus. Antikenmuseum
Staatliche Museen Preussischer Kulturbesitz, Berlin.

Actor in costume, holding his mask.
Martin von Wagner Museum der Universität Würzburg.

(Above) Mask being held by an actor. Martin von Wagner Museum der Universität Würzburg.

(Left) Mask of a young tragic heroine or chorus member. Agora Excavations, American School of Classical Studies at Athens.

Chorus members putting on their costumes. Courtesy, Museum of
Fine Arts, Boston.

The Theater of Dionysus at Athens. Reproduced by permission of
the Greek National Tourist Office.

The theater at Epidaurus. Reproduced by permission of the Greek
National Tourist Office.

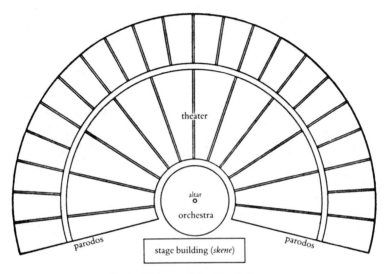

theater

altar
orchestra

parodos

parodos

stage building (*skene*)

Basic features of the Greek theater.

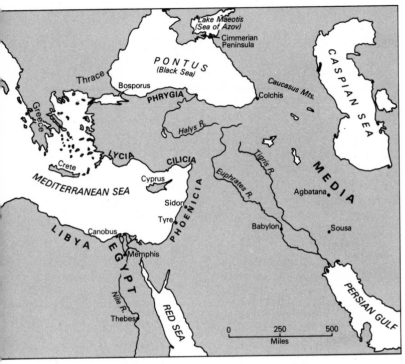

Ancient Greece in relation to Asia Minor and Egypt.

Ancient Greece and the Aegean world.

PONTUS
(Black Sea)

H R A C E

Bosporus

PROPONTIS
(Sea of Marmara)

nos

Hellespont
Tenedos

TROAD

PHRYGIA

Troy
(Ilium)

▲*Mt. Ida*

MYSIA

Lesbos

Chios

LYDIA

▲Sardis

Mt. Tmolus

SEA

os

Ikaros

Samos

Mykonos

elos

CARIA

Naxos

os

Knidos

LYCIA

Rhodes

0   50   100
          Miles

A NOTE ON THE COMMENTARY

THE NOTES PROCEED through the plays line by line. The line numbers in the margins of the translations are those of the Greek text, and occasionally the English version has fewer or more lines. When extra lines occur, I have used the adscripts a, b, c (149a, 149b, 149c). Where fewer than the full number of lines occur, I have numbered from the lower figure. Thus at *Ag* 215–20 only three lines intervene between 215 and 220 and no line 219 will occur in my numeration. The Greek text, however, is not defective here, and the reader who happens across a reference to *Ag* 219 in another book should expect to find the substance of the Greek in Lattimore's translation of lines 217–18.

Although I have tried to take up problems and definitions as they appear, the reader should consult the index when a proper name or technical term appears without explanation. The index also offers more comprehensive surveys of major topics, such as metaphor and staging.

Translating Aeschylus is not an easy business. My respect for these excellent translations has not kept me from offering alternative versions or from discussing at some length the meaning of a word or phrase. Often, of course, there is no English equivalent for a Greek word; in such cases alternative phrasing and synonyms help to establish the connotations of the Greek. I have made extensive use of cross-referencing in order to give the reader a better sense of contextual meaning and significant thematic patterns. If the reader studies one of these notes, he will sometimes find great variety in the way the English translators have rendered the same Greek word. This is inevitable: the English versions must vary to accommodate context, rhythm, and English syntax. My assumption has been, however, that the function of both the translation and commentary is to help us grasp the art of Aeschylus. Consequently, I have not hesitated to draw attention to verbal patterns in the Greek that are not so evident in the English

versions. For example, when the reader finds a note like the
one at *LB* 429 ff., where **all-daring** is said to characterize
Clytaemestra, he should assume that the additional passages
cited contain either this Greek compound or other words in
which the Greek root for "daring" is present in much the
same sense. When I indicate in that note that "all-daring" =
"unashamed" (*Ag* 1237), the equals sign means that the same
or essentially the same Greek word—for example, a verbal
cognate of a noun—appears in Aeschylus' Greek text. Similarly, the word "echoes" in my notes usually means that a
Greek word or phrase is repeated or is virtually the same in
the additional passages noted. When I note that a word or
phrase is "interpretative"—for example, an article or pronoun
must often be used in the English translation where the Greek
lyrics have none—the reader should understand that the English version contains a word or phrase that is not explicitly
present in the Greek text. The absence of articles and pronouns is a common source of ambiguity in the text of Aeschylus, and the reader should not assume that the translation
is deficient just because it chooses one path of meaning rather
than another. Yet another occasion for notes on style derives
from the fact that, as an inflected language, Greek can arrange
words and phrases with greater freedom than English can.
When I note, for example, that **soiled** (*LB* 1017) is the last
word in that line, I refer to the Greek text, where a thematically significant word has been postponed to a final, emphatic
place in the line. The English translator often cannot achieve
such effects simply because of the limitations imposed by English word order. My comments on such matters are not intended as criticisms of the translations but are offered by way
of bringing the reader closer to the tone, rhythm, and emphasis of the Greek.

   The following abbreviations are used throughout: *Ag:
Agamemnon; LB: Libation Bearers; Eum: Eumenides; Pers: Persians; Suppl: Suppliant Maidens; Sev: Seven against Thebes;
PB: Prometheus Bound.* The plays of Sophocles and Euripides
are cited from the Chicago translations.

   In transliterating the Greek alphabet I have distinguished
the omega (long *o*) from the omicron (short *o*) and the eta
from the epsilon by the use of the macron for the long vowels

(thus $\bar{o}$ = omega; o = omicron; $\bar{e}$ = eta; e = epsilon). Upsilon has been transliterated with a y in most cases. The reader will notice different spellings of the same word. In a few cases, such as that of Clytaemestra (also spelled Clytemnestra), this difference originates in Greek usage. Most of them, however, are due to two different systems of spelling Greek proper names. While the Greek system transliterates names directly from the Greek (so Athēnē, Kronos, Phoibos), the Latin system first gives Latin values to the Greek letters and then brings them into English (so Athena, Cronus, Phoebus). The three translators of these plays have not used the same system, but the reader will have few problems if he remembers that such differences merely reflect individual preference. The index of proper names will also help to clarify some variations in spelling.

Most of the materials for this commentary are taken from the work of my predecessors. The bibliography records my particular debts and lists all works specifically cited in the text, but I have not attempted a more comprehensive acknowledgment. Consequently, there are, for example, few references to standard encyclopedias and commentaries on other Greek authors. A few emendations are cited from the critical apparatus of the Oxford editions and not from the original editions. The fragments of Aeschylus are cited from Lloyd-Jones' appendix to volume two of Smyth's Loeb edition. My debt to Italie's *Index Aeschyleus* was constant but is largely unnoted. I trust that modern scholars, realizing the nature of this work, will understand the absence of more detailed bibliographical references. The reader will occasionally find references to notes on projected commentaries on Sophocles and Euripides; in the meantime, I hope the relevance of these cross-references will be self-explanatory.

Because of its popularity and peculiar significance as the sole surviving Greek trilogy, I have treated the *Oresteia* more fully than the other four plays. For the same reasons it is featured at the beginning of my commentary, though the probable historical order of production is *Persians, Seven against Thebes, Suppliant Maidens, Oresteia, Prometheus Bound*. I confess to sharing with several modern scholars doubts about the authenticity of the *Prometheus Bound*.

Agamemnon

THE PART OF A GREEK PLAY that precedes the entrance of the chorus (the *parodos*, which in the *Agamemnon* begins at line 40) is traditionally called the prologue (Aristotle, *Poetics*, chap. 12). Neither the *Persians* nor the *Suppliants* has a prologue, and only in the *Eumenides* and *Prometheus Bound* is it more than a monologue. This watchman will not appear again in the *Agamemnon*, though the actor who plays him will re-appear in the roles of the messenger and Cassandra (cf. the priestess in the *Eumenides*). Unlike some Euripidean pro-logues, all initial scenes in Aeschylus' plays are fully dramatic. While this watchman conveys essential information concern-ing place, time, and his own function (lines 3, 5, and 8), he also takes on some shape as a character: he is tired, a little impatient, intimidated, hopeful, and loyal but cautious. His most important function, however, is to hint at Clytaemes-tra's treachery and thus to establish through metaphor and image the themes and motifs that will pervade the trilogy. He speaks, that is to say, in the dramatic language of the play and not in a personal idiom; though he is a credible character, his primary function is to initiate the action and the conceptual language of the play.

It is often assumed that the watchman is on the roof of the stage building (the *skēnē*). The textual evidence for this stag-ing (line 3) has been disputed. Arnott argues that he might be on the ground before the palace (Arnott, pp. 118 f.), but the language does not forbid use of the roof.

2 The expedition to Troy lasted ten years (line 40). Various expressions for time, timeliness, opportunity, and crisis run through the play. See 40, 196, 727, 785–87, 1356, 1378.

3 Atreidae means "the sons of Atreus." Lines 399–402 in-dicate that Aeschylus thought of the brothers as occupying the same house. Both the Homeric and later tradition gave them separate homes, Agamemnon in Argos (or Mycenae, as in Homer), Menelaus in Sparta.

10 f. Aeschylus likes to highlight themes by means of figures of speech. Here the oxymoron (a figure that uses antithesis and contradiction for emphasis, as in **lady's male**) introduces a frequent motif, i.e., Clytaemestra's usurpation of the male role. See also 348 ff., 479–84, 592, 606–12, 918, 940, 1231 f.

16 For metaphorical language from medicine see the note on 1170. **Mince** refers to incising a wound to effect healing.

19–21 In the Greek, "redemption from distress" = "respite from weariness" (1). Such repetition of a word or phrase, known as ring composition, is a frequent literary phenomenon from Homer to Herodotus. Ring composition articulates parts of a speech or narrative, marks transition, and stresses ideas and form.

One reason for differences among translations stems from Aeschylean ambiguity. For example, in line 20 **from the blackness** is one sense of the adjective, while another and common sense is simply "black," as in Euripides' "blackest night" (*Orestes* 1225). The second sense cancels the **good augury** (no "black flame" would be a "good augury"). Of course the watchman "intends" the meaning in our translation, but any Greek who knew Homer's "murky night" would hear the ominous connotation "indistinct."

Torch races were common in Athenian festivals (see on 281 ff.). The trilogy begins and ends with torches (*Eum* 1005, 1022). The usual connotations of light are evident here and from *Ag* 522 and 602, but its natural association with the hearth (*Ag* 1435) and sacrifice (*Ag* 594–97) allows this imagery to become perverse and treacherous, as at 387 f.

The double spacing between lines 20 and 21 indicates a slight pause before the watchman sees the light. The italicized notes in parentheses are the translator's, which often, as here, also reflect the views of the ancient commentators (the scholiasts).

24 Argos: in the Homeric epics Agamemnon's home is Mycenae, Menelaus' is Sparta. Since Athens had made an alliance with Argos in 462/1, most scholars see topical political references in this change. See further on *Eum* 290, 670–73.

28 Ilium = Troy. Ilus founded the city and gave it his name.

32 In a game similar to our backgammon, three dice were thrown to determine the player's move. The watchman celebrates his master's perfect cast.

35 The **ox on the tongue** is proverbial. Cf. Theognis (late sixth century):

> An ox has stepped on my strong tongue and checks
> my chatter, though I know well enough.
> (815–16; my trans.)

36 The house itself represents more than personification, for the house is identified with the vital interests of the living and the dead. House and family are often interchangeable: both are cursed as a result of the crimes of Tantalus, Pelops, Atreus, and Thyestes. Cf. 1090–93. At *LB* 12 f. Orestes speaks of the house taking a "new wound." On this theme see Jones, pp. 82 ff. For the sentient house, see Euripides' *Andromache* 923 f. and *Hippolytus* 418 f. and 1074 f.

40 The parodos is the entry of the chorus. Twelve men, accompanied by a flutist, recite anapestic lines (40–103) as they take their places for the lyric proper (104 ff.). These anapests were delivered in a chant or recitative. Both the *Persians* and the *Suppliants* begin with these marching anapests, but they are not required, as the subsequent plays in this trilogy show. What follows is the longest choral utterance in extant Greek tragedy.

Contestants is a law term (= "adversary in a trial"). The kings are viewed as one in this joint venture for revenge on Priam, king of Troy, whose son Paris carried off Helen.

44 Kings have their scepters and power from Zeus (*Iliad* 2.100–108, of Agamemnon's inherited scepter), or, in Hesiod's straightforward way, "kings are from Zeus" (*Theogony* 96). Though the Athenians and many other Greek states had long since given up monarchy, their mythical past was aristocratic and monarchic, so that something very like the divine right of kings is an implicit social rule in most plays. Thus as kings the Atreidae claim Zeus's help, but they also can claim that support for another reason: Zeus protects guests and oversees the reciprocal rights of host and guest. Since Paris has violated Menelaus' hospitality by abducting Helen, he has incurred the moral wrath of Zeus (see on line 60).

48 ff. Since the **eagle** is the bird of Zeus (cf. *PB* 1022 and, below, 135) as well as a martial predator, a comparison of the king to **eagles stricken** offers several analogies: they are famed for their **shrill cry**, for their valor, and as birds of omen from Zeus himself. These eagles also have literary antecedents; in the *Odyssey*, Telemachus and Odysseus

> . . . cried shrill in a pulsing voice, even more than the outcry
> of birds, ospreys or vultures with hooked claws, whose children
> were stolen away by the men of the fields, before their wings grew
> strong; such was their pitiful cry and the tears their eyes wept.
>
> (*Odyssey* 16. 216–19)

The word translated as "vultures" in these lines is the same as the one rendered here as "eagle" (in line 49; apparently identified with the more common word for eagle, which appears at 137). Aeschylus seems to have borrowed the motif of the **young perished** from Homer; but whereas Homer keeps distinct the two men and the birds of the simile, Aeschylus fuses them. When the **Fury** (59) is introduced, we realize that the distinction has collapsed, i.e., the formal comparison of the simile ("as eagles") has come round to a new view of the kings, who, first compared to suffering birds, have now become agents of vengeance for the birds and for themselves. Much of Aeschylean imagery derives its dynamics from this kind of interpenetration.

56 Neither **Apollo** nor **Pan**, god of the mountains and wild animals, seems to have any place in the moral argument, and the disjunctive **or** dissipates the force of the image a little, although the manner is natural to Greek poetry (cf. "ospreys or vultures" in the Homeric simile cited in the note to 49). Clinton suggests that the audience would think of shrines of Apollo and Pan on the northwest of the Acropolis, but that is the wrong slope for an actor's gesture, even if a shrine to Apollo was there.

59 **Fury** (*Erinys*)—here singular but often plural—is the spirit of vengeance regularly associated with bloodguilt (so Cassandra at 1190, the chorus at *LB* 650 f.). The chorus of the *Eumenides* is composed of Furies. They are also mentioned in the *Agememnon* at 463, 645, 749 ("a vengeance"), 991, 1119 ("demon"), 1190, 1581. According to Aeschylus they are chil-

dren of Night (*Eum* 321), whereas Hesiod says they sprang
from the blood of the mutilated Uranus, who had been cas-
trated by his son Cronus (*Theogony* 178–85). Hesiod's genealogy suits their function, the punishment of those who have
slain kin (cf. *LB* 276 ff.). The present passage, like 749, where
Helen is a Fury ("a vengeance"), metaphorically extends their
function to righteous retribution generally, as in *Antigone*
1076–77.

60 "Zeus Protector of Strangers" (*Odyssey* 14. 283–84) is
the **great guest god**; he is "hospitable" (748), god "of the
guests" (362), who looks after "the guest's right" (402). Yet
drives (57 and 60) may be a little strong if it implies in English that Zeus forces or commands the expedition (note the
chorus's criticism in **promiscuous**, 62). "Sends" is also a possible translation, and the point becomes critical for our understanding of Agamemnon, at least as the chorus sees him, if
with Peradotto (*Phoenix* 23, p. 251) we observe that, while
Zeus sends them (we might say the god "gives them his blessing"), he does not command them to pursue Paris (= **Alexander**: Homer also uses both names for the son of Priam).
Agamemnon, as reported by the chorus (205–16), would
seem to have convinced himself that he must make the expedition. But Greek moral thought did not see man used by the
gods as a scourge to punish other men; the gods were able and
willing to punish if they saw fit to do so (cf. the prologues to
Hippolytus and *Bacchae*). So we should not confuse, as Agamemnon may have, the righteousness of the cause with the
necessity of the expedition. For example, according to legend,
the Greeks who went to Troy were bound by an oath, made at
the time of the courting of Helen, to "defend the favoured
bridegroom against any wrong that might be done him in respect of his marriage" (Apollodorus, *The Library* 3. 10. 9). In
the *Iliad* Hera and Athene do everything they can to further
the Greek cause; but neither they nor Zeus, who often seems
more favorably disposed to the Trojans, has required the
Greeks to seek vengeance.

62 Cf. 448 and 800–804 for aspersions on Helen and the
expedition; other allusions to Helen occur at 225, 823, 1455 ff.
Before her marriage to Menelaus, Helen had been carried off
by Theseus (Apollodorus 3. 10. 7); later she was the woman

of Paris and, after his death, of Deiphobus, his brother. The chorus is loyal but still critical of the man and the cause.

66 Homer refers to the Greeks as **Danaans**, Argives, and Achaeans (184); the Danaans take their name from Danaus, king of Argos (see *Suppliants* 11).

67 f. This tag apparently means something like "that's the way things are." The next sentence (68) means "this business moves toward its necessary end" (in **end** we have the first of many appearances of the Greek *tel*-stem; see on 972). The first sentence seems colloquial, like Oedipus' "Well, let my fate go where it will" (*Oedipus the King* 1458), and it characterizes the chorus as evasive, perhaps afraid to speak; the second sentence is sententious, portentous but noncommittal, and also musical, since Aeschylus repeats words and varies their form and meaning in much the same way as a composer repeats, elaborates, and extends a note or phrase.

70 This line is probably an intrusive gloss. Greek sacrifices were of two classes: things burned, e.g., animal sacrifice, and things unburned, e.g., wine or cakes. Greek **tears** did not function as atonement. The cryptic Greek phrasing (in which neither the subject nor **the gods'** is expressed) first attracted a scholiast's marginal note or gloss, and this explanatory note was later incorporated in the text by a scribe who was making a new copy of the manuscript.

72–82 The chorus describes itself as too old to have joined the army, in need of crutches (**on staves**), very like a baby in that neither the extremely aged man nor the child can manage perfect warcraft (78). Aeschylean metaphor ranges from abstract, personifying figures of thought to the most concrete sorts of metonymy (the substitution of one name for another, e.g., of concrete for abstract or cause for effect). Here **young vigor that urges** translates Greek words meaning "bone marrow" that "leaps"; with **leaf withered** compare the imagery at 966 f. and *Pers* 617 f.

82 Another translation of this line is "a dream, an ephemeral thing, that wanders." See the note to Sophocles' *Ajax* 126 for other variations on this figure. Cf. Euripides' *Heracles* 108 ff. for a similar description of old men (especially the imagery of 111 f.). Other imagery from dreaming occurs in the *Agamemnon* at 420–26, 491, 891–94, 983, 1218.

83 Whether Clytaemestra is in fact onstage now, or indeed before 258, remains disputed. That the chorus addresses her does not, to judge from Greek dramatic practice, indicate that she is necessarily present (cf. *Ajax* 134 ff.), nor does her silence prove that she is not present (cf. Danaus' silence at the beginning of the *Suppliants* and Electra's wait through the parodos of the *LB*). Taplin argues against her presence: her silence is inexplicable, and such a protracted silence would be without parallel in extant tragedy. Others have found her silent presence manipulative. (The loss of so much Greek tragedy makes argument from practice and parallels of uncertain value.)

The possibilities are these: (1) she is offstage now and until 258; (2) onstage now, she departs and returns at 258 (and still more silent entrances and exits may be added); (3) she is onstage now and remains present throughout the song.

To some extent a decision on this problem depends on your view of the style of the trilogy. If Clytaemestra is onstage during all or part of this choral song, she must necessarily distract us from the chorus, and not only from its song and dance but also from the significance of its views. Commentators who think this song essential for defining the tone and thematic lines of the play leave the chorus to dominate the stage; those who think that the actors, and particularly the interaction of chorus and actor (Clytaemestra), are primary are inclined to put the queen onstage, ignoring the chorus, tending to small sacrifices in preparation of one great sacrifice, tacitly manipulating the chorus and the action, as she will later verbally manipulate chorus and king.

89 f. The **high and deep spirits** are the gods above and below the earth (Olympian and chthonic); cf. *Suppl* 22. Because **to them of the sky** (90) appears redundant, it has been emended to "to them of the house (door)."

94 Simple means "guileless," "without duplicity," which is hardly near the mark so far as Clytaemestra's purpose is concerned.

99–103 For **healer** see on 1248. **Hope** is a common motif; cf. 262, 266, 505, *LB* 194.

104 Here the lyric proper begins. What follows was sung and danced, a fact that surely did not make these allusive, and

elusive, lyrics any more intelligible. The great thing to remember for the spirit of the piece is that it is operatic, com-
bining music, dance, and lyric poetry into a single mood that
is serious, to some extent mysterious (as memory attempts to
recall the past), and altogether stylized and traditional. Although a kind of narrative is present, as well as an occasional
sententious patch, the prime impulse is **singing magic**, the
power of incantation. As Hesiod says of the Muses,

> they breathed voice into me
> and power to sing the story of things
> of the future, and things past.
> (*Theogony* 31–32; trans. Lattimore)

The **wonder at the wayside** is the omen at Aulis, the **wild
bird portent** (108) described at 114 ff. **Magic** = "persuasion"
at 86 (see on 385).

    113 Teucrus (also spelled Teucer) was a legendary king of
Troy.

    114 The eagle is the **king of birds** and the bird of Zeus
(48 ff.). What was a simile in the anapests (49 ff.) is transformed into an omen (a sign of divine favor) in the lyric.
A pair appears on the right—a favorable sign—then seizes
and tears apart a pregnant hare. For the equation of 114 cf.
Orestes' description of his "eagle-father" at *LB* 247.

    121 This refrain (cf. 138 and 159) is taken from the ritual of
mourning.

    122 The **seer** Calchas (156; see *Iliad* 1. 69 ff.) reads the
omens for Homer's Achaeans. He recognizes (**knew**) in the
twin eagles a correspondence to the two kings, who may thus
be said to feed on the hares. This seems the sense of an ambiguous passage. Unexplained is **to the hearts divided**, a difficult expression because it would apparently indicate a division
in will or courage between Agamemnon and Menelaus. Such
a division is neither germane here nor so pronounced in the
tradition as to make it necessary.

    Lines 126–55 are in direct speech, the report of Calchas,
but note the recurrence of the refrain (which belongs to the
chorus) and the ambiguity about who is speaking lines 140–
45 (see the note to 144).

    127 With **shall stalk** (or "takes"), an oracular vision of the hunt becomes vividly present to the seer. Cf. the metaphors from hunting at 358 ff., 695, and 1184–85.

129 Greek has a number of words for **Fate** or destiny. One of the most common is *moira*, which in its root sense denotes "lot" or "portion." So the Latin *fate* is misleading if we take it always of fatal consequences or see in it a mechanistic notion of the universe that denies man his free will. Cf. *Ag* 1026 ("fate . . . against fate"); *Eum* 172 ("distributions"), 476 ("work," i.e., their assigned task); *Sev* 948 ("share"); and see Nilsson, *History of Greek Religion*, pp. 167 ff.

131–38 A controversial passage, in part because the allusive style of the chorus does not tell as much about **Artemis'** motive (why is she angered?) as we would like to know, in part because a number of interpretations seem plausible while none is absolutely compelling. As for her **anger** (Greek *phthonos*; see the note on "malice," 904), two views contend: she hates the **feasting** simply because, as goddess of wild animals (140–44 describe her), she pities the innocent hare and its young; on the other hand, she hates what the feasting (the omen) portends, i.e., the destruction of Troy and all the innocent lives it holds. The first view accepts, and stops with, a literal interpretation that identifies Artemis simply and exclusively with her traditional care for wild animals; the second view sees her anger and demand for a **second sacrifice** (151) in a larger context of justice and morality. The innocent hare and her young, on the second view, symbolize the innocents of Troy; the feasting of the eagles portends the savage and unnecessary brutality of Agamemnon's revenge, which will exceed the proper limits of justice. So Agamemnon will be forced by Artemis to sacrifice his daughter, Iphigeneia, at Aulis, to make a decision and take an action that will irrevocably signify his guilt and, of course, insure his own punishment in the end. If he will go so far to punish Paris, then he must accept the murder of his daughter as a price for success—a price that in the course of destiny must come back on him.

In such symbolism a harsh equity is exacted from the king. The theologically more primitive view, that Artemis acts solely out of indignation at the slaughter of innocent wild things, should also have its turn. Like many Greek divinities,

Artemis enjoys autonomy in her own cultural sphere. Zeus
sends his eagles for a sign that he sanctions the expedition, but
when that sign happens to anger another divinity (Artemis),
Zeus does nothing to protect Agamemnon. Yet the king must
respond to Artemis' demands. As it turns out, Agamemnon
must sacrifice his daughter if he would appease the goddess.
So he is caught, as the Greeks often are, between the powerful
claims of opposed divinities. In the *Libation Bearers* (269 ff.)
Orestes is caught between Apollo's instruction to kill his
mother, and thereby avenge his father's death, and the certain
vengeance of his mother's Furies if he does murder her. It is an
old story, more humorously treated in the *Odyssey*, where
Odysseus complains to Athene that she never helped him
after his departure from Troy. The goddess offers this excuse:

> But, you see, I did not want to fight with my father's
> brother, Poseidon, who was holding a grudge against you
> in his heart, and because you blinded his dear son, hated
> you.
>
> (*Odyssey* 13. 341–43)

Euripides, thirty years later, utilizes yet another conflict between divinities in the *Hippolytus*.

Finally, we know from a summary of the lost epic *Cypria*
that Aeschylus chose to ignore a tradition that made Agamemnon (and Atreus) responsible for Artemis' wrath. Proclus reports that in the *Cypria* Agamemnon went hunting, shot a
deer, and boasted that not even Artemis shot so well. The angered goddess checked the fleet by sending storms. Calchas
explained that the goddess demanded the sacrifice of Iphigeneia, to which Agamemnon agreed. When Iphigeneia was
placed on the altar, the goddess snatched her away and substituted a deer. This version is reported by Sophocles (*Electra*
564–77); see also the note to 248, below, and cf. the account in
Apollodorus, *Epitome* 3. 21–22.

132 f. The army is likened to the bit for a horse (**huge
iron . . . curb**). **From inward** seems to translate a participle
that means "from the army" and modifies **iron**, so that, as if
to answer the riddle posed by the two preceding lines, we
learn that the bit is (metaphorically) the army. **Darken upon**
means "to cast a cloud over." To paraphrase: "May no divine

anger express itself in some action of the army that might darken its triumph over Troy."

144 Grant meaning is very uncertain. Lattimore and some editors emend the verb and assume that we have a prayer by Calchas. On this view the translation means "grant that these signs may be fulfilled, even though they presage both good and ill." The manuscripts, however, give us a verb meaning "ask" or "pray," and some editors assume the meaning to be "Artemis prays (to Zeus) that these signs may be fulfilled." **You** (140) represents the translator's interpretation and should not influence the analysis.

146 ff. Apollo is a god of medicine and healing (see on *Suppl* 260 ff.) and brother of Artemis. As the chorus represents the matter, Calchas anticipates that Artemis will send **cross winds** to prevent sailing until the Greeks pay a **second sacrifice unholy**, i.e., the sacrifice of Iphigeneia. Aeschylus uses the Homeric Calchas,

> who guided into the land of Ilion the ships of the Achaians through that seercraft of his own that Phoibos Apollo gave him.
>
> (*Iliad* 1. 71–72)

151–55 He calls it a **second sacrifice** because the eagles are said to be sacrificing (= "eating," 136) the hare and her young. For sacrificing see 231 ff., 1056 ff., 1235 (note), 1433. **Untasted** because it is a human sacrifice (this word, like line 137, makes us think of the human flesh fed by Atreus to Thyestes; see 1504, 1600); **in the blood** refers to the house of Atreus and the curse hanging over it; **faith lost** is literally "fearing no man" and would naturally refer to Clytaemestra, from whom the sense of the words is transferred to the sacrifice of her daughter, which will in turn cause the queen herself to "fear no man." What Aeschylus does in this sentence and the next is to string out a series of nouns and adjectives, all in the same case, with almost no grammatical subordination. The effect is that of a linear collage that grows in complexity and suggestiveness as it accumulates. So 154 f. might be: "it remains, fearful, returning, the household steward guileful, remembering anger child-avenging." Perhaps **anger** is personified; cf. 1433 and *LB* 292 ("wrath").

158 f. This time the refrain (159) is neatly integrated as a cap to the ambiguous auguries of Calchas.

160 ff. The following passage, traditionally known as the hymn to Zeus, presents a number of particular and general problems. With 160 a new lyric meter and a new subject (the power and wisdom of Zeus) begin, but after three sections of the lyric (160–66; 167–75; 176–83) the second antistrophe returns to the narrative of events at Aulis, even though the new lyric meter continues. Thus the beginning of the section is marked by an abrupt turn in meter and thought, but the transition back to events at Aulis (184) is not marked by a similar metrical change.

Coherence is the chief problem here. Do 160 ff. have any immediate and particular relevance to the preceding narration? Why does the chorus begin as if to make a prayer, only to proceed descriptively? Do 176–83 apply to a particular person (Agamemnon? Paris?), or has the chorus strayed too far from the thread of the narrative for any precise application? If the chorus continues to think of events at Aulis, why is its theological moralizing phrased so elliptically, so vaguely?

Line 160 is apparently the beginning of a prayer, but we never get the vocative. **Whatever he may be**: in prayers, naming the god accurately, according to attribute and function, is necessary for procuring attention and aid. Cf. "I will protect him, because he knows my name" (Psalm 91 : 14). See on *Sev* 399 ff. and *LB* 948.

163–66 Lattimore's English is easier than the Greek, where, after **I cannot find a way**, the syntax fails because no object is supplied for the verb (**to cast this dead weight . . . out** represents a conditional clause: "if one must cast out"). The question turns in part on the meaning of the verb here rendered **cannot find a way,** in part on what object we should supply with the verb.

Peter Smith has recently argued that the chorus is still thinking of the events at Aulis, particularly of the sacrifice of Iphigeneia, but so horrible is that murder that they cannot understand how and why it came about. In Smith's view the chorus suppresses the mention of the sacrifice, with the latent thought being something like "I can find no means of explaining this horror save by reference to Zeus." **Dead weight of igno-**

rance, on Smith's view, may refer both to the moral horror felt at the murder of Iphigeneia and to their inability to find a sufficient cause for it, save by reference to Zeus. Smith (p. 16) finds this assignment of causality "a morally adequate cause: Zeus' determination that Paris and Troy be made to suffer for their offense, whatever the costs entailed by such Justice."

In Lattimore's version Zeus is the source of comfort and solace, especially for our inability to comprehend events such as that at Aulis. This view of the passage seems a reasonable middle way between Smith's interpretation and the notion of Fraenkel (and others) that **this dead weight** "is the burden of the folly which induces men to believe that Zeus is not the almighty ruler" (Fraenkel, 2:103).

167–72 The allusions in 167 and 171 are, respectively, to Uranus and Cronus, grandfather and father of Zeus, rulers prior to the reign of Zeus. The metaphor in **master** (172) is from the three falls in wrestling, as at *LB* 339 and *Eum* 589. Hesiod's *Theogony* tells of the succession in rule of these three and emphasizes the violence of Uranus and Cronus, the strength and wisdom of Zeus.

176–78 This is Aeschylus' variation on a proverb that can be illustrated from Homer, Hesiod, and Herodotus. In the other versions the proverb does not praise learning that is to be purchased only from experience. For example, in *Iliad* 17. 32 Menelaus tells Euphorbus (a Trojan who wants a fight):

> So I think I can break your strength as well, if you only
> stand against me. No, but I myself tell you to get back
> into the multitude, not stand to face me, before you
> take some harm. Once a thing has been done, the fool sees it.
> (*Iliad* 17. 29–32)

The last line seems to mean "if you have to learn from experience, you will regret it."

A similar moral is drawn by Hesiod, who, after haranguing his brother to be just and avoid *hybris*, concludes:

> For Justice [*dikē*]
> wins over violence [*hybris*]
> as they come out in the end. The fool knows
> after he's suffered.
> (*Works and Days* 217–18; trans. Lattimore)

In both passages the word for "fool" is the same; it denotes childish inexperience, and the implication is that a man of any sense does not need suffering ("experience" also seems a good translation) to learn what to do and what to avoid. Herodotus (1. 207) has Croesus vary the proverb thus: "My suffering, though hard, has become a source of understanding.

Consequently, unless Aeschylus has inverted the usual meaning of the proverb, it seems advisable to modify the translation in the direction of Denniston and Page's "[Zeus] who set men on the path to understanding, who laid down the law, 'learning through suffering,' to hold good." This version does no violence to the sense of the Greek, and it eliminates the positive connotations of Lattimore's English (especially the **wisdom . . . alone**), for which the context gives no specific justification. Of course, Aeschylus might have intended to invert, and so transform, the meaning of the proverb; but if he did, we might expect to be able to find, in the play or in the trilogy, some application of his new formulation. Yet Agamemnon certainly learns nothing, Clytaemestra goes down swinging, and Orestes' learning is in the first place too much a matter of divine dictation and, in the second, too little the focus of action in the *Eumenides*. In later tragedy, e.g., Creon in the *Antigone*, the motif of learning-too-late does come into play, but, generally speaking, wisdom from suffering seems more honored in word than in action; the practical Greek, unlike the moralizing Christian, would rather avoid the suffering.

It is usually assumed that the chorus has a specific person in mind, someone who has learned, or will learn, through suffering. For this role, Agamemnon (Page and Lloyd-Jones), the chorus (Lebeck, *Oresteia*, pp. 25–26), and Paris (Peter Smith) have all been nominated. If Aeschylus had a specific "learner" in mind, he has proved to be too cryptic for a modern consensus. Other passages relevant to this motif: *Ag* 250 f., 1425, *Eum* 521; Sophocles, *Oedipus at Colonus* 6 f.

179–83 Again, we may wonder if a specific application is intended or, perhaps, a multiple application. The "our" and "we" are interpretative. Another version:

> Still there drips in place of sleep before the heart
> labor painful with memory. Even to the unwilling

> temperance comes.
> From the gods who sit at the helm
> grace comes somehow violent.

This passage is not easier for its use of contradiction and oxy-moron: temperance is an intellectual virtue and an odd visitor to the unwilling; violent grace, as if we had a "brutal favor," does not clarify. Perhaps the compression of this last phrase represents "A favor to us from the gods comes down violently on Paris" (the grace or favor to one party consists of the violent treatment of an enemy). On the other hand, the transition to Agamemnon in the following antistrophe implies that he is the nearer subject.

184 ff. The **elder king** (cf. 205) is Agamemnon, who does not fault (**no more strict**) the prophecy. Seers like Calchas were not thought infallible; the audience would remember how, in book 1 of the *Iliad*, Agamemnon rails against Calchas because the seer's interpretation will cost him his prize. Cf. 206.

186 Turned with the crosswinds of fortune might also be translated "breathes together with the blasts of fortune." Like the image at 218, this line implies a physiological harmony uniting the man and the events; unlike 218, there is as yet no suggestion of moral choice. Cf. *Sev* 707 (note to 705–9b), *LB* 775.

189 Aulis is on the coast of Boeotia, three or four miles south of **Chalcis** on the island of Euboea. The channel is narrow enough for a bridge, and the tide is extraordinarily strong. Aulis is the traditional gathering point for the expedition against Troy.

191 The winds are from the northeast; **Strymon** is in Thrace.

198 The **bitter wind** is a winter storm, a frequent image in the play: lines 5, 563, 627, 634, 649, 656, 969; cf. *LB* 202–3.

200 Another medicine: the chorus will not speak directly of the sacrifice of Iphigeneia, already alluded to at 151 ff. In several Greek myths the sacrifice of a child is required to appease an angry deity: Andromeda (in the story of Perseus) is offered to a sea monster (Apollodorus 2. 4. 3), as is Hesione, daughter of Laomedon (Apollodorus 2. 5. 9); in both cases the girls are victims of parental vice, and in both cases oracles declare that the land will be delivered from pestilence if the child is sacrificed. In Euripides' *Phoenician Women* Creon's son, Menoeceus, must be sacrificed:

> and so give libation blood
> for Cadmus' crime, appeasing Ares' wrath
> who now takes vengeance for his dragon's death.
> (933–35)

The chorus of Euripides' *Heracles* calls Procne's murder of her son Itys a "sacrifice to the Muses" (1023). Thus the murder of children (e.g., in the *Heracles* and *Medea*) is a related motif (for Agamemnon, Iphigeneia is a sacrifice; for Clytaemestra, she is a victim of murder).

206 Of the several Greek words for **fate**, *kēr* is perhaps the least mechanical and the most personalized. In vase paintings the *kēres* (plural) are represented as birds with human heads; they are daimonic death-spirits. Everyone has a *kēr* from birth (*Iliad* 23. 78 f.), and on the battlefield they are omnipresent (*Iliad* 12. 326 f.). When Zeus weighs the fates of Hector and Achilles (*Iliad* 22. 209 ff.), he puts two *kēres* ("portions of death") onto the scales. Since in the present passage fate = *kēr* and **angry** = "heavy," Aeschylus modifies the Homeric figure: he keeps the personalized death-spirit and transforms the scales into the image of counterpoised weights, as if Agamemnon possessed a double *kēr*, each of which pulls him down fatally. Elsewhere Aeschylus equates the *kēr* with the Sphinx (*Sev* 778) and with the Fury (*Sev* 1055), both agents of vengeance. More imagery involving scales at 250, 573, and 706; see also on *Pers* 346. For the motif of the heavy daimon see *Eum* 712 and the note on *Eum* 372–76.

209 This **stain** is the pollution that marks any murderer of kin; it is "the guilt stained upon him" that Clytaemestra mentions at 1420. The word and its cognates are most frequent in the *Eumenides*, where "the blot of matricide" (*Eum* 281) on Orestes is finally purged.

213 Lose my faith of battle means "fail my comrades-in-arms."

216 The word for **right** (Greek *themis*) denotes approval in light of religious custom and belief; it is, at best, self-deceptive, as the following wish indicates. **May all be well yet:** cf. the refrain at 121, 138, and 159.

217 The Greek makes this active: "when he put on the yoke of necessity," which more bluntly places the decision and its consequences on Agamemnon's choice, however impossible that choice may have appeared to him. Cf. 1071. For "yoking" see *Pers* 49a; for **necessity** see *PB* 514. The yoke of necessity is a commonplace: Pindar, *Second Pythian* 93; Sophocles, *Philoctetes* 1025 ("by constraint"); Euripides, *Orestes* 1330.

As for the guilt of Agamemnon, scholars have divided between two views: (1) Agamemnon is the victim of the curse on the house of Atreus and is himself essentially innocent; (2) Agamemnon of his own free will sacrifices his daughter and thus drives Clytaemestra to her revenge. Though these views are sometimes argued dogmatically, as if they were mutually exclusive, it seems probable that Aeschylus saw both the curse (which a modern poet might see as a genetic factor, as, e.g., in Oswald Alving in Ibsen's *Ghosts*) and personal responsibility at work in Agamemnon's fate. The spirits of vengeance are ingrown (1190), yet Orestes is finally able to escape them, and his absolution may be attributed not simply to divine intervention but also to a finer moral sensibility than his father possessed.

218 For **the breath** see 186 (note), and cf. the imagery at *Sev* 706 ff. (note).

225–26 Cf. 62. The focus is very tight, since **first offering** denotes the sacrifice preliminary to marriage (the same word occurs at 65 in "in the onset"); so we have daughter (marriage vows violated), whore (vows betrayed), and marriage ritual in three lines. The same Greek stem (*tel-*), with more ambiguous allusions to marriage, is discussed at 972. For a radically different treatment of Iphigeneia as bride see Euripides' *Iphigeneia in Aulis* 87 ff.

235–37 They stifle her cries to prevent a curse.

238 The shedding of her **saffron mantle** alludes to the ritual in the Attic cult at Brauron, where little girls, five to ten years old, "played the bear" in a sacrificial ritual in which Artemis appeared as a bear. As the culmination of the ritual the children shed their robes and danced for the goddess. In the fifth century a goat was sacrificed to the goddess, but the ceremony seems likely to have commemorated a time when a girl was sacrificed. See Parke, *Festivals of the Athenians*, pp. 139 f.

242 The Greek verb used here suggests she "stood out," was "clearly distinguished," and Fraenkel observes (2:139): "This passage of the *Agamemnon* is our earliest evidence for the clear definition of the individual figures being regarded as an essential quality of painting."

245–47 Iphigeneia tries to call the individual chieftains by name; she had known them from her father's banquets, where she sang. **Third cup** (247) refers to the after-dinner custom of pouring drink offerings (libations) to a trinity of gods and singing hymns. There is an allusion here to "Zeus the Savior," "the god to whom the third libation was offered at the close of the feast, and he [Zeus] was regarded at this moment as the god who dispensed all good things, as the 'good daimon' of the life of man" (Farnell, *Cults*, 1:61). Zeus the Savior appears again in line 1386 (note); cf. *LB* 1072 f. and *Eum* 759 f.

248 They will not mention the actual slaughter, but one implication of line 249 is surely that the sacrifice appeased the goddess, so that the fleet was freed from the unfavorable winds.

The version reported from the *Cypria* (see note on 131–38), which Aeschylus ignored, focuses on *hybris* punished: Agamemnon vainly boasts and, like Niobe and many another infatuated victim, pays for his arrogance. (On *hybris* see the note to 763–71.) The version reported in our chorus (lines 133–37) shifts the goddess's anger to the omen and thereby renders Agamemnon's culpability more ambiguous. In his *Iphigeneia in Tauris* (19 ff.) Euripides offers yet another motive for the sacrifice when Calchas (as reported in the prologue by Iphigeneia) explains the storm by telling the king

> there can be no way
> Of setting your ships free, till the offering
> You promised Artemis is given Her.
> You had vowed to render Her in sacrifice
> The loveliest thing each year should bear. You have owed
> Long since the loveliness which Clytemnestra
> Had borne to you, your daughter, Iphigeneia.

Given these variants, we can see that Aeschylus deflected his tale from the simpler, more direct motifs of folktale and legend to an oblique account, rendered all the more problematic by the impressionistic style of this lyric.

250 Justice is *dikē*. The translations of this very common word vary according to context, but Justice (384) and Right (*LB* 244 and 949) are the two most frequent renderings; see on *LB* 935 f. Virtually every character in the trilogy invokes *dikē* at one time or another: Agamemnon (815), Clytaemestra (911 and 1432), Aegisthus (1611), Electra (*LB* 244), Orestes (*LB* 497, 988–90), the Furies (*Eum* 490 ff.), Apollo (*Eum* 615–19), and Athene (*Eum* 891). It is not a constitutional principle but rather an order of things proper to nature and society, as at 259, 761, and 772 ff. (Righteousness). *Dikē*, the daughter of Zeus (*LB* 948 f., *Sev* 663), is a principle of balance and proportion, the image for which is the scales of Zeus (**moves** = "inclines"; see on 206 and cf. *Suppl* 402–6). As early as the Homeric *Hymn to Hermes* we find that, after a dispute, Apollo and Hermes approach Olympus and their father Zeus,

> for there for both of them the scales of *dikē* were placed.
> (line 324)

This traditional association of justice with Zeus (see particularly *Eum* 614 ff.) provides the moral and theological backbone for many of the lyric passages and, in a general way, for the largest thematic line of the trilogy. But apart from this abstract meaning of justice and how it is to be achieved, and apart, too, from its relation to vendetta and retribution and its value when Olympian and chthonic powers clash, the word *dikē* has more specific value at the forensic level; for its legal meanings ("case," "trial," "judgment," and "action" are a few) lend the play a variety of familiar, concrete extensions into the everyday life of the fifth-century Athenian. *Dikē* as "justice" is traditional, literary, easily allied to myth; *dikē* as "trial" is immediate, personal, historically present. For this second type of language see *Ag* 40 (note), 813–18. For a discussion of *dikē*, see Nilsson, *Greek Piety*, pp. 35 ff.; Podlecki, *Political Background*, pp. 63–80; Lloyd-Jones, *Justice of Zeus*, pp. 59–61.

In its language the present passage clearly recalls 176–78. Here we much more naturally think of Agamemnon and of events subsequent to the sacrifice than of Paris. As at 176–78, translation and interpretation of the proverb vary; cf. Fraenkel's: "Justice weighs out understanding to those who have gone through suffering." As with "alone" at 178, **only** interprets (i.e., adds a meaning that is not in the Greek) and seems to me unduly restrictive.

257 Apian: The Peloponnesus (and so Argos) was once named for a mythical seer and physician, Apis (see *Suppl* 260 ff. for his story).

If Clytaemestra has not been onstage, she enters with these lines (255–58).

264–65 The proverb she refers to is unknown (Hesiod speaks of Day being born from Night [*Theogony* 124], but Dawn is the daughter of Theia). Her **angel of blessing** echoes "messages of good hope" (262). She transforms the proverb into a wish, even though she knows exactly what the Day brings and the Night has brought.

268 Strictly speaking, these iambic trimeters in stichomythia (dialogue in which two characters speak alternate lines) should be attributed to the leader of the chorus (called the coryphaeus). With the possible exception of a line in the *PB*, there is no stychomythia by half-lines in Aeschylus. One of stichomythia's most common functions is interrogation (cf. *Ag* 538 ff., *Pers* 232 ff., 715 ff.); but that ostensible purpose does not preclude argument, such as we find here, and, in fact, inquiry in this naturally more dynamic, excited mode often leads to anger and recrimination. Syntactically, the lines may be relatively independent, as here, or varying degrees of linking may be had from grammatically dependent exchange, as in the next instance (538 ff.).

271 Despite the formality of stichomythia, subtle and realistic psychological effects are often achieved. Here a slightly hostile, skeptical coryphaeus does not convince the queen of his loyalty. **Betray** may suggest simply "indicate" or, as in legal contexts, "accuse"; in the latter case she impugns his sincerity. Their tilting also appears in some cognate words denoting belief and persuasion (268; "evidence" in 272; 274; cf. "proofs" 352) and in the word "lied" (273), which also means "tricked" or "deceived" (see note to 886). "Hope" (262 and 276) implies that she is credulous and easily deceived.

275 Cf. *LB* 37 ff., 523 ff., where Clytaemestra's dreams are omens of her own fate.

281 ff. Hephaestus (the god of fire) carries news of Troy's fall by a series of relays, varying from about fifteen miles to over a hundred. Mt. Ida is southeast of Troy; the Hermaean horn (283) is a promontory on the island of Lemnos (west of Troy); Mt. Athos is northwest, on the Thracian coast; Macistus (289) is unidentified but must be down the coast, perhaps on the island of Euboea; Euripus' streams (292) are the straits separating Euboea from the mainland; Messapion (293) is in Boeotia, opposite Euboea; Asopus (297) is the main river of the Boeotian plain, which is bounded by Mt. Cithaeron (298) on the south; both Gorgopis' marsh (302) and Mt. Aegyplanctus are unknown (it has been suggested that Mt. Aegyplanctus is on, or at least calls to mind, the island Aegina because Aegina is near enough to Argos to serve as the next-to-last link in the chain); finally, Mt. Arachnus (309) is near Argos. Some of the proposed distances seem at least implausible, though the historically-minded have argued that the relay is feasible. Note the significant names **Gorgopis** ("Gorgon-faced") and **Aegyplanctus** ("roamed-by-goats"). Cf. the description of Io's wanderings at *PB* 706 ff. and the herald's description of the Persian rout at *Pers* 480 ff.

In a personal communication Noel Robertson writes: "The transmission of the fire-signals is described as a torch-race, i.e., a race of relay teams, each passing the torch. In 458 B.C. the torch-race was fairly new in Greece and both then and later was especially favored in Athens. At this time torch-races were certainly conducted at the Panathenaea and at the festival of Pan, probably at the Promethia, possibly at the Hephaestia. Before lines 312–14 the principal allusions are in lines 281, 282, 287, and 296." Robertson cites Herodotus 8. 98 (description of the Persian couriers): "The first, at the end of his stage, passes the dispatch to the second, the second to the third, and so on along the line, as in the Greek torch-race which is held in honour of Hephaestus."

320 Like a clairvoyant and prophet, the queen first describes Troy's last night (320–37), then turns to the dangers attending success (this sort of talk is ominous: it names that which is to be avoided; see on *Sev* 257 f. and *Ag* 1652). The Greek audience knew how the gods, and especially Athene, had turned against the victors because of their sacrilegious pillaging of the city's temples and altars (see the prologue to the *Trojan Women* and book 2 of the *Aeneid*) and how the fleet had been destroyed by storms on its return (*Odyssey* 3. 130 ff. and 4. 495 ff.).

333 The image is taken from the habit of drawing lots from a helmet.

341 Passion would call to mind Locrian Ajax's rape of Cassandra at the altar of Athene:

> *Athene*
>> Did you not know they outraged my temple and shamed me?
>
> *Poseidon*
>> I know that Ajax dragged Cassandra there by force.
>>>> (*Trojan Women* 69 f.)

Cassandra will be brought home by Agamemnon to be his concubine (950–55; cf. 1438 ff.).

343 f. The Greek racecourse is marked by a pole that the horses or chariots must double round before returning to the start.

345–47 Lattimore has made these lines a little easier than the Greek, where the last line would naturally read

> may never sleep, if only no fresh wrong be done!

Their threatening quality is not mitigated by the ambiguity in **these slaughtered**, which might include Iphigeneia, and in **anger**, which may also allude to Clytaemestra's pain. With 346 cf. *LB* 278.

355–487 The first stasimon (the choral lyrics that divide the scenes). Despite the absence of any exit cue for Clytaemestra, most commentators have taken her offstage. While her departure would be in keeping with the normal practice of clearing the stage during a choral lyric, there are sufficient exceptions to this rule (e.g., Cassandra later in this play, 975 ff.) to leave the matter open for discussion. If she goes off, the lyric focus is more narrowly concerned with Paris, the revenge taken on him, and the mysterious yet inevitable revelation of divine wrath on human wrong. On the other hand, much here (e.g., the net imagery and the destruction "of things inviolable" in 371) clearly has a double reference, so that we think of Agamemnon's destiny even as that of Paris draws the primary reference. For this reason Scott argues for her presence: "As the chorus sings of the law which calls determinedly for revenge, she visually represents the law as its agent" (*TAPA* 108:266). For Scott, Page, and others her presence enhances dramatic tension by visually doubling the focus. It might also be argued, however, that her solitary, silent figure would distract attention from the chorus, both from what it has to say and from our perception of, and concentration on, its anxiety and moral ambivalence.

355 All the heavenly bodies are divine. **Night** is **beloved** because she gave aid to, i.e., was the occasion of, the Greek victory. Line 356 probably refers to Night's possession of the stars and planets (cf. *PB* 23).

358 The imagery of the **net** pervades the play and finds a perfect symbol in the robes Clytaemestra throws over Agamemnon before killing him (1375, 1381 ff.). For Aegisthus these murderous robes are "the tangling nets of fury" (1581) that bring down on Agamemnon retribution for the crime of Atreus. The variety of ways Aeschylus managed to introduce this imagery makes "levels" of metaphorical meaning a more accurate descriptive term than it sometimes is. Cf. Clytaemestra's rumor (868); Cassandra's "net of death" (1115) and "folded web's entanglement" (1126–27; for her the robes and web are one, which in fact proves to be the case); and the chorus's perception of Cassandra as herself "fenced in these fatal nets" (1048). The imagery carries over into the *Libation Bearers*: at 506 Electra compares the children to "corks upon a net"; at 980 ff. Orestes displays the robes used to kill his father, and at 997 ff. he makes explicit the metaphorical connection between hunting and nets. Cf. *LB* 492 f.; *Eum* 112, 147, 460. Elsewhere in Aeschylus: *Pers* 98 (note), *PB* 1078, *Sev* 609 ("snare").

364–67 Cf. the similes from archery at 628 and 1194; note at *LB* 380. Zeus is compared to an archer; but since he usually accomplishes his purposes with thunder and lightning, the metaphor is eased into that more natural mode with **stroke of Zeus**. See on *Pers* 740, and cf. "strokes of life" at *Eum* 933. Such language denotes both external misfortune ("the blows of fate") and intellectual derangement, as at 479, where "reft of wit" might be translated "knocked senseless."

368 Trace it shifts the metaphor to tracking (cf. 127 and 463).

369–72 This is an old chestnut of Greek morality: Do the gods in fact punish wrongdoing? The *Iliad* offers little comfort to moralists (but see the first chapter of Lloyd-Jones's *Justice of Zeus* for a vigorous minority opinion), the *Odyssey* a bit more, Hesiod more still. Aeschylus is more inclined than either of his successors to justify the ways of god to man. At 399 the focus returns to Paris, but it is not easy to say what **delicate things** he trampled on—not that an allusion to the sacrifice of Iphigeneia is particularly clear either. **Trample** will occur again, however, in 957, when Agamemnon tramples (= "crushes") the purple (cf. 1356).

374–76 The text is uncertain: neither **curse** nor **wrings atonement** will be found in all texts.

378 ff. A variation on the topic of limit; cf. 1001 ff. and Solon's

> My desire is to have riches; but win them unjustly
> I will not, for retribution must then come my way.
> (1. 7–8; trans. Lattimore, p. 18)

381–84 But great good fortune tempts man: cf. 751 ff. and 1331 with their notes on **perdition** (= "excess" or, better, "surfeit"). **Spurns** (in **spurns the high altar**) more concretely also means "kicks," an image Aeschylus likes (see the note on 371 and cf. 885 and 1601; *Eum* 150).

385 f. Although many connections were traditional, the Greek poets enjoyed great freedom in creating new genealogies among the various abstractions, daimonic powers, and divinities that populated both the popular and the poetic imagination. **Persuasion** was said by Sappho to be a daughter of Aphrodite, a natural affinity Aeschylus plays with at *Suppl* 1039 ff.; see the note to *Eum* 885. That erotic tie may be latent here, inasmuch as Paris is both the last and the next actual person mentioned; but two other connections—one with various kinds of persuading in the trilogy, the other with **Ruin**—also increase the thematic complexity.

(1) **Persuasion** as a theme has already been anticipated: 86; 106 ("magic"); 268, 272, and 274 (on these see the note to

271); and 352 ("proofs" are persuasive evidence). Dramatically, Clytaemestra's ability to control the chorus and to manipulate Agamemnon are correlatives in the action to the verbal emphasis on this theme. Cf. *LB* 726, *Eum* 885.

(2) How variously **Ruin** is treated may be seen from the fact that Homer makes her a daughter of Zeus (*Iliad* 19. 91), whereas Hesiod calls her the child of Strife (*Eris*, at *Theogony* 230). But these genealogies simply reflect varied ways of thinking about the same phenomenon, the infatuated delusion that leads man to folly and his own ruin (see the discussion at *Pers* 93–101). For the Greeks a single word, *atē*, epitomizes this idea, which is difficult to translate because it often suggests both cause (delusion) and effect (ruin) and because it is often personified as a kind of daimonic power ("personification" is, generally, a literary word and so not the best term to designate a dynamic process that is both external and internal for man). In the *Agamemnon* this noun *atē* occurs fifteen times, in connection with everything from the "disaster" that falls on Troy (361) to the "Wrath" to whom Clytaemestra claims to have sacrificed Agamemnon (1433). Cassandra finds it everywhere in this cursed house: it is the "sin" sung by the Furies (1192), Clytaemestra herself ("a secret death," 1230), the "hate" that Orestes will culminate (1283), the "disaster" she herself would avoid (1268). The several translations reflect decisions about nuance in each passage and necessarily refract only a small part of the spectrum that is *atē*.

This type of metaphor may be analytic, i.e., it may ask us to look at Persuasion and Ruin as components at work within a particular situation. So we might say in this case that any man who has lost his good sense (is a victim of *Atē*) will be easily persuaded to self-destruction. In some cases, however, the association is less analytic than expressionistic, in which case the metaphor simply asserts an intimate tie between two or more ideas. Here we would say that Persuasion (temptation) and Folly (ruin) go hand in hand. In other cases the chronological and parental bonds have special value; this is true, for example, in the sequence "Prosperity, satiety, Hybris" (750 ff.), while the idea "Zeus the father of Right" (*LB* 948 f.) draws its power from neither chronology nor biology so much as from social acceptance and poetic tradition. In the case of Persuasion and Folly/Ruin, we are hard pressed to say which precedes the other, since *atē* may suggest either end of a sequence beginning in folly and ending in ruin. Erotic temptation, from an analytic viewpoint, might just as well be called mother of delusion as daughter of delusion.

387 Medicine picks up a metaphor begun at 16, continued ironically at 99, applied to Agamemnon (222 f.), and continued variously through the trilogy (see on 1001 and 1170; *Eum* 987).

The sin translates a medical term meaning "hurt" or "lesion," a sense prominent here after **medicine**.

390–93. Recent commentators do not believe that there is a reference to **touchstones** or to testing in this passage. **Cheap bronze** contains lead, which shows black as it spreads over a surface subjected to wear.

The man tested (or rather "judged," "brought to trial," a legal metaphor continued in "wickedness" at 398; both words are from the *dikē* stem) reveals, like bad metal, the black stain of the moral cancer he bears. **This man** is a generic, not a particular, reference; **shows vain** means "shows his black nature."

394 This line is drawn from a proverb (on the futility of chasing a flying bird) and is only loosely attached to the preceding image. If 394 f. are applicable to Paris, they point to the vanity of his life and the shame it brings on Troy.

409 After the preceding lines these household **prophets** might be expected to be Trojan, but the following lines show that they belong to Menelaus' establishment.

410–19 Lattimore ends the lament of the prophets at 419; other modern editors extend it through 426.

415 As so often, an aura of the demonic shadows **phantom queen**, a phrase that combines verb and noun from the Greek (which reads "a ghost will seem to rule the house").

416–19 Such is the concision of these lyrics that the commentators differ over whether the **eyes** belong to the **images** (statues), to Helen, or to Menelaus. The **where** suggests that Lattimore takes it of the statues. The Greek belief that the glance of the eye sheds love is illustrated by Hesiod's description of the Graces:

> and from the glancing of their lidded eyes
>   bewildering
> love distills; there is beauty
>   in their glance, from beneath brows.
>   (*Theogony* 910–11; trans. Lattimore)

422 f. Vain . . . vain: cf. the play on "daring" at 409. This vanity (or futility) is a favorite motif, already expressed in lines 165 ("dead weight") and 387 (see notes on *LB* 846, *Eum* 142). Cf. *Medea* 1261 f.

435 The dead were burned and their ashes collected from the pyre, to be sent home in **urns**. By contrast, bodies at 452–55 are buried in the ground.

437 f. Ares is the **god of war** imagined as a **money changer** doing business with scales (**the balance**; cf. note on 206 and the next occurrence at 573).

448 They fight because of another man's wife; cf. on 62.

451 Quarrels represents another legal term (cf. on 40), something like "the advocacy of the sons of Atreus."

457 Paid for by whom? Apparently the people **curse** the sons of Atreus for the losses suffered; so a scholiast thought that Agamemnon was the person to do the paying (the question is more pressing in the Greek, where the sentence has the form "*x* pays a debt for the curse of the people"). Fraenkel understands the "speech of the people" as the subject that will pay, the idea being that a formal curse has been contracted which the city must "pay out." Neither view of the sentence is completely compelling—but *someone* must pay.

463–67 Cf. the more specific application of this idea at *Eum* 264–75. Just as they claim in the *Eumenides*, the **Furies** are here imagined as agents of retribution who correct malfunctions in the natural order of justice (**right** = *dikē*). The Greek text adds "in time," allowing for the late stroke of retribution, and suggesting attrition: the Furies wear a man down with bad luck until he is nothing. **Among the ciphers** means "in Hades," i.e., even after death (as at *Eum* 273–75).

468–71 The moralizing passes from the inevitable punishment of "those who have killed many" to the dangers of **high glory** ("reputation") and **envied wealth**. These are commonplaces of Greek morality, applicable to both Agamemnon and Paris (cf. the notes on 904 ["malice"], 751, and 922). For the

thunderbolt as instrument and symbol cf. 367 and *Pers* 740.
Towering mountains is an emendation. Lloyd-Jones sticks
with the manuscripts and translates: "for by the eyes of Zeus /
the thunderbolt is hurled." Cf. the divine "evil-eye" at 947
and see *PB* 358 f. (Typho). Marlowe offers a parallel to lightning from the eyes:

> For he shall wear the crown of Persia
> Whose head hath deepest scars, whose breast most wounds,
> Which being wroth sends lightning from his eyes,
> And in the furrows of his frowning brows
> Harbors revenge, war, death, and cruelty; . . .
> (2 *Tamburlaine* 1. 4. 74–78)

475 ff. The preceding meditation on the fall of Troy now
yields, surprisingly, to doubt: who but a woman would fall
prey so readily to credulous belief in these beacons? If we
view the chorus as a character, as a single, unified personality,
then only some psychological explanation—a natural ambivalence, perhaps, which desires the announced fall but from
long and frustrated waiting has grown skeptical—will serve
to explain this reversal. Some scholars, like Dawe, reject psychological explanations in favor of a stress on the dramatic
contrasts to be had from such inconsistencies (the chorus's
doubt is immediately rebuffed by the herald's appearance).
Such arguments have their own psychological dimension in
that they recognize that the dramatist is trying to manipulate
our expectations, i.e., set up a contrast for someone (the spectator). Similar inconsistencies between word and action have
been felt in the third stasimon (975 ff.) and in the scene between the chorus and Cassandra. See on 1100 ff.; see also
on 1650.

This last section (475–87) is called an epode (it is astrophic,
i.e., nonresponsive). Its division among several members of
the chorus is not obligatory. Hemichoral divisions do occur
(see *Suppl* 1013 ff.), but there is apparently no certain case of
more than two parts in such lyrics.

483 f. In the Greek the first line says "it suits the spear of a
woman . . ." Some take "spear" to mean "temper," but a
more literal sarcasm is possible, with obvious overtones of
sexual contempt. Cf. the echo at *LB* 630.

485–87 As at 272 and 276, the chorus alludes to the con-

ventional notion that women are preyed upon by foolish
hopes. She responds at 590–92.

489–500 The manuscripts assign these iambic lines to Clytaemestra and 501–2 to the chorus. Most modern editors give
the lines to the chorus, but Lloyd-Jones and Page retain the
distribution of the manuscripts, which most scholars agree
have very little authority in the matter. Two specific points
suggest that the speaker changes at 489: (1) there is in the
Greek at 496 a pronoun meaning "to you," which, if it is retained (and it is often emended away), must indicate the presence of two parties; (2) the transition at 501 is very awkward if
the lines are attributed to the same person. Accepting the arguments of Page for giving the lines to Clytaemestra, A. M.
Dale adds (p. 215): "it would be altogether abnormal for a chorus to speak at such length, or indeed in such highly wrought
metaphors. No chorus ever *said*, though it might have *sung*:
'my witness is mud's sister and next-door neighbor, thirsty
dust,' whereas Clytaemestra constantly speaks in that style."
Dale's italics call attention to the iambic (spoken) meter of
these lines. Against these difficulties and the attribution in the
manuscripts we must weigh the awkwardness that many have
felt when faced with a present but silent Clytaemestra (503–
86), just the sort of "portentous silence" for which Aristophanes lets Euripides chide Aeschylus (*Frogs* 913 ff.).

If, however, we compare the messenger scene at *Pers* 249
ff., we find that the queen is certainly present, yet not addressed, and silent for forty lines during a lyric dialogue between the messenger and the chorus. Absence of personal address and a prolonged silence may also be found at Aegisthus'
entrance at *Ag* 1577 ff. Since convention and the formality of
Aeschylean theater seem to admit the prolonged silence of a
present character, we can probably safely attribute 489–500 to
Clytaemestra and 501–2 to the chorus.

494 The garland signifies good news; cf. *Oedipus the King*
83 f.

495 Aeschylus' metaphorical style sometimes makes connections of a forced and artificial kind, so that the effect is
bombastic, inflated, and turgid. The present figure is in-
famous (see Housman's wonderful parody). The genealogical
connection is characteristic (cf., e.g., 385 f.). Cf. Clytaemes-

tra's "rippling springs" (887 f.) and the more violent tears of Electra (*LB* 183–86, where Lattimore's "like" in 186 softens the metaphorical rush a little). Aristophanes had some fun with this sort of language.

502 Because mistakes or sins are often imagined as being sown, growing, and reaching fruition, **reaping** the harvest of **crime** (*hamartia*: the same root as "sins" at 537; see the note to 1194–97) is the natural metaphor for the culmination of this process. **Reaping** occurs again at 1044, 1655. Cf. also *Suppl* 71 ("We gather blooms of sorrow") and *Pers* 821.

503 Here, as in the *Persians* and *Eumenides*, Aeschylus does not hesitate to telescope time for dramatic effect. The herald's announcement confirms Clytaemestra's beacons and silences the doubting chorus.

The herald or messenger is a standard role in Greek tragedy, the origin of which may go back to the earliest differentiation of actor from chorus. In Aeschylus' plays this part is already managed with such variety and sophistication that we can hardly learn much about the primitive beginnings of tragedy from this, our best evidence. Messengers report offstage events (the defeat of Xerxes, the victory of Agamemnon), they announce entrances (the coming of Agamemnon), they give occasion for lyric reflection (*Ag* 681 ff.; cf. *Suppl* 625 ff., after the report of Danaus, who has a messenger's function), they may admonish, exhort, or otherwise affect the tone of a scene (very seldom in Aeschylus is the report simply a matter of bringing information). Though no messenger in Aeschylus is drawn with the realism of the guard in the *Antigone* (223 ff.), we may find in the detail of 555 ff. and in the hesitant, evasive, but finally ominous prologue of his third speech (636 ff.) sufficient personal matter to make this a credible character in his own right.

The division of his report into three speeches by means of intervening dialogue and the speech of Clytaemestra demonstrates a studied effort to gain the greatest dramatic potential from this scene. We are not merely prepared for Agamemnon's arrival but are advised of the misfortune and bad omens accompanying his victory. We are shown Clytaemestra hypocritically announcing her loyalty and the chorus backing off from public exposure of her liaison with Aegisthus. Thus the scene serves in several ways to foreshadow Agamemnon's arrival and to set a problematic tone for it. It is worthwhile to compare *Pers* 249 ff., our earliest messenger scene but one already structurally complex, where the elaborate structure is devoted to a single unambiguous issue and tonality. Antagonistic messengers, like the Egyptian herald (*Suppl* 824 ff.) and Hermes (*PB* 944 ff.), who serve as representatives of their masters, are a distinct species; like Danaus, they illustrate the variety Aeschylus has already achieved, and we may add Orestes, who in the *LB* assumes the role of a messenger.

Note that the herald addresses neither the chorus nor Clytaemestra but the land (503), the Sun (508), Zeus and Apollo (509), the "gods . . . assembled" (513, with possible reference to statues of divinities before the house; cf. 518 f.), Hermes (515), the heroes (516), and, finally, the house (518).

509–12 He thinks of Zeus the Savior (see on 245–47). The **Pythian king** is Apollo, so called after he had killed the dragon Pytho at Delphi (see on *Eum* 1 ff.). He was **grim beside Scamandrus** (the river on the Trojan plain) in that he favored the Trojans. When he is addressed as the god of healing (512), the audience may think also of the plague he sends on the Greeks in book 1 of the *Iliad*; for **healer** compare the prayer at 146 and the note on *paiōn* at 1246–48. As the god of medicine and healing, Apollo naturally finds a place in the metaphorical language of the sick house, but in the *Libation Bearers* and *Eumenides* he will take on a more personal, and problematic, role. Cf. Sophocles, *Oedipus the King* 149 f.

515 Hermes protects all travelers, especially professionals; see on *LB* 1.

516 f. The Greeks worshiped at the graves of **heroes**, great men who, they felt, continued to have power from the grave. Darius in the *Persians* and the spirit of Agamemnon summoned in the *Libation Bearers* are examples of what the chorus in the *Suppliants* calls "ancient gods below possessing the tomb" (*Suppl* 22 f.). The Athenians felt that Theseus rose from his grave to fight beside them at the Battle of Marathon.

518 f. It is assumed that the **seats of sanctity** are thrones for the kings and elders before the house. The **divinities that face the sun** would include the images, like Apollo's, that were placed before the eastern front of the palace. See on 1081–83.

525 f. Sophocles borrowed **the spade of Zeus** and found himself in turn parodied by Aristophanes. In the following lines Iris is threatening Pisthetairos:

> Most frenzied of fools, rouse not
> The vengeance-wreaking wrath
> Of the gods, lest Justice armed
> With the fateful fork of Zeus
> Raze to the dust your race
> And pulverize your palaces.
>   (*Birds* 1238–41; trans. Dickinson)

Vindictive translates a word meaning "bringing justice (*dikē*)," which appears again in Aegisthus' exulting "day of doom" (1577) and in Electra's "give them punishment" (*LB* 120). Aeschylus apparently coined the word for the *Oresteia*.

529–31 The king, who put on the yoke as a requisite for capturing Troy (217), has yoked the city. The language is very grand; the man is blessed by a happy, benevolent daimon (**fortunate**); see on 1660. The praise is altogether appropriate, the irony palpable.

533–35 The sentiment is one of several variations on the theme discussed at 1560–66 (note). Legal language again, not only in **guilty** and **theft** but also in **prize captured** (i.e., Helen), which in Attic law was anything seized by way of compensation for wrongful seizure or theft.

537 Because of its Christian connotations, **sins** is a good word to avoid; cf. the note to 502. As Nietzsche says, "Foolishness, not sin."

539 Another interpretation of this line would give: "I am content and will no longer refuse to die." For the thought cf. *LB* 438.

548 Cf. 35 ff. The chorus darkly alludes to troubles at home but deflects the herald's inquiry; cf. 808–10. **Silence** is a "medicine" against disaster; cf. 848.

551 ff. This second speech turns mainly on remembering the hard campaign and on gratitude for survival. It has been admired for its characterization of the herald, though in fact no anecdote or incident unique to this man is related. Thus, while the speech lingers for a moment on his experience and not on the immediate dramatic issues, it is nonetheless generic, placing him in a class of soldiers and survivors. By contrast see Odysseus' recollection of a night raid while he was at Troy (*Odyssey* 14. 462–506), which, though it is all a lie, could have happened only to one particular man.

553 f. It is a commonplace that pain, grief, and uncertain fortune distinguish man's life from that of the gods. Cf. the sentiment at *Sev* 626.

573 Cf. the image at 437 f.

577 f. Nailed the spoils: it was a custom to dedicate spoils of war in the temples of the gods and to advertise the donor's name and the occasion with an inscription.

584 f. The phrasing of the English might suggest that this news must be reported to her and that therefore she is not present, but we could also translate: "This news is the particular interest of Clytaemestra and the house."

586 The **cry of joy** announces victory or auspicious omens and was previously raised at 27 ("raise the rumor of gladness") and is mentioned again at 595. So "howled aloud" (1236) reflects Cassandra's vision of the victorious Clytaemestra. It occurs again, and prematurely, at *LB* 942, and finally it is justified by events at *Eum* 1043 (note).

590 She may refer to 479 ff. or to 261 ff., when she is certainly present.

594 This cry is **womanish** because it was usually uttered by women; but here that fact of ritual merges with the theme of sexual antagonist and the queen's duel with the hostile chorus. For the theme cf. 10 f. (note), 1625, *LB* 304 f.; cf. *PB* 1003 ff. (deprecation of feminine weakness), *Antigone* 61 and 484, *Medea* 230 ff.

597 Still (= "putting to sleep") may refer to dousing fires with wine.

603 When we find **spread the gates** in Aristophanes (*Lysistrata* 250), there is little doubt of the sexual significance. Cf. the "unbroken seal" of 610 and Clytaemestra's excitement at 1446–47.

604 ff. Fraenkel argues that the message precedes rather than follows 604, which makes sense if 605–12 are as ambiguously threatening as they seem. For example, **longs for** is an erotic word (the city's "darling"), perhaps mocking the great man. Wilamowitz quite rightly doubted that Clytaemestra intended 606 ff. as a message for the king. They are, if not an aside (see on 1646–48), only for the chorus. The ambiguity of **true** is patent: "true to him" (ironic, or simply a lie); "true to her own purpose" (i.e., to kill him); so "trusting" and "to be trusted" are equally possible. The translation **watchdog** interprets, for the Greek says simply "dog of (or for) the house," which is extremely brazen in light of the common meaning of dog as "bitch" or "slut" (so Helen at *Iliad* 6. 344 describes herself as a "bitch"). The Greeks were not so sentimental about dogs as we are (see the note to *LB* 621). Aegisthus has not been mentioned, but in the tradition he is there in the wings, waiting to howl (1577 ff.), and that fact, so far withheld, would seem one reason for the darkling murmurs of the chorus.

610–12 Some modern commentators have doubted that this line ambiguously plays on the **seal** of a storeroom and the seal of chastity, but the second meaning leads most naturally to the grand lie of 611. Finally, **to temper bronze** offers a double ambiguity: (1) one tempers steel, not bronze, which melts if excessively heated (Clytaemestra means: "I would deny my liaison with Aegisthus as soon as I would melt the dagger saved for Agamemnon"); (2) the phrase may also refer to dipping bronze in order to dye it (she means: "I shall soon show you how well I can dye [with blood] this bronze, just as well as I can enjoy my man"). Both readings make sense; it seems likely that Aeschylus played on both meanings.

613 f. These two lines probably belong to Clytaemestra. Mocking the chorus, she has exulted in her triumph, and now she concludes with language so edged with double meaning that it virtually challenges them to reveal their distrust. In response the coryphaeus merely stumbles (615 f.). She sweeps off the stage with grand confidence and disdain; the audience is left in suspense, wondering what her next move will be. She returns at 855.

615 f. Lattimore's version, more intelligible than some, captures the awkward indirection of these lines. We expect something like "you heard her; a good interpreter would understand her well enough." But that is not exactly the sense.

624 f. In the epic versions (e.g., *Odyssey* 3. 130 ff.) the Atreidae quarreled and left Troy separately. Aeschylus need not have accounted for Menelaus, and he probably introduced him here only to anticipate his satyr play *Proteus*, which concluded the tetralogy and returned to the happier theme of Menelaus' adventures. For the present, however, such talk of disaster can only be ill-omened; it will "stain the blessing of this day" (636 ff.).

632 f. The witness of the Sun is invoked at *Iliad* 3. 277 in an oath and at *Odyssey* 8. 270 f., where the Sun betrays Ares' seduction of Aphrodite to her husband, Hephaestus. Cf. *LB* 985.

634 f. For **the wrath of divinities** see the note to 320.

637 Such gods are honored apart: a much-disputed phrase, which Lattimore apparently takes as referring to honor for the Furies (645). In times of disaster and bad omens it would be natural to placate the Furies, but today ought to be one of thanksgiving. Otherwise we may interpret the line to mean "honor appropriate to the Olympian gods stands apart from such talk." This second view would be preferable if the herald did not continue with such a thoroughly black picture of what he styles as "life-giving fortune" (664).

641 Slain may mean "selected (consecrated) for sacrifice"; if so, the verb is another example of the perversion of religious language.

642 Imagery from the **whip** or scourge is frequent: see the notes to *Sev* 609a and *LB* 375. This sort of whip had a double barbed point. Note the three **doubles**: Ares drives his victims with a whip with two barbs, which is for them a double disaster (*atē*), for they are like a bloody pair (of horses yoked to Ares' war chariot). The compression of the image defies full translation.

645 Song of triumph: the paean (*Pers* 393) would normally be offered to the Olympian gods, not to agents of vengeance. It is a song of thanksgiving (= "song," 246), not of misgiving.

649 Though the herald cannot know it, his narrative verifies Clytaemestra's forecast (338 ff.), thus making the signs favorable for her business. For the **storm** see the note at 320.

654 A **Thracian stormwind** blows from the north.

657 Fraenkel suggests that **shepherding** comes to mind after the metaphor of "gored" (655: of being struck by the horns of a bull). Cf. 668 f. Here the **wicked shepherd** is probably the storm.

659 Stanford (*Greek Metaphor*, pp. 111 ff.) calls attention to
the wide variety of uses the Greek poets make of *anthos* (**blossoming**). He argues that "when Euripides and Aeschylus
used the word of corpses on the sea they were primarily
thinking of 'that which rises to the surface' and secondarily
perhaps of hideous *scum* and the dark *dye* of blood—grim realism indeed but not cynicism—while the note of 'blossoms'
must have been the least prominent meaning in their minds"
(p. 114). Stanford has in mind Euripides' imitation of this line:

> blossoming like a sea of blood
> (*Iphigenia in Tauris* 300; my trans.)

The metaphorical sense is much more common in Aeschylus
than the supposed literal meaning "flower." Cf., e.g., "pain
flowers for him" (*LB* 1009) or "Insolence, once blossoming"
(*Pers* 821); in such abstractions the sense of "coming to the
surface" or "erupting" is certainly prominent. But the "plaited
flowers" (*Pers* 618) and the use in compound adjectives at *Pers*
612 ("honey-working") and *PB* 452 ("flowering spring") suggest that the equation with "flower" is valid at times. In the
Oresteia, where perversity of human and natural phenomena
is so common, a sea that blossoms with dead men is at home
with a "harvest of crime" (502).

676 f. A wordy way of saying "if he is alive"; cf. *Pers* 297.

681 ff. The second stasimon. It is not the disaster that has
all but destroyed the Achaean fleet that stirs this meditation
but rather the fate of Troy and the ways of divine retribution
evident from it.

Aeschylus' interest in etymology, i.e., in significant naming, provides material for a small monograph. He is not scien-
tific by modern standards (Helen's name cannot be connected
with "death," as his punning at 687 f. implies), but enough of
his etymologies are obviously playful, fanciful, and artificial
to assure us that the poet himself would not have made scien-
tific claims for them (cf., e.g., 1081 f., *LB* 948 f., *Suppl* 41–
48, and their notes). But these puns and wordplays are true in
another sense, in that they aim to reveal the essence or true
nature of the person or thing and so to demonstrate a cohesion
between word and deed, between action and idea. Helen's
name **fatally** (i.e., truly) names her function, which is to de-

stroy. See also the pun at 699 f. (note), the note to *Sev* 821–31, and *Alcestis* 636.

681–84 The **you** and **your** are not expressed in the Greek, so that there is no hint of the answer until Helen's name comes at 687.

688 The triple **death**—of ships, men, and cities—is contained in three Greek compounds in the same line: *hele*nas, *hel*andros, and *hele*ptolis.

697 The **Simoeis** is the second, and less frequently mentioned, river of the Trojan plain.

699–702 Here a second elaborate verbal play at Helen's expense turns on a homonym meaning both "object of care" and "connection by marriage." To try to bring out the ambiguity we might translate: "Wrath drove this truly named care on Troy." **Wrath** was "anger" at 155, and it is, throughout the trilogy, associated with the anger of the dead; cf. *LB* 292 f. and *Eum* 314 and 888 (the last two of the wrath of the Furies).

708 Changing its song's measure, i.e., learning a lamentation to take the place of the bride-song. Cf. other references to singing to this point: 28–30, 57, 106, 121 (repeated), 246, and 645.

716 ff. The next strophe and antistrophe tell a parable of a **lion cub** that is taken into a house and nurtured, only to turn murderous against its people. In the context the first referent for the parable is Helen, but Knox (*CP* 47:12–25) has demonstrated that language and imagery in the parable proper (716–36) and in the moralizing stanzas that follow it draw our attention to both Paris and Agamemnon. That is, all three agents participate in the image of a murderous "priest of destruction" (736). The following notes offer a few of the specific connections Knox has studied.

718 Lions are first mentioned in Calchas' prayer (140–42); Artemis' care for "tender young" and "sucklings" (= **craving the breast**) includes Iphigeneia, the child dear to Artemis, who is the goddess and protectress of young animals. Agamemnon implicitly likens himself to "a wild and bloody lion" (826 f.); Cassandra compares Agamemnon (1259), Clytaemestra (1258), and even Aegisthus (1224) to lions (the lion may have been the dynastic emblem of the house of Pelops). Cf. *LB* 938. Here the motif of nurturing the cub recalls the child and thus involves the lion father, who will become a priestly destroyer of his own kin.

720 First steps repeats "in the onset" (65) and "first offering" (226, with note); the phrase is a metaphor from the wedding ritual, so that it alludes to the adultery of Helen and Paris, while the connection with line 226 evokes the king's morbid marriage to murder. Both king and lion **played with children.**

727 f. As the lion at length shows the character it has from its parents, so the vice of Tantalus and Pelops recurs in yet another generation.

731 The **grim feast forbidden** (more than the mere murder of sheep) recalls the "second sacrifice unholy, untasted" (151). After 730 it seems clear that people of the house, not sheep, are the lion's victims.

734 The language echoes "those who have killed many" (462) and "sin" (387, with note).

735 f. With **priest** compare 223–26, where Agamemnon presides at sacrifice, and 1384–87, where Clytaemestra does the honors. On **destruction** (*Atē*) see the note at 385 f. and compare Clytaemestra's claim that "the old stark avenger" offered up Agamemnon (1501; 1502 alludes to the feast prepared by Atreus).

Graham Greene seems to have imitated this parable in *Brighton Rock*: "She wouldn't attempt anything with Dallow; but a man of law—when he is as clever as Drewitt was—was always frightened of the law. Drewitt was like a man who kept a tame lion cub in his house: he could never be quite certain that the lion to whom he had taught so many tricks, to beg and eat out of his hand, might not one day unexpectedly mature and turn on him; perhaps he might cut his cheek shaving—and the law would smell the blood" (New York: Viking Press, 1953, pp. 301 f.).

741 Cf. "do shoot enchanted arrows from their eyes" (*Suppl* 1003) and the note to *Ag* 416–19.

743 f. Fraenkel points out the riddling character of 737–44: it is not until **she** that Helen is returned to the lyric. **Consummation,** i.e., of the marriage ritual.

748 Zeus hospitable: cf. 60 and note.

749 The god of guest friendship sends the least-wanted

guest of all, a Fury (**vengeance** translates Erinys). By a common figure of thought, effect (vengeance) is substituted for cause (Helen), and then the effect is incarnated as a demonic agent. See on 1268 and *LB* 649–51.

751 ff. Cf. Pindar's variant on this maxim:

> Grand wealth keeps envy to match its bulk
> (*Eleventh Pythian* 29; trans. Lattimore)

The dangers of prosperity are a commonplace (cf. 1331 ff.). The man of good fortune cannot, as we say, get enough (that is the point of **quenchless** [756], which is the same as "slakeless" at 1331). The biological metaphor implies both the innate character of evil and its pernicious ability to grow and reproduce itself.

755–61 If this passage moralizes the parable, then **in the blood** directs us to the house of Atreus (cf. 771), because **act of evil** (i.e., act of impiety) more aptly fits Agamemnon's sacrifice than it fits either Paris or Helen. Culminating this line of thought are **houses** (plural for singular, as often) and **children in all loveliness** (the Greek singular here must remind us of Iphigeneia). It is characteristic of these oblique, allusive lyrics that we cannot be sure if the chorus *consciously* ponders the king's lot.

763–71 Pride translates *hybris*. The Greeks viewed pride and excessive self-confidence not so much as "sins" but as vices that inevitably led to violence. It is what man does, not what he thinks or feels, that gets him into trouble. So Darius (*Pers* 820 ff.) connects "thoughts too high" with the insolence that led Xerxes to make his foolish expedition against Greece. *Hybris* for the Greek is not the beginning of the chain but the manifestation of a reckless, outrageous disregard for others, whether god or man, that results from man's lack of regard for his own limitations. *Hybris* is regularly a violation of someone's rights. Thus in the *Suppliants* the Danaids think that their Egyptian cousins, who want to force marriage upon them, are acting hybristically, and in *Prometheus Bound* Might says that Prometheus acts hybristically (*PB* 82), and he defines that term by charging Prometheus with "plundering the Gods' privileges." Later on in the *Agamemnon* the chorus will accuse Aegisthus of *hybris* ("this strong vaunting," 1612). So "pride" does not adequately translate this word, if only because *hybris* regularly denotes an action, whether it be the insolent speech of Aegisthus, Paris' rape of Helen, or Agamemnon's sacrifice of his daughter. We need to remember that for the Greeks a donkey or a vine could be hybristic and that Athens passed a law against *hybris*. So it is better not to impute "the ancient flaw of pride" (Heilman, *Tragedy and Melodrama*, pp. 23 f.) to either Aeschylus or Aristotle (*hybris* is not mentioned in the *Poetics*).

Both Paris and Agamemnon have been violent men; both pay for it. Their violence, at first successful, begets fresh violence (767), which encourages yet more **Daring** (769), which is here identified with the mental infatuation known as *atē* (= **the black visaged Disaster,** reading a singular for Lattimore's plural). This is traditional moralizing, which in this instance may go back to a specific contrast in Hesiod between *hybris* and *dikē* ("justice"). Aeschylus begins the antistrophe (772 ff.) with *dikē* (= "Righteousness"), thus giving a stanza to each concept, while Hesiod weaves the two through several lines. Hesiod addresses his brother:

> But as for you, Perses, listen to justice [*dikē*];
>   do not try to practice
> violence [*hybris*]; violence is bad for a weak man; even a
>   noble
> cannot lightly carry the burden of her,
>   but she weighs him down
> when he loses his way in delusions [*atē*]; that other road
>   is the better
> which leads toward just dealings. For Justice
>   wins over violence
> as they come out in the end.
>   (*Works and Days* 213–18; trans. Lattimore)

772 For **Righteousness** (*dikē*) see the note on 250.

776–78 The **simple in heart** are the pious, who are contrasted (as clean) with those with **reeking hands.**

780 Stamped false means coin debased or counterfeit; cf. the imagery at 390–93.

782 At this point the choral song ends and anapests introduce Agamemnon. After the herald's announcement, he is expected, though the preceding lyrics can hardly be said to cele-

brate either him or his victory. The anapests (which continue
to 810) are marked by reserve, indirection, and something less
than refreshing candor.

The chariot in which Agamemnon enters is mentioned at
906. No attendants are mentioned, but we might expect a
nominal escort; they should exit when the king enters the palace. That Cassandra returned with Agamemnon as part of his
booty would be known to the audience from *Odyssey* 11. 405–
34, where the dead king tells Odysseus how Aegisthus, with
the connivance of "my sluttish wife," slaughtered him and his
companions at a feast in Aegisthus' house. Tradition did not
oblige Aeschylus to include Cassandra in the play, however;
and when she fails to speak for almost three hundred lines, the
audience will probably decide that she is merely decoration,
playing the kind of mute role that was not uncommon in the
Greek theater. A similar apparent mute will be found in the
character of Pylades in the *LB*.

786–94 For the motif of finding the proper mark see 364–
67. **Time's graces** means "the proper degree of favor." This
preamble, ostensibly on propriety in praise, reveals an anxiety
easy enough to link with the preceding lyric. **Breaking justice,** for example, recalls the contrast of 763–81; it might also
be translated "transgressing the limits of what is right [*dikē*]"
and so it recalls the same idea that surfaced immediately after
the sacrifice of Iphigeneia was described (250). The chorus's
stress on specious sympathy (790–94) may also seem too rhetorically self-conscious for simple decorum.

795–800 Good shepherd recalls the Homeric "shepherd
of the people" and directly invokes Agamemnon as a man
who must study his flock. Each successive line echoes recent
imagery: "shepherding," 657; the revealing "eye," 418. **Water**
refers to mixing wine and water, i.e., to dilution, while
feigned is "fawning," used of a dog (see on 1228 f.) and lately
of the lion cub (= "broken" at 725). All this sounds like a
warning; then they turn (799 ff.), not to Clytaemestra or any
other danger at home, but to their own ill will, harbored so
long, which they now wish to reveal and write off.

802 The metaphor is from steering a ship, as at 781 and,
more fully, at *Sev* 3.

803 f. Sacrifice refers to Iphigeneia, but the word is an emendation. **Wild spirit** refers to Helen, but this too is suspect. Page interprets: "restoring (courage through sacrifices) to dying men."

811 The entire play points to this scene, which is only 165 lines long and falls at the very center of the plot. Its dramatic significance cannot be disputed, but its meaning, both for the play and for the trilogy, has aroused much controversy, largely because of different views of the character of Agamemnon. As often happens, divergent critical readings turn not on the sense but on the tone of a speech, and this is particularly true for the king. He has been described as everything from a true gentleman to a pompous, besotted murderer. No doubt we should look to his Homeric characterization, if only because the audience's expectations would certainly be conditioned by that familiar figure; but we may also admit that neither all readers of the *Iliad* nor all characters in that poem agree with Achilles' assessment:

> O wrapped in shamelessness, with your mind forever on profit

> (*Iliad* 1. 149)

—a line in which Achilles is angered because Agamemnon has threatened to take his prize, Briseis, a girl who, like Cassandra, has been taken in a raid. Their quarrel, and Agamemnon's seizure of Briseis, triggers the plot of the *Iliad*, and because so many deaths may thus directly or indirectly be laid at his door, it is easy to fault the king of Mycenae. If he is selfish, callous, and brutal, these are faults few heroes are exempt from all the time, and perhaps they are required for survival. He is nonetheless the acknowledged leader of an elite, aristocratic band of knights, who are not readily manageable at the best of times. Like all kings, he is "near to Zeus," from whom his authority and power ultimately derive. He may be duped and betrayed by the highest god, yet his standing with both gods and men remains more or less stable. In this regard he is not unique, for all the heroes enjoy divine protection and aid, and certainly in the *Iliad* Achilles seems nearest of all to the gods. As we see from *Ag* 40 ff., Aeschylus portrays, in the words of Nestor, a "sceptred king to whom Zeus gives magnificence" (*Iliad* 1. 279). In addition, Agamemnon is particu-

larly identified as father and head of the house. Such status
carries sacral as well as political and social responsibility. Because of the power invested in this status, the man, regardless
of personal failings, assumes in ancient Greece a merit and
consequence out of proportion, as we may think, to his character or achievement. Endowed with this aura of social and
familial nobility, Agamemnon need not be extensively characterized by the dramatic poet. He upholds, for good or ill,
the order of things; to murder him disrupts that order and defies the divine *dikē* within the world.

Such generalizations should always be checked against the
facts. Here there are two kinds of fact, one the thematic concerns of the play and the trilogy, the other the particular
speech, decision, and action of this scene. For the first, justice,
both human and divine, and the survival of a viable house will
not be disputed as major themes. For the second, we need not
expect Agamemnon to step out of the pages of Homer, since,
all else aside, Homer never has the occasion to show him in
the hour of triumph. In our play he is full of himself, satisfied
that he, the agent of justice, has taken care of one city and can
now handle matters at home. A little pompous, complacent,
circumspect, but with a yielding vanity, he is lured into her
den by a more masterful ruler of the house. Some writers
have found his yielding too easy, even stupid, and so have invoked the curse on the house or a malignant *atē* as an explanation for his precipitate fall. Certainly the air is full of evil,
daimonic evil; but little in the text compels us to see Agamemnon as the helpless thrall of divine malice. If his reasoning (930 ff.) is none too good, it is still intelligible, his error
human. If the man does not live up to his rank, that too is
perfectly credible. In a way, modern problems with this scene
may stem from the accurate perception that the man, the personality evoked dramatically, does not live up to his billing.
Having lost the sense of social caste, we expect more from the
agent of Zeus's justice. The more realistic Greeks, always
alive to the danger of overstepping human limits, perhaps
found his dilemma more natural, even inevitable.

Compare Agamemnon's opening words (811), **to Argos
first**, with the herald's address to the "Argive earth" (503).
Agamemnon, responding to the choral antithesis of "just"

and "reckless," uses the *dikē* stem three times in the first four lines of his speech (what is **due,** his **vengeance,** and the **justice** heard by the gods).

815 ff. Votes within the urn: at the end of a trial each Athenian juror would put a marker in one of two urns, one for condemnation, the other for acquittal. To maintain a secret ballot, the juror passed his hand over both urns, so that it was not evident how any individual voted.

819 As often, the irony derives from a double application of the sentiment. Since the word **their** is not present in the Greek, the sentence may also apply to the ruin (*atē*) hovering over the speaker.

822–25 Toils: of hunting nets (cf. 1375 f.). Here the city is hunted by **the beast of Argos,** i.e., the Trojan Horse, which hid the **fierce young** (the Greek warriors). Agamemnon is again the victim of his language: the Greek word translated as **beast** would normally be a serpent (as at 1232–33 and *LB* 530), and Clytaemestra is the snake in the grass waiting to destroy him.

826 The setting of the Pleiades would apparently indicate a time of year, the autumn, but it is hard to find much relevance in that, despite the herald's descriptions of storms at sea, which the audience would naturally associate with the end of the sailing season. Otherwise the phrase may simply be a periphrasis for "an attack by night," a vague lyricism, as Fraenkel puts it, for the traditional hour.

829 f. Agamemnon's **prelude** tacitly recognizes that he has so far ignored the chorus (we may suppose that Clytaemestra is not in his view, even if she is "onstage"). By contrast with the herald's list of divinities (509–19), Agamemnon has wandered off in a grandiose description of Troy's ruin, his thanks to the gods (821) being nearly overwhelmed by the metaphor. To what **thought** does he refer? Perhaps to the sentiment elaborated by the chorus in 785 ff., i.e., that sincerity and candor are seldom companions. Note, in these sententious reflections on envy and prosperity, how little of the truly personal is evident; only the reference to Odysseus (841) ties this portion of the speech to a particular man, Agamemnon, and to the Trojan War.

839 Companionship (social experience) is a mirror in

which the knowledgeable man may read the truth; on this view, **shadow's ghost,** though grammatically in apposition to **mirror,** refers to the impermanence of such companionship, i.e., to the **seeming** friendships contrasted with the true loyalty of Odysseus. See on *Sev* 592.

841 In the *Iliad,* Odysseus often acts in Agamemnon's service, e.g., by leading the embassy to Achilles in book 9. Line 843 may be an allusive anticipation of the satyr play *Proteus,* which followed the *Oresteia.*

845 The following lines are calculated to show that the king is no tyrant.

850 Beat down corruption's pain may also mean "to keep the pain from becoming a corrupting disease." Cf. 866 ff. Sickness is such a common metaphor that some commentators are inclined to dismiss its force. See on 1170.

851–54 Clearly, he now intends to enter, and the translation **I take my way** may suggest that he is moving toward the house; but he has not, and indeed he does not even leave the chariot, as we discover from 905 ff. So he remains in the chariot, and only her speech cuts him off. If she has been present, which seems unlikely, he cannot have noticed her. Taplin (p. 307), following Reinhardt, says: "Before he is able to move towards the doorway, Clytemnestra is standing in it. She blocks the way, she occupies the threshold: Clytemnestra controls the way into the house, and Agamemnon can only leave his temporary transport and enter the house on her conditions." This interpretation offers a strong dramatic confrontation at the threshold; but I cannot see how she can literally "block the way" if he never leaves the chariot, and he surely does not leave it and then step back into it. Carpets will be laid between him and the door, and the length of her speech (958–72) as he walks on them implies some distance separating them.

855 Why does Clytaemestra address the chorus and ignore Agamemnon until 877? Though the chorus has expressed its reservations about the expedition to Troy, it shows its loyalty to the king in its initial words of greeting and, later, in its reaction to his murder. Implicit in that loyalty runs the threat that the chorus may expose her liaison with Aegisthus (allusively present as early as 34 ff.). She has faced them down with her triumphant prediction that Troy has fallen, but they still hold the trump card. So now she brazenly, and ambiguously, asserts her wifely fidelity and, by ignoring the king, as much as says that she will deal with him in her own time; meantime, they should beware of meddling. The question is important because its answer bears on the tone of her speech and the degree of psychological realism that is involved. Although some scholars have doubted the presence of covert motives indicating psychological tensions beneath the surface of dramatic gesture, there are far too many and significant ambiguities for us to rest content with rhetorical analysis. The speech is shot through with irony. For example, she speaks of herself as shameless (856), of her love (857, with a word used at 411 of Helen), of lapsed modesty (858). More in the following notes.

857–62 The love . . . husband also means "my man-loving ways." **Modesty** (858) also means "dread" or "awe," i.e., of her husband; **with no man by** (862) suggests that she is alone and defenseless, which is far from the case. Of course the audience does not know that Aeschylus will bring Aegisthus onstage, but it does know the tradition of their adultery and conspiracy.

863 Thus she skirts the truth with brazen *double entendres*: the line also means "ominous words of hatred rising again."

870 Geryon was composed of three bodies joined together at the waist. He ruled over Erythia in the far west and had a herdsman, Eurytion, and a two-headed dog, Orthus, who guarded his cattle. Heracles killed all three and drove away the cattle.

879 The delay in pronouncing the name **Orestes** underscores his absence, which she knows may arouse suspicion. The Greek order runs: "therefore our child does not stand here, pledge of your trust and mine, as is right, Orestes." Fraenkel observes (2:395) that this "hesitant and piecemeal confession provides the dexterous Clytemnestra with a means of appearing reluctant to utter her excuses."

880 Phocis is in central Greece; Sophocles follows this version in his *Electra* (see on line 45), though he has Orestes stolen away by a slave. Cf. Orestes' story in *LB* 561 ff. and 674 ff. and the exchange at *LB* 913 f.

886 Subterfuge appears again in the lyrics of 1495 (as "treachery"), where Clytaemestra responds by accusing Agamemnon of the same (1522 ff.). Cassandra recognizes her "guile" (1129), and the queen will be held accountable, herself the victim of guile (*LB* 555–58, 955, 1003). Here she persuades guilefully, which is also Orestes' way (*LB* 726).

891 Untended left forever modifies **beacons.** Had they been tended, she would have had, as finally she did have, a signal of victory.

892 She slept so lightly that the buzz of a gnat woke her.

893–94 In her dreams she imagined more wounds than he might have actually taken during the time she slept. There is some ambiguity here, for the **wounds** (or suffering) she dreamed might have been those she planned for him.

896–902 Note how she piles up a series of examples, without conjunction, to illustrate a commonplace, "one best hope." Cf. the elaborate figure at *Heracleidae* 427–32, where the comparison focuses on "hope that charms and cheats you" (433 f.). The **stay** is the forestay or tackle tied from the mast to the forward deck of a ship. The **post** is the central pillar or supporting column of a house. All this is laid on with a magnificent literary trowel, as Agamemnon observes (915 f.), but Headlam and others have suspected that one or more lines (900–902) may have gotten into the text from marginal glosses. Line 902 is certainly an insipid climax. To the audience the irony and hypocrisy are patent, but Agamemnon does not know the story and will not survive her rhetoric.

904–11 It is exactly divine **malice** that Clytaemestra is attempting to bring down on Agamemnon. Cf. 921 and 947, where "jealousy" and "hatred" translate the same word (*phthonos*). As at 832 ff., this word often denotes envy, divine or human, and the following passage from Herodotus (7. 10) illustrates Greek thinking: "You see how the god strikes with lightning the great among things that live, nor does he allow them to posture, but small things do not provoke him. You see how he blasts with his bolts great houses and trees. For the god is accustomed to check the powerful. Thus even a great army is destroyed on this account, when the god from envy throws panic or thunder on it, on account of which it is destroyed from no fault of its own; for the god grants great ambition to none but himself."

What she means by **harm that went before** remains vague and ambiguous. He will take **harm** to mean the specious suffering she has just described; she thinks of Iphigeneia. So **where Justice leads** may refer to the *Dikē* that has triumphed at Troy and brought him home, but, for her, *Dikē* here means Retribution. In the Greek the clause (910 f.) denotes purpose: "that Justice may lead him into a house he never hoped for." Clytaemestra is going to persuade Agamemnon to do what he knows he should not do. Cf. Hedda's persuasion of Eilert Loevborg to drink (second act of *Hedda Gabler*).

909–11 Carpets, tapestries, and robes are the means (1126, 1382 f.) and symbols (**crimson**) of destruction, the continuity between the hunt offstage and its mirror onstage. As nets have bound Troy (357 f.), so Agamemnon will be brought down by the nets woven at home (1115, 1375). Cf. *LB* 982–84, *Eum* 1028. These are deep red, blood red (note at 957).

912 f. Agamemnon's first words (811 ff.) claim that his triumph has been through the **gods' aid.** She concludes her speech by claiming that right (*dikē*) and the gods are with her. Both see justice as retribution, both are successful, neither will survive to prove that this view of *dikē* is truly and completely authorized by the gods.

914 Leda, the wife of Tyndareus, was loved by Zeus, who took the form of a swan or goose to seduce her. Clytaemestra and Helen, Castor and Pollux, were her children.

918 For a **woman's ways** cf. 940.

919 Luxury (**make me delicate**) and absolute despotism were generally associated with **Asiatic** rule.

922 The tapestries (909) are inviolable, not because of any sacral character but because walking on them indicates a presumptuous character, such as one expects from an Asiatic despot (919); see on 904.

925 For the topic **a man, not a god,** see on *Pers* 819c ff.

926 Radically different versions of this sentence will be found, e.g., "There is a difference between (walking on) footmats and embroideries" and "My fame calls out (its quality) without such finery." I prefer this last version.

928 Decency of mind is the antithesis of the "great ambition" condemned in the passge from Herodotus cited on 904. This is commonplace morality in the fifth century, the kind of thing discussed by Solon in Herodotus 1. 31–32. Both happiness and unhappiness are "gifts of the gods," but divinity is less likely to be offended by the man of decent, restrained ambition. Great success, such as Agamemnon's, may lead a man to take honors for himself that are rightly the gods' (922) and so incur divine jealousy (921). When god is the source of both good and bad judgment and good and bad luck, the reasoning is clearly circular, but the Greeks were not so fatalistic as to think that a man had nothing to do with his own lot. Agamemnon would seem to have in mind the last line of Solon's discussion: "Often enough God gives a man a glimpse of happiness, and then utterly ruins him" (Herodotus, trans. de Selincourt).

Maxims answering the question "What is true prosperity?" are frequent; see, e.g., Darius' admonition at *Pers* 825–27. For later examples see *Oedipus the King* 1524–30. Variations on the "blessed man" are at 941 ("mighty"); 471 and 751 ("wealth"); and 837 ("bliss"). The Greek is *olbos* (see Subject Index, under prosperity).

931–35 These lines are at once crucial to the play and extremely difficult to interpret. The fact that no interpretation holds the field stems not from studied ambiguity but rather from the compression and terseness of the Greek. To give but one example, in 931 **my** is "your" in some translations.

Since the Greek leaves the noun (**will**) unmodified by either an article or possessive adjective, whose will (or "judgment" or "thought") is not specified. Similar questions of syntax and diction plague 933 f., lines which are apparently central to Agamemnon's decision to change his mind. The main objection to Lattimore's interpretation, which is similar to Smyth's, is that Greeks were not in the habit of vowing to the gods *not to do something*, whether they vowed from fear or in order to gain divine aid. I suggest the following translation as an alternative:

> C.: Tell me this, and give me your true opinion.
> A.: Be assured I shall not change my mind.
> C.: Would you, in fear of something, have vowed to the gods to do this?
> A.: Certainly, if someone from sure knowledge had declared this my duty.

Whether we translate this last word as "duty" or "rite," he is referring to walking on the tapestries. Agamemnon's "someone" is understood to be a seer or prophet (see 963–64). Clytaemestra induces Agamemnon to act from a false premise: he was not in fact required to make such a vow and did not make it, yet he proceeds to act as if he had.

937 Bitterness means "censure" or "blame." **Shame** ought to inhibit action. See 948. When his wife Andromache urges Hector to avoid the dangers of battle in the open field, her husband responds:

> All these
> things are in my mind also, lady; yet I would feel deep shame
> before the Trojans, and the Trojan women with trailing garments,
> if like a coward I were to shrink aside from the fighting.
> (*Iliad* 6. 440–43)

939 See on 904. Cf. 947.

943 She appears to move from argument to entreaty, but **yield** translates the commonest verb for "persuasion" and so in fact climaxes her argument.

947 ff. Cf. 951 f. Agamemnon is conscious of the fatal significance of his act and would wish away the evil eye of divine envy. And though Cassandra, mentioned for the first time at 950, has quite another dramatic purpose, her presence as a slave recalls the dangers attendant on the fluctuations of power, which he has himself now experienced (**my will** is **bent,** 956). One cannot but think of the cursed house, so strangely beguiled is the king, aware of the **yoke** yet compelled to put it on.

957 Purple (cf. 960) translates the same root as "crimson" (911). Goheen (pp. 115 ff.) argues that the Greek connotes a blood-red color, the dark hue of congealed blood and dust. Does this dark carpet prompt the chorus's lines at 1017 f.? "Blood for blood" embodies a law central to the trilogy (*LB* 400–402). In the *Eumenides* the Furies track the trail of blood (245–48, 253); the cycle of blood vengeance is resolved when the Furies no longer demand that the "dry dust drink blood" (*Eum* 978–83). In the crimson ("purple stained") robes worn in the concluding procession (*Eum* 1028), Goheen sees a visual correlate of the verbal imagery, which has, in the course of the trilogy, been converted from ominous and polluting to beneficent and fecund.

958 The ostensible connection between **sea** and the preceding lines is the fact that shellfish from the sea furnish the purple dye for coloring these magnificent tapestries. For Clytaemestra, however, dyeing calls forth dying, while **dipped** (960) recalls Iphigeneia's "saffron mantle" (238). Lloyd-Jones brings out that connection by translating "her robe of saffron dye." See on 612.

Agamemnon enters while she speaks, not to him, as Fraenkel notes, but "as if soliloquizing" until the "you" of 968, where she slowly turns to watch him advance through the door. He exits at 972, when she turns to address a prayer to Zeus. The length of her speech (958–72) implies some little distance for him to walk (see on 851–54).

966 f. As Silk notes (p. 140), the subject (Agamemnon's return to the house) intrudes into the comparison. So, instead of saying "while the root lives, the leaves may yet return," the poet writes "while the root lives, the leaves may yet come home." Sirius, the **Dog Star**, marks the beginning of the hottest summer days.

972–74 The words **master** and **accomplisher, accomplish** and **bring these things to pass,** all bring the same root (*tel-*) into play, and the first two are the same adjective. Verrall noticed the ambiguity of applying this word to Agamemnon, since it may denote **master** but also describes the "perfect" victim. Clytaemestra applies it to the dead (sacrificed) king at 1504, where it is translated "last blood." Giving both husband and Zeus the same epithet is seemingly honorific, especially because "Zeus the accomplisher" is invoked in ritual as the god of marriage (*Eum* 214 f.). See above on 225 f. She silently prays that the god may aid and accept her sacrifice of the man nearest on earth to the god. Of course Clytaemestra is perverse in thinking that the Olympian gods will accomplish such a prayer—or is she? But she cares nothing for Zeus or religion; her passion is all revenge, her whole character is to be an avenger. This *tel*-stem (as in the English "teleology"), one of the most frequent in Aeschylus, applies to an activity or process that is directed toward a goal (see Pindar's *Second Olympian* 18, cited in the note on 977 f.) and then to the person or thing realized or perfected by such activity. The activity may be a natural process or imposed by god or fate. Its associations with ritual give many passages a religious cast (it occurs at 934, where I have translated it "duty").

If Agamemnon exits at 972, preceding the queen, she may turn before her exit to speak this prayer. Contrast the bantering dispute of Aegisthus and Orestes over leading the way into the house (Sophocles, *Electra* 1501 ff.).

975 ff. Critics differ on the question of how self-conscious the chorus is. Is their foreboding truly vague and uncertain? Are they consciously trying to repress fears for Agamemnon, fears inspired by a vague (?) or specific (?) understanding of Clytaemestra's game? Or do such questions assert too much "character" for a chorus that is merely the medium for a lyric meditation? How can the chorus not perceive what she is up to, even if we dismiss as extradramatic any knowledge of the queen's adultery?

Fear and hope (980, 992, 999, 1031) are frequently paired (cf. *Ag* 1434, *PB* 250–52).

977 f. With **mantic heart** cf. 105 f. The **strain** is a song of insistent foreboding (the **it** of 982). Cf. 990 f., 1021. The magical property of song, both to reveal god's truth and to cure man's ills, is a commonplace (see on *Eum* 646). So the mortally wounded Heracles calls:

> Is there any singer of spells,
> any craftsman surgeon who can
> exorcise this curse, but Zeus?
> (*Women of Trachis* 1000–1003)

Unrepaid: no man would summon, much less pay, the Fury to sing (991). With **valor . . . seated** compare "fear beat its wings" (975 f.), "time has buried" (983 f.), "the spirit sings" (990), "strength . . . knows" (1001 f.), and "sickness chambered" (1002). Some editors capitalize these abstract nouns, and rhetorical criticism naturally labels them as personifications, but they are such an ingrained habit of Aeschylus' metaphorical thought—and different in kind from demonic "abstractions" such as Wrath, Vengeance, and Ruin—that it is perhaps closer to the poet's thought to view them as the animated agents of social and psychic experience. The line of distinction is often fine, as in the case of **time** (983), which the poets certainly did personify on occasion:

> Of things come to pass
> in justice or unjust, not Time the father
> of all can make the end unaccomplished.
> (Pindar, *Second Olympian* 15–18)

983 ff. The Greek text is defective here, but the sense seems to be that so much time has passed since the evil omens attending the fleet's departure that those omens may not be fulfilled. If that is the sense, the interpretative translation **Yet** in 988, introducing the antistrophe, draws an erroneous contrast. The nautical imagery comes up again in "whirl of drifts" at 996 and then elaborately at 1005 ff.

990 f. Here **spirit** translates a Greek word meaning not "daimon" but "inner spirit" or "heart." The song of the **Fury** (cf. Cassandra's vision at 1186 ff., where "spirits" [1190] does mean the Furies) may have for its theme the death of Iphigeneia or the slaughter of children of earlier generations, or both.

996–1000 Both **real** and **unfulfillment** carry on the *tel*-stem (note 972), i.e., the first word suggests that something must come of these forebodings, the second wishes that their anxiety may be vain. Cf. the similar language at *LB* 212 f.

1001 ff. Pope has a phrase, "the madness of superfluous health," that sums up the present theme. Though the text is defective and a line is missing at 1006, its main thematic lines are a variant on those of 751 ff., with latent allusion to *hybris* in **no . . . limitation.** The idea that **sickness** is the neighbor of good health (= **high strength**) is paradoxical, yet it was familiar enough to those Greeks who thought that any optimum condition was a mean between two extremes. Denniston and Page cite the Hippocratic *Aphorisms* 1. 3: "Good condition at its peak is dangerous, if it has gone to extremes."

1005 ff. Cf. another elaborate metaphor from a ship in a stormy sea at *Eum* 553 ff. Here the course of life is compared to the voyage of a ship, a commonplace from which all sorts of variants were created by the Greek moralists. Herodotus (3. 40 ff.) tells the story of how the tyrant Polycrates, whose luck and prosperity made him famous, attempted to avoid divine envy by throwing a valued ring into the sea. In a similar way the belabored ship of the present passage **throws overboard some precious thing** so that the entire ship will not be lost. Note how **not all the house** intrudes into the metaphor, momentarily focusing the chorus's fear even as it would escape that fear through metaphor.

1014–16 Ring composition (i.e., returning to a word or phrase that begins a theme or passage) is emphatic in **sick** (the last word in the stanza; cf. 1001 f.), just as **starvation** contrasts with the surfeit of 1002. **Zeus,** god of rain and so of abundant harvests, appears here because of his intimate connection with the house; but the imagery of compensating harvests after years of famine contrasts with the preceding nautical imagery. Such strong, almost violent, contrasts in imagery, while the thematic connection can yet be perceived, are characteristic of the poet.

1022–24 The allusion is to Asclepius, the famous physician celebrated in Pindar's *Third Pythian* as "the hero who warded sickness of every kind." According to a scholiast on *Third Pythian* 56, Asclepius raised Hippolytus, son of Theseus, from the dead, for which breach of law Zeus struck the physician dead. Cf. 1248. See Apollo's version of this story in the prologue to Euripides' *Alcestis*.

1026 Limits on human existence are imposed by the gods. There is some punning on fate: "lot" given by the gods; man's natural "portion."

1028–29 Reversing the usual figure, the poet suggests that the heart's grief might pour forth before the tongue could utter it. **Grief,** however, is interpretative, for the Greek says simply "pour forth *this*," and we might take the pronoun to mean "these apprehensions" or simply "what is on my mind."

1035 By now the audience may expect Cassandra to be a mute. Clytaemestra's unexpected return directs attention to her once again, but still she does not speak. Failing to command Cassandra's obedience, the queen returns to her sacrifice. Eventually, only after the tension of expectation has been prolonged for almost 300 lines, Cassandra voluntarily enters the palace. The rhythm of dramatic action, so slow in the first half of the *Agamemnon*, now gains pace and variety (neither

Cassandra nor Aegisthus is a necessary or expected character in the play).

1037 f. Lustral water is for cleansing those about to engage in sacrifice. Given the context, the **household god** (1038) may be assumed to be Zeus. Cf. 973 f.

1040 Alcmena's son Heracles was afflicted by disease because he had murdered Iphitus, son of Eurytus. The oracle at Delphi told him that to be cured he must be sold into slavery for three years, after which he must pay compensation to Eurytus. Omphale, queen of Lydia, bought the hero (Apollodorus 2. 6. 2–3). Such paradigms are, as Fraenkel notes, more in the style of choric speech than natural to the queen.

1044–46 Another passage in which the queen is so selfabsorbed that she seems to talk of what she plans rather than to the person addressed. She has **reaped success** beyond her hopes (cf. 1058) and will shortly be **savage** to this slave beyond any **need** or **standard.** Line 1046 seems to follow rather abruptly; some editors think that a line has dropped out after 1045.

1048 With **fatal nets** the chorus thinks of the fate of Troy, but Cassandra knows of other nets now being gathered (1115 f.).

1049 The line repeats its verb three times to achieve virtually absolute assonance and alliteration:

> *peithoi' an, ei peithoi' apeithoiēs d' isōs.*
> "You should if you would obey; could you?"

—a hopeless task in English. The point of the line is more than musical, however, for the queen now experiences her first failure to persuade a victim (**obey** at 1052 and 1054 repeats the same verb), as she herself recognizes (1068).

1051 It is not the **swallow** in particular but rather birds generally that are known for their incomprehensible speech.

1060 f. Perhaps this is not so silly as it sounds if Clytaemestra indicates by a gesture of her own hand that at least some gesture of reply might be offered.

1063–67 These lines imply that Cassandra's manner is wild; she is already possessed by her visions. Note **captured** after **captive** and her sense of analogy. The **curb** is a bit for a horse; cf. the similar imagery for the restraint of Iphigeneia (237).

1071 Compulsion = "necessity" (217); her fate is yoked to Troy's (see 1042, where "constraint of fact" translates the same word that is here "compulsion"), yoked to Agamemnon's, and now yoked to the fatal house. **Give way** is the yielding so often advised, so seldom practiced. Cf. *PB* 322, *Antigone* 472.

1072 The meaning of the word translated **earth** is disputed; it may be nothing more than an exclamation of grief.

In the following section of paired stanzas Cassandra sings in lyric verse, while the chorus responds, until 1121, in spoken iambics. The same style of paired stanzas in alternating lyric and iambic verse will be found at *Suppl* 347–416, where the chorus has the lyric verse, the king the iambic; see also *Pers* 255–96 and *Sev* 203–44. In extant tragedy this is the first scene in which the chorus—more likely the leader of the chorus—responds in iambics to the lyrics of the actor. Such scenes of dialogue in alternating lyric and spoken verse are called epirrhematic scenes. Taplin (p. 319) suggests that Cassandra "should be free to move and dance in accompaniment to her lyric."

1074 Loxias is a cult title of Apollo; it was taken to refer to the riddling quality of his oracles. Joyful song and praise are more customary for this god.

1081–83 Lord of the ways refers to an image of Apollo, often only a conical stone, which stood before many houses; apparently one stands before this palace (cf. the herald at 519 and *LB* 583 f.). Similar references at Sophocles, *Electra* 635 and *Women of Trachis* 209.

With **ruin . . . undone** she puns on Apollo's name, connecting it with a Greek verb meaning "to destroy" (*apōlesas*). For her first "undoing" see 1202 ff. The coryphaeus seems altogether benighted; is this senility or distraction?

1090 It is more likely that the compound represented by **God hates** is active and means "the house that hates god," with reference to the murderous crimes of Pelops and Atreus (1091 f.).

1093 Cf. the simile from hunting at *Ajax* 7 and the note to *Ajax* 5. More *hounds* hunting at *Eum* 131.

1095–97 The English, particularly the **there,** may suggest a visionary experience; the **witnesses** in which she puts her faith is apparently the vision of 1091 f. In 1096 f. she alludes to

Atreus' murder of his brother Thyestes' children, whom he then cut up and fed in a stew to their father (see 1590 ff.).

1099 They understand her reference and ask not to be reminded of such bloody business, which is too close to home to require prophets.

1100 ff. It is natural for us to wonder how the chorus can fail to understand Cassandra's visions. They are hardly predictions, for she literally sees what is happening in the house, at the altar, as Clytaemestra prepares and enacts the sacrifice. In the first place, the English is less opaque than the Greek. **She** (1100 and 1102) does not occur in the Greek text, where we simply find third-singular forms of the verb (perhaps an English passive would serve: "what is purposed now?"). So, too, the **your** of 1108 makes the line a little more specific than the Greek. Second, Cassandra has shifted abruptly from Atreus and Thyestes to Clytaemestra; these old men of the chorus are not agile enough to shift so quickly (some commentators think lines 72 ff. are included by way of anticipating their crucial senility in the last moments of the king's life). Third, the audience is well aware of the tradition that Cassandra was cursed by Apollo never to be believed (see the note on 1202 ff.). As in all Greek tragedies, the audience has a privileged knowledge, which puts it in the position of watching known events unfold. The audience understands what the characters only discover; it knows what they come to know.

Still, the chorus has not escaped censure for being both obtuse and inconsistent. "Equally remarkable is the contrast between the chorus' sensitive foreboding of death at *vv.* 975 ff. and the blunt unreceptiveness which they display in their interchanges with Cassandra not long afterwards. Can anyone seriously believe that Aeschylus is successively exploiting first the latent receptivity, and then the latent unreceptivity, of the chorus? Is it not obvious that he is using the chorus precisely as suits his purpose in developing the possibilities of the individual scene?" (Dawe, p. 45). To explain this putative inconsistency, Dawe says that Aeschylus, indifferent to psychological verisimilitude, was simply trying "to heighten the effect." We may wonder, however, whether the reaction of the chorus would then be convincing. If their reactions are inconsistent, can the audience take them seriously? Aristotle (*Poetics*, chap.

15) calls for lifelike and consistent characters, presumably because otherwise they will be of little interest and so unable to rouse pity and fear. See the note to 475.

1105 The rest seems to refer to 1096 f. They understand allusions to the past but not to the present and future.

1107–9 Both in **can do this thing** and **end** the Greek shows the *tel*-root (see on 972), denoting accomplishment of a goal. The idea of an innate, organic goal for Justice and Retribution has been built into word, image, and action. Cassandra sees Clytaemestra as she bathes Agamemnon (cf. 1128 f.; he must be clean before sacrifice); she senses the queen's purpose but does not yet see the instrument (1115).

1115 f. For the **net** see 1126 f., 1382, and 1581.

1117 f. Although Erinys (**Fury**) does not appear until the choral response (**demon**, 1119), most commentators take the Greek as Lattimore has. **Howl aloud**: see on 586, 1235 f. **Monstrous death** more specifically means "a sacrifice that deserves stoning" (Fraenkel); cf. 1615 f. Stoning was a traditional means of public punishment (cf. *Iliad* 3. 57 and *Antigone* 37).

1121–24 Here the chorus breaks into lyric song, following Cassandra's example. Cf. the image at 179. Lattimore's version from 1122 to 1124 is no more obscure than the Greek.

1125 ff. The inversion (we expect "keep the cow from the bull" but Aeschylus has "keep the bull from the cow") is odd, since the king is threatened, not his mate. No less odd, at least to our ears, is the homely metaphor. In fact the king, who would normally make the sacrifice, is now himself the victim, caught in the very robes he would have worn as priest of the sacrifice, and struck down by the queen, whose **black horn** seems metaphorically borrowed from the bull for his own destruction. If this view is correct, the whole stanza reflects an inversion of normal experience and custom.

1130 ff. To paraphrase: "I cannot claim to understand these prophecies in detail, but they plainly bode no good. That is the nature of prophecy, always in bad times to inspire fear."

1138 f. Is this addressed to Agamemnon or to Apollo? **With him** might also be "with you" and does not preclude Agamemnon, since the pronoun is not expressed. Recent opinion seems to incline toward Apollo.

1143–46 Procne killed her son **Itys** to avenge her husband's savage rape of her sister Philomela. Tereus, her husband, pursued her, but in answer to her prayers the gods transformed Procne into a nightingale (see Ovid, *Metamorphoses* 6. 426 ff.). The nightingale's grieving cry became a paradigm (cf. Sophocles, *Electra* 148). The textual problem in **fate like hers,** where fate ought to mean "death" (though we know of no story concerning the death of the nightingale) seems to have been solved by Page's transposition of the Greek words for "life" (1144) and "fate" (1146). This transposition gives us a nightingale grieving the death of Itys and a response in which Cassandra envies the life of the nightingale. The error, in which the Greek *bion* and *moron* in successive lines were interchanged, illustrates a common source of corruption in these texts.

1150 ff. Whence: also "why, for what reason?" Something of the chorus's confusion may be seen in **cries,** which translates a word normally used of animal cries or the confused cry of a mob, or a scream, either of an archer's bow or an animal. **Singing,** too, suggests a high shrill sound. Though we cannot be certain of the manner of acting and singing here, such words imply wild, distraught speech and gesture.

1154 Marks may be limits, boundaries, or indications of such. The commentators assume that the question means "who marked out for you the path . . ." and that it is finally answered at 1202. Earlier, however, they had recognized Apollo as the source of her inspiration (1083 f.), and "driven of God" (1150; cf. 1140) implies their acceptance of her divine inspiration. Perhaps, then, these questions look to the immediate occasion for her ecstatic prophecy and not to the divine agency responsible for all her visions. So, to paraphrase: "What signs inspire you to sing these terrible, god-granted prophecies?"

1157–61 The **Scamandrus** is both a river (cf. 511) and the tutelary deity of Troy, who in the *Iliad* (bk. 21) nearly overwhelms Achilles. **Drank and grew strong:** see on *LB* 6 f. **Cocytus** and **Acheron** are rivers in Hades.

1163 Since they understand her revelations concerning the past and her predictions for herself, they seem especially ob-

tuse in only vaguely penetrating the references to Agamemnon (1125 ff.). Winnington-Ingram (*CQ* n.s. 4 [1954]) will
grant some obtuseness but argues that the portrait is psychologically consistent and true: "Broadly speaking, what they
display in this scene is a reluctance, amounting to refusal, to
face facts" (p. 26). He does not reject what Murray calls "the
curse of disbelief" (cf. my note at 1100 ff.) but finds this disbelief made psychologically credible in a chorus that has been
intimidated by Clytaemestra and is both fearful for the king
and unwilling to face squarely their own forebodings and
Cassandra's intolerable prophecy.

1170–72 As at 387 and 1103, the medical metaphor domi-
nates. The sacrifices could not cure the morbid condition that
Paris had carried to the city. Cassandra's **brain ablaze** can di-
agnose but cannot cure. At this very moment Clytaemestra is
preparing another sacrifice, one that will itself only perpetuate
the disease (see *LB* 470–74 and 538 f.). In the *Eumenides* the
struggle to cure the house pits Apollo (*Eum* 645) against the
Furies (*Eum* 499–506).

1178 Cassandra turns from song to the iambics of spoken
verse; her first words discard the veil of ecstatic vision.

1179–82 Glance is the verb to both **prophecies** and **girl;**
then **bright and strong** modify **prophecies,** which shares
with **winds** the verb **shall wax.** In the intervening line (1180)
the prophecies are compared to winds rising in the morning,
and this figure is continued in 1181, where they have raised a
great wave, on the **swell** of which the prophecies gleam in
the morning sun (here we have the familiar fusion of thing
compared and comparison; see on 1005 ff.). The compression
and ambiguity of the English (do we take **to burst** with
bright and strong or with **the swell** or with both?) reflect
the Greek.

1183–85 Cryptic speech ("riddles") translates the same
word rendered "darkness of her speech" at 1112. Line 1184 is
addressed to the chorus. She compares herself to a hunting
hound (cf. 1093) on the track of old wrong. A closer translation would be: "bear then witness for me as I run close on the
scene of those brutal things done long ago."

1186–92 The **choir** is revealed as the **vengeful spirits**

(1190), i.e., the Furies, whose song takes as its theme the **old sin** (*atē*; see on 385 f.).

1193 Thyestes **spoiled his brother's bed** by seducing his wife; although Thyestes' son Aegisthus has also seduced the wife of his cousin Agamemnon, the prophecy is here strictly applied only to their fathers.

1194–97 Archery continues the hunting metaphor of 1184 f. **Go wide** is echoed in **wickedness** (*hamartia*, the Aristotelian "flaw" [*Poetics*, chap. 13], and a very common word, in both literal and figurative senses, in Greek tragedy; see *LB* 519 ["the act done"], *PB* 6 ["sin"], *Philoctetes* 1249, *Antigone* 927).

1195 Seers and prophets were not necessarily considered honest or infallible, either in or out of drama. Thomson, in his edition of the play, cites Plato: "There are itinerant evangelists and prophets who knock at the door of the rich man's house, and persuade him that by sacrifices and spells they have accumulated some kind of divine power, and that any wrong that either he or his ancestors have done can be expiated by means of charms and sacrifices and the pleasures of the accompanying feasts" (*Republic* 364b, Lee's translation).

1202 ff. In the following stichomythia Cassandra tells how Apollo fell in love with her, gave her the gift of prophecy, and, when she reneged on her promised favors, annulled the gift by ordaining that no one would ever believe her (1212). In Greek myth the divinities are usually bound by their own promises, oaths, and decisions; so Apollo cannot revoke his gift, though he can turn it to bitterness by making all her prophecies incredible. Rape and flight are common motifs in Greek myth, but Aeschylus would probably not so emphasize Apollo's persecution of Cassandra except for the prominence of the god in the remainder of the trilogy.

1205 One reason we are tempted to read subtle psychological nuances into characters and chorus lies in Aeschylean repetitions and echoes. Here **airs of vanity** repeats the verb "make me delicate" (918 f.) with which Agamemnon describes Clytaemestra's temptation. Since the verb occurs only in these two passages in the trilogy, the chorus may, at least unconsciously, be circling the king's fate as it talks to his concubine. The word suggests the kind of effete, enfeebling self-indulgence regularly attributed by the Greeks to oriental rulers (cf. *Pers* 41).

1217–22 She sees above the house the ghosts of Thyestes' children, slaughtered by Atreus to make a meal for their father (1222).

1224 This puny **lion** is Aegisthus; for the metaphor see 716 and 1258 (of Clytaemestra).

1228–30 The fused image (a flattering tongue, a dog, Clytaemestra) has led to a variety of readings and translations. In **like a secret death** the themes of ruin (*atē*) and justice (*dikē*) are introduced. In part the ambiguity derives from the use of *dikē* in the accusative case, where it may be prepositional, as in Lattimore's "*like* a secret death," or a direct object, as in Lloyd-Jones's "drawing out at length . . . its plea."

1233 The monstrous **Scylla** ate six of Odysseus' men as his ship passed beneath her cave:

> Right in her doorway she ate them up. They were screaming
> and reaching out their hands to me in this horrid encounter.
> (*Odyssey* 12. 256–57)

Apollodorus (*Epitome* 7. 20) described her as having the face and breasts of a woman and, growing from her waist, the heads and feet of six dogs. Her bestial qualities fit nicely into a passage populated with a feeble lion, a distempered dog, and a viper. Cf. *LB* 248 f.

1235 f. The profoundly ambiguous line 1235 is not made easier by some uncertainty about the last word (**hate** or "Curse"?). **Smoldering** may also mean "sacrificing"; **relentless** may mean "without libation." When we add that **howled aloud** is yet another (cf. 586, 1118) cry of victory, usually associated with ritual sacrifice, it is hard not to see a vision of Clytaemestra (the **mother of death**) taking upon herself the role of a vengeful, sacrificing Curse (cf. 1431 ff.). Cf. Zeitlin's translation (*TAPA* 97:648); "a sacrificing hellish mother and a curse-Fiend blasting trucelessly against her near and dear ones," where "trucelessly" means that she, as the mother of death, i.e., of/from Hades, will not be appeased by libations. Cf. her words at 1386 ff. Euripides offers a pun of a similar sort when Dionysus says to Pentheus,

If I were you,
I would offer him a sacrifice, not rage.
(*Bacchae* 794)

1237 Unashamed echoes "daring" of 1231; this willingness to dare all is male, dangerous, and peculiar to Clytaemestra (cf. *LB* 996).

1238 As so often, the pronoun (**his**) is not expressed in the Greek; Cassandra's prophecy is clearer to us than to the chorus.

1241 Words were true echoes "true prophecy" (1215).

1246–48 There is nothing ambiguous about 1246, but the choral leader's reaction (**peace, peace**), which simply deprecates sinister speech of any kind, hardly tells us whether the chorus cannot believe her (because of Apollo's curse), or refuses to face her assertion, or is, perhaps, too distracted by her manner and their own doubts. Cassandra is too quick for them: when they respond **peace,** she links that verb with singing the *paean* (a song of victory) and then puns on "paean the song and Paion the god of Healing" (Denniston and Page). Some form of healing (*paiōn*) occurs at 99, 512 (of Apollo), and 1199 (in "do any good").

1249 This may dazzle them a bit, but not so much that they fail to respond with a wish that she may be wrong. The audience will take the **it** (1249) to refer to Agamemnon's death, but the chorus cannot express such a thought.

1251 Beastly thing is an emendation for "grief": "By what man will this grief be prepared?" The verb ("prepared") is a Homeric euphemism for sexual intercourse, as in "the woman prepares a bed for a man."

1252 Mistake suggests both being driven off the track (hunting metaphor) and being deranged. The wordplay and mocking tone may suggest that Cassandra is a little tired of the obtuse chorus, which recognizes oracular tone but not plain sense (1255).

1257 The cult title **King of Light** (*Lykeios*) is of disputed meaning; some connect it with "wolf," as Aeschylus does at *Sev* 144. Here that sense would point (1) to the most common cult meaning and (2) would suggest "destroyer." Cf. 1259, **wolf.** On the other hand, **flame** (1256) and her inspiration argue for Lattimore's translation.

1258–59 The riddling quality of these lines is clearer in the Greek, which reads, literally, "This is the two-footed lioness" (cf. *Suppl* 895), a phrase that recalls the riddle of the Sphinx (*Oedipus the King* 393).

1260 ff. Wife is a clarifying addition. If the text is sound, the mixed metaphor fuses the ideas of preparing a drug and paying someone a wage by describing the wage (which is the **drug**) as being put into **wrath** (rather than a cup or drink, which would maintain a more distinct image). There is some ambiguity here, not least in 1263, where the Greek could mean either "she exacts vengeance from me" or "she exacts vengeance from him (for my arrival here)." Of course, Clytaemestra had planned Agamemnon's murder before she knew that Cassandra would accompany him.

1264–70 Fraenkel thinks that the words **these mockeries** refer to her garments, which she tears and throws to the ground. The **staff** and **flowers** (= ribbons of wool around her head) would then be additional symbols cast aside. On this view she means, by 1269 f., "that in this action of hers the god himself is operative, just as throughout she feels herself his instrument and sacrificial victim" (Fraenkel, 3 : 584). Fraenkel also passes on a suggestion of Wieseler and Sommerbrodt that Cassandra's garment is a kind of open netting that covers the entire body. An illustration of such a garment, obviously suitable to the imagery and metaphor of the play, will be found in the dictionary of Daremberg-Saglio, 1 : 165.

1268 The text has been questioned by those who cannot believe that Aeschylus wrote "make someone else the wealthy Ruin (*atē*) in place of me." Cf. 1460 f., where Helen is called "a demon of death," and 1501, where Clytaemestra identifies herself with "the old stark avenger"; 736, where the lion turns out to be "a priest of destruction (*atē*)"; and 749, where Helen is "a vengeance" (Fury). Creon calls Antigone and Ismene "twin destruction" (*atē* in the dual, *Antigone* 533).

1270 The watchfulness of the gods, whether for good or ill, is to become particularly prominent in the next two plays (see, e.g., *LB* 985 ff., *Eum* 531). The notion that the gods and spirits keep watch ("have an eye on") covers both beneficent and malignant influence (*Eum* 1045, of Zeus, and *Eum* 220, of

94 AESCHYLUS

the Furies). All of this is traditional but still thoroughly integrated into the trilogy.

1271–76 Charging the god with responsibility for human suffering was not felt by the Greeks to be blasphemous. **Dearest . . . hated** = "by dearest enemies," a nice example of Aeschylean oxymoron. Cf. "strengthless lion" at 1224. The verbal artifice and stylized expression of the play cannot be too much stressed. In 1275, e.g., **seer** and **prophetess** are immediately juxtaposed in the Greek (*mantis mantin*), so that the identity and hostility of god and mortal are welded by grammar, syntax, and position. Similar inflections occur at 1026, 1288–89, and 1374.

1279–85 She foresees the revenge of Orestes. These lines foreshadow dramatic problems set for the *Libation Bearers*. Cf. 1317–19.

1291 The **gates of death** are the "gates of Hades." Cf. 408 f., 603.

1292 **True stroke** is precisely what Agamemnon receives (= "deadly blow," 1343).

1298 The perfect sacrificial victim voluntarily approaches the altar and so may be said to be **driven of god,** since no man may force it to its death. There seems to be an allusion to the Athenian sacrifice known as the *bouphonia* ("a slaughter of the oxen"): oxen were allowed to approach an altar on which sacrificial cakes had been placed; if an ox ate the cakes, it had violated the sacred place and signified its willingness to be slaughtered. See Harrison, *Prolegomena*, pp. 111 f.

1300 This line means that the last moments of one's life are the most precious.

1312 For Cassandra the house gives off the odor of blood; for the choral leader, the scent of **frankincense.** Her fine sense makes him seem inane.

1315 The call to **friends** (which is echoed in "stranger's grace" at 1320) and **bear witness** (1317) draw on legal custom: unless a person wronged calls out for help and invokes as witnesses those present, a subsequent appeal before a court will be invalid. Such considerations for proper testimony may also prompt Orestes at *LB* 972 ff., esp. 987; cf. *Suppl* 904.

1316 The bird fears the bush because of the Greek habit of

setting traps in bushes. The commentators cite Shakespeare's
3 *King Henry VI*, 5. 6. 13 f.:

> The bird that hath been limed in a bush
> With trembling wings misdoubteth every bush.

1322 The **not** is a conjecture; perhaps the line runs: "I wish
to speak once more, a dirge for myself." The **Sun,** source of
light and life, is invoked as a certain witness. Cf. *LB* 985.

1328 f. Cf. the figure at 839; for the ephemeral character of
human affairs cf. 82.

1331–42 Twelve lines in anapestic dimeter, chanted or re-
cited, mark the division between this scene and the next. *LB*
855–68, in the same meter, have a similar function.

1331 Slakeless and what follows recall the argument of
369–84. Man never turns away from prosperity, no matter
how close prosperity may be to the surfeit that breeds disregard for human limitations.

1338–41 These lines take the form of a condition: If Agamemnon, for all this success, must now pay with his life for
blood shed (**generations gone** may include Iphigeneia as
well as the children of Thyestes), who then would claim that
his **angel** (*daimōn*) is always benign?

1343–45 Taplin (p. 323) notes that "outside the *Oresteia*
there are no instances in Aeschylus of words heard from offstage, and assuming that the skene [stage building] was still
new, it is quite likely that this was one of the very first uses of
the device." Cf. the cry from within the house at *LB* 869. As
here, the shouts from within at *Hippolytus* 776 ff. prompt in-
decisive questioning from individual members of the chorus.

Note the play on **deadly** and **to death; struck, stabbed,
struck** reflect the same stem four times in three lines, an effect
that is further intensified by the repeated exclamation (**Ah**).

1348 ff. Although no absolute proof exists that the Aeschylean chorus numbered twelve, the twelve pairs of speeches
attributed here to individuals strongly suggest a chorus of
twelve. No chorus in Greek tragedy leaves the orchestra to
enter the stage building, and some commentators are content
with this convention as a reason for the inconclusive delibera-
tions that precede Clytaemestra's appearance. Yet Aeschylus

certainly prolongs the choral dialogue more than the later dramatists do and much more, too, than he himself does at LB 869, where the messenger explains the cry from within only five lines after it is first heard. The confusion and uncertainty (is the king really slain?) should be noted. The individual voices may be intended to reflect this disorganized reaction. Apart from their doubt about the fact of murder, their reaction to the possible usurping "tyrants" (1355, 1365) unifies their purpose and anticipates a primary theme in the LB (cf. "twin tyrannies," LB 972). Some readers may feel, with Dawe (p. 46), "a tinge of the comic," but there seems little dramatic point to that sort of break in the tension here, whereas the nurse's scene in the LB, which Dawe compares, is both more obviously realistic in style and integrated more concretely into the play.

1355 On **tyrants** see Lattimore's note 6 to his Introduction, p. 10.

1356 f. Headlam detects in **deliberation's honor** an allusion to a proverbial statement celebrating cautious delay. So: "while we waste time, they ignore deliberation and act."

1372 ff. The audience may have expected a messenger to announce and describe the events within (cf. LB 875 ff.). Instead, Clytaemestra appears, covered with blood (1389) and displaying the body of Agamemnon. Taplin suggests that we are even to take 1539–40 literally, i.e., the king's body is not only wrapped in the robes that Clytaemestra threw over him but is also in the tub. Clearly, we have a tableau of the death scene, and we must ask how this scene was represented on the Aeschylean stage.

The possibilities seem to be three: (1) the doors of the palace are thrown open, and the chorus sees Clytaemestra standing over the body; (2) the body, nets, and tub (?) are carried on by attendants, who set up the scene for the queen's speech; (3) the eccyclema (a wheeled cart or revolving platform) advances the tableau through the doors to display the scene described by Clytaemestra. The last is clearly the most immediate and efficient, but we do not know whether Aeschylus had the eccyclema for use in such scenes. At an early stage of Greek theater the second possibility must have been the means of showing interior scenes, yet the time required for setting up the tableau may seem at odds with the incisive introduction of Clytaemestra (but does the modern demand for illusion intrude in such a judgment?). As for the first possibility, the tableau within the doors could hardly have been visible to all of the audience, most of whom were well up the slope from the orchestra. Whatever staging was used here, it was probably the same as that adopted at *LB* 973. See Flickinger's discussion of the eccyclema, pp. 284–89.

1375 Like a hunter, she has surrounded the game with **nets** too high to leap over. For the imagery see the note on 358 and cf. 1382 ff.

1386 The **third blow** comes by analogy: as Zeus the Savior is the third god offered libation in **thanks and reverence** after dinner, so here the third blow is dedicated to him. See the note to 245–47; for another variation see *LB* 577–78. Hades, ruler of the underworld, is often called the **Zeus of the dead** (*Suppl* 157). Fraenkel observes in the passage "grandiose blasphemy," "harsh impiety," and "travesty of ritual language to enhance a gruesome effect."

1392 The commentators compare:

> But his anger
> was softened, as with the dew the ears of corn are softened
> in the standing corn growth of a shuddering field.
>
> (*Iliad* 23. 597–99)

In the present passage the blood-spattered queen likens herself to the earth joyfully receiving rain just when the young plant most needs it. **Of God in glory** means "god-given," as if the victim had been presented for sacrifice by god.

1395 f. Lloyd-Jones cites Odysseus' admonition to the nurse after the slaughter of the suitors:

> Keep your joy in your heart; old dame; stop, do not raise up
> the cry. It is not piety to glory so over slain men.
>
> (*Odyssey* 22. 411–12)

It was in fact customary religious practice to pour a libation of wine to the dead. The repeated **deserved** represents the *dikē* stem, as does "righteousness" (1406). In Euripides' *Electra*, Electra protests that she is ashamed to insult the dead, but Orestes encourages her to freely vilify Aegisthus (900–906).

Earlier in that play she accuses Aegisthus of dancing on her father's grave (326–31).

1401 Vain means "senseless."

1407–1576 Clytaemestra's first speeches, until 1462, are in spoken iambics; from 1462 on her speeches are in anapestic dimeter. Throughout this (epirrhematic) scene the choral responses are in sung lyrics.

1409 f. Words for sacrifice and curse, as in 1413, make an alternative translation possible: "you have taken upon yourself this sacrifice and the roaring curses of the people" (Zeitlin, *TAPA* 96:474). **Hate** is the same as "curse" at 1235 (see note there). After **cast away** and **cut away** an object must be supplied, either "hate" or "your civic rights" (implicit in **homeless**). Death or banishment was the traditional penalty for murder.

1419–20 By sacrificing his daughter, Agamemnon incurred the **stain** of pollution (cf. 209). This is the same guilt suffered by Orestes, "the blot of matricide" (*Eum* 281).

Pollution is dangerous because, like a disease, it can be had from contact. So the polluted man is an outcast whose mere presence endangers others. He requires ritual purification, without which he is cursed forever; see on *Eum* 236 ff., 276 ff., for the ordeal and cleansing of Orestes. For pollution from the shedding of a kinsman's blood see *Sev* 681 f.; Oedipus is a pollution on Thebes (*Oedipus the King* 98). In the *Oedipus at Colonus* (1374) Oedipus curses his sons and predicts the pollution they will bring on their land. Cf. *Heracles* 1232 ff.

1425 This looks like a variant on "suffering and learning" (note on 176), which for the queen becomes a threat: "test me and you will learn to suffer!" **To keep your place** = "to behave yourselves" in Aegisthus' speech at 1620, both with a sneer at this middle ground of discretion, so often recommended in Greek tragedy, so little practiced. Ajax uses the same verb to put Tecmessa in her place:

> Don't probe and question! It becomes you to submit.
>
> (*Ajax* 587)

And Phaedra plots the destruction of Hippolytus:

> he will have his share in this my mortal sickness
> and learn of chastity in moderation.
>
> (*Hippolytus* 730 f.)

1427 f. These lines seem to mean that the bloody madness (**fury**) of the murder is reflected in a bloodshot **eye**.

1429 f. Clytaemestra, **forlorn of friends,** must pay.

1431–34 Right (*themis*: see note at *Suppl* 359–64) translates the same word used by Agamemnon to sanction the sacrifice of Iphigeneia (note on 216). **Sacrament** translates "oaths" (sworn to avenge her daughter). She swore by her three "divinities," **Justice** (*Dikē*), **Wrath** (*Atē*), and **Fury** (*Erinys*); having taken an oath, she made Agamemnon the victim to fulfill her vow. After the trinity of 1432 f., it is tempting to capitalize **hope** and **fear.**

1435 Aegisthus is mentioned for the first time; as master of the house, he tends the sacred **fire** of the **hearth**.

1439 Clytaemestra puns on the name of Chryseis, the **golden** one, daughter of the priest Chryses and given as a prize to the king by the army. The audience would remember Agamemnon's praise of Chryseis:

> because I for the sake of the girl Chryseis would not take
> the shining ransom; and indeed I wish greatly to have her
> in my own house; since I like her better than Clytaemestra
> my own wife, for in truth she is no way inferior,
> neither in build nor stature nor wit, not in accomplishment.
> (*Iliad* 1. 111–15)

1442 In the compound translated **who yet knew the feel,** Koniaris and Tyrrell have detected a sexual obscenity; literally, it is "she who wears down the mast."

1444 Swanlike for two reasons: the swan was thought to sing before its death, as at *Heracles* 110 ("our song the dirge of the dying swan"); second, the swan was sacred to Apollo.

1446 f. A disputed line, but probably more lewd than Lattimore's translation suggests. Cf. Lloyd-Jones:

> when he brought in
> a side-dish for his bed, he pandered to my delight.

The play is certainly not about Clytaemestra's adultery, much less her lust, but her passionate hatred of Agamemnon can be expressed sexually. The king, not the queen, has been the plaything of sexual desire (1453 f.).

1453 That is, for the sake of Helen he has now died at the hand of a woman. The chorus does not care to think of Iphigeneia, for whom he was hardly a "shield, kindest of men."

1455–60 Wild heart may be a shade sentimental: "deranged" or "mad" is closer to the intellectual tone of the Greek. Similarly, **to shine. . . as blood flower** hardly praises: she has crowned herself with a garland that flowers because of blood never to be washed out. Whether the **blood** is Iphigeneia's, Agamemnon's, or the multitude's, or all of them, is not indicated. For the image see the note on 659 and cf. *LB* 150.

1460 Demon is "strife," perhaps personified.

1468–71 Kneel = "fall," the common metaphor of a daimon (**divinity**) stepping or trampling on its victim. Cf. *Eum* 370–76. The **two strains** are Menelaus and Agamemnon, victims of two daimonic women. The alliterative assonance of **steer . . . strength** reflects the Aeschylean *kratos . . . kardiodēkton . . . kratuneis.*

1473 f. More vile crows at *Suppl* 751. **Crippled song** recalls "wild lyric" (1142). Both are out of tune. With Clytaemestra's hymn contrast Cassandra's lamentation (1445).

1477–80 The Furies are like vampires that feed on the blood of the house (cf. *Eum* 302 ff.). What is the referent for **thrice**? Tantalus, Atreus, Agamemnon? Pelops, Atreus, Agamemnon? Tantalus (1469) seems less in focus than Atreus and Agamemnon; Pelops, for all his vices, did not sacrifice children. If she is referring to victims claimed, then Agamemnon, Iphigeneia, and the children of Thyestes come to mind (cf. 1500 ff.). Aeschylus' play with the number three is too varied to be systematized; cf., e.g., 870 f., 247, 173 (where "victor" means "winner in the three falls" of a wrestling match), *LB* 876, and the note on *Eum* 759 f.

Lines 1478–80 mean that the love for drinking blood is constantly renewed by the **spirit** (*daimōn*: the Curse/Fury).

1485–88 On **all through Zeus** Guépin comments (p. 102): "It is a logical consequence of the religious attitude of the tragedians that every tragedy that does not end in conciliation must necessarily end with an accusation at the gods responsible." His examples: Theseus accuses Aphrodite, *Hippolytus* 1460–61; Agave accuses Dionysus, *Bacchae* 1375–76; "Jason accuses Medea, who appears as a goddess," *Medea* 1405–7; Theseus and Heracles accuse Hera at the end of *Heracles* (1313–19). Guépin also cites Sophocles, *Women of Trachis* 1264 ff., and *Ag* 1485–88. See also *Eum* 198–200. Such blame is not blasphemy but a realistic recognition of divine power.

So **God's blessing** means not that god sanctifies the deed but that his power is evident in it.

1489 ff. Besides the accusation and argument of this dialogue, the entire scene is one of lamentation for the dead king. See the notes on *LB* 306–475 and *Pers* 905 ff.

1492 The female **spider,** like the viper called echidna (see on *LB* 550), devours her male partner (cf. our "black widow"). See *Suppl* 887. The **web** is another net.

1500 This may also be translated "appearing in the likeness of his wife." **His revel of hate** (1503) explicitly refers to the feast Atreus offered Thyestes (see 1590–98).

1504 Last blood means "perfect victim." See the note to 972–74 for the same Greek stem. "First offering" at 226 (the same phrase occurs at 65) and "consummation" at 745 are other occurrences of the *tel*-stem that pertain to religion and ritual.

1507 f. The **fiend** (*alastōr* = "avenger," 1501) "guides" Clytaemestra, i.e., joins in to help her fulfill the curse. While the queen claims that she is merely the instrument of justice, the chorus insists that, though an avenging daimon may be at work, she is also responsible. This seems the same sort of thinking discussed at *Pers* 742: where the human agent is ready and eager, the god joins in to speed the work along. In allowing that a daimonic power may also be involved, the chorus assents to some degree of justice (**requital** = *dikē*) in her revenge. So the queen has beaten them back and left them to lamentation (1513 ff., 1537 ff.) and confusion (1530 ff.).

1513–20 The ephymnion, i.e., a part of the song not in strophic responsion, repeats 1489–96.

1532 Their focus is on the house; cf. 1468, 1482, 1554, 1565.

1533 ff. A storm of blood rains down on the house; cf. 1390 and the note at 198. The image changes radically in 1535: **fate** sharpens its **blade** (of justice) to continue the cycle of retribution.

1537 Cf. *LB* 43.

1540 For later references to his death in the tub see *LB* 999 and *Eum* 633.

1545 For **graceless grace** see on *LB* 42. Proper burial, mourning, and continued tendance of the grave are religious obligations of the family and are calculated to insure the good will of the dead. The first half of the *Libation Bearers* takes up this theme. To refuse lamentation (1554) is to leave the ceremony incomplete. Proper tendance for the dead is a significant thematic issue in Sophocles' *Ajax* and *Antigone* and in Euripides' *Suppliant Women* and *Phoenician Women*.

1557 Clytaemestra ironically imagines the reunion of father and daughter in the underworld (a common motif in Greek myth). The Greeks thought that the dead must be ferried across the river Styx in order to come within the actual bounds of the underworld.

1560–66 The stanza sums up the law of retribution: he who acts will in turn suffer (1564). Variations on this idea will be found at 532 f. (of Paris), 1527, *LB* 313 (see note to *LB* 306–14), *Pers* 813 f. Lattimore translates a Pindaric variant

<blockquote>
nothing
is accomplished without loss to the man who does it.
(Fourth Nemean 32)
</blockquote>

Aristotle takes reciprocity as a traditional principle of justice and quotes both the Pythagoreans and "the judgment of Rhadamanthys": "If a man suffers what he has done, strict justice is accomplished" (*Nicomachean Ethics* 5. 5. 3).

1567 ff. This first line means that she recognizes the oracular truth of their pronouncement. While she realizes that her claim for the Spirit's agency is doubled-edged—for just as she struck, so now she must expect the blade—she attempts to placate the daimon by praying it off onto another house (1571–73). Commentators differ considerably in describing the tone of this speech: Is she anxious? resigned? ironic? practical?

1577 Taplin (p. 327) notes that Aegisthus' arrival is all the more unexpected for coming so long after the last choric song marking a division of scenes (1331–42). Normally a scene begins following a song, and all the actors who play the scene appear immediately or very soon after the song. Taplin compares the late entry of Orestes at *LB* 212, but in that case Orestes and Pylades are "concealed" nearby, i.e., they are visible to the audience though not to Electra and the chorus. Later staging is more flexible, as, e.g., at *Philoctetes* 974.

With **splendor** cf. Clytaemestra's language at 1435. **Day of doom** = "the day that brings *dikē*."

1581 In what may be a conscious imitation of this line, Sophocles has Heracles call the shirt of Nessus an

> encircling net
> of the Furies, by which I am utterly destroyed.
>
> (*Women of Trachis* 1051 f.)

1583 ff. Atreus and **Thyestes** vied for rule of the city (**king's right**). Thyestes was at first victorious, since by seducing Aërope, wife of Atreus (see 1193), he had got the golden lamb, possession of which brought the kingdom with it. But the gods favored Atreus and told him to exact an agreement from Thyestes that if the sun changed its course to set in the east, Atreus should be king. Thyestes agreed, the gods reversed the course of the sun, and Atreus won the throne and banished his brother.

1588 The **hearth** is the center of domestic sacrifice (= "central altarstone" of 1056), and so it is the ideal place for the suppliant to bring himself within the protection of the gods. The **grace** he won from his brother consisted in not being slain and thereby polluting the house of his fathers. Tantalus had cut up his son Pelops and offered him as a feast to the gods; now Atreus serves the flesh of his brother's sons to his brother. Cf. the story of Harpagus and Astyages in Herodotus 1. 119.

1601 f. The **curse** of the dead or of those offended by the death of kin (cf. 457 and the note to 1409) was felt to have a binding power that the person cursed could hardly escape; cf. Rigoletto's reaction to Monterone's curse. By a kind of sympathetic magic the fall of the house is tied to the fall of the table, i.e., Thyestes binds his curse to an act and condemns Atreus and his **seed** to suffer a similar fate. No doubt most Athenians, like the chorus (1565), believed that the curse could not be torn from the blood. It is fixed on the accursed the way pollution is fixed on the house and land. Such ritual cursing long survived in the commination rites of the Anglican church, more than one of which might have been used by Thyestes:

> Cursed is he that taketh reward to slay the soul of innocent blood.
>
> (*Book of Common Prayer* of 1559)

For the curse in Aeschylus see also *Sev* 70, 655, *PB* 912; in the *Oresteia*, see *Ag* 1235, *LB* 145 f. (where "prayer for evil" is *ara*, "curse"), 406, 912, *Eum* 417.

1602 Pleisthenes has also been mentioned in the Greek text at 1570 (translated in the phrase "in the house"). His place in the family tree is uncertain (some sources make him the son of Atreus and father of Agamemnon, but that is not the version Aeschylus used in this play). If he is the ancestor of Atreus, then Thyestes curses his own line in cursing Atreus, perhaps, as Whallon (p. 61) suggests, in ignorance of the fact that his youngest child survives.

1604 Another translation: "And I was the just stitcher of this murder." He claims to be the deviser of the net, the one who "pieced it together" (1609). Cf. "cords," 1611.

1612 Vaunting = "to speak hybristically."

1616 For **stones of anger** see on 1117 f.

1623 The mocking tone is clear from the commendatory use of **wise surgeons and exemplars** at *Eum* 62 (note).

1624 "Kicking against the goads" is proverbial for futile resistance; cf. Dionysus' use of the same phrase in Euripides' *Bacchae* 795.

1625 Because Aegisthus has admitted premeditated complicity in the murder, he is legally as guilty as Clytaemestra. Yet it seems strange to use **woman** abusively when a woman has actually murdered the **lord of war.**

1629 f. The singing of **Orpheus** was so entrancing that it moved trees and stones. Cf. *Bacchae* 560–64.

1639 The **yoke** is a commonplace for subjection, e.g., at *Pers* 49 f.

1640 f. Free traced: The trace horse is the third and unyoked member of a team of three. Since his work is largely at the turns in a race, he is for the most part free and unrestrained, unlike his steady companions under the yoke. At 842 the trace horse Odysseus is the man for critical turns.

1644 f. Murder pollutes (**curse**), and murdering blood kin is still more polluting, which makes the present argument odd, since it is Aegisthus who is Agamemnon's cousin. This at least would be the argument of the Furies, who do not persecute Clytaemestra, the reason being that "the man she killed was not of blood congenital" (*Eum* 605).

1646–48 Though to be **in sunlight** is the common idiom for being alive, light also symbolizes victory (1577), survival (900), and delight (602).

The Greek says **these** two **murders,** which, as Fraenkel observes, indicates that the coryphaeus turns and speaks "aside" what is practically a prayer for Orestes' return. Note that Aegisthus does not pick up the reference to the natural avenger, which he surely would do if he heard it. Bain (p. 67) disagrees.

1650 The **henchmen** are his bodyguards. Lines 1650 ff. have been attributed variously by different editors, some of whom object to the chorus having swords (cf. 75), others finding **henchmen** more appropriately referring directly to the chorus. The belligerence of these men, "old in our bones" (72), has surprised some critics, but Vergil did not shrink from letting old Priam arm to face outrage (*Aeneid* 2. 509 ff.), and Euripides has the chorus of his *Heracles* (253–74) imitate them.

1652 f. Among the various kinds of omens, one particularly suited to drama is the one that takes a chance utterance, whether a word or a phrase, as predictive of the future. Here the chorus hears Aegisthus pronounce a **death** sentence on himself and ratifies his last word by designating it the **word of fate** (the chance word that suits the occasion, whether for good or ill; see notes on 624 f., 637, 1246–48, and *Sev* 257 f.).

1660 Or: "struck to misfortune by the heavy heel of the daimon." Cf. "heavy spirit" (1482), the spirit that falls on the house (1468), the imagery of kicking (e.g., 1624) and trampling (923, 963; cf. on "ridden down," *Eum* 150). This is the sort of imagery that makes Aeschylus' vision of the daimonic world so physical and concrete. *Daimōn* occurs in 1663 (= "destiny and power") and 1667 (= "God's hand").

1663 f. See on *LB* 513. **Sober opinion** echoes "behave yourselves" (1620).

1665 Grovel = "fawn." More dogs at 1672, where "howls" = the "whimperings" of line 1631, as if they were puppies.

1668 Proverbial. Cf. "The saying is that exiles feed on hopes" (Euripides, *Phoenician Women* 396, elaborated through 405). Cf. *Ag* 899 and *PB* 252.

Clytaemestra and Aegisthus take possession of the house.

The Libation Bearers

THE FIRST LINES OF THE MANUSCRIPT have been lost, and the text is patched together from parodies of it in Aristophanes' *Frogs* (1126–28, 1172–73) and quotations from it found in ancient scholia. Most editors print the text with one or more gaps between the various fragments, but Lattimore's welding of lines 1 through 9 does not violate the separate quotations.

In Lattimore's stage directions "downstage" probably indicates the central part of the orchestra. The tomb of Agamemnon is also the altar at which sacrifice is offered to the dead. Orestes and Pylades enter from one parodos, Electra and the chorus from the other.

1 Hermes escorts the souls of the dead to the underworld and is thus the proper god to call upon for intercession with the dead (cf. 123 ff.). The Aeschylus of Aristophanes interprets the **powers of my fathers** as "powers of your father," i.e., he watches over the powers given him by Zeus. The Greek admits either reading; in Lattimore's view Orestes thinks of his rights of inheritance (see note on 6 f.). Hermes is also the god of stealth and deception (726 ff.) and the god of contests (811 ff.). Since the Greek also includes the word "ally" (**stand by**), Orestes would seem to have this god of contests particularly in mind.

6 f. Two locks are offered. The first derives from the custom of young men cutting their hair at the age of maturity, and so this lock suggests that Orestes has reached the age to vindicate his rights. It is dedicated to **Inachus,** god and river of the Argive plain, **who made me grow to manhood.** Rivers are credited with begetting and nurturing children (*Suppl* 1025 ff. and note). The second lock signifies his mourning. The hair and head symbolize strength and life, and so the cutting of the hair indicates grief and submission. Cf. *Ajax* 1168 ff.

10 ff. With these accurate conjectures Orestes in effect introduces the chorus and his sister.

17 f. A brief prayer, which, like 1 ff., reasserts his purpose. **Fight beside me** = "stand by" of line 2—an example of ring composition (see the note to *Ag* 1014–16). For Orestes as a warrior cf. 497.

19 Pylades is the traditional companion of Orestes (Sophocles' *Electra* 17, Euripides' *Electra* 1284, and a speaking part in Euripides' *Orestes* 729 ff.). See on 561 and 900–902. As for the staging, they need not be hidden from the view of Electra and the chorus. They simply stand aside, probably to the rear, until at 212 they reenter the action. Their eavesdropping is imitated by Euripides at *Electra* 11 ff., and Sophocles has Orestes suggest that he and his companion (an old slave) overhear the talk of Electra and the chorus (*Electra* 80–82). The most famous eavesdropping in Greek tragedy occurs at *Hippolytus* 601 ff.

21 ff. The parodos, without introductory anapests. The women of the chorus are slaves in the house, perhaps brought back by Agamemnon from Troy (76 ff.). From the outset their sympathy is with Electra. Now they carry **libations** (liquid offerings; see on 92) to the dead king, whom they still lament in the traditional manner (tearing the face, hair, and clothing). Cf. the appearance of the queen at *Pers* 598 ff. (note) and the lament at *Sev* 914 ff.

31 Whence smiles are fled, a single word in Greek, a privative form like our "*un*happy."

32 Fear and terror (cf. 35, 46, 59), dread and apprehension, color the initial scenes of every play save the *Prometheus*. Cf. *Ag* 14, *Eum* 88, where the fear is subsiding, *Pers* 115 and 205, *Sev* 45. This **terror** has been inspired by Clytaemestra's dreams (523 ff., 929), which, interpreted by divination (32, 37), signify the **wrath** of the dead Agamemnon. Just as Orestes and Electra believe that they can evoke the aid of their dead father's spirit, so Clytaemestra hopes to placate it (cf. *Ag* 1568–73).

42 f. Grace without grace: cf. *Ag* 1545. Her sacrifice is apotropaic, i.e., calculated to **turn aside** the harm threatened by the dream; thus the chorus can speak of grace ("favor," "good-will") without the substance of grace, for Clytaemestra acts from fear, not from kindness.

Other invocations of **earth** occur at 399, 489, 540, 722; cf. *Suppl* 890.

Terror is on me: they fear to offer any prayer commissioned by Clytaemestra to propitiate the spirit.

48 ff. Pollution is physical (66 f.); **blood spilled** demands more blood, and a polluted **hearth,** the focal point of family worship, cannot be purified by offerings made by murderers.

54 ff. Pride is not the usual meaning of the Greek word *sebas* (e.g., it is "reverence" at *Eum* 690). Thomson translates: "Reverence for royalty, once indomitable and unconquerable, passing through the ears and hearts of the people, now stands aside, and they are afraid: success—among mankind that is God and more than God." The sequence of thought in the stanza may be the following: when reverence is gone, men will live in fear, and then good fortune, the gift of the gods, replaces piety and regard for divine power; yet finally the scales of justice bring a reckoning.

61 ff. For the imagery of the scales see on *Ag* 206. The **beam** is explicitly "the beam of *Justice,*" and it strikes (or "watches over," a reading preferred by several editors) three classes: those in their prime (**in the brightness**), those who are aged, and those who are dead (**Desperate** = "utter," i.e., the darkness of Hades).

67 Gore is caked also means that the murder is fixed, or planted, as in the earth, and probably also that "the penalty is determined."

69 Ruin = *atē*, here with some feeling that "his own infatuation carries him away" until he is ripe with **infection.** This metaphor of brimming infection leads naturally to a comparison with the violation of a maiden's virginity, for which there is **no cure.**

72 f. Cf. Lady Macbeth's "all the perfumes of Arabia will not sweeten this little hand."

76 f. Resisted fate = "necessity" (cf. *Ag* 217, *PB* 514 ff.); in all three passages necessity is simply the constraint of fact or an irrevocable decision.

83 The vanities that have killed my lord: the Greek is vague, offering something like "the vain fortune of my masters," and it is not clear whether they lament Agamemnon's death or, as Lattimore's version suggests, the adultery that led to the murder.

84 Electra's silent presence throughout the parodos is worth noticing. Cf. Danaus' long silence during the parodos of the *Suppliants*. The scene beginning at 84 runs for 500 lines, very long by Greek standards. The iambic dialogue is interrupted by a long lament (the kommos of 150 lines, beginning at 306). The tomb is the central focus of the scene, and it must have been near the center of the orchestra, put in place during the interval between the plays. The palace is in the background, near enough to recommend caution (see 264 ff.). There is no need for a stage, the use of which would even impede the corporate lament; here actors and chorus mingle freely in the orchestra, around the tomb.

84–105 Aeschylus' Electra is young, uncertain, innocent, not yet the petulant outcast of Euripides or the hateful cancer of Sophocles. Since she has no part in the second half of the play, it is clear that the poet wanted to limit her scope to the recognition and lament at the tomb. Drink offerings for the dead, tendance of the grave, and lament were customary for the Greeks. Such care maintains the ties of the family with its past and, particularly, with the dynamic spiritual powers of the dead, who, as so much of this play presupposes, take an active interest in the living. Electra fears that sacrifice to Agamemnon may actually accomplish Clytaemestra's wishes, and so she asks if, and how, the prayers and offerings should be given.

92 The **liquid** might be pure wine or wine mixed with water. Odysseus offers "honey mixed with milk, . . . sweet wine, . . . water" (*Odyssey* 11. 27 f.). A trench or vase fixed on the grave receives the liquid, so that it enters the earth (cf. 164).

95 Electra has only to substitute *kakōn* (**evil**) for *kalōn* (good) to pervert the customary formula and to show her disposition.

106 ff. Burton (pp. 260 f.) compares *Oedipus at Colonus* 465–92, where the coryphaeus instructs Oedipus in the proper form of local ritual.

109–11 My friend? / Yourself first is an odd sequence in

English. **Those of good will** are those loyal to the memory of Agamemnon, not merely her friends, though in this case they happen to be the same: "Pray for those well disposed (to your father). Who among those dear to him are these? Yourself first, then all who hate Aegisthus."

113 The coryphaeus (= chorus) is not trying to shirk responsibility for the suggestion. The meaning is, as Thomson says, "you take my meaning."

119 More than man = *daimōn*, i.e., some spiritual power; both the dead Agamemnon and the Furies qualify as daimonic powers. The "charmed spirits" of 125 are daimons.

123 This response reflects popular morality (cf. *Ag* 608, *Sev* 144–46, 1049). Her question has more point than the coryphaeus allows it, as Clytaemestra's appeal at 912 shows ("are you not afraid?" = "do you not have pious regard for . . ."). Still, Orestes' morality, though sanctioned by Apollo, is also expressed in terms of quid pro quo (e.g., at 930).

124 f. See note on line 1. As the guide of dead souls, **Hermes** may intercede with the powers of the underworld. **Earth** must release Agamemnon's spirit, but she is also claimed as an avenging power (147 f. and 399).

129 The Greek here normally does mean **lustral waters**; but in the present context that does not make sense, so we should probably understand "libations."

130 The play begins with Orestes' prayer; at 156 the chorus will add its prayer. See the note to 306–465 for prayers in the kommos.

131 ff. The motif of dispossession also appeared in Orestes' first lines (cf. 915). It is not merely materialistic (135 f.) but is especially cast in the form of saving the house (e.g., 235 ff., 264); for not only has rightful political rule been usurped but also rightful spiritual succession (this is the force of Electra's claim at 244 f.).

137 For the idea in **high style and luxury** see *PB* 437 ("pride").

140 f. Contrast the Sophoclean Electra's attitude at *Electra* 308 f., where "moderate and restrained" echoes **more temperate of heart** and "pious" echoes **purer.**

143 f. Avenger looks at the most straightforward expression of the dramatic issue, while **as they deserve** invokes *dikē.* More subtle is the simple **in turn,** which translates a prepositional prefix (*anti*) frequently used to express nuances of reciprocity. Its basic meaning, whether as preposition or prefix in compounds, denotes "exchange" (*x* for *y*). Already it has occurred at 94 ("return"), 121, 133, 135 ("in the place of a slave"). Its most studied form occurs at 309–13 (see the note to 306–14). Other examples at 498 f., where "like those" and "in turn" reflect two *anti* compounds in successive lines. Unique compounds like "that once were men" (*Ag* 444, which might also be translated "ashes *for* men") and "cross winds" (*Ag* 147; elsewhere only at *PB* 1087) imply a special poetic interest in this common preposition. Cf. *Eum* 264 and 268, and also *Eum* 982–84, where the double use of *anti* marks the resolution of the demand that blood repay blood.

150 f. This is addressed to the chorus. **Incantation** = "winner's song" (343); the meaning is, roughly, "let the dead triumph."

152 ff. This brief lyric begins with lines difficult both for the text and sense. Dodds, accepting Weil's emendation of the Greek text (he substitutes a Greek word meaning "stream" for the word translated here as **mound**), translates: "let your tears fall splashing, and perish for a perished master, upon this stream which sought to avert things good or evil, the pollution we pray against, pollution of an outpoured drink-offering" ("Notes on the *Oresteia*," p. 15). Here, as also in Lattimore's version, "to avert things good and evil" involves looking at the libation first from Clytaemestra's point of view (for her it is an "averting of evil"), then from Electra's point of view (for her it is an "averting of good"). Clearly, mother's evil is daughter's good, and the double focus ("bold paradox," as Dodds puts it) makes sense, however difficult; moreover, it is not an impossible compression for Aeschylus. Such compression introduces ambiguities, which inevitably lead to scribal error and textual corruption. Many of these ambiguities are deliberate and are due to the typically Aeschylean parataxis of word and phrase, i.e., the cumulative modification of a single idea, suggesting, without differentiation, the chorus's ambivalence about sacrifice of any sort, about death, and about contact with polluted ground, where the angry spirit may make too little distinction between friend and foe.

161 The **Scythians,** who lived in what is now the Ukraine, were famous riders and archers. Here Ares, the **god of war,** stands, by metonymy, for the man who epitomizes the god's attributes.

169 Deep-waisted refers to dress, the manner in which the sash or girdle is worn, usually of the dress of foreign women ("in ample folds adorned," *Pers* 156, of the Persian queen).

172 Aristotle (*Poetics,* chap. 11) does not prize recognition by tokens so much as those from circumstance, but even among material and physical signs some are more plausible than others. Electra's credulity, her willingness to believe that the hair and the footprints (206) are those of Orestes, has been parodied by Euripides (*Electra* 518 ff.) and defended by Aeschylean enthusiasts; see the sensible reading by Kitto, *Greek Tragedy,* p. 83. Electra's vacillation between hope and skepticism and her recognition that she may be deluded by hope (194) make it clear that the poet finds these tokens no more than adequate, while the brevity and directness of the scene, compared with the lament that follows, imply that recognition is not the central dramatic purpose. By contrast, both Sophocles and Euripides suspend recognition and at the same time draw more emotional life from the reunion. See Sophocles, *Electra* 1098 ff.

176 Lloyd-Jones notes that Menelaus, speaking to Helen, compares Telemachus to his father:

> I also see it thus, my wife, the way you compare them,
> for Odysseus' feet were like this man's, his hands were like this,
> and the glances of his eyes and his head and the hair growing.
>
> (*Odyssey* 4. 148–50)

They are all the readier to think of Orestes (and the audience is ready to follow them) because they have been praying for an avenger—specifically, for Orestes.

183 Bitter wash introduces imagery from a storm at sea ("tempest" or "flood," as at *Pers* 599). Cf. 186, 202 f.

185 Thirsty drops has not been explained.

187 f. She reasons against the likelihood that the hair might belong to some other citizen or to Clytaemestra (189).

201–4 A number of editors would transpose these lines to the end of the speech, after 211, on the grounds that Orestes responds to her prayer (**we call upon the gods**). Thomson urges that 211 must end the speech, and some editors transpose 201–4 to follow 210.

Note how the imagery modulates from **seafarers** through **live** to **tree**. The key term is **live**, which is a variation on "savior" (2) and "salvation" (236). So if the ship lives (is saved), the house will spring to life once again. Similar imagery and compression occur at 260 f., where "the stump . . . shall (not) sustain altars" moves in the opposite direction from the present imagery.

205–10 Thomson observes: "I have myself seen Irish peasant girls sitting round the fire and comparing their family likenesses in feet."

212 Orestes reenters the action: where was this "place of concealment"? Since the second half of the play takes place at the gates of the palace (653 ff.), Orestes may have stepped back into the door of the stage building. But quite possibly he and Pylades simply stepped aside, remaining still until this "reentry." Actual concealment argues more realism than we generally find in these plays.

219 f. Or: "Here I am. Seek for no nearer friend than me" (Smyth). Very emphatic, but she, who has been so hopeful, sees cunning (**net**).

222 For laughter and hostility cf. *Eum* 788 f., *PB* 152–59b.

225 ff. Orestes' patient criticism clearly demonstrates that Aeschylus realized the hopeful nature of Electra's reasoning, and, of course, we have her own self-conscious critique at 194.

231 After being accused of weaving a net of treachery (220), he offers a **piece of weaving** for assurance.

234 f. A conscious paradox, since **those nearest** means "our dearest friends" as well as our "nearest kin." Electra responds with the same word (**dearest**). Orestes' line looks like a variant on Solon's commonplace:

> So shall I bring pleasure to friends and pain to enemies.
> (Solon, Frag. 1, line 5; trans. Lattimore, *Greek Lyrics*)

Cf. *Pers* 1033.

238 ff. The motif goes back to the *Iliad* (6. 429–30), where

Andromache, who has lost all her family save her husband and child, says to Hector:

> Hector, thus you are father to me, and my honoured mother,
> you are my brother, and you it is who are my young husband.

Cf. the variations at *Antigone* 906 ff., *Alcestis* 646.

240 In **turns** (= "falls" or "inclines") the metaphor of the scales momentarily surfaces (cf. 61 ff.).

244 Honor denotes someone worthy of reverence (= "majesty," 157); cf. note at 54 ff. and Sophocles, *Electra* 685. For the **third** and Zeus see *Ag* 1386. **Right** = *Dikē* ("Justice" at 148).

246–63 The prayer carries two traditional motifs: (1) "Zeus sees the end of everything" (Solon 1. 17); (2) "Zeus the father":

> The kin of the gods,
> those near to Zeus, theirs is the altar of Zeus
> the father in the clear air on Ida's slope.
> (Aeschylus, Frag. 162; my trans.)

Zeus protects the family and clan and so the house (254, 263), and he watches over the sacred tie between parent and child. Just as the dead father is honored by his children, so Zeus the protector of the family can be honored only if the family survives from father to son (255 f., 261). Latent in this passage is "Zeus the father of Justice" (see 948 f.). If Zeus does not accomplish just retribution, man will have no sign of divine order in the world (258 f.). Without denying to Orestes some sense of personal loss and suffering, I would say that the central focus is the time-honored Greek feeling for patriarchal order, continuity of the family, and the subservience of personal desires to those of the family. So Electra can mention Iphigeneia "pitilessly slaughtered" (242) without much censuring her father, on whose "sacrifice and high honor" (256), however sordid in our view, she and Orestes so depend that no affection for Iphigeneia can divert them from reasserting the father's right.

247 The play is full of animals: **eagle father** (cf. note to *Ag* 122) naturally has fledgelings (255), but the mother is a **viper** (249; again at 994), the son a wild bull (275); the mother a fawning dog (420), the son and daughter wolves (421); Electra has been treated as a vicious dog (447); Clytaemestra has dreamed she gave birth to a snake (527), and Orestes will "turn snake to kill her" (550). Cf. 585 ff.

249 Herodotus reports a bit of natural history about this **viper**, the *echidna*, which Aeschylus seems certain to have had in mind: "when [*echidnai*] pair, and the male is in the very act of generation, the female seizes him by the neck, nor lets go her grip till she has devoured him. Thus the male dies; but the female is punished for his death; the young avenge their father, and eat their mother while they are within her; nor are they dropped from her till they have devoured her womb" (Herodotus 3. 109; trans. de Selincourt). Borthwick adduces numerous examples of this belief (e.g., *Antigone* 531, *Iphigeneia in Tauris* 287) and points out the obvious analogy between the mating snakes and their young and the house of Atreus. The sexual animosity and the **coils** (248), extensively elaborated in the net imagery, also suit Aeschylus' themes. Cf. Orestes at 549 f., Clytaemestra at 928, and *Ag* 1231 ff.

251 To bring to **their shelter slain food** ambiguously plays on several meanings: the slain food is "paternal prey," i.e., prey hunted either by or for the father; since the word translated as **shelter** means "tent" and may have referred in Aeschylus' time, as later, to the stage building behind the orchestra, the line could also suggest "we cannot bring our father's prey (to justice) onstage." Lattimore's translation keeps the phrase within the metaphor of the eagle and snake.

260 Stump continues the metaphor of the house as tree (204). Since this word may also mean "foundation" or "base," it becomes at 646 "Right's anvil" (= "the foundation of Justice").

264–68 House = "hearth" (cf. 48 ff.). The warning clearly indicates that the palace is not outside our dramatic perception. Line 268 refers to a form of execution in which the victim is tarred and then set on fire.

269–96 Does Orestes feel any personal anxiety and doubt about the revenge? Is he simply reporting Apollo's command, which he has already accepted as binding, or do the several lines devoted to the terrible suffering to be experienced if he refuses Apollo's charge reflect a subjective scruple? Critics have argued for both views, but they are not mutually exclusive.

Increasingly in the Archaic age Apollo embraced and advocated ritual purification as a means for criminals, and particularly for homicides, to escape the endless cycle of bloodguilt (see 1059 f.). That aspect of Apollo's jurisdiction becomes clear in the *Eumenides*, but in this play he has sanctioned, even demanded, blood for blood (cf. 1030 ff.). The greater part of this important speech describes the terrors awaiting Orestes if he fails to exact retribution from his mother. The obvious irony is that the same Furies (283) will drive him, crazy, into exile if he *does* kill Clytaemestra.

270 Forsake = "betray."

272 Disaster (*atē*): of physical and psychological affliction.

274 Cut them down in turn (see note to 143 f.).

275 Bull's fury: cf. *Ag* 1125 ff.

278 Thomson compares *Ag* 345–47. **The angers from the ground** are the spirits of the dead (285; cf. 292 f.). In book 22 of the *Iliad* the dying Hector threatens Achilles, saying that he will become an "anger" that will pursue Achilles to his death. A hundred years after Aeschylus' time Plato tells an "old tale," according to which

> the man slain by violence, who has lived in a free and proud spirit, is wroth with his slayer when newly slain, and being filled also with dread and horror on account of his own violent end, when he sees his murderer going about in the very haunts which he himself had frequented, he is horror-stricken; and being disquieted himself, he takes conscience [memory] as his ally, and with all his might disquiets his slayer—both the man himself and his doings. [*Laws* 865d–e; trans. Bury]

And a little later:

> And should the nearest relative fail to prosecute for the crime, it shall be as though the pollution had passed on to him, through the victim claiming atonement for his fate; and whoever pleases shall bring a charge against him, and compel him by law to quit his country for five years. [*Laws* 866b]

279–83 "Aeschylus was either borrowing from some doctor's clinical knowledge or else shows himself as an attentive observer of symptoms. This whitening of the hairs [**leprous fur**] on a dangerous ulcer was recognized by the Hippocratic school as a grave sign" (Stanford, *Aeschylus in His Style*, p. 56). Others understand the punishment to be a scabrous itch.

283–88 The **avengers** are the Furies, which also occurs in the singular (402, 577) and is translated "Vengeance" at 650. For his **terror** see 1023 ff.; for his vision of the Furies see 1048–50.

290 Bronze-loaded lash has been suspected. If it is sound, it suggests a scourge tipped with bronze. He will be an outcast from his city (290), from communal libations (291), from the altars of the gods (293 f.). These penalties for not avenging his father are exactly those the Furies demand that he suffer for murdering his mother (*Eum* 653–56).

The motif of the cursed exile may be found in a number of later tragedies. Oedipus curses the murderer of Laius (*Oedipus the King* 246 ff.), and Thebes suffers a plague because it harbors the murderer of its former king. Heracles describes the cursed fate awaiting him as murderer of wife and children (Euripides, *Heracles* 1280 ff.; cf. *Orestes* 46 ff.). For Orestes' escape from the pollution of murder see *Eum* 448–52.

297 ff. Obedience is obviously still open. The reasons to **trust such oracles** are clearly negative rather than positive. **Work that must be done** is euphemistic: he does not want to speak plainly of matricide. In what follows, four reasons are given for revenge; they are: divine (Apollo's command), familial (his **father's passion,** the positive side of "wrath of the father," 292 f.), personal (his **estates**), and social/sexual (**brace of women** recalls the theme of sexual antagonism so prominent in the *Agamemnon*).

306–475 This lyric section is called a *kommos*, literally, a "striking" (the word occurs in 423), which refers to the beating of head and chest during lamentation. Aristotle (*Poetics*, chap. 12) defines the kommos as "the common lamentation [*thrēnos*] of the chorus and actor[s]." Formally, this lyric is made of songs alternating between the chorus and one of the two children (for two actors sharing the lament cf. *Sev* 875–960). In content, the songs include lament; prayer and appeal to the dead Agamemnon (e.g., at 332 ff.); and invocation of Zeus (394), Earth (399), and the rulers of the underworld (405). Lament is combined with petition, invocation with sacrifice; the spiritual goal is to conjure the aid of the daimonic powers for the children as they try to reclaim the house for themselves. Their supplication subverts Clytaemestra's attempt to appease the dead and aims to capture the attention and dynamic power of the underworld for their revenge. Cf. the successful conjuring of Darius, *Pers* 619a–80.

Metrically, the pattern of responsion of 306–422 is the following: A aba A cbc A ded A fef, where A represents anapests. A second section, 423–455, has the pattern a b c c a b. Each letter represents a stanza metrically responsive to the stanza designated by the same letter.

306–14 Destinies = Fates (*Moirai*).

The balanced pattern of these sentences illustrates the interlocking and reciprocal nature of retributive justice. Only to illustrate the pattern of the Greek, we may translate 309 f. "for hateful word, hateful word" (ABAB), while 312 might be turned "for bloody stroke, stroke bloody" (ABBA). Both sentences begin with the preposition *anti* (**for;** see note on 143 f.); both end with a verb (third-person imperative). Choice, action, suffering: the inevitability of this pattern, here in the variant **Who acts, shall endure** (cf. *Ag* 1564), is reflected in the structured, interlocking pattern. Word embodies action: the thing and its name are one. Cf. 461: "Ares against Ares falls, Right against Right" (AA, verb, BB) where the Greek, without prepositions, has but five words.

Who acts, shall endure: the agent will endure suffering (experience) similar to what he has caused. The meaning of this commonplace in our play is well glossed by the following passage from Plato's *Laws*:

> The myth or story (or whatever one should call it) has been clearly stated, as derived from ancient priests, to the effect that Justice, the avenger of kindred blood, acting as an overseer, employs the law just mentioned, and has ordained that the doer of such a deed [i.e., willful murder of a kinsman] must of necessity suffer the same as he has done: if ever a man has slain his father, he must endure to suffer the same violent fate at his own children's hands in days to come; or if he has slain his mother, he must of necessity come to birth sharing in the female nature, and when thus born be removed from life by the hands of his offspring in afterdays; for of the pollution of common blood there is no other purification, nor does the stain of pollution admit of being washed off before the soul which committed the act pays back murder for murder, like for like, and thus by propitiation lays to rest the wrath of all the kindred. [*Laws* 872d–873a; trans. Bury]

(In "come to birth . . . female nature" Plato is referring to reincarnation of the soul.)

315–22 Orestes begins the search for the right word, the
right gesture, to rouse his father's spirit. What is the relation
of the second sentence in this strophe to the question that precedes it? Most translators seem to interpret it as adversative
(Lattimore's **yet**), perhaps because the following choral stanza
reassures Orestes and thus implies that his sentences have expressed doubt about the efficacy of his prayer. I am inclined to
think the meaning may be: "All the same, a lament, glorious
to the great lords of the house of Atreus, is an action of
grace." That is, Orestes recognizes that the dead are honored
by his mourning (even if they do not respond), which is
styled **an action of grace** because it is freely given, without
obligation, and so the greater honor.

323–31 Cremation does not destroy the spirit or its wrath.
The killer will come to light (328). This very **deathsong** (the
"mourning" of 321), with its just claim (**stern**), will search
him out. The song not only summons the dead spirit but has
the magical power to ferret out the malefactor.

332–39 Electra likens the tomb to an altar at which suppliants and exiles (the children driven from home and paternal
rights) seek safety. The absence of a pronoun in 339 makes it
possible to take **disaster** (*atē*) of the ruin that lies on the house
or of the daimonic Clytaemestra who possesses it.

340–44 The subject of **bring home** is **winner's song** (the
paean). The object is ambiguous; it is either a person, **the beloved**, or "a newly mixed bowl of wine" with which the victory would be celebrated.

345–53 The wish is traditional. Telemachus speaks of his
lost father:

> I should not have sorrowed so over his dying
> if he had gone down among his companions in the land of
>   the Trojans,
> or in the arms of his friends, after he had wound up the
>   fighting.
> So all the Achaians would have heaped a grave mound over
>   him,
> and he would have won great fame for himself and his son
>   hereafter.
>
> *(Odyssey* I. *236–40)*

Lloyd-Jones compares Achilles' speech to Agamemnon in *Odyssey* 24. 30–34. The **Lycians** were Asiatic allies of the Trojans.

352 f. Lattimore takes the adjective **doubled** of the Hellespont; others take it to mean "beyond the sea," i.e., at Troy. The burden of such a grave would be a **light lift** because it would be a glorious memorial.

354 ff. Imagining Agamemnon as a lord among the dead, subservient only to the **Kings of the under darkness,** the chorus continues the thought of the preceding strophe. As we see from Odysseus' visit to Hades in the *Odyssey*, book 11, one strand of Greek thought represented the dead as joined together in a society much like the one they had known in life. Such a view was aristocratic and thus suitable to this play, but it was hardly universal in Greece; in fact it is not even the only belief reflected in the *Odyssey*, where we also witness Tantalus and Sisyphus paying, in the underworld, for their vices in this world. The chorus's present worship at the grave also reflects another view of the dead, one that subscribes to ghosts and the soulful unease of creatures such as Hamlet's father, spirits restless and revengeful because they have been foully murdered. So here the wish implies that the manner of Agamemnon's death and burial (cf. 429 ff.) has wronged his status and left him unable to take his proper regal place in the world below.

Since the Greeks did not enjoy a single, universal belief about death and its consequences, we should not dig too carefully with logic's pick. Nor should we question the emotive force of the scene because of the evident literary influence or question its religious spirit because of the compressed and metaphorical lyric. We have here not life but the condensed, passionate evocation of an essential ritual of life. The only thing that keeps Aeschylus from showing us the ghost of the dead king is the fact that his drama isn't going that way; the ghost could only be vindictive and still soiled with his crimes, whereas Orestes, though he seeks paternal aid, has been sent by Apollo and must not be tainted by the old motives or the old vices.

369–71 By those they loved is a supplement in a metrically deficient antistrophe. If correct, Electra would mean they should have died, as Agamemnon did, at the hands of their kin (we naturally think of Orestes and Electra as the kin, but neither the Greek nor the analogy requires that). **The distant story** refers to the hypothetical suffering of Agamemnon's murderers.

372 Dreaming in the sense that she wishes for great good fortune, even greater than that brought by gold, greater than that known to the Hyperboreans (**the Blessed Ones north of the North Wind**). Bolton (p. 7) summarizes Pindar's description of the Hyperboreans: "Theirs is an idyllic life passed in song and dance, feasting and worship of their god Apollo. They know not disease nor old age, though their span of life is a thousand years. Toil, war, and Nemesis are strangers to this holy race." See Pindar's *Tenth Pythian* 30–44.

375–78 Imagery from the **lash,** goad, and spur abounds in Aeschylus; cf. *Ag* 642, *Suppl* 109, *PB* 325–26. The commentators are inclined to explain **twofold** from the two children or from the "double reproach" (Thomson: of murder and adultery charged against Clytaemestra), or from two hands striking the tomb; but it also seems to anticipate the antithesis that follows, between the **powers under ground** and the **unclean lords,** both of which may be said to be lashing the children to action.

380 ff. Cf. the **arrow** at 285, 184 (translated "sword"), 162; archery at 1033, *Ag* 364, *Eum* 676.

Lattimore has regularized the syntax of the sentence at 382–85, which in the Greek may indicate Orestes' inability to name the act he plans: "Zeus, Zeus, sending up from below a delayed destruction on the hard heart and the daring hand—yet it will be accomplished for (our) parents." (This version is closer to the manuscripts, but Lattimore's imperative, **force up,** is a small change that brings syntactical normality.) Since later speeches (554 ff.) and actions (899) give us a son who has some moral scruples at the thought of murdering his mother, a broken version here appropriately suggests a certain reluctance to look the act in the face, to say what he must do: kill his mother.

386–92 The **man** and **woman** are Aegisthus and Clytaemestra. **Deathsong chanted in glory:** see *Ag* 586. **Flitters:** something flies about, as "fear beats its wings" at *Ag* 975–77;

this image of agitated movement modulates into a storm **wind** striking aslant the prow (= **stem**) of a ship. **Thin** means "piercing"; the hatred is **burdened** because it is a long-felt grudge.

393–97 Lattimore has apparently emended the Greek to render **from all shoulder's strength.** Tucker's bold interpretation of the Greek gives us "the god of both parents," but no interpretation seems to have gained the day. **Smash** means "split" and probably looks to the lightning of Zeus (cf. *Ag* 367, 469), as Thomson says. The land will **believe** when it has a sign from Zeus that he crushes usurpers.

400–404 Law means customary usage. Blood on the earth becomes a pestilence (= **death act**) which summons the chthonic Fury to renew the cycle (*atē* on *atē*, 404).

406 Perhaps, since they are addressed in prayer, the **curses** (see on *Ag* 1601) should be capitalized; cf. *Eum* 417. In the *Eumenides* the Curses of the Dead (i.e., the Furies) oppose Zeus and his agent Apollo, but here the same prayer calls Zeus and the Curses to avenge father and king (the provinces of Zeus) and the murdered kin (the domain of the Furies). The word for curse also occurs in 146 ("evil prayer"), 692, 912.

409 Implicit in the invocation of the dead is some sense of need and perhaps, too, some lack of confidence and anxiety at killing his mother (cf. 434 ff.). So while the kommos both laments and celebrates the dead, it also strengthens Orestes' resolve. Strictly speaking, he knows where to turn, for Apollo has commanded the revenge; but that knowledge does not lessen the personal trauma. On the other hand, the primary emphasis is on the dispossessed son of the house, not on the personal dilemma of Orestes, and the Greek is more closely rendered "where should one turn?" (By contrast, we find the first-person "where shall I turn?" at *Ag* 1531.)

420–22 For the **fawning** dog see *Ag* 1228 f. **Softens** (= "charms") at first may suggest that the object of the fawning is the dead spirit, whose anger she would charm away with libations; but the following comparison implies that it is the children, whose savage purpose, wolfish as their mother's, cannot be charmed away. As usual, Aeschylus probably had both referents in mind. For the motif comparing parent and child Thomson cites Sophocles, *Electra* 608 f., and *Antigone* 471 f.

423 Herodotus says that the Medes were called **Arians** until the visit of Medea of Colchis, from whom they took their new name. **Cissia** was the Persian district known as Susiana (the ancient Elam). Asiatic lament was reputed to be the most passionate; cf. *Suppl* 67 f. (note).

The lyric now turns to the death and rites of Agamemnon.

429–33 All daring characterizes Clytaemestra several times (cf. *Ag* 1231, *LB* 384, 594–97), and, at the crucial moment of decision at Aulis, this word also describes Agamemnon (*Ag* 221). Agamemnon's burial (*Ag* 1541 ff.) has been accomplished, but without the customary honors and ritual mourning. Line 431 means that no citizens attended the procession; **no sorrow** suggests the absence of prescribed lamentation, as does **unbewept.**

434–38 Orestes' resolution may seem uncertain from the interrogative, though I don't think Lattimore intended the question to read that way. Line 435 might also, then, be rendered: "Then she must pay for this dishonor . . ." In 436 f. the parallelism and anaphora (repetition at the beginning of a sentence or clause—here of the word **for**) are wonderfully succinct, something like, as a vow, "God willing, my hands able." Line 438 seems no less vigorous for being a commonplace of the "see Rome and die" variety (cf. *Ag* 1610 f.).

439–44 Sophocles' Electra (*Electra* 444 ff.) also reports this mutilation. Thomson cites Frazer's description and explanation: "Greek murderers used to cut off the extremities, such as the ears and noses of their victims, fasten them on string, and tie the string round the necks and under the armpits of the murdered men. . . . It appears to be a widespread belief that the ghost of one who has died a violent death is dangerous to his slayer, but that he can be rendered powerless for mischief by maiming his body in such a way as would have disabled him in life" (Frazer's note to Apollodorus 3. 5. 1, Loeb ed., 1 : 328–29).

Such mutilation is the obverse of the binding power of magic and the dead man's curse (see on *Ag* 1601): the magician mutilates a representation of the living target and thereby hopes to maim or kill him; the murderer cuts off the hands of the corpse and thereby hopes to make it impotent. Such belief probably accounts for the head-hunting in the *Iliad*.

450 This is spoken to her father.

459 Cf. *Pers* 630–32.

461 Warstrength = Ares; **right** = *dikē*. For the structure of the line, see the note on 306–14.

466–75 A pair of responsive stanzas ends the kommos. The central metaphor is medical: the house is like a living person, with a congenital **pain** from the **stroke** of *atē* (**disaster**). The **cure** is a medical plaster (here translated by **there lies**), which must be homemade. Cf. *Ag* 1190, and see Jones, p. 96.

475–78 Cf. *Pers* 619–30.

480 Few lines in the play offer more cogent evidence for arguing that the house and the dynasty, with the political and social power they entail, are more urgent for both Orestes (and the dramatist) than personal feelings about revenge. It need not be a question of either/or, however, and it may be fairer to say that for Orestes the interests of the house clearly demand a murder that he must find personally repugnant.

481 f. The second line is corrupt, having lost at least one word; emendations vary, and **murder** represents Hermann's supplement. At any rate, her thought turns to Aegisthus, not to the woman who dominated the *Agamemnon*.

483–85 If they succeed in their vows, he will be honored perpetually at the feasts devoted to the dead; if not, nothing.

486–88 As Kitto observes (*Form and Meaning*, pp. 48 f.), this would be stylistically offensive if Electra were thinking of a husband and children. On the contrary, like Orestes she thinks of a rightful return of status and estate; the bridal dowry and commemorative libations symbolize her return to a proper degree and order.

490 Persephone, daughter of Demeter, is invoked as queen of the underworld.

491–93 Cassandra foresaw the **bath** (*Ag* 1109); Clytaemestra described the **net** (*Ag* 1382), which leads to **a beast in toils** (more vivid if we omit the word **like**); cf. 997 ff. and 1072 for later echoes.

495 The items and events just mentioned are **challenges** in that their unavenged memory reproaches the king's honor. The dead do lose their strength, so that tendance is required to keep their influence vital and beneficent. Agamemnon has slept for some years and must be reminded of his own interests.

497 Despite his use of guile, Orestes is much more a warrior, a man for **battle;** cf. the language at 2, 17, 461, 478, 489 f.

498 Holds offers another metaphor from wrestling (cf. 339, 866–69). The Greek match had three falls; Clytaemestra won the first, Orestes will win the second.

501 Cf. 247 ff., 255.

503–9 It often happens that the manuscripts either do not specifically designate the speaker(s) or are clearly mistaken in their disposition. Here we have a patch of almost thirty lines (497–523) without specific attribution, with the added problem that lines 505–7 were attributed to Sophocles by Clement of Alexandria. Various editors have responded variously. The most obvious reason for breaking up the present speech (500–509) is to continue the pattern that begins with line 479 (two speeches of two lines; two speeches of three lines; eight lines of stichomythia; one speech of three lines). To keep this design, Page assigns 500–502 to Electra, 503–4 to Orestes, 505–7 to Electra, and 508–9 to Orestes. This attribution neatly extends the scheme of line distribution that began at 479 and gives for the whole sequence from line 479 to 509 the following pattern: 2:2:3:3:1:1:1:1:1:1:1:1:3:3:2:3:2. If 505–7 can be dropped (assuming they are Sophoclean lines, interpolated here from a marginal gloss), then, beginning with 497, assign: Or. (497–99); El. (500–502); Or. (503–4); El. (508–9). This arrangement gives a perfect symmetry from 479 to 509.

503 The **Pelopidae** are the descendants of Pelops.

505–7 The **for when** introduces these lines in the Greek. **Voice** also means "omen" (cf. *Ag* 926 f.) and "fame." All three meanings may figure in this line. In the following simile the **net** recalls Clytaemestra's fishing (*Ag* 1381 ff.). The children, then, **like corks,** mark where the net has sunk and serve to buoy it up, thus saving it from sinking into the depths. If the lines are interpolated, they were well chosen.

510–12 Cf. *Ag* 914–17; Sophocles, *Electra* 1334–38 (speech/action).

513 Prove your destiny = "daring destiny and power" at *Ag* 1663, where Aegisthus' taunt suggests our "trying your luck." Since **destiny** translates the word *daimōn*, they may also be said to be testing the ghost, to see if it will help them, to see if they have actually gotten its attention.

The choral transition at 510–14 marks a new stage, from lament and evocation to exposition and planning.

517 f. As Thomson says, **wretched grace** does not make sense unless we understand Orestes to mean "a poor enough offering for such a crime." Even this view leaves unexplained the emphasis on **dead and unfeeling:** if the dead are unfeeling or unconscious, the entire kommos has been vain and futile.

519–21 Another significant use of "exchange" (see note on 143 f.). **Atone** = "compensate for."

521 Reason says probably refers to a proverb ("as the saying goes").

523 On **dreams** as omens see *Pers* 177 ff. The lyric poet Stesichorus in his *Oresteia* told of Clytaemestra's dream of a serpent. Stesichorus is probably Aeschylus's source; cf. on 733.

527 So Hecuba dreamed that she gave birth to a firebrand (*Trojan Women* 921 f.). Cf. *Ag* 824 (on "beast," see note to *Ag* 822–25), 1232 f.; *Suppl* 895 ff.

533 Athene tricked Hera into nursing the baby Heracles, who gave his stepmother a good bite, having sucked her immortal milk.

539 Medicinal also means "surgical." Cf. *Ajax* 583.

548–51 Aeschylus had a reputation for the marvelous (see on *Suppl* 570). **This hideous thing** belongs to the same class as Typhon (*PB* 355–56), the son Zeus may get (*PB* 923), and the transformed Io (*Suppl* 570). **Interpreter** (= "reader of marvels") also applies to Cassandra (*Ag* 1440 f.), whose visions baffle the chorus; to the chorus itself, when the signs are ominous (*Ag* 977, "mantic"); to Apollo (*Eum* 62), who will see the horrid Furies; and to Calchas, who sees the sacrifice of Iphigeneia (*Ag* 125).

550–53 The association of snakes with death, the underworld, and the cult of heroes deepens the image, which plays on the paradox that Clytaemestra more naturally fills this role (see 249 and 994) and will find snake monsters to be her avengers (1048–50 and *Eum* 126 f.). Orestes' interpretation, together with the imagined marvel of "turning snake," causes the coryphaeus to regard him as a diviner (**interpreter**) able to expound cause, effect, and proper ritual. Thus the language of the Greek borrows from ritual, and the self-consciously dramatic language of **rehearse** and **parts** misleads.

554 ff. With this speech the intrigue proper begins. For continuity with the *Agamemnon* see note to *Ag* 886 (**treachery**). The attention to **disguise** (560), proper **dialect** (564), and the contingencies of reception (565 ff.) implies dramatic realism. Orestes' concern for how he will get into the house and his preoccupation with Aegisthus (569 ff.) are not justified by the event, for he has no trouble gaining access, and Aegisthus is killed almost immediately. (See the note on *Pers* 528–30.) Clytaemestra will give her son more trouble; perhaps Orestes does not want to think of his mother and so makes the killing of Aegisthus the pressing difficulty. Yet outwardly he is all confidence, which is another aspect of the speech that proves misleading (cf. 899).

Despite the vague instructions, the audience might expect Electra to have some part in the plot, but we hear nothing more of her after 579, unless she speaks 691–99.

557 Net also means "noose."

561 Orestes puns on **Pylades'** name: "to the outer gates with Mr. Gates."

563 ff. Mt. **Parnassus** towers above Delphi in central Greece, in a district known as **Phocis**. The language of our text does not reveal any trace of a Phocian dialect.

566 In a curse of ills = "possessed by a *daimōn*."

571–74 The text at 574 is disputed. Page accepts Dodds' emendation, which for 573–75 yields: "or if he comes back and says to me face to face (for you may be sure he will actually summon me into his presence), then before he can say . . ." (Dodds, "Notes on the *Oresteia*," pp. 17 f.).

578 For the third time: see on *Ag* 1386.

583 f. The identity of **the god** has been debated, since the Greek ("this one") may refer by gesture either to Agamemnon or to the statue of Apollo before the house (*Ag* 1081). Because he wants a clear-cut shift of scene, Taplin (p. 584) favors Agamemnon, but 264 ff. seem to have more point if the palace is imagined as immediately present. Also bearing on this issue is the exit of Electra (Lattimore would apparently take her into the house). For her to exit into the palace seems to draw attention to it prematurely, in a much more emphatic fashion than Orestes' nod to Apollo. She probably does not return (see on 691) and should now exit with Orestes and Pylades. The stasimon which follows thus divides the play into two large acts, each with a separate focus (tomb, then palace) but without complete disregard of their mutual proximity. No new scenery is required.

585–651 The first stasimon. With the opening lines compare *Antigone* 332 ff., where "Many the wonders" = **Numberless . . . dangers** here. **Sober thought** might also be rendered "anxiety." **Torches:** of various atmospheric phenomena, and perhaps here of meteors.

594 ff. The first word of the antistrophe (594–602) marks a climax and contrast with the list of "dangers" in the strophe and gives the antistrophe a thematically as well as metrically responsive form. **Daring, stubborn,** and **all-adventurous** are variants on the same root. For the theme of daring see 630, 996, 1029, and *Ag* 1231. Despite the general character of these lines, it is hard not to think of Clytaemestra, the **female force** (perhaps both "force that conquers woman" and "the conquering force of a woman"), whose **desperate** (= "loveless") **love** has destroyed Agamemnon.

603–11 This strophe and the following antistrophe (613 ff.) offer examples from myth of perverse love. **Althaea** was the mother of Meleager. At his birth the Fates declared he would live until the brand then burning in the fire had burned out. His mother saved the brand and hid it in a chest, but when in an argument over division of the spoils from the Calydonian boar hunt Meleager killed her brothers, Althaea threw the brand back into the fire, thus condemning her son to death (Apollodorus 1. 8. 2). Both Sophocles and Euripides made plays from the Meleager story.

612 ff. The **girl of blood** is Scylla, daughter of Nisus, king of Megara. Apollodorus (3. 15. 8) and Ovid (*Metamorphoses* 8. 44 ff.) make her love for Minos, king of Crete, Scylla's motive for cutting her father Nisus' **immortal hair,** thereby killing him and condemning her city to servitude. Aeschylus makes her the dupe of bribery (**seduced by the wrought golden necklace**), like Eriphyle, wife of Amphiaraus (see Sophocles, *Electra* 837–39).

621 Foul wretch = "with the instincts of a dog." Cf. "dog-hearted" at *Suppl* 758.

623–30 A particularly corrupt stanza, especially from 624 through 628, but it seems that the allusions are to Clytaemestra rather than to a third example from myth (the **treacheries** then are hers, and the **lord** is Agamemnon). **Not inflamed** (transferred from Clytaemestra?) makes a strong oxymoron after **prize the hearth,** since the fire on the hearth should always be kept lit. **Woman's right** (= "woman's spear") recalls the phrase at *Ag* 483 (note), with more respect this time.

631–38 A third example of woman's sexual perfidy. "The Lemnian women did not honour Aphrodite, and she visited them with a noisome smell: therefore, their spouses took captive women from the neighbouring country of Thrace and bedded with them. Thus dishonoured, the Lemnian women murdered their fathers and husbands, but Hypsipyle alone saved her father Thoas by hiding him" (Apollodorus 1. 9. 17). Kranz (p. 152) notes a number of strophes ending with "rhetorical" questions: *Suppl* 125, 807, 823 f.; *Sev* 157, 356; *Eum* 525. For another standard technique of closure see the note below on 649–51.

640–45 There is some textual uncertainty here. Perhaps the first **right** (*dikē*) is personified. In Lattimore's translation **that which had no right** (*themis*) must refer to the murder of the king. Other versions take the meaning to be: "Right, though trampled into the ground, will strike those who transgress Zeus's majesty."

646 ff. Right's anvil: see the note on 260. **Right, Destiny,** and **Vengeance** (the Fury) conspire for the homecoming and for the cleansing of the house.

649–51 The last sentence has a structure worth noting: in the Greek, **child** is the first word, **Vengeance** the last, with the entire last line (of the three lines) modifying and celebrating the Fury. "A child it brings home, of ancient blood's pollution to avenge, in time, the famed, pensive Vengeance."

This sort of postponement to final position is easy in the inflected Greek and is common in Aeschylus. Krantz (p. 152) compares *Sev* 791 and *Ag* 749, in both of which Erinys ("Vengeance" and "Fury") is the concluding word in a lyric stanza.

652 The scene shifts from the grave to the house; no new sets are needed, for, as Taplin says, the action simply changes its focus.

At 560 Orestes spoke of disguise, but he did not reveal his plan to report his own death (681 f.). His own (hopeful?) forecast that he would find Aegisthus at home may lead us to expect the master of the house; on the other hand, the preceding lyric is all Clytaemestra.

660 Many primitive peoples imagine the heavenly bodies moving in **chariots** or in some other form of human locomotion. By an easy extension, especially easy for the Greek personifiers, atmospheric conditions such as night are given vehicles for travel. Cf. *Phoenician Women* 1563, "chariot of the sun."

665 A number of words and phrases in this passage ambiguously resonate with earlier and later passages. **Delicacy** (*aidōs*), e.g., is exactly the idea invoked by Clytaemestra at 896 ("take pity"), and it causes Orestes a momentary scruple ("be shamed," 899); see the note on 896 ff.

670 A similar resonance may be found in Clytaemestra's offer of a bath to the travelers, quite traditional in itself but here inevitably recalling the king's last bathing (cf. 491). So, too, in her odd phrase **the regard of temperate eyes,** the word **temperate** (from the *dikē* stem) connotes a proper, civilized reception. Yet another variant on this stem is Orestes' "carefully" at 681, which also means "with complete justice" (the same word at 241 was translated "as she deserves").

674 ff. Contrast the long circumstantial account of Orestes' death that his servant delivers in Sophocles' *Electra* 680 ff.

679 Strophius: cf. *Ag* 880.

691–99 Some editors assign this speech to Electra; today most give it to Clytaemestra. If it is Electra's, the feeling is necessarily feigned; if it is Clytaemestra's, the grief may be completely feigned (see the nurse Cilissa's comment, 737 f.), or it may be sincere, expressing at once her relief and regret. She has reasons to be ambivalent about her son, but some critics have found any sincerity incompatible with her manner elsewhere. If the speech is given to Electra, she has a role in the intrigue, yet no great role. Telling against assignment to Clytaemestra is the tone of her next speech (707 ff., cold and formal) and the sense of lines 715 and 717: without Electra on stage, Clytaemestra must give the command at 715 to a slave, and the Greek at this point, which suggests legal accountability, would be odd if put to a slave, but perhaps right, in a nasty way, if put to her daughter; also, 717's allusion to "our numerous friends" is hard to reconcile with the present speech, for it either contradicts the loss claimed here or treats that loss sarcastically. Against giving the lines to Electra are the facts that we don't know when she came in, we hear nothing else from or of her, and the part is very slight and undeveloped for a major character.

On balance, I think the lines are Clytaemestra's. Assigned to her, the scene maintains an economy and directness that Electra's presence only muddles. The question of her tone, i.e., her sincerity, is difficult but not insuperable. Since there is no dramatic reason to feign grief—and unnecessary dissimulation is hardly the way of this woman—we may accept her sense of loss as authentic, even if, unlike characters in Euripides, she does not fall completely apart from remorse. She pulls herself together quickly enough, and we need not wonder that the servant Cilissa disbelieves her mistress, while her hostile witness deserves no special credulity. For some modern critics this view will be altogether too "psychological," which means out of keeping with the austere formalism of Aeschylean rhetoric and the narrower, less-rounded characters that such a style supposedly entails.

692–99 For **curse** see 406 and 912; **antagonist** continues the imagery from wrestling (cf. 339, 498, note). A remarkable number and variety of images turn on seeing (cf. the notes on 246 and 985 ff.). Metaphors from **archery** are common, especially in contexts of hunting (cf. *Ag* 1194), and not least because both Apollo and Artemis are hunters with the bow. **Of all I ever loved** is a little strong for "you strip me of those dear to me" (the plural ["those"] for the singular is common but hardly adds force to the sentiment). Can the woman who calls this house a **swamp of death** call for "an axe to kill a man" (her son, 889)? These last four lines are much more difficult to attribute to Clytaemestra than the first five. **Hope** as a **healer** would seem language more natural to Electra (cf. 194, 236, 539). Of course, if Clytaemestra is faking it, she might naturally preempt Electra's metaphors.

Set down as traitor: the translation represents a commonly accepted emendation. Lloyd-Jones's interpretation saves the received reading, which he translates:

> now the hope that existed in the house as medicine
> against the evil revelry you must write down as present and
>   awaiting death.

His comment: "When criminals were condemned to death in Athens, they were entered in the register as 'present' or as 'absent' because only if they were present could the sentence be carried out." Thus a legal metaphor is retained. Lloyd-Jones "*evil* revelry" is itself an emendation that hinges on whether we take "revel" with "healer" or "hope," i.e., as "a hope of bright revel" or as "a healer of an evil revel."

708 Clytaemestra is the unconscious victim of her own irony. **Our friend** translates the same word as "all I ever loved" (695), so that she is made to say, "You will be no less dear for reporting my dear one's death." So Orestes speaks of their relationship as one between strangers (703), while his mother unconsciously speaks of him as kin.

710 It is the hour also means "it is the crucial (or opportune) moment." Cf. note to *PB* 379–82.

711–14 The rest they deserve = in manner worthy: the same abstract phrase, meaning "what is fitting," ends both lines. She might be thinking of the amenities of entertainment, but he can take it as a good omen, since the person he intends to kill unconsciously acquiesces in what is fitting and proper for all concerned.

713 Some modern editors emend **men** to a singular. The plural must refer to attendants carrying baggage and the like; the emendation is easy, and there are no other references to these attendants. Taplin suggests that the plurals are a deliberate alteration for a later production. Subsequent producers, he says, found Aeschylus "too bare for their taste; and they took any easy opportunity to introduce more colour and spectacle" (p. 342). Lines 712–15 are addressed to a slave or to Electra (see on 691–99).

717 f. Smyth's translation, ". . . and—since we are in no lack of friends—will take counsel touching this event," brings out the contradiction some readers have found between these lines and 691–99. **Friends** continues the irony (note on 708).

719–31 An interlude in anapestic meter; cf. 855–68 and *Ag* 1331–42.

722 f. No distinction should be made between **Lady Earth** and **Earth Queen;** so, "who now *lies* mounded."

726 f. For **Persuasion** see on *Ag* 385; for **stealth** see *Ag* 886 ("subterfuge"). **Go down to the pit** suggests both descent to the underworld and the wrestling metaphor. The chorus assumes, as the audience probably would, that Orestes is now dealing with Clytaemestra. The nurse's appearance surprises them and diverts the action.

733 This, for us, rather inflated way of referring to the nurse's grief is a natural result of Aeschylus' penchant for animating things and personifying feelings and ideas. The scholiast on 733 says that Pindar called the nurse Arsinoë and that Stesichorus called her Laodameia. For the Pindaric passage see *Eleventh Pythian* 15–37. Stesichorus may have invented the nurse's role.

737 f. Character can be read in the **eyes;** cf. *Ag* 796. The nurse's judgment is commonly accepted as true and so as necessarily implying Clytaemestra's hypocrisy at 691 ff. But no one in the house loves the mistress, and there is no compelling reason to think that this nattering old woman knows her mistress through and through.

749 ff. The nurse's recollections, not anecdotal, not specific to Orestes, take us momentarily into the world of comedy, an interruption of the tragic rhythm that is more characteristic of Euripides than of Aeschylus. Cf. Cadmus and Teiresias in *Bacchae* 169 ff. and also the guard in Sophocles' *Antigone* 223 ff. The problematic moral burden Orestes carries is suddenly, and unexpectedly, thrown on the shoulders of a baby not yet potty-trained. Orestes himself cannot be embarrassed by these lines, but for a minute the audience must balance the incongruent problems of child and man. Cf. Bergson:

> The bashful man rather gives the impression of a person embarrassed by his body, looking around for some convenient cloakroom in which to deposit it. This is why the tragic poet is so careful to avoid anything calculated to attract attention to the material side of his heroes. No sooner does anxiety about the body manifest itself than the intrusion of a comic element is feared. On this account the hero in a tragedy does

not eat or drink or warm himself. He does not even sit down
any more than can be helped. To sit down in the middle of a
fine speech would imply that you remembered you had a
body. [*Comedy*, p. 94]

Bergson goes too far, but still his point bears on the present
issue. Rose finds the passage comic, but many scholars find
little or no comedy in any of the plays, one reason being that
the style remains "tragic" even as the content turns mundane;
e.g., **he needs to make water** is in the Greek even more euphemistic and remote from childish peeing, being a single abstract noun that occurs only here in Greek literature. Thomson
compares *Iliad* 9. 485–95, where Phoenix reminds Achilles
how he played the nurse and father.

762 In his *Eleventh Pythian* Pindar says that the nurse
snatched Orestes away and out of the house while Clytaemestra was killing the king and Cassandra. At *Ag* 877–81, however, Clytaemestra says that she sent the boy to Phocis, and
nothing in the *LB* contradicts that.

766 ff. Here the coryphaeus follows the Aristotelian in-
junction to join in the action (*Poetics*, chap. 18). By persuading Cilissa to alter the message (770), the chorus makes the
way for Orestes' revenge easier and more plausible. Since this
motif of the **bodyguards** (768) is otherwise gratuitous, Aeschylus clearly sought dramatic involvement of these secondary characters.

773 A proverb.

775 The same metaphor from changing winds at sea occurs
at *Ag* 219 ("changed") and *Sev* 707 ff.

783 ff. The prayer to Zeus continues for three stanzas. The
entire lyric is plagued by such corruption that the translator
must necessarily choose among emendations.

786 Temperance is much more in accord with the style of
these avengers than of those in the *Agamemnon* (cf. the note on
"discretion," *Ag* 1425).

791–97 Because the final word (**you**) is not expressed in
the Greek, the stanza offers a nice ambiguity and an ominous
foreshadowing of Orestes' suffering. **Blithely he will repay**
means, in the context of Zeus's aid, that Orestes will gener-
ously repay Zeus with honor and sacrifice; but since the **you**
is not expressed, and because the language here is normally

used of penalties (as at 935 f., "Justice . . . heavy and hard"), the line also means "he will pay recompense" (with this meaning, **blithely** makes a tidy paradox). This second sense of the line leads to the metaphor **harnessed to the chariot of suffering**; cf. *Ag* 217. The Greek says "orphaned **colt**" (cf. 247), thus intruding actual description into the metaphor. Cf. *Ag* 1640, *LB* 1022 ff. The imperatives (**See, Set, Make**) continue the address to Zeus.

800 ff. Their prayer turns to the household gods (**gods of sympathy**). **Fair-spoken:** another common reading would yield "fresh," i.e., new and untainted, which may explain the transition to **breed** in the next line.

807 ff. The **cavern** is assumed to be the inner sanctum of Apollo's temple at Delphi (cf. *Eum* 39 f.). Apollo and Hermes (next stanza) make a pair of sons of Zeus, one from light, the other for darkness, to guard the son of the house.

811 The son of Maia and Zeus is Hermes (whom Orestes invoked in line 1); in the following lines he is credited with power to bring favorable winds (with a metaphor from both sea and travel), a power not usually his but his father's.

815–18 Line 815 is deleted in some editions. **Markless** means "enigmatic." The text and meaning of 816 vary so much that some editors have taken all reference to speaking out of the line. Lines 817–18 are said by Lloyd-Jones to refer to the "cap of Hades," the possession of which makes the wearer invisible (see *Iliad* 5. 845). Hermes the "lucky" would be useful for any duplicity, and disguise and darkness suit him as well as Orestes' project.

819 ff. Zeus, the household gods, Apollo, and Hermes willing, then the chorus may sing a song of deliverance. The ship, aided by a fair wind (cf. 775, 813), will have weathered the storm (cf. 202 f.).

826 ff. But success depends on Orestes (**your turn**), who must be able to remember his father when Clytaemestra cries **Child** (cf. 896 ff.). **Innocent murder** ("an *atē* that cannot be blamed") echoes **wreck and ruin** (*atē*) of 824 f., which is repeated in the next stanza ("disaster," 836).

831 ff. As **Perseus** had to steel himself to face the gorgon Medusa, whose glance turned men to stone, so Orestes must face and murder his mother. Perseus serves as a type of intrepid courage; both heroes are helped by Hermes, which may explain the comparison. (Persons and stories from myth often serve as paradigms, i.e., as examples of moral and social behavior.) **What their bitter passion may desire:** corruption of the text makes the sense uncertain, but the idea seems to be that Orestes will do a favor for the bitter anger of father and house. **Make disaster a thing of blood** = "wreak havoc on those in the house." As they say **the man stained with murder,** Aegisthus enters; the song summons and announces the victim.

838–930 This passage has five entries by speaking characters, a brisk pace for Aeschylean drama.

838–47 That even Aegisthus feigns grief (**no delight**) may make it easier to believe that Clytaemestra is also posturing (note to 691–99). Like its more legitimate heirs, he worries for the **house,** which has been **bitten and poisoned** (the first verb suggests that the wound is from a snake; the second may also be translated "festering"). With **dripping fear and blood** compare the image at *Ag* 179 f. Lloyd-Jones suggests that the metaphor in 845 f. is "from sparks leaping upward from a bonfire." **Empty** means "in vain," i.e., to no effect, a favorite word (= "wastes" at 926; cf. *Eum* 142, 144).

855–68 These anapests, like those at 719 ff., divide the scenes. The anxious chorus turns to Zeus, but not in song.

864 f. Domain refers to political succession, **treasure** (*olbos*: see on *Ag* 928, *Pers* 706) to general prosperity.

869 Cf. *Ag* 1343, 1345, where the wounded and dying Agamemnon is given two lines to speak.

870–74 "How does it stand? How has it been accomplished for the house?" Line 872 seems to indicate that the chorus will now divide and **stand aside** so that the dramatic focus will be directly on the house.

878–79 The **women's gates** may imply a stage building with two doors, the servant having used one, Clytaemestra the other; but the slave may, for all we know, be calling into the house about doors within. Thomson, referring to 579 f., suggests that Electra has bolted the doors to the women's chambers. The slave's excitement, however, as well as the pace of events, hardly gives us time to worry about these arrangements.

883 f. The **razor's edge** is proverbial but has been emended to "on the block" by editors who find the nonmetaphorical use bizarre. Emending, Lloyd-Jones gets:

> Now, it seems, near her consort
> shall her head in turn fall, smitten by the stroke of justice.

885 Two conventions of the Greek theater come into play now, one that keeps all killing offstage, another that keeps all the action outside the house. We do not know why the Greeks restricted killing, suicide, and mutilation (e.g., the blinding of Oedipus) to offstage action. The exception to this rule, the suicide of Ajax in Sophocles' *Ajax*, indicates that the reason was not a religious taboo, which, had it existed, would probably also have prohibited bringing on the dead. In fact there seems a pronounced inclination to display, after the offstage horror, the bodies of the slain and mutilated (e.g., the dead children and blinded father in Euripides' *Hecuba*, the head of Pentheus, carried by his mother in the *Bacchae*, the bodies of Haemon and Eurydice in the *Antigone*). Though some religious inhibition might have influenced the pre-Aeschylean theater to avoid onstage bloodshed, other factors, such as the difficulty of staging a convincing killing and the awkwardness of murder in the presence of an interested chorus, should also be considered. We may also guess that in the earliest theater there was more rather than less narrative (this would explain the prominence of the messenger's role in fifth-century drama), so that the habit of reporting offstage events, and particularly supernatural phenomena, contests, dragon-slaying, and bizarre crimes, became an easy, convenient, and acceptable way of dealing with theatrically tricky episodes. Imitation of epic narrative may also have influenced dramatic practice. Even in the Homeric epics, which are definitely dramatic in style, long speeches report episodes that a modern novelist would not hesitate to present dramatically within a total narrative structure.

As for the absence of interior scenes in Greek tragedy, the most obvious determinant may be the theater itself. The spacious stage and orchestra are not easily constricted, even in the mind's eye, to a room. There is also the chorus, whose presence disturbs the realism of any scene the director would take inside. Hence the locus of most plays *before* a public building—a palace or temple—and the use of the trolley (eccyclema) to present tableaux of interior scenes. If we think of the present example in terms of naturalism, we shall see that the slave (the "Follower") would not run out to call Clytaemestra, who is inside. Nor would she come out to discover from a household slave that Aegisthus has been killed within. If she wants an ax (889), she should stay in the house. But Aeschylus did not want to report the confrontation of mother and son; he wanted to dramatize this crisis, and to do that he had to bring all the characters out from the natural locus of the action, i.e., from the great hall, where they were standing over the body of Aegisthus. Both Sophocles and Euripides stage this scene more realistically, but in doing so they sacrifice the vivid emotional and moral dilemma that culminates the present play.

886 f. Clytaemestra calls this line a **riddle** because the line, taking advantage of natural syntactical ambiguity, means either "the living man is killing the dead" or "the dead are killing the living."

888 "We shall perish by treachery, just as we killed."

889 The question posed by what follows is whether or not Aeschylus made use of four actors to manage the parts of the follower, Clytaemestra, Orestes, and Pylades. Although some commentators have thought the follower could exit as early as 886 and return dressed as Pylades six lines later, such a quick change of costume has seemed to other critics impractical. Even a costume change in ten lines, assuming that Pylades does not enter until 900, is very rapid. Thus, if we accept Lattimore's stage directions, we must entertain the possibility that Aeschylus used four actors for this scene, which would make it unique in extant Greek tragedy. The argument for four actors is perhaps the stronger for our expectation that the two men will appear together: Orestes' question at 899 and Pylades' violation of his role as mute might be thought all the more surprising if Pylades had continued the role of onstage mute until the last conceivable moment. Some critics, however, find his appearance only after Orestes' appeal equally dramatic.

Aristotle tells us that Aeschylus introduced the second actor, Sophocles the third, with which, Aristotle says, tragedy reached its natural, mature form (*Poetics*, chap. 4). Yet no inherent propriety or external rule seems to preclude more than three actors, and the present scene, on the face of things, demands four actors.

896 ff. Oh take pity translates a verb repeated in **be shamed** (899); the idea in the Greek (*aidōs*) is regard for normal usage and public opinion, not so much conscience as a sense of propriety, which, of course, Clytaemestra threw to the winds when she killed a king and a husband.

In Plato's *Euthyphro* Socrates quotes a poet who says "where there is fear, there also is shame [*aidōs*]"; then Socrates corrects this description to "where there is shame, there too is fear," a conversion that points out the negative, inhibitory nature of *aidōs* (*Euthyphro* 12a–c).

The gesture (**before this breast**) recalls Hecuba trying to keep Hector from facing Achilles; she too bares her breast and invokes *aidōs* (translated here in the word "obey"):

> Hector, my child, look upon these and obey, and take pity
> on me, if ever I gave you the breast to quiet your sorrow.
> (*Iliad* 22. 82 f.)

Cf. *Suppl* 641 ("respect"), *Eum* 680, 709 (where "think on" = "have respect for"), and see the note on 665, above.

900–902 Cf. 269 ff., *Eum* 798 f. Orestes' appeal to Pylades would be unexpected, since by now the audience will have assumed that Pylades is a mute character, as he is in the Electra plays of Euripides and Sophocles. If we ask why Aeschylus introduced this dramatic surprise, several considerations come to mind. We have noticed that in the first half of the play Orestes has little to say about the prospect of killing his mother and prefers to talk of Aegisthus. His present hesitation confirms the view that a personal, moral scruple is indicated by his earlier evasions. There is no doubt of what he must do, but that does not mean that he wants to do it. Such a scruple gives Orestes a more decent human instinct than either his mother or father has displayed. In fact, we may say that he displays in this gesture and question a deeper moral sense than Apollo, whose counsel, after all, continues the law of an eye for an eye, whose terrors are no different in kind from those of the Furies, whose law and argument in the next play will offer no truly satisfactory moral solution to Orestes' dilemma. Orestes is caught between the hard primitive law and a more refined sensibility and ethical sense; and though he acts according to the old law, his personal reservations, which the austerity of Aeschylean characterization will not elaborate, signify his right to ultimate acquittal.

902 Cf. the sentiment at *Antigone* 453–59.

904 With **kill,** Orestes continues the language of sacrifice; the same verb occurs at *Ag* 1433 ("sacrificed"). Cf. notes on *Ag* 1409 f. and 1419–20 and the language of the Furies at *Eum* 303 ff., where "cut down" in 305 is again the same verb.

909 Some part in that reflects language that has frequently called attention to responsibility (Greek *aitios*), particularly the responsibility of Aegisthus ("who helped," 134; "the man of guilt," 70; "the man stained with murder," 837), but also of the pair ("the murderers," 117 and 273), while Orestes has looked for help ("stay with me," 100) and the chorus has used the stem negatively ("not seem to be accountable," 873). It occurs again in 1031. This language carries over to Orestes' trial—very emphatically at *Eum* 199 f., in the accusation of the chorus, and then in his defense (465 ff.).

915 f. The dispossessed Orestes speaks figuratively; his mother would take him literally, for purposes of refutation.

917 f. Apparently he is ashamed to mention her sexual infidelity—odd after 906; she catches his point and alludes to Agamemnon's **vanities** (Cassandra? Chryseis?). Cf. Euripides, *Electra* 1030–34, for plainer language.

924 Curse is correct but more explicit than our text: "take care for the angry hounds of a mother" (she refers to the Furies; the same phrase occurs at 1054). Cf. *Eum* 131 f.

926 The line apparently plays on a proverb that compared an insensitive man to a tomb.

928–30 Cf. 523–27, 550. His last line here echoes the moral doctrine of *Ag* 1564.

931–71 Moralizing on the motif of time is a commonplace in Greek poetry, and a fragment of Pindar (Frag. 159 Snell) might serve as a motto for this lyric:

> For just men time is the best savior.

Aeschylus marks the motif in 935, 956, 963, 965 (some form of *chronos* occurs in each of these lines).

934 For the **eye** of the house cf. *Pers* 169 f. Here, more literally, "that the eye of the house shall not utterly die." Cf. 962 f.

935 f. As Gagarin (p. 71) argues, **hard** (936 and 947) lends to *dikē* (**Justice** and, at 949, "Right") the sense of "retribution," which Gagarin thinks is the primary sense of *dikē* in the trilogy. Cf. on 791–97 and the sense of passages such as *Ag* 699 ff.

938 Lloyd-Jones suggests that **double** refers to Orestes and Pylades.

942 High cry is the cry of good omen after a sacrifice, as well as the cry of victory; see on *Ag* 586.

944 It is the **stain,** the pollution on the house, that is emphatic here.

946 f. The first line has been emended, so that the person returning is Hermes rather than Orestes.

948 ff. Aeschylus' penchant for etymology reaches its fanciful zenith here. *Dikē* has been the daughter of Zeus since *Theogony* 902, but not by deriving her name from *Dios kora*, "daughter of Zeus" (*Dika = Dikē*), an impossible derivation but good fun.

950–51 Her wind is fury: she breathes fury on those she hates. Cf. *Eum* 136–39.

952–60 Textual problems in this stanza have led to very different solutions. I take Lattimore's **All that** as subject of **returns now** . . . (with general reference to the last stanza). Heath's emendation makes a link with the preceding stanza and asserts Apollo's concern for Right: "she (Right) whom Loxias, who on Parnassus holds the huge, the deep cleft in the ground, lifted up and restored, by guile, though she was wronged and hurt. Now in her time Right returns." **Loxias** is Apollo. **Parnassus** is the high peak above Delphi. On **guile no guile** see the note on *Pers* 527.

962 The **bit** of a horse's harness, as at *PB* 54 (note). Cf. 794.

966 ff. References to the **stain** of pollution (*miasma*) on the house increase in the second half of the play: 651, 859 ("bloody"), 944, 1017 (Orestes' "soiled victory"), 1028. Cf. *Ag* 1420, *Eum* 445. For the physical cleansing and purification of a house after blood is shed see *Odyssey* 22. 480 f.

969–71 Textual corruption and emendation lead to extraordinary differences in translation, as Lloyd-Jones' version illustrates:

> In the light of a fortune fair to look on can we
> see the whole, as we cry out,
> "The tenants of the house shall be cast out."
> Now we can see the light!

These "tenants of the house" are the Furies. No dice are mentioned, but the metaphor may be present in the verb and noun (a "fortunate cast"); cf. *Ag* 31–32.

973 This scene is analogous in its staging to *Ag* 1372 ff., where Clytaemestra, standing over the bodies of Agamemnon and Cassandra, glories in her triumph. For the possible ways of staging, see the discussion there. How many attendants are present is not specified, but no great number is necessary to display the net (983 f.). The address to the audience (980) may be directed only to the chorus and attendants; on the other hand, this is clearly one of those situations where the audience in the theater may become a part of the drama. Cf. Athene's speech to the men of Athens at *Eum* 681 ff. Such address violates dramatic illusion, which is assumed for Greek theater by Aristotle and most modern critics. But cf. Bain, "Audience Address in Greek Tragedy," p. 22, n. 1.

980 As Taplin says (p. 358), the **again** "is not merely a resumption of line 973, it harks back to the scene in *Ag*." While the staging of this scene ought to mirror the earlier one (two bodies, man and woman, the nets, the confession and defense), Orestes' language is more restrained, less defiant, more composed, less metaphorical, than Clytaemestra's.

985 ff. Unlike his mother, Orestes anticipates the trial to come (*dikē* occurs three times in four lines); so now he invokes Sun, symbol of purity and universal presence, to **witness** the justice of his work. For the **Sun** cf. *PB* 87 ff. (note) and Agamemnon's invocation before he takes an oath:

> Father Zeus, watching over us from Ida, most high, most
>   honoured,
> and Helios [the Sun], you who see all things, who listen to
>   all things,
> earth and rivers, and you who under the earth take
>   vengeance

on dead men, whoever among them has sworn to
    falsehood,
you shall be witnesses, to guard the oaths of fidelity.
(*Iliad* 3. 276–80)

Orestes wants only some witness, and he will not invoke the
powers of darkness, for he knows that *they* will be his adver-
saries. As in English, "seeing" in Greek is linked with overseeing, surveying, insight, and guidance. Cf. line 1 (Hermes
"watches over . . ."); 125 f. (where Electra invokes spirits
who "watch over . . ."); and *Eum* 739 (where "lord" = "he
who watches over").

990 As in some places today, so in Athens, the killing of an
adulterer is not held to be a criminal act.

992 f. Underneath her zone means beneath her sash and
is not so odd or precious as the English may seem.

994 For the sexual significance of **viper** see the note to 249.
Borthwick (p. 252) says of the **water snake** that "it is likely
that the comparison with the [water snake] is introduced here
along with the echidna because of the belief that the female
came on land to mate with the male viper . . . , and according
to Athenaeus 312 D the offspring of this union are the only
ones whose bite is fatal."

997 The gaps in the text at 996–97 and above, at 990–91,
recognize much-disputed problems in the text. The Greek
here translated **this thing** would most naturally refer to
Clytaemestra, though the subsequent description clearly describes the net; consequently, transposition of 997–1004 to
follow 982 or 990 has been favored by some editors. If we
don't transpose, we must recognize that the language moves
almost seamlessly from the woman as viper to the woman as
net and trap to the actual nets displayed from Agamemnon's
killing. If the woman can be called a spider (*Ag* 1492) and a
net and trap (see *Ag* 1115 f.), the move in the present passage
from snake to trap and net is possible, given the boldness of
Aeschylus' imagery. The difficulty here stems from the presence of Clytaemestra's body and of the actual robes that en-
tangled him (the **bath curtain** echoes *Ag* 1540). Orestes has
not yet gone mad (cf. 1023–24), a condition he recognizes; so
it seems improbable that in this speech we should see the be-

ginning of a psychological collapse, though that would explain, for some commentators, his confused referents. Nor should we commend Fraenkel's condemnation of 991–96 as an interpolation ("rant," he calls it); the lines are too in touch with earlier images and themes.

998–1000 His catalogue is taken from the *Agamemnon*: **trap for an animal** (*Ag* 1048), **bath** (*Ag* 1540), **net** (*Ag* 1115), **robe** (*Ag* 1126, 1581).

1009 On **pain flowers** see note to *Ag* 659. **Pain** = "the death" in 1016.

1010 ff. Conscious of the necessity of killing her and of guilt for having killed her, he begins to sink into terror (1024).

1017 Soiled (*miasma*: see on 966 ff.) is in the Greek the last and key word in the line. **Has no pride** = "unenviable."

Aeschylus' manner of depicting Orestes' ambivalent moral revulsion may be compared with Euripides, *Electra* 967–87 (guilt before the murder) and 1177 ff. (violent reaction after the murder).

1021 Various problems arise when we consider Orestes' madness. Unlike Cassandra, Orestes does not have any lyric speech; his iambics imply more control than the rhythms given her. Yet he is driven from the stage in terror of the Furies. We know very little of how the masked actor would play this hallucination, but the dialogue from 1048 on implies vivid realism, and the entire scene suggests a gradual intensification of emotion, beginning with confession, justification, turning to an obsessed regard for the net, then to his own polluted hands, and finally, as he senses his failing self-control, the vision of serpentine Furies. By the end of the century a purely moral explanation could be offered for such psychoses (cf., e.g., Euripides' *Orestes* 394 ff.), but, from Homer well into the fifth century, poets represented such mental aberrations as the result of external daimonic intervention (see the first two chapters of Dodds, *The Greeks and the Irrational*). Lacking in this scene the objective representation of the Furies (this is saved for the *Eumenides*), we are naturally tempted to find in Orestes' madness a manifestation of his moral guilt. For Orestes the daimon is Apollo. But the god does not knock him crazy; rather, his oracles have commanded an act so morally abominable that they can be called "spells" (1029): only a man under a spell could risk such physical and moral pollution. So we seem now to be given a deeper view of the hero's psyche, a view that earlier in the play was masked by Apollo's command, by Orestes' willing surrender to ritual and to the duplicity necessary for accomplishing the revenge, and by the poetic focus on the house. Now for a moment—perhaps more so than ever in the *Eumenides*—the contingency of the house's existence is revealed in the moral revulsion and madness of its single surviving heir.

1022 ff. Charioteer: For the image cf. 794 ff. and the note to *PB* 879–87 (where Io's madness evokes similar imagery), *Antigone* 801, and Euripides, *Heracles* 880 ff., where the demon Madness mounts a chariot to hunt down her victim.

With this **singing and dancing of wrath** cf. 166; at *Heracles* 892 ff. imagery of dance and song describes the attack of Madness.

1032 This line alludes to his father's Furies (cf. 276 ff.).

1035 For **branch** (of olive) **and garland** cf. *Suppl* 19 f. and *Eum* 39, 43–45.

In the *Eumenides* Orestes still carries his sword, "with blood dripping from his hands" (42; see note there). Does he carry a sword in the present scene? If so, does he put it down to take the branch with the garland on it? It would seem visually distracting for him to carry the branch and garland from the beginning of the scene. Perhaps an attendant brings them to him now (1034 clearly marks a transition in thought and action). **Centrestone:** See *Eum* 40. The action is now turning toward the scene of the *Eumenides*.

1041 Orestes insists on the legality of his act and has repeatedly appealed to witnesses and to the procedure of the courts (987, 1010, 1026 f., 1030 f.).

1042 The homicide was the most impure and polluted of the profane; even a dead murderer was cast out beyond the boundaries of the state. Now Orestes must seek purification, and he turns to the god who commanded the murder, and so his pollution, and who is preeminently the god who purifies (see on 1059 f.).

1044 Bind = "yoke."

1047 f. The reference to **snakes** leads to his vision of the Furies, who are like the snake-wreathed **gorgons.** Cf. 831 ff. (note); *Eum* 48 f.; Euripides, *Heracles* 883 f.

No! is his frightened reaction to his vision, not a rejection of 1046 f.

1052 Fancies: the Furies do not appear onstage; only Orestes can see them.

1054 Bloodhounds, just as she threatened (924).

1058 All the imagery of *seeing* (see notes to 246–63, 692–99; various references to eyes, etc., at 99, 125 f., 185, 288, 671, 738, 809, 817) culminates in a vision of horror by one who has been styled the "eye of the house" (934). Such attention to varieties of vision quietly prepares the spectators for the Furies' repulsive appearance in the next play (*Eum* 52 ff.).

1059 Clean has reference to the catharsis (purification) provided by Apollo to Theseus (after he killed his cousins, the sons of Pallas), to Heracles (who had killed his host Iphitus), and to Achilles (who killed Thersites). Orestes' purification was the most famous.

1065 ff. The **storm** (cf. 183 ff., 775) has not abated; **inward race** refers to the genetic history of the house: Atreus murdered Thyestes' children (cf. *Ag* 1096 f.); Clytaemestra killed Agamemnon (no mention of Iphigeneia); now the savior of the house is driven into exile. For **Third is for the savior** see on *Ag* 245–47.

1075 f. Fury of fate = the strength of *atē* (the last word in the play).

The Eumenides

IN ORDER TO TAKE SERIOUSLY the religious and ethical issues that are involved, the reader of the *Eumenides*, as of *Oedipus the King*, must grasp certain Greek notions about the consequences of murder—notions that are entirely alien to our own experience. First among these consequences is the obligation of the immediate kin (as far as first cousins) to avenge a murder. In the heroic age imagined in this trilogy, that obligation was entirely private, for the law of primitive Greece made no provision for criminal prosecution in the courts (there were none). So Orestes takes justice into his own hands, kills his mother, and thus becomes himself a murderer. Such a man becomes liable to vengeance from his mother's kin or, failing that, from spirits of retribution known as the Erinyes (the Furies). A second and equally significant consequence of murder is that the murderer is "polluted"—literally stained and defiled by the blood—so that his very presence contaminates any person or place he touches. Hence the necessity of purification, a physical act of cleansing that washes away the noxious infection—the *miasma* or defilement. In *Oedipus the King* we find an entire city ravaged by plague and famine because it is unknowingly harboring a murderer, the present king. Before the plague will abate, that man must be driven into exile and the city must be ritually purified.

In the *Libation Bearers* Orestes has recognized his need for absolution (Apollo had advised him of this even as he had commanded the murder!) and so flees into exile, to Apollo's temple at Delphi, in order to escape the wrath of his mother's avenging spirits. These spirits—chthonic and thus indifferent to the Olympian world of Apollo—have as their sole business the hounding of Orestes to a mad grave. This is the testimony of the *Eumenides*, where their confidence in the absolute privilege of their office, which they repeatedly style "justice," may be difficult for modern readers to understand, given these creatures' horrid appearance and implacable demand for blood.

We can hardly sympathize with such demons, but it is important to understand that for the Greek audience the reality of
their existence and the fear it inspired were as certain and
compelling as any claims that Apollo might make for having
freed Orestes from the bloodguilt. For the world of darkness
does not recognize the law of the world of light.

As it happens, we have good evidence apart from poetry
for Greek belief in these matters, for Herodotus, Thucydides,
and the orators all testify to public concern for a defilement
that is private in origin. See, e.g., Thucydides 1. 126–35 and
Rohde, *Psyche*, pp. 174–82. So we can be sure that Aeschylus
has not created the Furies out of some poetic fancy, nor has he
merely adopted them from literary tradition, although they
are securely at home there as early as Homer and Hesiod.

Knowing about Greek beliefs is one thing, but grasping the
sensibility and dynamics of an essentially irrational belief is
another. For this reason, modern readers may find more sensational spectacle than dramatic conflict in the play. Perhaps
Aeschylus himself sensed the problematic nature of his enterprise, for when he pitted the primeval, retributive *dikē* of the
Furies against lawyer Apollo and persuasive Athene, the deck
was stacked against the *lex talionis*—the law of an eye for
an eye.

Texts of interest in connection with the *Eumenides* are Pin-
dar's *Eleventh Pythian* (lines 15–37), a lyric version of the
Oresteia in which Clytaemestra's infidelity shares billing
with the sacrifice of Iphigeneia as her motive for murdering
Agamemnon, and Euripides' *Electra* (lines 1250–72), where
Castor tells the fate of Orestes after the murder of his mother.

1–139 The choral song does not begin until line 140,
which makes this the longest prologue in Aeschylus. It is also
striking for being broken up by the departure and return
of the priestess, her second exit, a brief exchange between
Apollo and Orestes, followed by their exit, and, finally, the
appearance of the ghost of Clytaemestra, who comes to rally
the Furies to their pursuit. In effect, then, three distinct scenes,
involving one, two, and one actor, respectively, occur before
the first lines of the chorus at 140.

Our picture of this rapid, excited scene is complicated principally by an uncertainty about when the chorus enters. Many ancient and modern commentators have agreed with Lattimore that at line 64 the door opens to reveal Orestes surrounded by the sleeping Furies. The textual evidence for this traditional staging rests on the sentence at lines 66 f. and on Clytaemestra's vigorous, direct address to them (94 ff.). Normally, however, choruses do not appear before they speak; if the Furies are onstage, or on an eccyclema, they are silent until their whimpering begins at line 117, and they say nothing articulate until line 140. As Taplin argues, this silence may seem to mitigate the horrid impression promised by the priestess (46 ff.). As for **See now** . . . (66 f.), the line might be accompanied by a gesture toward the interior of the temple, or the verb might be used in the sense of "understand" (Taplin, p. 373). If, as Winnington-Ingram asserts ("The Delphic Oracle in Greek Tragedy," p. 486), the wheeled trolly (eccyclema) was used, then a few members of the chorus might have been on it, with the rest to appear later. They would be slumped over in such a way that their hideous masks would not be revealed. Such staging gives us visual reference for Apollo's lines without premature revelation of their grotesque appearance.

If the chorus is not visible when Apollo addresses Orestes, can it be absent when Clytaemestra's ghost appears? Flickinger argues, and Taplin considers this view seriously, that we do not see Clytaemestra but only hear her voice, speaking from the inner temple to the Furies, who are still within. This interpretation certainly requires the Furies to be offstage, for Clytaemestra can hardly ask them to look at her wounds (103) if they are onstage and she is not. Though her voice, inciting them to action, might produce a spooky effect, it is a little difficult to deny Aeschylus the spectacle of the ghostly queen rousing her vengeful dogs to the hunt. And if they are present at the exit of Apollo and Orestes, then they must be visible at their entrance. See Flickinger, pp. 286 f.

Other ghosts will be found in Aeschylus' *Persians* (681 ff.) and Euripides' *Hecuba* (1 ff.).

1 ff. Apollo and his priestess are called **Pythian** after the dragon Python, which the god killed on this spot. She enters from the side and delivers this prologue as she prepares to enter the shrine, where, filled with divine ecstasy, she will prophesy to those who have come to Delphi seeking the god's advice (29–33). As for the list (1–8) of previous tenants of the Delphic site, that is natural both to her prayer and to the ritual that is preliminary to prophecy. Note, however, that the killing of Python does not figure in her narrative, probably because it would implicate the god in murder and pollution (every eight years a festival at Delphi represented Apollo's slaughter of Python and his subsequent trip to Tempe to be purified for the crime).

Themis is the daughter, hence natural successor, of **Earth** (*Theogony* 135; cf. *PB* 211 f.). **Phoebe,** on the other hand, lacks a secure place in the family tree. Hesiod makes her a Titan, maternal grandmother of Apollo. Phoebus ("bright") is an old epithet of Apollo, and Phoebe is simply the feminine form; but whether Apollo gave the name to this shadowy figure or got it from her cannot be said. The **Titans,** children of Earth and Uranus, are the old gods. Cronus, their leader, was Zeus's father. Hesiod connects their name with "strain" because they strained against the rule of Zeus, who displaced them from power.

9 ff. Apollo was born on **Delos** and traveled to Delphi by way of Attica, the land of **Pallas** Athene. The Athenians are **Hephaestus' sons** out of respect for the smith god (*PB* 12 ff.), who was the father of Erichthonius, an early king of Athens. They are probably styled **builders of roads** because they constructed the sacred way by which Apollo journeyed from Attica to Delphi.

16 Delphus was an early king who gave his name to the land.

17 Full with godship means that he was inspired by divine guidance to practice the craft of prophecy. Cf. 616 ff. for the thematic significance of Zeus's authorizing Apollo's pronouncements.

21 f. Pallas-before-the-temple refers to a temple of Athene nearby; Athene will be prominent when the scene shifts to Athens. The **Corycian Rock** is a cave high up on Mt. Parnassus, sacred to Pan and the nymphs; cf. *Antigone* 1126 f.

24–26 Bromius refers to Dionysus (Bacchus) and is a common epithet meaning "the thunderer." Aeschylus wrote two trilogies taken from Dionysiac myths, one treating Lycurgus, king of Thrace, the other **Pentheus,** king of Thebes, both of whom were destroyed for resisting the advent of the god. Euripides' *Bacchae* takes as its subject the futile resistance of Pentheus. The **Bacchanals** are the female followers of the god who in ecstatic madness tear Pentheus limb from limb. Apollo shared Delphi with Dionysus, who controlled the temple during the winter.

27 f. The **Pleistus** is a nearby river, whose spirits would be sacred to the town. Pausanias (2. 33. 2–3) reports that Delphi once belonged to **Poseidon**, who was also said to be the father of King Delphus; both Poseidon and Dionysus enjoyed exceptional honor in the inner temple (an altar for the former, the tomb of the latter). **Final . . . Zeus:** for the epithet, from the *tel*-stem, see the note on "Zeus accomplisher" at *Ag* 972–74 and at 214, below; at 384c it is translated "authority."

29 ff. The priestess who utters the prophecies is possessed, in ecstasy; i.e., she is a medium through whom the god speaks. Those wishing to consult the oracle drew lots to determine the order in which they would ask their questions, with Greeks (**Hellenes**) having priority.

37 Extraordinary realism for the Greek stage, if, as seems likely, she is literally crawling from fear.

38 The line means that a terrified old woman is no better than a child.

39 ff. The **wreaths** belong to suppliants, who have left them at the shrine to honor the god. The **centrestone** is the omphalos marking the center of the world ("Navel-of-Earth" at *Sev* 746; cf. *Oedipus the King* 480). Fontenrose (pp. 374 ff.) considers it the marker of an old tomb of Python or Dionysus. For representations on Greek vases of the omphalos, the sanctuary, and the supplication of Orestes see Webster and Trendall.

42 ff. Orestes appears with the **branch** and garland (**wrapped in a great tuft of wool**) that he carried from the last scene (*LB* 1034 ff.). It is so soon after the murder that we must think, when we see this **sword,** that it is still bloody from Clytaemestra's death, which would be an extraordinary profanation of Apollo's temple. In fact, as we must assume from Apollo's manner at 64 ff. and as we learn from 281–85,

Orestes has already been purified. The sword is bloody from the pig slain as part of the purification.

48 ff. Cf. the description at *LB* 1048 ff. Having thought of the snake-wreathed **gorgons,** she thinks to compare them more accurately to the Harpies who ravaged the table of **Phineus,** a blind king of Thrace. The Harpies were "winged female creatures, and when a table was laid for Phineus, they flew down from the sky and snatched up most of the victuals, and what little they left stank so that nobody could touch it" (Apollodorus 1. 9. 21). Here too their **breath** is disgusting (53). For their **eyes** see *LB* 1058.

62 f. Three epithets designate Apollo as (1) "healer-diviner" (also of Apis, son of Apollo, at *Suppl* 263; abusively at *Ag* 1623); (2) as "diviner of signs" (cf. "mantic," *Ag* 977, of portentous intuition); (3) as "purifier" (**clears out the house**), which is the last, emphatic, word in the speech. Cf. 276 ff.

64 Some editors, finding Apollo's words abrupt, have transposed 85–87 after 63. The naturalism of an entry in mid-conversation is exceptional, perhaps unique in Greek tragedy. Taplin (p. 364) compares *Hippolytus* 601 ff., *Iphigeneia in Aulis* 305 ff., and *Philoctetes* 1222 ff., all scenes of animated conversation, none in prologue or without some preliminary introduction of the main characters.

Apollo's first sentence represents exactly (with change of person) Orestes' first words about Apollo at *LB* 269 f. ("will not forsake me"). There is also in **give you up** the connotation "betray" (the god is bound to help the suppliant).

66 The **see now** may be literal, or it could mean "you perceive how . . ."

69 For **aged children** see on 1034.

70 Will have to do often means "have sexual intercourse with," and after **lewd** (67) and **maidens** (68) Apollo enjoys a coarse *double entendre.* Cf. Talbot's line,

> Well, let them practice and converse with spirits.
> (1 *Henry VI*, 2. 1. 25)

72–73 The **Pit below Earth** is Tartarus.

74 ff. Despite his purification, Orestes must endure a difficult and long journey, which may be a part of his purification (cf. 276 f.). Apollo styles this a "labor" (**hard march = af-**

fliction, 83), a word customarily used for the trials of mythical heroes. The emphasis on travel by sea (77) and on his being hunted (75) also stresses greater endurance than an actual journey to Athens would require. The metaphor at 78 (**be herdsman**) implies a radical reversal in role, i.e., from animal pursued to one who protects a flock and wards off beasts. **Circle-washed:** "surrounded by water."

80 The **ancient idol** is the wooden statue of Pallas Athene in her old temple on the Acropolis, the present Erechtheum (cf. 409).

81–82 Cf. the description of Persuasion at 885 f., where "beguilement" = **magic** here.

85–87 As Sidgwick observes, Orestes sounds to us too bold, but "the Greek is not so meant, nor does Apollo take it so." Lloyd-Jones notes that Orestes' language suggests a legal distinction between criminal offenses and those due to negligence. There is also, in **mistrust,** a commercial and legal metaphor ("surety"), which Aeschylus favors (see on *Sev* 398).

89–91 Hermes' presence would seem justified by the frequent references to him in *LB*. If he is actually onstage, he is yet another indication of divine favor for Orestes. In **guides . . . Shepherd** Apollo puns on *pompaios . . . poimaínōn* (Hermes was both guide for dead spirits and guardian of shepherds).

92 f. The Greek is odd, for **wanderer** might also be translated "outcast" or "outlaw," meaning one beyond the pale of civilization. Suppliants and strangers are under the special care of Zeus; if the suppliant has good luck on his journey—and he will, with Hermes to help—this good fortune is a sign of divine protection.

94 Because Clytaemestra's ghost addresses the Furies, their presence has generally been assumed (but see the last paragraph to the note at 1–140). If they are visible through the door (unlikely), then she rallies them to pursue the escaped Orestes. She would not come out of the temple to speak to persons in it, so she must come from a side entrance. If, however, some of them are already out on the eccyclema, she might enter from the temple, though this seems to me a little awkward, since the majority of the Furies must still be within, and there is some question of how much room the actor will have to maneuver around them. She is a dream (116, 155), come from the dead (96), and now she hunts them out and stalks around the lethargic forms. Bring her on from the side.

95–96 Greek religion, if we except the Mysteries (like those celebrated at Eleusis), did not anticipate rewards and punishment for all the dead in Hades. Famous villains such as Ixion, Tantalus, and Sisyphus suffer for having assaulted the gods, but the average man, if he believed in any sort of personal survival, did not expect to pay for each and every sin. So Clytaemestra's complaint that she is **dishonored among the dead** is to some extent a convenient, intelligible literary fiction; on the other hand, it also represents the natural disquiet of an abused spirit. Her anger and desire for revenge on Orestes is the same sort of feeling that Orestes and Electra expect from the dead spirit of Agamemnon. She is a little incoherent—fair enough for such an avenging devil.

102 Slaughtered also suggests "sacrificed."

104 f. These two lines may be a gloss. Line 104 would seem to be literal and refer to their sleep, despite which she says that they can see her suffering. Line 105, where **future** = "fate" (*moira*), is at best tangential to the context.

107 Without wine: a mixture of water, honey, and milk was offered to the Furies; cf. *Oedipus at Colonus* 101, where Oedipus is addressing these same spirits.

111–13 For the **fawn** cf. 247; **nets:** 147, 460 ("gyves"); hunting: 131, 138, 147, 231, 245 ff., 676. It is characteristic of Aeschylus' imagery that the subject of **laughing merrily** is at once the fawn and Orestes.

114 The word **life** is odd, coming from a ghost; one Greek notion of death viewed it as the separation of spirit (breath, Greek *psyche*) from the body. Hence *psyche* is often translated "soul" and here as **life,** by which she seems to mean "I'm speaking of my very being."

119 In an uncertain text Lattimore has accepted an emendation that displaces a Greek word meaning "suppliant." It may be closer to the received text to assume that the sense is something like "suppliants have friends, more than I have."

125 Or: "What is your business but to do harm?"

127 The Furies are more commonly described as hounds (e.g., 131). Harrison thinks that even the singular **mother-**

snake is significant in that it recalls a much older conception of the Erinyes: "The Erinyes as ministers of vengeance are indefinitely multiplied, but the old ghost-Erinys is one, not many; she is the ghost of the murdered mother. Clytaemnestra herself is the real 'dragoness,' though she does not know it, and by a curious unconscious reminiscence the Erinyes sleep till she, the true Erinys, rouses them" (*Prolegomena*, p. 233); cf. Dietrich, pp. 139 f.

130 Get him may mean "catch the scent," "mark the trail" (Thomson).

131 For the Furies as dogs see *LB* 924. Cf. the "fleet hounds of madness" exhorted at *Bacchae* 977, and see also *Heracles* 898.

135 There is justice (*dikē*, here translated in **well deserves**) in her scolding both because of the sacrifice she has offered to the Furies (106 ff.) and because of their natural function as avengers of kindred blood.

136 With **spur** compare "counterspurred" at 466.

142 Morning-song is a prelude (= "choral prelude," *Ag* 30); cf. *Sev* 7, *PB* 740. There is quite a lot of such self-conscious rhetorical reference in Aeschylus; cf. *Oedipus the King*, 895 f. On **vanity** cf. 144, *LB* 846.

143–77 The parodos begins in responsive lyrics, without anapestic prelude.

150 According to the traditional genealogy of the gods, Apollo, **a young god,** belongs to the fourth generation; by contrast, the Furies, children of Night (321), belong to the very beginnings of things (at *Theogony* 181–85 they spring from the blood of the mutilated Uranus, a reminder of their tie to sexuality and bloodguilt). Conflict between old and new, young and old, takes a variety of forms in this play; see 68 f. (Apollo's contempt), 162, 172, 393 f. (the issue of power), 727 f., 848, 883, etc. **Ridden down** specifically suggests a horse (and rider) trampling over someone or something (three times in *Eum*; see 731 and 778). This may be related to the chariot imagery (e.g., at 155 ff.) and to the imagery of trampling or kicking underfoot (110, 141), all violent, kinetic figures for driving and knocking down.

151 A **godless suppliant** is clearly a contradiction in terms, an ethical and religious oxymoron.

154 The Furies will not hesitate to commit their case to trial because they are from the beginning confident that **right** (*dikē*) is with them. Cf. 163, 186 f.

156–60 Goad = "spur" (136, with note). **Executioner's whip** describes Clytaemestra as the "public scourger" who, like a lashing charioteer, drives them on and whips them for lagging. Cf. *Ag* 640–43.

162 Such are the actions jumps back to the argument of 149–54. In this stanza, as in the next, Apollo's flouting of tradition is more the focus than Orestes' guilt: how can a god, of his own will (170), tolerate and condone pollution ("spoiled," 168) of the sacred shrine devoted to his own worship?

171 f. Violating the law (custom) of the gods, Apollo honors **man's way** and thus destroys the ancient **distribution** (a good example of "fate" [*moira*] in the sense of "allotted function").

177 Murderer = "polluter" (echoing "spoiled" at 168); yet another avenger will arise to destroy Orestes and so continue the cycle of renewed *miasma*. The Furies are obsessive, unforgiving, implacable—instinctively and unalterably bestial in their vengeance.

183 f. They are blood-sucking vampires (cf. 264 ff.). Maxwell-Stuart (p. 83), studying the evidence for their appearance, compares them to bats: they "were dark, had membraned wings (51), and shrivelled, ugly faces like those of old women or ancient children—a possible reflection of their size, too; they may have been small creatures—and yet had something also of the grotesque facial distortion of the Gorgon."

186 ff. A list of tortures the Furies would likely enjoy; **the spoil of sex** is castration; **mutilation** is the cutting-off of other extremities, such as the hands and nose.

195 Filth responds, more or less ad hominem, to 168 f.

199 f. After his name-calling they insist on establishing responsibility: Apollo is not partially but completely responsible (**guilt** and **accessory** are both forms of *aitios*; see the discussion on *LB* 909). Cf. 465–67.

202 Orestes is an **outlander** (*xenos*), both as "fugitive" and as "guest" received by Apollo. Zeus *Xenios* protects outlanders (see on *Suppl* 628).

203 Price = "retribution" (see on "repay," note to *LB* 791–97). The same word occurs at 322 and 464 (where in both cases it is translated as "vengeance") and at 981 ("revenge").

212 The woman marries into the house but is not related by blood; the Furies score a point in that Greek law made just such a distinction. Apollo attempts an analogous argument at 658 ff.

214 Apollo invokes Zeus and Hera as god and goddess responsible for the consummation of marriage. Of the cult epithet **of consummations** (*teleios*) Farnell says: Zeus "is *teleios* not only in the more general sense as the god who brings all things to the right accomplishment, the god to whom under this title Clytemnestra prays for the accomplishment of her hopes (*Ag* 973); but especially in the sense of the marriage god" (*Cults*, 1:53). Cf. *Suppl* 623 f. and the next note.

215 Aphrodite is called **Cypris** or the Cyprian because the island of Cyprus was particularly sacred to her. Farnell (*Cults*, 1:53) quotes Plutarch: "those who marry are supposed to need five divinities, Zeus Teleios and Hera Teleia, Aphrodite and Peitho [Persuasion], and Artemis above all."

218 f. The qualifier **of nature** is interpretative, for the Greek reads simply **by right** (*dikē*). Though Apollo's argument does turn in part on what we might call a law of nature, the question of what the law is, or should be, will be defined by the action of the play. Given the allusion to cult epithets of Zeus and Hera, one might argue that his appeal is to the sanctions of religion, which would not exclude an appeal to natural law.

234 A departure of the chorus during the course of the play occurs four times in extant fifth-century tragedy: *Ajax* 814 (the chorus leaves to search for Ajax), *Alcestis* 746 (the chorus attends the funeral cortege), *Helen* 385 (the chorus accompanies Helen into the house), and *Rhesus* 564 (the Trojan chorus exits to change the guard, thus clearing the way for Odysseus and Diomedes to come onstage) (Taplin, pp. 375 f.). Only in the *Ajax* does departure signal a change of place, as here, and only here is some length of time explicitly recognized. If we follow Lattimore's stage directions at line 63, then the omphalos ("centrestone" of line 40) must now be replaced by a statue of the goddess (80, 242, 259 f.). Historically, this particular ancient wooden image of Athene was kept within her temple on the Acropolis, so the present scene must be imagined as taking place inside the sanctuary; then, at 565, the scene shifts (immediately after a lyric) to the Areopagus. It is possible that this first scene was staged within the stage building, with a large curtain revealing Orestes at the image, but this seems an undue regard for realism, as does Pickard-Cambridge's caveat concerning the Furies' dance around Orestes; he suggests (*Theatre of Dionysus*, p. 44) that the "binding song" at 307 ff. cannot take place around Orestes because he is within the temple. He enters from the parodos, as do his pursuers.

238 By a familiar figure, **blunted** is transferred from the guilt ("the edge of the guilt," i.e., its "bite") to the agent.

245 ff. The hunting imagery continues (cf. 111 and 252) and is developed so self-consciously that we may have hints of the manner of the chorus. They are spent, exhausted from the chase. There is a curious insistence in the language of Orestes and the chorus on the long and difficult labor of the pursuit (cf. Apollo at 74 ff., 83), but I cannot find any particular thematic point or any relevance of these afflictions to his absolution. The same word (for "labor," "affliction," "trouble," etc.) occurs in 59, 78, 83, 126, 132 ("hunting"), 133, 226, 555 f., 771. This word (*ponos*) is very common elsewhere in Aeschylus and hardly peculiar to the *Eumenides*.

252 Gone to cover is the same verb as "crouched down" in a simile from the *Iliad*:

> But swift Achilleus kept unremittingly after Hektor,
> chasing him, as a dog in the mountains who has flushed
>   from his covert
> a deer's fawn follows him through the folding ways and the
>   valleys,
> and though the fawn crouched down under a bush and be
>   hidden
> he keeps running and noses him out until he comes on him.
> (*Iliad* 22. 188–92)

253 Cf. 183 f. The Greek is bolder than the English; cf. Smyth's "The smell of human blood makes me laugh for joy." A ghoulish group, as lines 264 ff. attest.

254–75 After the iambics of 245–53 (spoken by the coryphaeus), a song in an excited, astrophic lyric follows. Perhaps their dance mimes the hunt.

260 That is, he seeks to put himself in the hands of the goddess. A *dikē* compound here means "liable to legal action," so that we could also translate "he is willing to stand trial for the work of his hands."

261 The stain of **blood** that pollutes and demands, through revenge, yet more pollution; cf., e.g., *LB* 1055 and *Ag* 1017 f., 732, 215.

265 The word translated here as **blood** denotes any viscous liquid and is used elsewhere (e.g., *LB* 92, "liquid") of a sacrificial offering; so here we may understand his blood as a sacrificial offering they demand.

269 This sentence may be more intelligible if a new clause is marked here: "you will see, if another mortal goes astray by dishonoring god or dear parents, each [such criminal] with the pain upon him his crime deserves" (the omnipresent *dikē* occurs in the last line: "the reward Justice ordains," Lloyd-Jones).

273–75 Reckoning introduces a favorite Aeschylean metaphor from public life (see on *Pers* 212 f.), which also occurs in "Zeus . . . a grievous corrector" (*Pers* 829) and "tiller's governance" (*Suppl* 718). For judgment by Zeus (or Hades) after death see *Suppl* 229 ff. In a fragment from an unknown play by Aeschylus (Frag. 282, Lloyd-Jones) *Dikē* speaks of rewards and punishment and of writing "their offences on the tablet of Zeus," a phrase with verbal affinities to **his recording mind** (cf. *PB* 789–90).

276 This looks like a variation on "suffering and learning" (*Ag* 176–78).

280–85 Dulls . . . fades might also be rendered "sleeps . . . dries up," as if the blood, with a life all its own, has finally grown tired and drowsy of its work. The blood is literally **washed away** by the blood of the sacrificed pig, held over the suppliant so that its blood drips down and over him and carries away his infection (**blot**). The acid test for the efficacy of purificatory rites (**absolved**) is contact with others; for since the *miasma* is physical and infectious, it will be transmitted to anyone near the polluted person. Therefore, in noting that no one has been **hurt by being with me,** Orestes argues that he is clean and absolved.

286 This line is probably a tag originally written in the margin and later erroneously assumed to be part of the text.

287 Cf. "in all eloquence" at *LB* 997 f., where, as here, the idea may be proper, decorous speech.

290 The first of three allusions (cf. 670–73, 762 ff.) to the contemporary political alliance between Athens and Argos.

Aeschylus has changed the scene of the play (see on *Ag* 24) from the Homeric Mycenae, apparently for no other reason than as a compliment to Athens' new ally against Sparta.

292–95 Libyan land and **rescuing there her friends** allude to Athenian ventures at the time of the play's production; the Athenians had an expeditionary force in Egypt in support of a revolt led by Inaros, king of the Libyans (Thucydides 1. 109–10). **Triton** is a lake in Libya. From one of Athene's Homeric epithets, Tritogeneia, which is still unexplained, the ancients conjectured, among other possibilities, her birth from this lake (**her father's crossing** may be the stream where she was born). Herodotus (4. 188) mentions her worship around Lake Tritonis.

294 f. Tragic elevation for "whether she sits or stands" (her foot would be shrouded by her gown if she sat). In the battle of the giants and the gods at **Phlegra** (see on *Sev* 424 ff.) Athene vanquished Enceladus and Pallas.

302–5 Aeschylean oxymoron describes the living Orestes as a "bloodless **fattened** calf for the powers of death, a wraith." **Chewed dry** and **blood drained** anticipate the effect of their blood-sucking sacrifice. Cf. 264 ff. Line 303 implies a gesture of contempt on the part of Orestes.

306 The Fates themselves are spinners and binders (cf. "destiny spun," 335); the Homeric Sirens' name may be connected with "rope," and their song casts a magic spell over anyone who hears it (*Odyssey* 12. 39 ff.); so the song of the Furies **binds** the victim (cf. 332 f.), magically rendering him helpless (see Onians, pp. 369–72). Something of the Furies' power to restrain, though in a very different and metaphorical context, may be seen in Fragment 94 of Heraclitus:

> Sun will not overstep his measures; otherwise the Erinyes, ministers of Justice, will find him out.
>
> (Kirk and Raven, No. 229, p. 203)

As Kirk and Raven observe, this fragment illustrates "the principle of measure in natural change; . . . the sun is restrained by Dikē, the personification of normality and therefore regularity." For a man to kill his mother is to overstep his limits, defined by *dikē* (justice), just as a change in the course of the sun would be a violation of the *dikē* of nature; both are corrected by the Furies.

For other passages on the magical power of song: *Ag* 1021, 1418, *LB* 475.

307 Choral means "dance," and if they do not actually dance around Orestes, the spirit of the piece imagines them surrounding him (note the word "over," 328). If the statue of Athene has been placed in the orchestra, there is no reason for the hunt not to circle the prey (325 f.).

310 Rights of office is a primary theme of this stasimon; cf. "purpose" 334, "such lots" 347, and "duties" 385, all translations of the same word. References to fate (335), to their distinction from the Olympians (323 f., 350–52), and to their authority (382, 391 ff.) are other variations on function and privilege, the mode of *dikē* they preserve (312).

315 Unscathed also means "innocent" and "without hurt or lesion"; the medical metaphor is the same as that at *Ag* 387 ("sin") and *LB* 1019 ("unhurt").

318 ff. They judge, bring **witness,** and execute the penalty, an efficient legal system. There is another legal term at 362, where "appeal" also has the technical meaning "preliminary examination" prior to a trial.

321 See the note on *Ag* 59 for **my mother night.**

325 f. With **the prey that crouches** cf. 252 and the note there.

328–33 = 341–46; 354–59 = 367–69c. The second repetition is conjectural.

328 Doomed to the fire translates a verb used of burned sacrifice (as in "smoldering," *Ag* 1235), a natural move after likening Orestes to a (wild) victim who may serve as an expiation for bloodshed (325–27).

329 f. Note the alliteration and assonance in these phrases (the Greek has three compounds for the three English phrases: *parakopa, paraphora, phrenodalēs*, all descriptive of the chant). After an initial prepositional phrase (**over the beast**), the entire stanza is built up by apposition to **chant,** with the effect of placing the grammatical structure *over the victim*.

334–35 Purpose = "office" (see on 310); more concretely, **all-involving** means "piercing" or "running through" (Hippocrates uses it of ligaments running along the spine). The adjective may be transferred from **purpose**—which penetrates and runs through all life—to **destiny.**

339 f. Cf. the thought at *Suppl* 413–16 and here at 175, 603.

347–52 The stanza stresses the difference between them and the Olympians (**the immortals**), for whom **white robes** are the appropriate ritual dress, while the chthonic deities prefer black. In sacrifice (**feasting**), white animals are offered to the Olympians, black ones to the chthonic deities.

354–59 In an uncertain Greek text Lattimore's version suggests that the chorus identifies itself with the **Battlegod** (Ares) when that god enters a house and kills kin. **For the blood** means "because of the blood."

360 ff. There is little agreement on the meaning of these lines. Some commentators take Zeus to be the one **in haste.** Lloyd-Jones sees an allusion to the story of Ares' murder of Halirrhothius, son of Poseidon, for which Ares was tried by a jury of Olympians summoned to meet on the Areopagus (= "Ares' hill," a name it received from this first trial). See Apollodorus 3. 14. 2. The point of this interpretation lies in the antagonism between Zeus and the Furies. Lloyd-Jones' version:

> Eager to exempt some one of the gods from his concern,
> denying to our prayers fulfillment
> and forbidding us to make inquiry,
> Zeus has held our bloodstained, hateful race
> unworthy of his converse.

Lattimore's version moves the argument more directly from the preceding stanzas. **All others** are presumably any gods who would meddle. **Devisings** may mean "anxious concern," euphemistic and ironically understated. **Appeal** suggests that the gods should not even have a part in the preliminary inquiry. The final clause (365 f.) asserts their permanent alienation from Zeus.

To understand why translations can differ so much, the English reader should remember that most of the pronouns in these lyrics are derived either from suffixes attached to verbs, as in 360, where the form of the verb is disputed, or from implied relationships. The Greek is terse and elliptical, so that an intelligible English version adds the words **to them, our,** and **with us** to clarify, and also to interpret, the last two lines.

367 The ephymnion after 366 (= 354–59) is not repeated in the manuscripts (hence the irregularity in the line numbers), but several modern texts accept the repetition conjectured by Schneider. The same is true of the repetition following 380.

369d–71 The metaphor in **melt** may be from medical pathology and refer to putrefaction of a corpse. So we might also translate "high opinion, ever so proud and grave beneath the sky, yet falls away and melts into the earth." This unnatural melting is caused by the **pulsing** (= "dancing"; cf. 307) feet of the Furies (cf. 372 ff.). Typically, the Greek transfers **vindictive** from **feet** to **pulsing**: "the vindictive pulsing of feet."

372–76 The daimon jumping down on its victim is a commonplace; see on *Pers* 346, 516–17, *Sev* 791; cf. "weight" 712. So the chorus in Sophocles, *Oedipus the King* 1301:

> What evil spirit leaped upon your life

378 Or: "Such a cloud and mist of infection hovers over man."

384c–d Hold memory of evil: at *PB* 516 Prometheus speaks of the "remembering Furies." For **stern** see on 1041.

387 Ways = "paths," the common metaphor from travel. The following line is a variant on 322 f. Thomson takes the meaning to be that they visit their punishment on both the living and the dead; could it also apply to premeditated and accidental crimes?

396 Athene enters walking, not in a chariot. Line 405— omitted from this and many texts—indicates arrival in a chariot, which contradicts 403 and should probably be attributed to a later production.

398–402 Scamandrus and **seisin of land** refer to an Athenian dispute with Mytilene over the possession of Sigeum, a town in the Troad, about five miles from Troy. Herodotus' account (5. 94–95) puts this business in the sixth century, well before the production of the *Eumenides*, but such territorial disputes are seldom definitely settled. **Achaean lords of war** takes her claim back to the Trojan War (Homer's Greeks are **Achaeans**), when the **sons of Theseus,** legendary founder of Athens, joined the expedition and thus gave their city claim to share in the booty.

404 The **aegis** is the shield of Zeus, often borrowed by Athene and described by Homer as the

> betasselled, terrible
> aegis, all about which Terror hangs like a garland,
> and Hatred is there, and Battle Strength, and heart-freezing Onslaught,
> and thereon is set the head of the grim gigantic Gorgon,
>
> (*Iliad* 5. 738–41)

407 From the point of view of legal procedure, Athene serves as the officer of the court who makes the preliminary examination, determines the charges, identifies plaintiff and accused, and recommends whether or not the case will go to court. This process has been anticipated by the word translated "appeal" at 362. See MacDowell, pp. 293–42.

413 f. The grotesque aspect of the Furies momentarily makes Athene forget her business, i.e., an impartial inquiry. **Mates** = "neighbors."

415 Daughter of Zeus recalls *LB* 948 f. and the pun on *dikē* there.

417 The Furies are also equated with **Curses** at *Sev* 69a ff. (note), which is to call the effect by its cause. Cf. *LB* 406.

419 Position means "place" (394), "office" (209), "privilege" (227), which for the chorus is fixed and established, although its range and definition become a central question in the second half of the play, as at 894, where the same word (*timē*) is translated "powers."

424 Blast may also signify a scream or shriek; Thomson takes it as a hunting word for "hallooing on the hounds," and "hound" is a sense offered by Hesychius in his Greek dictionary.

426 I take this to mean: "from some (physical) constraint, or was it fear . . ."

427 Spur = "goad" (156).

429 In the Homeric poems as well as Attic law an **oath** was a valid means of determining guilt or innocence. A solemn oath was taken as prima facie evidence of innocence, while refusal to take an oath could be entered on the record of the trial by the plaintiff. Orestes cannot swear either that he did not murder his mother or that he did so unwittingly. **Technicalities** (432) = "oaths."

435 Such acceptance of Athene and Zeus may seem odd after 360–66, but the Furies have full confidence in *dikē* if it is **fair** (433).

438 Anger = "blame," perhaps not quite "charge."

440 f. Cf. 718. Aeschylus seems to have written a trilogy on **Ixion**, who murdered his father-in-law Eioneus. When neither man nor god would purify him, Zeus himself accepted that office and even raised the culprit to Olympus, where he tried to rape Hera. For this second offense he was lashed to a burning wheel in Hades.

445 He denies that the guilt described at 378–80 applies to him (**stain** = "infection" there). He speaks to this first because a truly polluted suppliant would desecrate the temple.

In his *Argonautica* Apollonius of Rhodes tells of Circe's ritual cleansing of Jason and Medea:

> First, to atone for the murder still unexpiated, she held above their heads the young of a sow whose dugs yet swelled from the fruit of the womb, and, severing its neck, sprinkled their hands with the blood; and again she made propitiation with other drink offerings, calling on Zeus the Cleanser, the protector of murder-stained suppliants. And all the defilements in a mass her attendants bore forth from the palace—the Naiad nymphs who ministered all things to her. [4. 704–11; trans. Seaton]

Circe seeks to "stay from their wrath the terrible Furies, and that Zeus himself might be propitious and gentle to them." Vase paintings show Apollo holding a pig over the head of the suppliant Orestes.

460 These **gyves** are hunting nets, a meaning clear at *LB* 998 and *Ag* 1048. For the **bath** see *Ag* 1540. A clean dying.

463 It is not so much that he **pleads guilty** as that he "does not deny" his role.

464–66 The idea of retribution is especially strong in this line, first in **vengeance** (see on "repay," *LB* 791–97), and then in **counterspurred** (see the note on *anti* at *LB* 143 f.).

465–67 In **responsibility** and in **the guilty ones** the same stem is present (see the note to *LB* 909).

468 Case = *dikē*; the language echoes 433.

470 ff. Athene summarizes her findings from the preliminary inquiry, decides that she cannot act as judge, and refers the dispute to trial.

476 In **work** we have a good example of a common word for "fate" (*moira*) used in a familiar sense of "portion," i.e., the alloted aspect of life in which they find their essential fulfillment. Cf. 172.

484 Lattimore's spacing reflects a pause in the speech. Corruption in the text at 483 has led some scholars to posit missing lines just before this point. For the sense cf. 572. Both lines emphasize the mythic foundation of a historical institution.

486 Under bond means "sworn and attested."

490 ff. The second stasimon. Does Orestes stay onstage throughout the lyric? Since the scene changes from the temple to the site of the Areopagus (see 683 ff.), some scholars have taken Orestes off in order to leave the transition untroubled by the presence of the suppliant before the statue. The statue of Athene would probably have been carried off by extras, a transition that might seem to point awkwardly at Orestes if he remained onstage. Yet Taplin suggests (p. 391) that he remains through the choral song and finds some "dramatic gain" in his presence when the focus shifts from the individual to the city. It is better to take him off. Yet another question: when does he return? With Athene and the jurors (565)? or with Apollo (573), if Apollo enters then!?

To avoid contradiction, we must understand **young** (491) in the common sense of "new," so that they express confidence that the newly founded **laws** (the word echoes "court," 484) will reaffirm their right to punish matricides. The judicial sense of *dikē* comes through clearly in **claim** (also "cause"), but, insofar as we also hear "*justice* of this matricide," they contradict themselves with a strong oxymoron (Sidgwick). On the other hand, the play's themes clearly include the cosmological sense of *dikē* (see on 306 and 310), so that one *dikē* against another also means one kind of order in the world against another. For the clash of new and old see on 150.

499–502 Through 516 the unexpressed premise is "if our power is dismissed, then . . ." In that case they will no longer **watch over** (cf. "watchful," 518) the **works of men.** Consequently, men will **indiscriminately** kill one another.

503–6 Man will be helpless and insecure if left to his own devices. Line 503 may also mean "one man will look one place, one another, prophesying his neighbor's evils, (looking for) a respite and remission from trouble." Such a person would be a **pathetic prophet.**

515 Now means "seeing that," i.e., if their powers are abrogated, the house supported by Justice must fall.

517–49 This is one of several lyric passages in which a general theme, more or less disassociated from the particulars of its context, is elaborated. Kranz (p. 161) compares the hymn to Zeus (*Ag* 160–83), *Ag* 1001–33 (not within but concluding the lyric), the mesode at *Pers* 93–100, and the hymn to Zeus at *Suppl* 85–100. The narratives at *Suppl* 547–89 and *Sev* 742–57 are similar but lack the generalized, gnomic quality of the first group. Kranz also includes *Sev* 321 ff.

Despite its generalized theme, the passage has affinities with the character and function of the Furies. Wrath (314) that inspires terror (*LB* 1024 f.) essentially defines their nature. Their watchfulness is restrictive; it keeps man within civilized bounds by threatening madness, and it instills piety by crushing *hybris* ("violence," 534). Athene's language and argument at 697 ff. reaffirm the sentiments of this passage.

517–25 This and the next stanza are more purely political than most moralizing on these themes. **Fear,** like shame, is praised for its inhibiting power. For **wisdom from pain** see on *Ag* 176–78. For the rhetorical question ending the stanza see *LB* 638. The last word in this antistrophe is **right** (*dikē*), responding to the last word in the strophe, Justice (*dikē*). Rhythm and music probably enhance such emphatic repetitions.

526 Cf. 696. Praise for the mean, or middle way, is a commonplace in poetic and political moralizing. So Pindar:

> for I have looked in the city and found the middle estate flowers
> in prosperity far longer. I scorn the destiny of tyrants.
> (*Eleventh Pythian* 52 f.)

Pindar's "prosperity" is the same Greek word (*olbos*) as the one that ends this stanza (537; see on *Pers* 706 and *Ag* 928). Similar language at 550 f. and 563. This praise of the mean falls in the middle of the stasimon and very near the exact midpoint of the play.

531 Ordinances reflects a verb signifying "overseeing,"

168   A E S C H Y L U S

as, e.g., at *Suppl* 628: "May Zeus Stranger *behold* . . . offerings." Other imagery pertaining to watching, overseeing, etc., at 220, 224, 500, 518, 970 f., 1045.

532–37 Violence = *hybris*. Cf. on *Ag* 763 ff. **Vanity** is the contrary of "respect" (525) and may also be translated "impiety." Cf. the metaphorical sequence at *Pers* 821–27.

539 For another **altar of right** see *Ag* 383 f.

541 f. Cf. the imagery at 370 ff., and see the note at 150.

544 Another version: "The destined end (*telos*) holds fast." Cf. *LB* 874: "The fight is done, the *issue* drawn."

553 ff. The metaphor likens the unjust man to the sailor who, gone off his true course, must strike his sail—but too late; the rigging is smashed.

558 ff. The preceding nautical image is continued, with a metaphor from wrestling added.

560 Spirit = *daimōn*.

564 For the Furies, **Right** is a barrier reef against which the ship that is off course must smash to pieces. Cf. *Ag* 1005–13.

566 The scene has changed to the Areopagus (the "Hill of Ares," 685), where, under the open air (so that no one would be polluted by the defendant), trials for murder took place. Athene presides, calls the jury, and, after each side has pleaded its cause, summarizes the case (681 ff.). The actual number of jurors is not specified in our text.

567 The **Etruscans** of north-central Italy were famous for their work in bronze and were thought to have invented the trumpet.

570 The Council of the Areopagus seems to have been originally a group of advisors to the king; it was probably composed of elders from the Athenian aristocracy. By the time of this play its prerogatives had been limited by the democracy to trials for "intentional homicide, wounding, arson, and destruction of sacred olive trees" (MacDowell, p. 27; see his discussion, pp. 27–29). Our play ignores this court's more extensive ancient jurisdiction in order to honor its preeminent rights in murder trials.

573 Case (*dikē*) is the last, emphatic word in her speech, just as "trial" (*dikē*) concludes Apollo's first response (581).

Since there is no announcement of Apollo's entrance, he (and Orestes?) may have entered at 566 with Athene and the jury. In this scene, as regularly in iambic dialogue, the chorus's part is actually spoken by the leader of the chorus.

580–82 Responsibility echoes 465–67 and 199 f. Both **initiate** and its repetition in **declare . . . opened** reflect technical legal terminology, as does **pursuer,** which means both "prosecutor" and "hunter."

589 In one style of Greek wrestling three **falls** made a victory; cf. 776.

595 Their tone is incredulous and mocking, since, as in the case of Oedipus, the oracle would be expected to warn of **matricide,** not counsel it. Cf. 615.

600 Dirtied refers to pollution (*miasma*). At first his argument seems more serious in tone than the choral taunt, but then we discover that he is counting his father **twice** (602).

605 f. When it comes his turn, Apollo will use this distinction between **blood congenital** and uncongenital against the Furies (660 ff.), as Orestes anticipates (606). Sidgwick points out that evidence from tragedy varies on whether the Furies limited themselves to relatives by blood: Sophocles' Electra invokes the Furies against her mother (*Electra* 112), and the chorus of the same play predicts that the Furies will avenge the murder of Agamemnon (489 ff.). Lebeck (*The "Oresteia,"* p. 135) and others have noted that in any case the Furies' reference to "parents" at 271 and 546 contradicts their present distinction. For Lebeck such contradictions may be explained by the parodic tone of the trial: "What a contrast between the lofty status of the litigants and the tricks to which they will stoop to gain their ends."

616–21 Apollo's claim to speak for Zeus can hardly be denied, but not a few Athenians might wonder if the pro-Persian, pro-Spartan god is not stretching his prerogatives just a little. If Zeus does stand behind Apollo, he is nonetheless the god of hearth, home, and marriage; in short, Zeus cannot ignore matricide, any more than he can condone patricide. As if Apollo had not simplified enough, he goes on to add that the juror's oath is not so binding as the will of Zeus, a very odd thing to say about "Zeus the God of Oaths" (*Philoctetes* 1325). In fact, something must give: the gods are pitted against one another, even against their own interests; and if the human jury is to judge that Orestes killed in justice and has been absolved, then it must forswear its duty to condemn intentional homicide.

623 This means: "told Orestes that, having avenged the death of his father, he should disregard the honor of his mother." For "honor" see notes to 419 and 780.

625 ff. Killing a man and a woman are not **the same thing,** particularly if the man is noble (= **a man of blood**) and a king, whose honor comes from god. Second, and also prejudicial to the comparison of the two crimes, the man was murdered by a woman—no honest Amazon!—and by deceit and guile. As Winnington-Ingram remarks ("Clytemnestra and the Vote of Athena," p. 142), it is not for Apollo to disparage craft (cf. e.g., *LB* 556–58). For **Amazon** see on 683 ff.

630 ff. As at 635, Lattimore's spacing marks a pause before Apollo turns to a brief narrative. One or more lines may have been lost after 632. In **better than worse** there may be an allusion—very odd from Apollo at this point—to the death of Iphigeneia. Who is the **fair judge**? The word thus translated might refer to Clytaemestra's "specious welcome" or, as Smyth takes it, to the welcome of his subjects. The missing line would perhaps have clarified this; I would prefer to take it of her welcome.

634 f. Cf. Orestes' description of the murder at *LB* 997 ff.

637 Why **solemn in all men's sight**? Winnington-Ingram ("Clytemnestra and the Vote of Athena," pp. 142 f.) suggests that this is ironical, since Agamemnon "had been so humiliated" by Clytaemestra; but irony would tell—like the allusion to Iphigeneia—against Apollo's case. As king and father, Agamemnon is owed a certain degree of "reverence," and there is no irony in that. Apollo is very confident of his case and so is perhaps a little indifferent to the impression that Agamemnon made onstage.

639 Inflamed suggests the bite or sting of a viper (as at *LB* 841 f. and 995); see note on *Ag* 1492.

640 ff. The Furies score one! The repressive rule of **Cronus** was terminated when Zeus threw him and the other Titans into Tartarus (*PB* 223 and Hesiod, *Theogony* 713 ff.). Zeus could not destroy his immortal father, but sending him to the underworld comes very close.

645 ff. If Aeschylus had wanted to give Apollo his sharpest retort, the god might have said "that was no murder" or "but Zeus freed Cronus from his **shackles**." Yet Apollo is more nasty than clever, and he only vaguely alludes to the story that Zeus freed Cronus to make him lord of the Islands of the Blessed (Hesiod, *Works and Days* 173a ff.; Pindar, *Second Olympian* 70 ff.).

646–50 The argument is essentially the same as that at *Ag* 1017 ff. (chorus). There too the idea of magic **spells** may point to popular superstition; cf.

> No good physician quavers incantations
> When the malady he's treating needs the knife.
> > (*Ajax* 582 f.)

650 f. Cf. *Suppl* 98–100 for similar praise of Zeus.

652–56 This is very much the same argument found at *LB* 291 ff., where Orestes tells the personal trials predicted by Apollo if he does not avenge his father's murder. **Brotherhood** calls to mind Nestor's description of the exile's lot:

> Out of all brotherhood, outlawed, homeless shall be that man
> who longs for all the horror of fighting among his own people.
> > (*Iliad* 9. 63 f.)

Brotherhoods (*phratries*) in classical Athens represented the people organized by clan; the Apatouria, the fall festival of induction into the clan, would have been an occasion for **lustration** (ritual washing), followed by sacrifice and communal feasting, all of which would naturally be forbidden to the polluted killer.

658 ff. A crucial argument, which has elicited diverse reactions from modern critics. In brief, Apollo argues that the mother merely carries the father's semen and has herself no physiological relation to the child; she is the receptacle and the nurse, but no blood tie exists. Aeschylus did not invent this theory, which is approved by Aristotle and may have been Pythagorean in origin. Later it appears in Euripides' *Orestes* (552 ff.). Yet it is difficult to say whether his audience would have found it novel, and it is not at all certain that Greek males, even given the claims of patrilineal descent, would so easily have dismissed the mother's part in procreation. Perhaps more cogent as argument and paradigm for the Athenian audience is the example of Athene (663 ff.): born from the head of her father Zeus, Athene, warrior goddess and guardian of the city, is present evidence that the male may reproduce without benefit of the female.

Modern readers have found the argument ludicrous and "astonishing" (Kitto, *Greek Tragedy*, p. 95); others, like Vickers, think it must be taken seriously, advice we can hardly ignore in light of Athene's acceptance of it (735 ff.). Yet if Athene likes the argument and is "always for the male" (737), it is hard not to agree with Winnington-Ingram's observation that "the inference which depreciates the relationship of mother and child . . . undermine(s) one of the bases of tragic emotion in his trilogy" ("Clytemnestra and the Vote of Athena," p. 143). He refers, of course, to Clytaemestra's love for Iphigeneia and, still more to the point, Orestes' hestitancy at killing his mother, a shame and regard that is at best ill informed if his mother is no more than a body nourishing the father's seed. When Aeschylus made Orestes, shamed by his mother's plea, turn to Pylades for advice (*LB* 899), the playwright underscored a moral and affective relationship between mother and son that is totally alien to the present argument.

There are some ambiguities we must live with. In this play Aeschylus has created an impasse from which, it seems, only such casuistry as Apollo's can find a way out. His plea frankly appeals to male prejudice and just as frankly ignores maternal affection, on which his trilogy pivots. It is no good, with Vickers, to speak of Clytaemestra as having been eclipsed, nor can we ignore, even if Apollo fails to use the argument, that Orestes has achieved a moral stature that to some extent justifies the verdict. That the argument is not overwhelming and unambiguous, however, clearly appears from the fact that only Athene's vote brings a tie and so acquittal. That tie would seem more than merely aetiological, i.e., explanatory of the historical fact that tie votes in Athenian courts brought acquittal. The issue is "resolved" but not dismissed; Apollo's physiology remains a male pathology; the Furies must still be placated.

663 Warned by Earth that Metis (Thought) was destined to bear a son stronger than his father, Zeus swallowed Metis, who was already pregnant by him with Athene. Subsequently Athene was born from the head of Zeus; hence she is the daughter **without any mother.** See Hesiod, *Theogony* 886 ff., 924 ff.

670–73 The emphasis on trust, alliance, and friendship points to a topical political allusion, i.e., to the recent alliance between Athens and Argos. So, too, does the oath of Orestes, 762 ff.

676–80 Lines 676–77 and 679–80 are attributed to different characters in different editions. After Apollo's depreciation of the oath (619–21), it seems a little incongruous to give him 679–80, and, as an archer god, 676–77 suit him. On the other hand, the metaphor from the hunt in 676–77 is natural to the imagery attached to the chorus (cf., however, *LB* 381: speech as an arrow is a common figure); yet they have been hounds rather than hunters. I would reverse the attribution of the translation.

682 The translation is either mistaken or unnecessarily emended; so read: "in this first case of bloodletting that you judge."

683 ff. Aegeus is the father of **Theseus,** who succeeded him as king of the Athenians. The name Areopagus was traditionally interpreted to mean **Hill of Ares** (see the note to 360 ff.); it may actually mean "hill of curses." The **Amazons** (cf. *PB* 723) invaded Attica after Theseus had joined Heracles in an expedition against them (Theseus' son Hippolytus by the Amazonian queen Hippolyte—or Antiope, as she is also known—gives Euripides' play its title). As warriors and descendants of **Ares,** they naturally sacrifice (**slew their beasts**) to that god (689). "And though he [Theseus] had a son Hippolytus by the Amazon, Theseus afterwards received from Deucalion in marriage Phaedra, daughter of Minos; and when her marriage was being celebrated, the Amazon that had before been married to him appeared in arms with her Amazons, and threatened to kill the assembled guests. But they hastily closed the doors and killed her. However, some say that she was slain in battle by Theseus" (Apollodorus, *Epitome*

1. 16–17). Since Aeschylus here connects the name of the hill with the Amazons, an allusion to the story of Halirrhothius at 360 ff. would seem at least mildly contradictory.

691 Cf. 517 ff. **Do-no-wrong** is made from a negative of the *dikē* stem.

693–95 These lines are generally thought to allude to the recent reform of the court by which its powers were restricted to trials for homicide. Dodds ("Notes on the *Oresteia*") goes further and sees an allusion to the admission of the third census class (small landowners and artisans known as the Zeugitai) to membership in the court (the reform bill actually made this class eligible for the archonship, the chief magistracy; membership in the court was limited to former archons). On Dodds' view, **foul infusions** would refer to "the influx or infiltration of the lower class into the aristocratic Chamber" (p. 20). Dodds does not believe, however, that Aeschylus protests so much what has been done as he warns against going too far. The metaphorical language makes all this more than a little uncertain, but Dodds' view is not incompatible with the subsequent (696 ff.) political advice exhorting moderation.

696 f. Cf. 526 f. The two lines may be taken together: "I advise my citizens to embrace and revere neither anarchy nor despotism."

698 f. Cf. 517 ff. Although the echo of the Furies' sentiment seems conscious and thus commendatory, the thought is a commonplace of Greek popular morality. The inhibiting power of shame and the fear of divine retribution are familiar variants on this theme.

703 The references to **Scythians** of the Russian steppes and the land of **Pelops,** the father of Atreus and Thyestes, may be simply a periphrasis for "east and west," but a fragment of Aeschylus refers to the "well-ordered Scythians," and there was always a party in Athens that admired the oligarchic conservatism of the Spartan constitution (**Pelops' land**). Lloyd-Jones argues that these references to laws, as distinct from homicide, imply a criticism of the recent revocation of the broader constitutional powers of the court. In the hands of the old aristocracy the Areopagus had served as a check against hasty constitutional innovation.

708–10 Athene's last lines instruct the jury, so we expect the balloting to begin. The exchange between Apollo and the chorus (711–33: eleven speeches of two lines each, excepting the three lines of the last) offers a natural pace and symmetry for twelve ballots, the last to be cast at 734. That exchange is not directed to the jury, however, and some scholars have postponed the balloting until 734, which hurries the process a bit if it is finished by 747. As in other staging problems, we must ask ourselves if their quarreling would distract attention from the solemnity of the voting. Let the voting begin now.

714 Apollo returns to the argument of 616 ff. **Make void the yield** = "render fruitless," a metaphor from harvesting.

717–20 For **Ixion** as paradigm see the note to 440 f. The line means: "Was Zeus then frustrated in his own purpose when he accepted the supplication of Ixion?" According to the Furies' argument, Zeus himself must be unclean for having cleansed the murderer. Some in the audience may have wondered about the cogency of this example, since the thankless Ixion subsequently tried to rape Hera. When the Furies respond **Talk!**, they as much as say "You said it!" They cannot attack Zeus, but even he is not immune to their argument.

720 Weight: cf. 712 and the notes to 372–76 and 730.

723–24 The story alluded to in **the house of Pheres** is explained at length in the prologue to Euripides' *Alcestis*. Apollo, because he killed the Cyclopes, was forced by Zeus to serve a mortal—Admetus, son of Pheres—for a year. In gratitude for Admetus' kind treatment, Apollo secured from the **Fates** a favor for Admetus, namely, that he should escape death if he could find someone willing to die in his place. In the *Alcestis* Admetus' wife offers herself. According to the Furies, Apollo persuaded the Fates by first making them drunk (727).

730 Void = "vomit" (as at 184) or "spew" (see on 800); **hurt** translates the same word that is rendered "weight" at 712, 720, and 932; for **poison** cf. 478 f. and 782.

731 See the note on 150.

733 The **state** is implicated in Orestes' guilt and pollution if its jury absolves him.

734 Final may mean "last," and there has for some time been an argument about whether Athene casts a vote that makes the ballot even or breaks an even vote by adding her vote for acquittal. The evidence of 741 and 751 might be taken either way, but Athene's argument at 795 f. depends on her vote breaking a tie. Her speech explains the custom in Athenian courts that granted acquittal (called "the mercy of Athene") when the vote was even. Whether she actually casts a vote, by dropping a pebble in the box, is not clear from the text; the announcement may be symbolic, but the demonstrative **this** (ballot) in 735 suggests that she at least makes some sort of gesture to indicate her decision. Cf. her statement at the end of *Iphigeneia in Tauris* (1469–75):

> Orestes, once I saved you
> When I was arbiter on Ares' hill
> And broke the tie by voting in your favor.
> Now let it be the law that one who earns
> An evenly divided verdict wins
> His case.

Thus there is no reason to assume an uneven number of jurors in the present court; Athene's ballot is the odd, probably the thirteenth. See Kitto, *Form and Meaning*, pp. 65 f., for an argument for Athene as the twelfth.

736 ff. Athene accepts Apollo's arguments (658 ff., esp. 663–66) that the male is more important than the female. Thus Orestes' acquittal hangs not on his guilt or innocence—these arguments ignore that question—but on a resolution of the male/female antithesis that has run through the trilogy. The forensic focus, stressing a social and sexual antagonism rather than the homicide, is but another dramatic strategy intended to make us feel that Orestes is less culpable than Clytaemestra. If we call Athene's pronouncement a resolution, it must be admitted that, however much the vote for male domination squares with the social realities of Aeschylus' Athens, the injustice of such a decision is equally palpable to most modern readers. Several commentators would like to think that Aeschylus knew better, and perhaps he did; but the curious fact remains that the creator of the overpowering Clytaemestra asserts male primacy.

743 For ballots, pebbles were placed in one or the other of two **vessels;** cf. the metaphor at *Ag* 815–18.

751 The **house** as a theme has been less prominent in this play than in the *LB* (cf. *LB* 480, 966), but cf. 754 ff.

753 If the interpretation at 734 is correct, the jury was divided evenly, and Athene's is the **single ballot** (751).

759 f. The **all-ordaining god the Savior** is Zeus, who is in the text explicitly marked as "the third" (see on *Ag* 245–47).

762 ff. Now Orestes takes an oath to bind Argos to Athens in perpetual amity, another allusion to the recent Argive alliance (see the note on 670–73).

764 Bigness reflects the extravagance and redundancy that occasionally afflict Aeschylus' style.

765 For the metaphor in **helm of my state** see on *Sev* 1–3.

767 Orestes imagines himself a malignant or gracious **spirit** (774) who will work from the grave to bind his people to his oath. The power of such spirits is recognized in the conjuration of Agamemnon during the kommos of the *Libation Bearers*. Herodotus tells how the Spartans, beaten by the people of Tegea, sent an embassy to Delphi to ask which god they should propitiate in order to defeat Tegea in battle. The Pythia replied that they must bring home the bones of Orestes, the son of Agamemnon. When the Spartans finally discovered a huge coffin in the territory of Tegea and managed to transfer the bones in it to Sparta, they were ever afterward victorious over the men of Tegea (the full story is in Herodotus 1. 67–68).

776 With **outwrestle** cf. 559, 589.

777 If Apollo's entrance was "disruptive, hurried, and informal," as Taplin says (he is so unhappy with the text that he argues for considerable corruption and the loss of several lines), then his present "disappearance" is odder still (Taplin, pp. 397 f., 406). If our text is sound (and there is in fact no obvious sign of dislocation or loss), then the question arises why absolutely no recognition is given to his departure. It is no answer to observe that the drama must now turn to placating the Furies, for which business Apollo is certainly not suited. Nor does it make sense to say that his silent exit plays down his role, which has been too significant to reckon him, at this late date, a minor character. I can find no obvious dra-

matic reason for Aeschylus' handling of this exit; but if the
text has not lost a speech after 777, we should probably bring
the god on with Orestes in the first place (note to 573) and
now take them off together. They are a pair, treated as one
advocate of a single cause; such staging hardly elevates the status of Apollo, but then neither do his arguments.

As an Argive, Orestes has no place in the Athenian ceremonies of the last scene, nor would his presence aid in placating the Furies, who have some trouble in forgetting their anger. No aspect of the plot better illustrates the significance of
thematic considerations for the poet, who is willing to dismiss
his central character for the sake of enhancing social and religious reconciliation. The departure of Orestes signals the conclusion of the revenge plot, but the avengers must be appeased. As so often in Athenian tragedy, the city is celebrated
for its hospitality and willingness to give sanctuary. Unlike
the Furies, Orestes cannot become an Athenian.

778 ff. The chorus sings four lyrics—actually two pairs of
roughly similar lyrics—each of which is followed by a speech
of Athene. Defeated but not pacified, the Furies threaten
Athens with their angry poison (780–87); Athene must find
some persuasive remedy (885) that will turn them into benign
spirits (1040 ff.).

778 f. The verb **ride down** occurs for the third time (cf.
150). No object is actually expressed with **torn,** so that we
have a violent mixed metaphor in which the **younger gods**
trample down the same thing they tear away. Of course they
tore Orestes away from the grasp of the Furies and thereby
rode down the old laws.

780 Disinherited is one of over a dozen appearances of the
timē ("honor") stem in the next 130 lines (cf. on 419); 791
("dishonor"), 797, 807 ("devotions"), 824, 833 ("pride of
worship"), 853 ("more dignified"), 855 ("eminence"), 868,
891 ("privilege"), 894 ("powers"), 915 ("estimation"), 917
("forget the cause"). At 747 it appears as "duties."

Heavy with anger = "a weight of resentment" (cf. 720);
the same stem is echoed by Athene in "grieved" (794) and is
virtually repeated by her in "angry . . . bulk" (800 f.).

785–87 Cancer = "ulcer" at *LB* 279–83 (note). **For the
right:** an exclamation invoking *dikē.* **Smear** is the taint of

bloodguilt, the word Oedipus uses when he thinks he may have killed his father:

> May I be gone out of men's sight before
> I see the *deadly taint* of this disaster
> come upon me.
>> (*Oedipus the King* 832 f.)

789 So often the victim feels **mocked:** cf. *LB* 222, *PB* 152 ff. Dionysus says of Pentheus:

> I want him made the laughingstock of Thebes
>> (*Bacchae* 854)

By a nice irony these horrid persecutors of mortal guilt are made, rhetorically, pathetic victims.

794 Athene begins to bring them round with a verb of persuasion (**Listen**), echoed at 826 ("I have Zeus behind me" = "I have put my trust in Zeus"), again at 829 ("be reasonable"), and culminating in 885 (". . . Persuasion has her sacred place"). What follows begs the question but also excuses failure, since the chorus cannot hope to beat Zeus and Apollo at their own game.

800 The reading of the line is disputed; one possibility offers a close variant on 730: "and shall you spew forth grievous wrath upon this land?" (Lloyd-Jones' version).

802 Pestilence and sterility are conventionally associated with divine anger. Cf. 823–25 and Oedipus' description of Thebes:

> On you I lay my charge to fulfill all this
> for me, for the God, and for this land of ours
> destroyed and blighted, by the God forsaken.
>> (*Oedipus the King* 252–54)

where "blighted" = **barren of fruit** (802); related imagery appears in 714 (note), 831, 834, 942. The **dripping rain** responds to 783.

804 f. In complete honesty and **yours by right** are modulations on the *dikē* theme; perhaps the first proleptically suggests "which you will occupy in perfect right." (Prolepsis is a figure by which an adjective applied now will have force later.)

There was a cave sacred to the Eumenides on the northeast

side of the Areopagus. Cf. the pronouncement at the end of
Euripides' *Electra* (1270−72):

> The dreadful goddesses, shaken in grief for this,
> shall go down in a crack of earth beside the Hill
> to keep a dark and august oracle for men.

808−22 This antistrophe simply repeats the strophe (778−
93), as good a way as any of exhibiting complete intransigence.

826−29 Not, perhaps, a threat but at least a reminder that
the power of Zeus's **thunderbolts** is available if persuasion
fails. So Hesiod describes the destruction of Typhon:

> So when Zeus had raised up his might and seized his arms,
> thunder and lightning and lurid thunderbolt, he leaped from
> Olympus and struck him [Typhon], and burned all the mar-
> vellous heads of the monster about him.
>
> > (*Theogony* 853−56, trans. Evelyn-White)

Lloyd-Jones compares Athene's speech in the prologue of the
Trojan Women (80−81):

> He [Zeus] has promised my hand the gift of the blazing
>   thunderbolt
> to dash and overwhelm with fire the Achaean ships.

830 Reckless also means "in vain," "futile."

832 Wave suggests the surge of the sea and, combined with
black and **bitter strength,** a surge of poisonous black gall
flooding the land.

834−36 As spirits of the earth, they will receive sacrifices
for fertility, both at marriage and in thanks for children. This
will be quite an about-face for the character of line 605.

839 Out cast, like dirt = "dishonored, filth," the second
word being regularly used of pollution (e.g., 378, "infection"); so they have become, as they see it, the "stain" (445)
that attached to Orestes, i.e., something Athene would get rid
of by condemning it to a hole in the ground.

840 The line refers not to the **fury** they inspire but to the
hatred they feel. The language of these lines suggests a violent
dance.

844 f. Cf. 321 f.

845−47 There may be a wrestling metaphor here, something like "they have come within an ace of throwing me, by
their underhanded tricks, from my old rights."

848 ff. Athene is now more conciliatory, with promises that they will enjoy the predicted glory of Athens.

852–54 Time will bring more honor (**dignified**) to this city and so to its tutelary deities. Get on the bandwagon!

855 Erechtheus was a legendary king, for whom the Erechtheum, a temple on the Athenian Acropolis, is named. The offer thus gives them a place of honor equal to that of the autochthonous founder of the city.

859 Stimulus is literally "whetstones," bloody from the sharpened knives; **raging** modifies, by another transference, the whetstone (not the Furies). So, though it hardly survives in English: "do not cast bloody whetstones, destruction for young hearts, raging in a fury not of wine" Cf. *Ag* 1535.

861 The image is drawn from the fact that cocks fight their own kind, so that to have such a heart is to be inclined by nature to civil war (863; cf. 866).

864 f. Lattimore may view this as an allusion to the contemporary war with Sparta (**the man**). Otherwise: "Let war be foreign—easy enough to find: in which there will be a terrible love for renown."

870–80 = 837–47.

883 Unfriended: "as a stranger and without honor."

885 Persuasion actually had a cult at Athens: "When Theseus brought the Athenians together into one city from being little towns of people, he instituted the worship of Popular Aphrodite and Persuasion" (Pausanias 1. 23. 3). Cf. *Suppl* 1040–41, where, as often, Persuasion and Desire are joined; see also *Ag* 385 and the note there. **Beguilement** (= "magic" at 82) denotes the magic power to charm that is regularly attributed to rhetoric. "Have your way with" (900) is another form of this stem. Cf. the effect of Odysseus' story on the Phaeacians:

> So he spoke, and all of them stayed stricken to silence,
> held in thrall by the story all through the shadowy
> chambers.
>
> (*Odyssey* 11. 333–34)

Later in the century the sophist Gorgias' *Encomium of Helen* excuses Helen on the grounds that she was a victim of Persuasion.

888–91 Justice here also means "in accord with a proper

or natural dispensation." Leaving behind the legal sense that it had in the trial scene, *dikē* now takes on the older meaning, "fair way." **Baron's portion** belongs to the landowner, one who has a vested interest in the country's welfare.

895 f. Prosperous = "be strong" (908), "fatten" (943); this verb, evoking flourishing plant and animal life, catches their ear: it is *euthenein*, while their **be strong** is *sthenein*; the two are not homophones, but they are too similar and too near together not to interact.

897 Straighten suggests both our "straight and narrow" as well as "standing upright." This common metaphor appears in "restored" (751), "steering" (961; cf. 993–95), and "upright way" (772); of speech, at *Ag* 1475 f. and 699 f. ("in truth . . . the name"). This stem (the *ortho* of the English word *orthodox*) provides the metaphorical antithesis for "stumbling" or "going astray" (e.g., *PB* 472). The polarity commonly defines moral, social, intellectual, and spiritual alternatives. See the nice combination of literal and figurative sprawling at *Ajax* 452; for straightening see *Oedipus the King* 50 f., 419, 691.

899 Lloyd-Jones says that "Athene expresses herself with a kind of wry humor."

902 For song as incantation see on 646–50.

903–10 Evil success is a victory that harms the victor. So she asks that they supervise a harvest from a benign nature, from land, sea, and sky. Good weather leads to a good harvest (907 f.) and so to the well-being of the people (909). Line 910 ties the fertility of the land to piety (cf. 897).

916 With the second forensic scene now resolved, a new mood prevails, which moves toward the final processional. From 916 to 1020 choral lyric alternates with Athene's anapests (an epirrhematic scene). This structure corresponds to 778–891 but contrasts markedly with that section both in tone and in dramatic point.

916–26 Quite a number of words and phrases echo earlier themes and imagery; with 916 cf. 833; 917 involves the "honor" theme (see on 780); **Ares** of 918 goes back to "battle" in 914; 924–26 accords with Athene's call for a fertile, happy land (904 ff.). There is a little flag-waving in 918–20.

930 ff. Their **weight** (cf. 372–76, 712, 720, 730 [see note],

965) is not displaced or forgotten; rather, it is transformed into a positive, though restrictive, function. For **strokes of life** see on *Pers* 740. Henceforth beneficent, they still will attend to the curses from **past generations.**

938 Cf. the image at 905 f.; see also 137 f., 840 (= 873).

940 The meaning is uncertain. Some editors take **nor cross . . . place** as a reference to the boundaries of Attica ("may no blazing heat cross these frontiers").

946–48 The **secret child** apparently alludes to the wealth produced for Athens by her silver mines. **Surprise** is "the luck of Hermes," i.e., whatever one chances upon (cf. *LB* 811). So the guard in the *Antigone* (397), with the same allusion, says

> mine was the luck, all mine.

949 Addressed to the jury but, like several other lines, equally applicable to the audience. Cf. 928, 997.

950–55 **Fury** (Erinys) is probably singular for plural, as often; such address is yet another indication that their natures are not so much transformed as integrated and redirected, so that they now will dispense both **singing** and a **life dimmed in tears.**

960–63 These **steering spirits** are the Fates (Moirai), who, like the Furies, are daughters of Night (cf. *PB* 516 and *Eum* 321).

964 They are **implicate in,** i.e., joined to, the fate of every house.

965 References to time have been fairly frequent, e.g., at 852, 898, 908, 946.

967 August = "most honored." **Bestow** means "grant our prayer" (that murder cease and that girls find husbands, 956–59).

970–72 Cf. 885. **Persuasion** is described as looking on (**eyes**) and overseeing (**guided**) her successful work. But the poets also represent various virtues as situated in the eye or aspect, as, e.g.,

> Oh, where now has the countenance
> Of modesty or virtue
> Any strength, . . .
>   (*Iphigenia in Aulis* 1089–91)

Cf. 990 and the note on 531; *Ag* 418.

974 f. Hesiod (*Works and Days* 11 ff.) distinguishes two kinds of **ambition** (or "strife," as the Greek *eris* [eristic] is also translated); one leads to war and destruction, the other to emulation and productive work. The allusion explains the choral response.

979 f. Cf. *LB* 577 f., *Ag* 1188 f., *Sev* 736 f. (virtually the same language as the present passage).

979–84 The balance and parallelism of Lattimore's translation reflect the new reciprocity of **grace for grace**. The former vampires reject the draught of **black blood, revenge,** and the hunt (**prey**). See the note on *LB* 143 f. (here *anti* is translated **for**).

987 Healed: the healing results from directing all hostility toward foreign enemies. For the metaphor see 506, 645, and *Ag* 1170.

990 Their faces "speak terror." Cf. on 970.

992 f. Good will . . . will shall be good: Greek manages this sort of punning by declining two adjacent adjectives (*euphronas euphrones*); the same kind of juxtaposition occurs at 999 in "beloved . . . loves" and at 1012 f. in "good . . . good."

998 They are near to Zeus because they are righteous. Sidgwick cites Plato, *Philebus* 16c: "the men of old, better than ourselves and living near the gods."

1003 Are those in attendance the jurors, or the women mentioned at 1024, or yet a third group, the torchbearers (1005)? The text gives no certain indication (it is not even clear that the women mentioned at 1024 are actually onstage). Athene is conducting the chorus to its new home, and it does not seem inappropriate that this first processional honoring the "grave goddesses" (see on 1041) should be augmented by a splendid display of civic respect. Taplin, as usual, regards more attendants as less dramatic, but this is clearly a time for pomp and circumstance (in antiquity that would have varied not only with the poet's conception of the play but with the financial generosity of the producer).

1006 f. A more likely version is Smyth's: "sped beneath the earth with these solemn sacrifices," the obvious meaning of which is that sacrificial offerings (animals) are present, perhaps brought on by those attending the torchbearers. **Plunge beneath the ground:** see 1023 and the note on 804 f.

1010 f. The Athenians are **children of Cranaus,** a legendary autochthonous king whose name means "rocky." **Who keep the citadel,** as Taplin points out, was used at 775 and again at 884 ("mortal"), certainly, in the second passage, of the jury; so Taplin argues that the jury provides the processional and that no new attendants are required.

1017 The verbs **hold** and **grace** convey the idea of reverential tendance (the former is translated "rule" at 919; for the latter see on 92 f.).

1018 Guestship echoes "guests" of 1011. Both words designate the Furies as immigrants or resident aliens, which in turn leads to the symbolic investiture alluded to at 1028 (note).

1024 Women: see the note to 1003. Despite some ambiguity (the Greek of 1024 does not require that attendants be present), this is the moment for a double procession of jurors and women to escort the new divinities to their new home. Thomson, in agreement with the earlier paper of Headlam, argues that the Athenian audience would have thought of the annual Panathenaic festival, when a new robe was carried by a magnificent procession to the goddess on the Acropolis. Lines 1024 ff., with reference to her image, women in attendance, and the procession, bid us stage the kind of grand and colorful celebration enjoyed by the people and their patroness.

1025 f. Flower is literally "eye," a common metaphor for what is precious (cf. *Pers* 169) and particularly appropriate to the imagery of seeing in this play (see 970–72; cf. 220, where "eye them" = "review," 224). **Flower** might be the object of the procession, i.e., the sacred place to which the procession goes, or, as Lattimore takes it, it might refer to the **companies.** Some commentators have greatly swollen the company on the stage at this point, on the assumption that Aeschylus actually brought on women and children. Once again, however, the Greek does not actually require a large gathering.

1027 f. The Oxford texts follow earlier editors in marking a lacuna here (to precede 1028). Who is **invested with purple stained robes?** The missing lines would probably make this clear, but it seems likely that the Furies now put on the scarlet (**purple**) robes similar to those worn by resident aliens (see on 1018) in the processions of the Dionysiac festival (see Pickard-Cambridge, *Dramatic Festivals of Athens,* p. 61). Thomson points out that in the Panathanaea (see on 1024) the metics (the "resident aliens" alluded to at 1018 in "guestship") carried trays with honey and cakes for sacrificial offering. In the procession to Athene's temple the metics, wearing purple robes, joined representatives of the Athenian tribes who carried torches (cf. 1022 and 1042) and sang a paean of celebration. For the color and its symbolic value see on *Ag* 957.

1032 As noted above (1003, 1010), we cannot be positive that the auxiliary chorus is composed of the women just mentioned. From the increasingly civic character and tone of this last scene, with its celebration of the city, its gods, and their happy prospects, it would seem apt to join all elements of the people in a joyous processional. Here Aeschylus had not only opportunity but dramatic reason for pageantry. He could manage what the prologue to *Henry V* laments it cannot, i.e., offer the proper spectacle to "the swelling scene."

1034 Aged children is a traditional oxymoron, also associated with the Graeae (see on *PB* 794–801). The common use of the privative (see on *PB* 905 f.) to make such phrases (here *paides apaides*) borders on cliché. Cf. *Ag* 1545 and *LB* 42. This figure is less frequent and more striking in English, as in Milton's

> Son in whose face invisible is beheld
> Visibly, what by Deity I am, . . .
>   (*Paradise Lost* 6. 681 f.)

1041 With the words **grave goddesses** the poet identifies the Furies with the Semnai, "the venerable ones," who "took rank with the great divinities of the Attic state, to whom thank-offerings would be consecrated after victory, and prayers proffered in times of peril. Their worship was of great local prestige, their shrine an asylum for slaves and suppliants; they have all the reality for the Athenians of concrete goddesses, and were doubtless of ancient establishment" (Farnell, *Cults*, 5:440). This identification is adumbrated at 384d (where "stern" = **grave** here) and 833 (where "share my pride of worship" is a compound meaning "gravely honored").

1043 Singing refers to the cry of victory and good omen, which has been raised frequently, and perversely, throughout the trilogy (see on *LB* 942). Here, finally, the omens are propitious, the cry justified by the event.

1045 Cf. on 1025.

> The eye of Zeus sees everything. His mind
> understands all.
> He is watching us right now, if he wishes to,
> nor does he fail
> to see what kind of justice this community keeps
> inside it.
> (Hesiod, *Works and Days*, 267–69; trans.
> Lattimore)

The Suppliant Maidens

THIS IS THE FIRST PLAY in a trilogy. For an outline of the plot and some speculation on the major themes and action, see Benardete's introduction. It is possible, as Benardete suggests, that Aeschylus wrote this play early in his career but produced it only in his last decade, but most modern scholars are reluctant to explain the play's primitive, primarily choral, form by such hypotheses. If the play was produced in 463, the most commonly accepted date, then these hysterical girls are only five years from the *Oresteia*, where, particularly in the *Eumenides*, the dramatic integration of chorus, character, and action seems light-years removed from the plot of the *Suppliants*. Of course not all critics find the play "primitive" in its plotting, and in any case we should note that many qualities of its poetry are comparable to the mature style of the *Oresteia*.

The Io story belongs to a common type of Greek myth in which a girl is raped by a god—Zeus is the culprit in the stories of Semele, Danaë, Alcmene, and others—and is then more or less abandoned to her hapless fate. With the girls of Zeus this fate often entails persecution by Hera. Io, daughter of Inachus, is raped by Zeus, is transformed into a cow, either by Zeus to protect her or by Hera to persecute her (see on 299), and is then committed to the tender mercies of the monstrous Argos (305). Escaping Argos but not his daimonic presence, the girl/heifer finally arrives in Egypt. There her son by Zeus establishes a line that will eventually produce both the chorus of the *Suppliants* and the greatest of Greek heroes, Heracles. Although the Greeks were not so keen on psychology as we are, myths such as the Io story reveal a lively sensitivity to the effects of sexual trauma as well as interesting intuitions about genetics. These girls, haunted by the fearful Io, reenact her flight and terror and thereby offer us a vivid "interpretation" of a typical Greek myth. Lacking the whole trilogy, we can only guess at many of the details of plot and theme that are finally resolved, as in the *Oresteia*, in a happy ending. Clearly in this first play, however, Aeschylus is especially intent on the portrayal of pathos, precipitated by group hysteria. There is also, though this subject is much disputed, room for lively spectacle, and in this respect we must regret even more than we usually do the loss of the choreography.

Like the *Persians*, the *Suppliants* opens with the entry (parodos) of the chorus, without prologue. During the first forty lines of anapests the chorus takes its place for the dance that begins the responsive lyrics of 41–178. There is an altar someplace here (83), or a mound serving as a sacred place (189). Arnott thinks a stage served for this raised area; Pickard-Cambridge (*Theatre of Dionysus*, p. 33) would put it near the south edge of the orchestra.

1 Zeus Protector is one of several cult epithets denoting the god of suppliants; cf. "Savior" (23, also from cult) and "Avenger" (42, a poetic title). See on 628.

7 Garvie points out ("*Supplices*," p. 171) that **self-imposed** indicates Aeschylus' concern to establish the independent nature of the girls' decision. The tradition offered another motive, i.e., that because of an oracle Danaus was afraid he would be killed by his nephews.

11 Danaus has entered with them but will not speak until the end of the parodos. He does not join the choral song and should remain backstage center until he speaks at 179. Cf. Arnott, pp. 22 f., for a different view on this and several other matters.

12 The term **counters** is drawn from dice or backgammon. See on *Ag* 32.

16–18 Argos, whence we boast to descend: cf. 273–74. They are descendants of Io, an Argive princess, who was transformed into a **cow** when Zeus's love for her was discovered by Hera. Driven mad (**wild**), Io fled to Egypt, where she gave birth to Epaphus (= **caress;** see 47 f.). For the story see *PB* 848 ff.

21 ff. They invoke the city, the gods of the sky, the heroes (**gods**) of the underworld, and Zeus. Take **respectful . . . land** as modifying **receive:** "receive with the compassionate spirit of the land these suppliant maidens" (trans. Smyth, Loeb ed.).

30 The **insolent** (= hybristic; see on 76–80). The **men** are specifically identified as the "race of Aegyptus." With **swarm** cf. 684.

36 On the issue of legal claims see the note to 388–91.

41 ff. Io as cow was identified with the Egyptian goddess Isis, after which it was natural to identify her son Epaphus with the Egyptian **calf**-god Apis. In 47 f. Aeschylus combines his interest in naming, puns, and homophones by means of a play on two words for "touching," *ephapsis* (**caress**) and *Epaphos* (**Epaphus**). The two stems differ only in their aspiration (the presence or absence of the *h*-sound), but the *ephap*-stem also appears in legal contexts in the sense of laying hands on someone or something by way of claiming it as one's own. The second stem, with which Epaphus is more naturally connected, simply means "touch," and **Caress** suits it well. But the first stem, with its sense of "claimant," offers more intricate metaphorical material for the play. See on 312–14.

51–54 The truth that will **witness** their claims is their knowledge of Io's story, which was well known in Io's native Argos.

60 Metis is sometimes emended away because the name usually given for the wife of Tereus is Procne. **Tereus,** a Thracian king, raped his wife's sister, Philomela, and paid for that crime when the women murdered his son Itys. Again, in what was to be the standard version, Tereus was transformed into a hoopoe, not a **hawk.** Metis (Procne) became a nightingale, whose lament for her son Itys became her song (*Ag* 1143).

67 f. Ionian songs seems to be an allusion to the laments of Asia Minor; cf. *Pers* 1054 and *LB* 423 f. **Eat** = "rend" and points to the custom, in mourning, of tearing the cheeks. Cf. *LB* 23 f. It seems to be an open question whether the masks worn by the chorus would have represented this disfigurement. Gesture might have sufficed to indicate this customary aspect of mourning, with the audience expected to credit the gesture imaginatively. If the choral masks showed bloody gashes, then of course they had to remain that way throughout the play, since the chorus had no opportunity to change masks.

71 Blooms of sorrow: for imagery connected with blooming see 539a and 663–65.

76–80 Justice: see 167–70, 437 f., 933 f. ("gives verdict"), and the note to *Ag* 250. Some form of "youth" (perhaps "to youth") should supplement line 80, thus making it clear that the **pride** (*hybris*) belongs to the lusty Egyptians. In this play *hybris* usually denotes the suitors' violent disregard for the girls' feelings; so "insolent" at 30 and "arrogance" at 486 have more the right tone than **pride** (which is also the translation at 101, 426, 528, 844, 880 f.). See on *Ag* 763 ff.

83 The girls are in a sacred precinct, before an altar (the **bulwark**); cf. 189, 222.

85–93 A frequently accepted transposition of the second and fourth pairs of lines gives better sense:

> May his will, if it's Zeus's, be well,
> His will not easily traced.
> Dark are the devices of his counsel,
> His ways blind to our sight.
> And so certain it falls without slips
> By sign of Zeus fulfilled.
> Everywhere it gleams, even in blackness
> With black fortune to man.

Traced carries a hunting metaphor.

94 ff. For deceptive **hopes** see *PB* 252. **No violence he armors** means that Zeus does not need to arm to accomplish his purposes. Cf. the praise of Zeus at 590–99. The present passage is more abstract and theological, less anthropomorphic, than many descriptions, e.g., 171, where the poet speaks of Zeus in a traditional way as having a "face now averted." With the present passage Rösler (pp. 7 f.) compares this fragment of Xenophanes:

> Always he [Zeus] remains in the same place, moving not at all; nor is it fitting for him to go to different places at different times, but without toil he shakes all things by the thought of his mind. [Kirk and Raven, No. 174, p. 169]

Even in the present passage **sign of Zeus** (91) is probably a variant on the Homeric "nod of Zeus" (to signify assent, as at *Iliad* 1. 527).

101 ff. The prayer continues with the request that Zeus look on the **pride** (*hybris*) of the Egyptians that flourishes in their desire for **marriage**. For the theme cf. *Pers* 821 and *Ag* 763. The passage is terse, the sense difficult, but the argument seems to be that *hybris* leads to a frenzy that drives a man on like the goad of a charioteer. Finally he repents his folly, but too late; he is the victim of *atē* (for deception and delusion joined see *Pers* 93–100).

116–20 For **Apian land** see 260 ff. **Sidon** was a Phoenician city whose merchants traded fine goods across the Mediterranean.

121 ff. The elliptical and allusive style leave us straining for connections. The preceding stanza dwells on the expression of grief; now they turn to the bountiful sacrifices granted the gods when things go well; but then suddenly they speak of **toils,** as if, recalling their plight, they imagine themselves at sea, stormstruck (cf. the imagery at 439 ff.). The figurative expression leads them to remember the sea journey.

131 ff. Linen-bound describes the manner of clamping the timbers (Tucker). The **Father** is Zeus, who is styled as all-seeing (**omniscient**). **Timely** may also be taken with **gracious end:** "May Zeus accomplish a gracious end in good time." **That** (140) indicates the result of the beneficent god's action: "so that the seed of Io may escape." They appeal to Zeus, who raped their ancestor, to save them from marriage.

144 ff. The **pure daughter of Zeus** has been identified as Athene (unlikely), Artemis (**pure** = "sacred" at 1031, of Artemis), and Dikē (so Lloyd-Jones ["Zeus in Aeschylus," p. 59], probably thinking of the wordplay at *LB* 948 f.). Artemis, the virgin sister of Apollo, who has three or four cult titles pertaining to gates and walls (Farnell, *Cults* 2:517), is the best candidate for rescuing reluctant virgins.

154 ff. For **Zeus of the dead** (= Hades) cf. 230 and *Ag* 1387. Later the Danaids will threaten Pelasgus with suicide at the altar if he does not give them sanctuary (460 ff.). If Zeus their ancestral father will not honor them, then Hades will surely accept their supplication.

161 ff. The text of the third refrain is uncertain at the point here translated **snake-hate,** but the reference to Hera's jealous persecution of Io is clear enough. **Snake** is literally "poison" but has also been emended to an exclamation of pain. In either case the poet puns on Io's name. Hera's vendettas after Zeus's philandering are the universal burden of Greek girls and their sons; cf., e.g., Heracles' complaint in Sophocles' *Women of Trachis* 1048 and in Euripides' *Heracles* 830–32.

Winter suggests storms and heavy seas.

166 f. If Zeus dishonors his son (Epaphus) by turning away from our prayers, will he not be guilty of injustice? Their fears triumph in these last two stanzas.

179 Only now does the text reveal that Danaus has been present all along. His admonition (**prudence**) reflects the increasing anxiety, fear, and withdrawn self-absorption of the chorus. They have evoked storms at sea; he responds that he will be a **trusted pilot.**

182 Crowds: there is no indication of the actual number. Taplin notices the plural at line 500 (where the Greek word for "men" has not been translated) and suggests that three or four chariots may have appeared in this scene.

189 Altar might also be "mound." See on 508.

191 White: the olive branch (cf. 19) is wrapped in wool to denote purity; cf. *Eum* 43–45.

207 ff. The following stichomythia is rank with textual problems. Numerous supplements and transpositions have been proposed. For example, line 208 is actually at 210 in the manuscripts. As frequently happens in these texts, the manuscripts do not indicate the attribution of specific lines to specific characters, and the sense does not always make attribution certain. The distich at 211 f. is anomalous amid the single lines (one or more lines may have been lost here). Despite the appearance of Benardete's text, there are no half-lines or part-lines in this exchange.

212 f. The **bird of Zeus** is the eagle (*Ag* 114). The **sun** god (Helios) does not belong in this invocation of Olympian divinities, but he does belong as a universal witness (cf. *LB* 985).

214 f. Apollo was banished from Olympus for killing the Cyclopes (see *Alcestis* 5 ff.). Fontenrose (*Python*, p. 386), however, thinks that Apollo's stay among the Hyperboreans is alluded to in **knowing this fate** (i.e., exile).

218 The **trident** is the symbol of Poseidon, the primary god of the sea.

220 It seems likely that Aeschylus was aware of the Egyptian god Thoth, who was identified with the Greek Hermes. **A Greek custom** may refer to the phallic image of the god: ". . . the Athenians were the first Greeks to make statues of Hermes with the erect phallus" (Herodotus 2. 51). If so, Danaus identifies the statue but ignores, for his delicate daughters, its sexual form (the typical herm, or statue of Hermes, was simply a block of stone with a head and erect genitals). Hermes was lucky (*LB* 815–18) and was a **herald** (*Ag* 515).

222 The chorus has now taken its place at the **altar,** which might have been represented by a wooden structure or a mound of earth. Though Johansen gives directions (at 209) for them to mount the stage, other recent discussions see no need for a stage or for a building behind it. Garvie compares the use of images of the gods at *Sev* 184 and 265.

223 ff. The agitated violence of this speech quickens the pace of the scene for a moment. For the imagery compare *PB* 859 ff., which make the same comparison of the same people. Tucker offers *Iliad* 22. 139 f.:

> As when a hawk in the mountains who moves lightest of
> things flying
> makes his effortless swoop for a trembling dove, . . .

But the brutal vigor of these lines derives from Hesiod's vision of the law governing the animal world:

> as for fish, and wild animals, and the flying birds,
> they feed on each other, since there is no idea
> of justice [*dikē*] among them,
> but to men he gave justice, . . .
>   (*Works and Days* 277–79; trans. Lattimore)

Pollution, a phenomenon of culture, not nature, intrudes from the human side of the analogy to heighten the violence, adding a confused, emotive tension similar to that of the chorus.

234 ff. Pelasgus, excited by the sudden and outlandish appearance of these foreigners, enters with attendants (there is no indication of their number). Note the attention to exotic dress. Danaus is all but ignored (cf. 319 f.) until 490. Taplin (p. 205) compares the presence but virtually complete suppression of Adrastus in Euripides' *Suppliants*, 263–734.

249 ff. In the view of Aeschylus and Herodotus (1. 57–58), the **Pelasgians** were the oldest inhabitants of Greece. **Palaechthon** means "ancient land," and he, like many founding fathers, is himself the son of Earth. His realm, as described here, extends far beyond the historical Argolid: the **Strymon** river is in Thrace; the **Perrhaebi** in Aeschylus' time occupied the territory west of Mt. Olympus; the western territory of the Perrhaebi is bounded by the **Pindus** range of mountains, which runs north and south; **Dodona** is in Thesprotia, west of the Pindus. If, as in Johansen's text, **Paeoni** and **Perrhaebi** are interchanged, then the former tribe, which lived west of the Strymon and north of Macedonia, falls into a rough northern boundary for the continental empire. At 253 f. the translation should read: ". . . through which the holy Strymon runs, in the direction of the setting sun" (Johansen's version).

260 ff. The land **Apia** derives its name from a founding hero **Apis** (cf. *Ag* 257). So the Pelasgians are named for Pelasgus (251). **Naupactus** is in Aetolia, a northwestern district. Apis, a healer and purifier, whose magic can cleanse a polluted land, is naturally made the son of a god who heals and purifies and who also purged Delphi of its monstrous serpent, Python.

273 f. While their supplication at the altar has intrinsic religious force, to establish kinship with those supplicated will double its validity.

276 ff. All these comparisons to foreign types suggest that the choral masks had a non-Greek aspect.

286 The **Amazons** are the famous virgin warriors of Greek mythology, usually said to live in central Asia Minor. The essence of Pelasgus' argument indirectly leads to the topic of words versus things: you say that you are Argive, but your appearance belies that word. Cf. 493 ff.

299 In Apollodorus' version (2. 3) Zeus rapes the girl and then, detected by Hera, himself transforms Io into a white cow. Cf. Io's own version, *PB* 640 ff.

305 Hermes received one of his epithets, Argeiphontes ("slayer of Argos"), from this killing. Cf. *PB* 567 ff. for Io's description of **Argos,** whose ghost she equates with the gadfly that hounds her.

312–14 The ambiguous punning described in the note to 41 ff. continues, first in **by touch**—which also implies that Zeus is the legal claimant who lays his hands on the prize he claims as his own—and second in a word in 314 not translated by Benardete, a word that Johansen translates as "taking prize." This word in legal terminology denotes something seized or taken as compensation for another thing, namely, as a "prize," or, as Benardete translates it at 411 and 727, "reprisals." The point is that Epaphus's name not only suggests the form of his begetting but is, more significantly, in itself a *pledge* of divine paternity.

320 For some scholars this reference to **fifty** constitutes evidence of a chorus numbering fifty, the number of singers in the dithyrambic chorus, from which Aristotle says tragedy is derived (*Poetics*, chap. 4). Most authorities, however, seem to agree that the number belongs to the myth and is not to be taken literally. Pickard-Cambridge (*Dramatic Festivals*, pp. 234 f.) notes Wilamowitz' observation that, while the number seven is repeatedly mentioned in Euripides' *Suppliants* as comprising the number of mothers, the chorus almost certainly numbered fifteen. Older studies of Aeschylus (e.g., Smyth, *Aeschylean Tragedy*, p. 51) accept fifty and, with it, a spectacular conception of Aeschylean drama.

322 f. The text of the best Aeschylean manuscript gives a reading here that more particularly recognizes the act of raising the suppliant and thus accepting responsibility. If this reading is accepted, the translation would be: "Now knowing my ancient lineage, you should act to raise up an Argive band."

327–31 The answer is evasive. The second line is, in a unique form, related to the "birds-of-a-feather" metaphor. The question that follows implies that they have landed in Argos by chance, while elsewhere they seem to have come in the good hope that the ancient tie of kinship would serve them well.

336 ff. Lost lines before and after 336 ("Who buys . . .") are conjectured by Wilamowitz, who thinks that the lost verses contained a clearer explanation of the claim the Egyptians had on the Danaids. What in fact is offered in the text is strong personal animosity coupled with evasion (cf., e.g., their reply to the king at 392). Aeschylus had more than a few opportunities to clarify their motivation, had he wanted to; therefore we should assume that for him their reasons for flight were not so important dramatically as the fact of their flight. This response may beg the question, especially since there are tantalizing threads of evidence for various explanations (e.g., they are the rightful booty of the Egyptians after a war in which Danaus was defeated; or the Egyptians have a rightful social and legal claim to marry their cousins and thus claim their estate), but on this point I agree with Garvie's careful and skeptical survey, which finds none of the theories advanced by recent criticism acceptable. Their motivation, like their prospects for salvation, is, at least in this first play of the trilogy, ambiguous and obscure. If we may assume that there is no lacuna, and if we accept a couple of emendations, the following translation gives a line of thought for lines 333–39:

> *King:* Why have you come as suppliants?
> *Chorus:* That I may not be a slave to the clan of Egyptus.
> *King:* [Do you say this] because of hatred, or do you refer to something unlawful?
> *Chorus:* Who, if she loved, would fault her master?
> *King:* [Yet] thus power is increased for men.
> *Chorus:* And when things go wrong, a change is easy.
> *King:* How then with piety could I act in your case?

This translation is influenced by Garvie's discussion. The change alluded to in 338 would be **desertion** (in Benardete's version) or divorce.

341 New might be some evidence for an actual loss of verses around 336, but, as Tucker points out, the word may also suggest the strange and unexpected, hence the dangerous.

343 Shared from the start seems to mean "if Justice was the issue from the beginning (and is not now introduced to serve an argument)."

344 Ship of state appears at *Sev* 2 (there "ship's prow"). What is the connection? The king's answer may imply they have pointed to the wreaths (**crowned**) on the altar, so that the sense would be: "the gods, here crowned by our supplication, guide the ship of state and should be revered by you."

346–48 The first line is in iambics and should be taken as a spoken response to the king's last line. Though the chorus cries for pity in the following stanzas, **wrath** (= "god's anger," 385 and 427) underlines the fact that they, having put themselves in the power of the god, have the strength that comes from the god's protection. A pious man, like the king, must beware of the god's indignation should he refuse a just and righteous plea; so at 478 he echoes their words in "wrath of Zeus [the god of] the Suppliant."

347–416 The chorus sings three pairs of responsive stanzas. The king has five lines in iambic trimeter, intervening between the stanzas; then comes his last speech, which is eleven lines long. Cf. the similar lyric exchange (an epirrhematic scene) at *Pers* 255 ff., where the concluding speech (a new speaker) also modifies the formal structure.

353–57 Crowd of gods refers to the images on the altar (cf. 189). In the third line **friendship** recognizes the claims of guest-friends; **no doom** ("without *atē*") is answered in the following stanza by **innocent** (same word). **For us** means "for the city"; this distinction between personal and civic responsibility is continued in his next speech.

359–64 Themis, in Hesiod, is the bride of Zeus, to whom she bore the Hours, Good Government, Justice (*dikē*), and Peace (*Theogony* 901 f.). Harrison (*Themis,* p. 485) calls her "the force that brings and binds men together . . . the collective conscience, the social sanction." When not a proper name, *themis* is translated "law." **Master of lots** was an epithet at Tegea for Zeus as the god who sanctioned land division (Farnell, *Cults,* 1:56), but here it apparently refers to the god who determines the lots of life. Pelasgus is addressed as one **ancient in wisdom.** Some words have been lost from the last sentence of the stanza.

366 ff. The king's relation to his people is thoroughly anachronistic: **the city** must decide. Cf. 399–400, 483 ff. For the possibility of **stain** see 412 ff. Their response (370–76) rejects his claim that he needs the city's sanction.

377–80 At the very word **pollution** he superstitiously tries to avert it by wishing pollution on his enemies. Their speech is for him ill-omened (see the note on *Sev* 257 f.). In the last line (380) Johansen's version more fully states the king's predicament: ". . . fear of acting, fear of not acting, fear of taking the chance."

381–87 Zeus is the **protector** who oversees the laws that guard suppliants. **Zeus the Suppliant** means "Zeus the god who protects suppliants."

He is **charmed by no pity** for those who violate the rights of suppliants. The idea that the god's anger is implacable and beyond the power of charms is also found at *Ag* 69–71.

388–91 Pelasgus worries that the Egyptians have a legitimate claim on their cousins. Some scholars have argued that the Danaids are heiresses and, as such, are subject to the claims of their cousins. Danaus is of course not dead; but since he is without male issue, he has in effect put his daughters in a condition of being without male protection (in a dramatic sense he has certainly left them to their own devices). If that is their status, then under Athenian law and, we may suppose, under the Egyptian law imagined by Pelasgus, their nearest male relatives have a right to marry them and to claim the estate. Thus in Athens it was not uncommon for an uncle or cousin to claim the hand of an unmarried daughter whose father had died without male issue. As Garvie (p. 220) notes, the herald's "what I lost" at 919 may imply such a claim. To the king's sensible inquiry—for the Egyptians are not hybristic if they simply claim what is theirs by right of law—the chorus responds wildly and evasively. Another complication: in the next play of the trilogy the girls for some reason do marry their cousins, if only a few hours before killing them; so perhaps a legal, if not moral, claim was established in that play.

393 The metaphor is drawn from navigation at sea. Cf. *Oedipus the King* 794–96.

397 Aeschylus loves wordplay. Here we have a triple play on the *kri*-stem (**choice . . . choose**): "Not easily decided the decision; don't choose me the decider." Greek tragic style is more tolerant of such stylized rhetorical effects than modern English.

401 Cf. the rebuke that Hector imagines will be cast on him:

> Hector believed in his own strength and ruined his people.
> (*Iliad* 22. 107)

402–6 Zeus is the ancestor of both parties. The imagery of the **scales** is derived from Homer; Sideras (p. 213) compares *Iliad* 8. 69 ff., where Zeus balances the golden scales. See on *Ag* 206 and compare *Pers* 346, *Sev* 21. This imagery occurs later, at 606, in "not doubtfully," and again at 822 f. and in "unhesitant" at 982 (something like "not tilting both ways").

407–11 Tarkow interprets the image of the **diver** as reflecting Pelasgus' inability to resolve problems that are beyond his element: his kingdom is continental ("oceans bound my rule," 256), so that when he faces a dilemma he is at sea (cf. "here I'm run aground," 439). **Unblurred:** if the correct reading is in fact "drunken," as several modern editors assume, the metaphor is the remarkable "an eye sharp and not too drunk." **Reprisals** and its verb of claiming clearly look back to 314 (see the note on "pledge" there).

414 Alastor (= "spirit of vengeance") is very strong here; see the notes at *Ag* 1507 f. and *Pers* 353. Pelasgus might seem to be safe so long as neither he nor his people violates their sanctuary, but clearly he worries that even in doing nothing he runs a risk. The danger he imagines is similar to that actually experienced by the Greeks in book 1 of the *Iliad*, when they reject the supplication of Apollo's priest Chryses. He offers gifts and begs the chiefs for the return of his daughter; refused, he invokes the wrath of Apollo, in whose name he had made his petition (1. 21). Apollo then brings a pestilence on the entire Greek army. Thus the passive role of supplication, in which Chryses and the Danaids humble themselves completely, entails for the persons supplicated the danger of incurring the active animosity of a vengeful deity.

417–38 In two pairs of responsive stanzas the chorus sums up its argument and appeal. Their insecurity can be seen from the contrast between **pious protector** and the threats to that protector in the last stanza. Some texts include a reference to Ares (war) in the last stanza, which would provide a transition to Pelasgus' **war** (441).

439–43 At least three, and perhaps four, nautical situations are imagined in seven lines: first, this business of the king has **run aground,** as if in a narrow channel with reefs of war on either side; second, the tension is likened to that of a ship drawn up (to shore or a dock) by a **windlass** (like the ship run aground, it is out of its element); third, back in the water, the ship can find no **anchorage** without pain (*anchorage* is ambiguous; the word might also indicate "turning," so as to take a new course, or "conclusion," the end of the course). Finally, one more metaphor from naval freight occurs in a line suspected by several editors and omitted by Benardete: someone seems to be "freighting ruin (*atē*) with a still greater cargo," though how and where this line should be placed and exactly what it means are much disputed.

443–46 The transition to **wealth** seems based on an acceptance of war, for whose losses Zeus will compensate. With **tongue has failed** new metaphors scramble for a place: "when the tongue has shot wide of opportunity, speech may (yet) become a charm of speech" (?). What is the sense of these two lines? Perhaps: "though the tongue may miss the mark, aiming to speak seasonably, yet more extended discussion may heal the wounds of speech that has erred." The passage is corrupt, cryptic, and too shifting for any certainty. All of these lines are full iambic trimeters in the Greek.

446 ff. Consanguine blood may refer only to the Danaids and Egyptians; but since the Danaids have claimed kinship with Pelasgus, their cousins, the Egyptians, have similar claims, so that Pelasgus too is endangered.

456 All of these are items of their clothing. They make a riddle of their purpose, which is to commit suicide by hanging themselves.

458 Another version: "from these, you know, a fine **device**."

463 A demonstrative pronoun ("these") marks the **statues** as being nearby, on the altar.

464 He prefaces **speak simply** with "the speech is riddling."

465 From these repeats the first phrase of 458, a kind of ring composition that solves the riddle.

466 The threat of blood pollution (cf. 472) agitates Pelasgus even more than earlier allusions to vague retribution from divine justice (e.g., at 434 ff.).

470 Given the metaphor of passage through a storm, **doom** (*atē*) implies subjective confusion.

471 ff. In balancing the alternatives, the king thinks of opposing forces as **debts** and **waste** (both are commercial terms). Where debts and expenses are thus balanced in antithetical clauses, we naturally think of the image of the scales (note at 402–6). To these weights on the scales line 477 adds "men against women." Since it is Zeus who traditionally holds the scales and whose **wrath** now tips the balance in Pelasgus' thinking, **height** (479) may subtly continue the latent figure of the scales (in the traditional weighing, the surviving portion or soul went *up*).

481 ff. He turns to Danaus. The **wreaths** must be other than those of the chorus (cf. 506). For **replace,** read "place."

490 f. In **stranger** we have the same word (*proxenos*) that is translated as "protector" at 418 and as "patron" at 241. It denotes the person who has accepted responsibility to act as host and so to offer his assistance and protection to aliens. At line 500 the king will assign some of his own bodyguards as **guides.**

493 Danaus recognizes the same differences in appearance that the king noted at 234 ff. and 276 ff. Their strange dress and aspect justify the king's hesitant ambivalence.

493–96 The contrast of nature and nurture was a commonplace in fifth-century philosophy and literature. Here Aeschylus takes **nature** in the sense of appearance and attributes the difference in appearance to the **nurture** provided by the two lands (represented by their respective rivers).

496 f. A typical compression: "don't let (your) rashness beget (our) fear."

508 The Greek suggests motion "down" (to the **grove**) and so provides some evidence for a raised mound or altar (see Arnott, p. 22).

509 Public indicates that the grove is not protected by religious sanction; they fear to leave the altar.

510 f. Schutz (cited by Tucker) explained the transition by interpreting **rape of birds** as an expression for the exposure of children. He compared Euripides, *Ion* 902, where Creusa describes her exposed son as "lost . . . snatched as food for birds." At the same time, we recall Danaus' comparison of the Danaids and Egyptians to doves and hawks (223 ff.) as well as other metaphors from the animal world that elaborate the hunt/prey motif (e.g., 350 ff., 751 f.). Moreover, the word here translated **rape** may mean either "prey," as in Schutz's interpretation, or sexual rape (cf. *Ag* 534). This latter sense prompts them to respond: "but would you turn us over to an enemy more hateful than **heartless snakes?**" Such imagery is ready-made for Freudian analysis.

512 He finds their speech ill-omened and advises them to speak **auspiciously.** This is what is called an apotropaic response, i.e., one calculated to avert any word or gesture that might inadvertently bring bad luck (see on 377).

522 f. Persuasion is echoed by "supple Rhetoric" (623 f.), the last words of Danaus' report and the first words before the next lyric. Cf. 615.

524–99 The first stasimon begins with a prayer to Zeus, turns to the story of Io, and returns in conclusion to celebrate Zeus.

526 f. In **obey and let it be** the first word echoes Persuasion (522), the second may pick up Fortune as a subject (Tucker). So: "listen (to our prayers), and bring us good luck."

529a–30 This time the sea imagery is literal and refers to the hot pursuit by the cousins. The sea is **purpled** from the dark turbulence of heavy waves. Cf. the Homeric rivers that

> dash whirling in huge noise down to the blue sea
> (*Iliad* 16. 391)

("blue" and "purpled" translate the same adjective). **Doom** (*atē*) is substituted for the ships: the ship means doom for them, and its occupants are, in their view, victims of doom, i.e., of *atē* in the subjective sense ("mad delusion").

Aeschylus has fused three ideas: "cast their ship into the sea"; "cast ruin upon them and their ship"; "cast mad delusion upon them."

531–45 The antistrophe (531–38) begins with one of several clear antitheses between male and female: "Look on the women's side of the cause" (Johansen).

For another description of Io's wanderings see *PB* 791 ff. The last two lines of the stanza allude to Io's crossing the Bosporus (literally "cow-ford"), but it is hard to see in what sense she **defines** the strait.

546 ff. She moves south through modern Turkey (**Phrygia, the city of Teuthras** [king of Mysia], **Lydia, Cilicia,** and **Pamphylia** are in order, save for the inversion of the last two) to the **land of Aphrodite,** which is Phoenicia, famed for its worship of Aphrodite under the Semitic name of Astarte.

555 ff. At *PB* 567 the gadfly is called "the ghost of earth-born Argos," the monstrous hundred-eyed herdsman Hera set to guard Io. It is not clear whether the present passage takes **cowherd** figuratively or alludes to the same ghost. The

groves of Zeus are in Egypt. For **Typhon** see on *Sev* 493.
Here his attack may be that of the desert sandstorms.

The **stinging pains** come from being "pricked by goads"
(*PB* 597) of the gadfly until she is frenzied like a **Bacchant,**
the possessed follower of Dionysus (*Eum* 24–26). She is called
a Bacchant of **Hera** because Hera's vengeance has caused her
mad flight.

570 Aeschylus' interest in **marvels** was noticed by Aristophanes (*Frogs* 833 f.). See further on *LB* 548–51.

574 The question ending the preceding stanza leads to a
celebration of Zeus, who brings an end to Io's suffering. A
few words are missing here, but apparently Zeus effects his
cure by **divine breaths** (cf. 17 and *Ag* 1206).

580 The scholiast notes a curious metaphor: **burden** means
"ballast," such as was used in ships.

582 Modern readers of Greek myths quite naturally see in
Zeus's philandering a series of casual rapes followed by Hera's
jealous persecution of the luckless mortal girl. Our perspec-
tive shares Euripides' skeptical and even cynical view, but the
older Greeks looked on these affairs as the origins of heroes
and distinguished families. Zeus may be the author of Io's suffering, but he also ends it and brings her a famous line of children. So the very earth, ultimate source of all fertility, celebrates the life-giving power of Zeus. Another way of viewing
this subject is Robert Murray's: "The Danaids atavistic obses-
sion that they are, in some sense, a reincarnation of Io, is a
determining and dominant element of their character. Yet
their perception of similarity between themselves and Io is
woefully limited and superficial; the first stasimon reveals
this" (Murray, p. 69).

592 The world without Zeus would be like a garden without tendance. He is the lord and **craftsman** (a metaphor from
carpentry, as at *Ag* 152) who shapes its course and gives it
meaning. **Propitious the wind** translates an epithet denoting
Zeus as the god who brings wind, rain, and dew. In connection with these epithets denoting fertility Farnell (*Cults*, 1:44)
observes: "Probably in every city of Greece men prayed to
Zeus for rain in times of long drought, and the official Athenian prayer has been preserved: 'Rain, rain, dear Zeus, on the
corn-land of the Athenians and their pastures.'"

600 Since Aristotle, critics have referred to the sections of the play between choral lyrics as "episodes" or "scenes." What follows is one of the shortest episodes in Greek tragedy—clear evidence, if more were needed, of the primacy of the chorus in this play.

605 ff. Several metaphors are continued in this brief speech. **Not doubtfully:** see on 402–6. **Bristled thick** likens the assembly to a field of grain:

> as with dew the ears of corn are softened
> in the standing corn growth of a *shuddering* field.
> (*Iliad* 23. 598 f.)

For the legal metaphor at 610 see the note to lines 312–14; for the **wrath of Zeus Suppliant** see on 346–48; for **defilement** (*miasma*) see on 466.

615–21 Cf. the following paraphrase for metaphor and image: He spoke of the wrath of Zeus, how the city should be careful lest it later fatten Zeus's wrath; he mentioned the rights of both stranger and citizen, how in this case they converge, threatening a twin defilement appearing before the city, to be an unmanageable fattened victim for pain. Note (1) that the city fattens the wrath of Zeus and (2) that the defilement is then identified with a fattened victim that is unmanageable and a source of pain. A similar metaphor occurs at *Sev* 769b and *Eum* 302.

625 ff. During the first seven lines (anapests) the chorus takes its position for the second stasimon. The themes of the lyric are traditional to thanksgiving: peace, health, and fertility are the blessings sought; war and disease are especially deprecated. Tucker compares the rewards of justice sung by Hesiod in *Works and Days* 225–37. Cf. the several prayers for Athens that conclude the *Eumenides* (beginning at 916 ff.). Against the usual practice, the actor (Danaus) remains present during the choral lyric.

628 Zeus Stranger (*Xenios*) is the god who *protects* strangers. Other titles and praise at 641, 646, 652, 671 f., 688 f. The repetitions in **good ... good** and **Stranger ... stranger** represent the poet's declension of adjacent adjectives. Throughout the lyric there is strong linkage through assonance and alliteration.

630 Zeus-born applies strictly only to Aphrodite, Apollo, and Artemis.

635 ff. War (Ares) is **wanton** because he is the seducer of Aphrodite (*Odyssey* 8. 266 ff.; cf. note below on 663–65); as the enemy of festivity he hates the dance. **Changed** = "foreign."

641 Respect (some form of *aidōs*) has occurred eight times prior to this line: 25, 193 (twice in the Greek), 344, 364, 454 ("reverent"), 479, 490. See on *LB* 896 ff.

643 ff. The male/female antithesis is even stronger in the Greek, since **us** translates the Greek text's "quarrel of women." Cf. 790, 798 f., and see note on 531. **Avenger** may mean "he who exacts payment." Zeus might be a **spy** (from the familiar image of the overseeing god, as in the prayer at 101 f.), but Page suggests that this "avenging lookout of Zeus" should be equated with the Alastor (see on 414). If Page is right, then in the following lines we have a vivid image of the daimon hovering over the house: "What house, having such a creature (the Alastor) on its rafters, could be light at heart" (accepting Weil's emendation for **stained**). This fits nicely with **heavily presses**, the usual attitude of an evil spirit (see note on *Eum* 372–76).

656 Shadowed might be transferred from the people to their **lips**, i.e., from the suppliants walking in the shade to their speech. But **fly** suggests a metaphor from the flight of birds coming from a cave or thicket (Tucker). Note the following verbal and thematic parallels between this second strophe and the first strophe (630 ff.):

First Strophe		*Second Strophe*	
"Hear our prayers"	(631)	"honorable prayers"	(657)
"never . . . fire"	(633)	"never a plague"	(658)
"Pelasgian land"	(634)	"the city"	(660)
"Never War"	(635)	"Strife never"	(661)
War as harvester	(635–38)	War as a harvester	(664 f.)

663–65 The association of Ares (**War**) and Aphrodite is both literary (e.g., Hesiod, *Theogony* 933 ff.; Pindar, *Fourth Pythian* 87) and religious (Farnell, *Cults*, 2:653), but that may not be the limit of its significance here. Burkert (*Griechische Religion*, p. 336) stresses the "polarity corresponding to the biological-psychological rhythm that binds together male aggression and sexuality." He points out that in the Theban myth the daughter of Ares and Aphrodite is Harmonia, a name that would seem to recognize the tension and attempt a reconciliation. All this might seem to wander a bit far from our present passage, but in fact this is only one of several passages ambiguous enough to draw attention to Aeschylus' psychosexual probing. The very conventionality of the imagery may serve to mask the repressed sexual neurosis of the suppliants (more conventional than it seems, since the Greek adds a Homeric epithet for Ares [untranslated here]: "man-killer"). The English reader should note that pronouns such as **their** (665) are seldom found in the Greek lyrics, so that ambiguous wishes (for the youth of Argos; for themselves) stand out more vividly in the original (the three lines of English translate eleven words):

> Flower of youth unplucked
> Let it be, nor [may] Aphrodite's
> Husband, man-killer Ares,
> cut [the] bloom.

Lines 643 ff. have indicated that the Danaids have not forgotten their hostility to men. Despite the conventional elements here—perhaps I should say through them—the tension and apprehension they still feel is evident.

666 ff. More corruption of the text. Two words in the Greek, however, mean "old." A transition by contrast, then, moves from youth to old men at the altars.

672 Zeus is here once again modified by *xenios* ("protector of strangers"; translated "Stranger" at 628). He **guides** fate.

674 Hecate is celebrated in *Theogony* 409 ff., where there is no hint of her later association with Artemis and Demeter, unless it is in the epithet "nurse of the young" (*Theog.* 450), which in cult she shares with them and several other goddesses. Her attributes are magical and chthonic. Here she is identified with Artemis in their mutual care for child-bearing and child-rearing.

676–87 Grammatically, it is the **plague** that is **arming Ares** and also arming internecine **shout**. Lycian (see on *Sev* 144) would to an Argive audience (also to an Athenian?) call to mind "the most glorious object in the city of Argos . . . the sanctuary of Wolf Apollo. The statue was made in our own day by Attalos of Athens, but this temple and its wooden idol were originally dedicated by Danaus" (Pausanias 2. 19. 3). Pausanias goes on to tell an anecdote about Danaus' claim on the kingship: the raid of a wolf on their herds convinced the Argives that Danaus should be king, and in gratitude he founded the temple.

698 ff. The stanza prays for good government, for which it looks to the people rather than the king. This reference to **Ares** ("before they arm for war"), the fourth in the lyric, is clearly tied to their standing as guests. Now we see that their prayers for Argos, though a commonplace in these circumstances, are personally rooted in their fears of Egyptian retaliation.

706 ff. The **laurel** belongs to Apollo; here it stands for nonburnt offerings. The complementary word for burnt offerings is not translated. Though they were not written, the **laws of Justice** may be the familiar "Honor the gods," "Honor strangers," and "Honor your parents."

710 Note that Danaus has been present throughout the preceding song. Taplin (pp. 209 f.) points out how exceptional Aeschylus' technique is in handling Danaus' entry and exits. It is usual for one or more exits to precede the stasimon (what Taplin likes to call the "act-dividing song") and for an entry to follow it. Cf., e.g., *Pers* 530, where the queen takes her leave, the chorus sings, and the queen then reenters at 598. Thus the song tends to mark the end of a discrete section, which the entrances and exits also mark. But in this play, where the chorus plays the leading role, we may ask whether its extensive songs should be thought of as act-dividing. Taplin points to the parallels with 179 ff., where Danaus plays the lookout and sights Pelasgus, then rehearses the girls in their role. The point of this second or "mirror" scene, as Taplin calls it, is, in his view, to highlight the parallels in the two confrontations, the first between the chorus and Pelasgus, the second between the chorus and the herald. Such parallels are yet another means of engaging the chorus in a crucial role, and the differences in the choral reaction to the two men provides some opportunity for contrasting thematic and ethical treatment (e.g., Taplin argues that "in the matter of the supplication the chorus was calm, proficient, and, in effect, in control of the situation," whereas, when threatened by the herald, they are "helpless and full of wild fear" (p. 211).

712 No special stage setting would be required for **this outpost**. Danaus is standing at the rear of the orchestra, perhaps directly by the altar.

720 This reference to the armament, like the earlier fears of war, would be more to the point if a war between Argives and Egyptians followed in the (offstage) action of the second play (the *Egyptians*). Cf. 740, 742.

722–24 Cf. his advice at 179 ff. ("prudence").

725 Defenders and **advocates** would more completely translate his phrasing.

727 For the sense of **reprisals** see the note to 312–14.

730 ff. The **refuge** is the altar. Danaus' ominous concluding lines bring back the justice (*dikē*) theme: **shall pay** is, in Greek legal idiom, "to give *dikē*," and here, as often, the last word in a speech is thematically significant. These lines foreshadow the murder of the Egyptian suitors.

734 ff. Here begins one of the epirrhematic structures, i.e., alternating speeches and lyrics. The first two lines of the chorus are in iambics, the next three (indented) form the strophe of the lyric. Danaus responds with two lines of iambic, which the chorus answers with two lines of iambic followed by three lyric lines (antistrophe, here indented). That is the pattern followed through to 764. Cf. 347 ff. and 825 ff. Kranz (p. 15) thinks that this type of scene is the "germ cell" of tragedy, preserved in the plays of Aeschylus but little used by Sophocles and Euripides. For Kranz the three epirrhematic scenes in the *Suppliants* are the "only three scenes of dramatic life" in the play.

741 f. Mad may also suggest "lustful." **I speak what you know** is one of those lines in the play that Wilamowitz (*Interpretationen*, p. 15) takes as evidence that Danaus fled Egypt after being defeated in battle.

751 Because crows and **ravens** scavenge altars, they are **impure**. Cf. *Ag* 1473.

755 Apparently they are looking at the symbol of Poseidon on the altar; plural for singular (Poseidon holds only one **trident**).

758 Gluttonous might have sexual overtones (same stem as "mad" at 741).

760 f. Since the comparison of **reeds** (Egypt was a great source of papyrus) to **wheat** clearly contrasts Egypt and

Argos, one might expect more relevance—e.g., of totem animals—in **wolves** and **dogs. Fable,** however, suggests a proverbial tale.

764 ff. The following description is abstract, impersonal, and sufficiently metaphorical to suggest something more than an awkward and vague narrative of the Egyptian arrival. We have it from Sophocles (*Oedipus the King* 1208) and from a fragment of Empedocles (Kirk and Raven, No. 441, line 3) that metaphors of anchoring and harboring carry sexual significance. In this passage it appears that Danaus is talking of two things: literally, of the arrival of the Egyptian fleet; figuratively, of the prospective union of the Egyptians and their cousins.

This covert second meaning, of which we may suppose Danaus is unconscious, derives from puns, ambiguity, and metaphor; it forecasts a union that is slowly achieved, that for safety requires persuasion, and that will reach its climax at night, when, with the sun set, the Egyptian pilots will find pain like that of childbirth, the very pain their lust would bring on the Danaids. Some crucial elements in this interpretation: (1) line 764 may refer not only to a fleet arriving, as in Benardete's version, but also to the preparation prior to sailing; (2) **ropes to be secured** puns on a phrase that may also mean "the security of persuasion"; (3) harbor (in the privative **harborless**) = woman as object of sexual desire; (4) **night** (**it** of 770) is a time of breeding; (5) the **pain** (770) is specifically that of childbirth. This reading of the passage veers close to allegory, but I imagine that Aeschylus intended no more than a covert foreshadowing; by abstracting from the concrete description of the naval landing, Danaus admits a second level of meaning.

Exit: Despite the promises of 725 ff. and 774 ff., Danaus will not return until the crisis has passed, nor does he bring the king; nor does Pelasgus himself, who comes in the meantime (911 ff.), refer to a summons for help.

777 The first word puns on Io's name (**O** = *iō*), and **mountainous** contains the Greek for "cow," so that we have something like a vocative phrase "Io, Earth, Cow." Cf. 162.

779a–82 The commentators cite numerous parallels to this figure of thought in Greek tragedy. Cf., e.g., *PB* 582, where Io's pain drives her to pray for any kind of death (three ex-

tremes of escape are listed). In both passages fantastic possibilities follow possible escapes ("possible" at least in light of
the transformations that occur so often in Greek myth). As in
Prometheus Bound the thought that there is no way out is what
leads to the wish. As *Medea* 1295–98 shows, this motif of impossible escape is akin to a riddle: Jason imagines that Medea,
if she is to escape, must hide under the earth or "raise herself
on wings into the height of air"; in fact, she does escape in a
winged chariot! Similarly, the Scythians sent Darius a bird,
a mouse, a frog, and five arrows, with no indication of their
meaning. Gobryas, advisor to the king, interpreted: "'My
friends,'" he said, 'unless you turn into birds and fly up in the
air, or into mice and burrow underground, or into frogs and
jump into the lakes, you will never get home again, but stay
here in this country, only to be shot by the Scythian arrows'"
(Herodotus 4. 132; trans. de Selincourt).

Aeschylus not only chooses more exotic images (smoke
and dust) than Euripides, but he also elaborates his second
term to the point of oxymoron, as Smyth's fuller translation
suggests: "or, soaring aloft without wings . . ."

738 f. My heart . . .: The sense is uncertain. Page's Greek
text, e.g., would yield "the *kēr* (death spirit) can no longer be
escaped."

792 ff. These lines, continuing the thought of suicide, return to a variant of the image at 779 ff. The **throne of air**
might call to mind Zeus throned on Olympus (hence the
"clouds of Zeus," 780).

794 ff. Perhaps only *Ag* 151 ff. has a comparable accumula-
tion of epithets. There variety expands and extends the image;
here the modification tends more to intensify the subject's
sense of isolation.

800 Cf. 758 and

> gave their bodies to be the delicate feeding
> of dogs, of all birds, . . .
>
> (*Iliad* 1. 4–5)

806 Means and its verb suggest a metaphor from crossing
the sea: "How can I cut a passage to free me from marriage?"
Metaphors from travel are common; Becker (p. 155) compares 468 ff. ("uncrossed"); cf. *PB* 476 (note).

808–15 The text here is very corrupt. The **Father** is Zeus, who is given an epithet (**Protector**) conventionally associated with Poseidon.

816–24 Several themes and images are continued: **Proud** = *hybris* (see on 76); **men** = male (cf. 644); **beam of the balance:** see on 402–6; **brought to completion** as a cult epithet would invoke Zeus as god of marriage! See on *Ag* 972–74.

835 ff. The same actor played Danaus and the herald. Some editors have assigned the lyrics of 835 ff., 850 ff., and 857 ff. to a chorus of Egyptians, with the actual herald not entering until 872. The choral exclamation at 834 apparently anticipates the king's aid, not the return of Danaus. Before we knew that the *Suppliants* was performed late in Aeschylus' career, the manipulation of the two actors seemed awkward. Perhaps the dramatic intention was to fully implicate the Argives in the suppliants' cause before the second play.

Other pursuers demand the return of suppliants; see Euripides, *Suppliant Women* 399 ff., and Sophocles, *Oedipus at Colonus* 728 ff. The number of attendants is not specified.

Taplin (pp. 213 f.) comments on the lyric exchange between the herald and the chorus: "for all its disfiguring corruption, it still conveys a vivid and startling impression. The outlandish language, interjections, and bestial imagery create a scene of violent yet colourful, alarming yet almost lewd, boldness, which it is hard to match in surviving tragedy, unless in *Eum.*"

841 According to Apollodorus (2. 1. 5), the Danaids cut off the heads of their new husbands.

853 Though it is mere speculation to interpret such a corrupt text, in **fruitful**'s two earlier occurrences (*Iliad* 18. 593 and the Homeric *Hymn to Aphrodite* 119) it means "those who bring in oxen" and is used of girls, presumably because they bring in oxen as dowries. If for Aeschylus' audience this word had even secondary connotations of marriage and dowry, they would not have had to strain to spot the not too subliminal sexual repression. But some editors emend the first-person **I** to "you" ("may you never see again . . ."), which would make it parallel to 863 ff.

865 Sarpedon is the Homeric king of Lycia. If "fruitful" (853) is a literary adjective put to new subjective use for revealing the girls' traumatic anxiety, the present passage seems just the contrary, i.e., traditional and ornamental, without any personal psychic resonance.

878 The **Nile** may be invoked as the specific god of Egypt, the lord of its sailors, who would punish, if he saw, their **violence** (*hybris*).

885–92 Caldwell notes the ambiguity of **father** (Danaus or Zeus?) and the analogous postponement of Zeus between 811 and 815. In Caldwell's Freudian interpretation, "Danaus is relevant to the play because he is the father upon whom the Danaids are tragically fixated; he is superfluous because in their fantasy his place has been taken by Zeus" (p. 52).

The herald may be trying to pull the girls from the altar, but line 910 implies that the present stanza is more a hysterical fantasy (one meaning of **black dream**). For the sexual connotations of **spider** (here specifically male) see on *Ag* 1492. **Black:** of the spider, of the swarthy Egyptians, of the dream. The scholiast suggests that Zeus may be called **son of Earth** because Rhea and Earth were identified. Possibly; but earth symbolized fecundity, so that to make Zeus her child approves the fertility that their own repressed sexuality constantly denies.

893 f. Greek piety would not hold with this line of thinking, for the divinities of the world appear in various guises in various countries. Yet local divinities take the side of their own people and so become the enemies of invaders.

895 ff. We could hardly want better evidence for the sexual value of the **serpent**. Cf. *LB* 527 ff.

906 Obviously sarcastic; the sense if not the pith can be seen in Johansen's version: "Be of good cheer—you will have no reason to complain of want of rulers!"

907 This might also be rendered "leaders, commanders, I am assaulted." For the legal import of such a public appeal see the note to *Ag* 1315. More legal language at 934.

911 ff. In effect their cries for help announce the king's entry. No other motivation, e.g., the appeal of Danaus, is mentioned, but aid for threatened suppliants is too natural to require explanation. With **trifle insolently** (the same verb occurs in 235–36) Pelasgus reveals the same initial response to the males as he had for the females. How Aeschylus resolved the ambiguities of sameness and difference, of common descent from Zeus, and of the role of Zeus himself (e.g., he protects suppliants and strangers yet will ultimately have a son, Heracles, descended through the line of these suppliants) remains a mystery. **Off the mark:** see *Ag* 1194. **Upright:** see *Eum* 897.

918–20 Stranger (*xenos*; cf. 628) means "you do not know how to behave when abroad." To this the herald responds with an "innocent" question: "How's that? Haven't I found my lost property?" The king's reference to a **patron** (*proxenos*; see on 490 f.) again urges the lack of propriety, but the Egyptian knows his Attic law; for in calling on **Hermes the Searcher** he is referring to "officers appointed to ascertain and get possession of the assets of public debtors and exiles in Athens" (Liddell and Scott). The Egyptians, that is, assert a legal claim to repossess their own property and, at the same time, as foreigners in Argos, ignore their lack of civic status. The same root as that in "searcher" appears at 161 (= 174) in "sought out," there of Io, here of the suppliants, and so offers another of the subtle verbal identifications of the Danaids with Io. Cf. 929 (and the note).

925 On the other hand, if they are not bold enough to claim by **touch,** from a legal point of view they have renounced their claim.

927 Thieves (from the gods) echoes the edict (610) that guaranteed them asylum.

929 Flock puns on "cow" (*bous*) and "unwilling" (*aboukolētos/aboulētos*).

942 Aeschylus refers to the suppliants as a "band of women" (= **them**), where "band" connotes a force or fleet prepared for a journey. That connotation may have suggested, in 943, the imagery connected with joining and bolting the various parts of a ship's timbers.

952 f. Greek vintners strike back at depraved Egyptian beer-guzzlers!

954 Your maids is an emendation for "friendly attendants." After the escort given Danaus (490–501) we expect the girls to have one. Since the Greek noun that appears here is more proper to male than to female attendants, I am inclined to go with the manuscript tradition that gives the Danaids a personal *male* bodyguard. (See also the note on 1017–24, below.)

The fact that the opinions of modern editors have been so divided on the composition of this escort tells us a lot about how little we know of the end of the play. Since the reference pertains to the existence, entry, and character of a second chorus, it may be just as well to review the issues and possibilities.

If "maids" is the correct reading at 954, we want to know if they are present, how long they have been present, and what they do, if anything at all. Despite the absence of any earlier reference, some editors have assumed that the Danaids have been attended by servants from the very beginning of the play. In the Greek text at 975 ff. (omitted in this translation; see the note), servants are addressed and asked to join in the action in some way. If servants have not been present all along, then those addressed at 975 ff. must come into the orchestra before that speech and, it would seem, before Pelasgus makes the present remark.

If, on the other hand, Pelasgus is referring to male attendants, they would be a bodyguard accompanying him (entry at 910) and now offered as an escort. The real problem with male attendants is their apparent redundancy: the chorus speaks to female attendants at 975 ff. (see note), and Danaus enters with his own male platoon (985). So, whether we have male or female attendants, no notice is taken of their entry: the bodyguard would enter with the king (910), while the female attendants would probably have been present all along (this is much protested by Taplin, pp. 230 ff.).

All kinds of problems attend this issue, the most significant of which is the composition of the secondary chorus (1035 ff.). Benardete and most editors take it to be the female servants of the Danaids. Johansen argues that the Argive bodyguard sings this part. Taplin thinks Danaus may take the part, and McCall has recently strengthened the case for assuming that the chorus divides into semichoruses for this dialogue. Role assignment is particularly important because Chorus B speaks critically of the Danaids as "careless of Cypris (Aphrodite)" (1035). If we put aside a number of textual difficulties (some of which are discussed below), the central question is:

Who would most naturally admonish the chorus to have
more respect for marriage and the power of love? There is no
unanimous answer. As I see it, we should not overrate the
contradictory nature of this "second voice." Lines 1035 ff.
may be taken as cautionary and admonitory, since within only
thirty lines a moderating unity has been achieved. To introduce any *new* role seems almost violent at this stage of the
play. The same argument applies to a division of the primary
chorus: for some of the Danaids to accept love and marriage
to anyone so soon after their terror before the Egyptians is not
only unexpected but out of place with anything we know of
future events in the trilogy. We are left with Danaus. If we
attribute the part—here marked Chorus B—to him, we not
only eliminate a late and alien role but also enable him to continue voicing—and more directly—the kind of concern for
sexual moderation we find at 994–1012. His part grew larger
in the next play, and this pacifying attitude may have helped
him win his daughters over to a necessary marriage with their
cousins (which would not preclude his acquiescing in, or even
planning, the murder of the Egyptians when their sexual violence proved too much for the girls). While there is no sure
footing in this quagmire, additional voices, whether a secondary chorus or a semichorus, only lessen the dramatic unity of
this final scene. Danaus is at hand, the part is suited to him,
and some clarity and unity are gained if he is the speaker.

969 Escort might also be translated "send," which at least
relieves him of returning with Danaus, whom he neither escorts nor sends.

975 ff. Benardete has omitted five lines testifying to the
presence of servants (and a second chorus?). Here is a modified version of Smyth's translation of 972–79:

> All the world is ready to cast reproach on those who speak a
> foreign tongue. But may all be for the best! [*Exit the King.*]

> And do ye, dear handmaidens, preserving your fair fame and
> provoking no angry utterances on the part of the native folk,
> take up your stations even as Danaus has allotted you to be a
> dowry and attendants for each of us.

Even if Pelasgus refers to these attendants at 954, the fact
that the chorus should speak to them now, for the first time, is
surprising. So far as we can tell, they have done nothing in the

play up to now (or we may complain with the vigorous Taplin that they are "a distracting and meaningless encumbrance"). That the maids are a dowry is certainly surprising, for the Danaids hardly seem ready for courting. But if Danaus speaks lines 1035 ff. and the remaining lines now attributed to Chorus B, this anticipation of marriage is linked both to him and to another passage in the text, and we may feel less eager to condemn 975–99 as an interpolation from a later production. Another difficulty: since "take up your stations" seems preliminary to the final choral song and dance, why are these arrangements brought up, only to be interrupted by Danaus' entrance? In short, if these servants do not form Chorus B, they seem at best irrelevant to the action. If they are present—whether from the beginning of the play or only now—simply to dance, we have some unhappy evidence for how little we may know of Greek tragedy. Some editors have suspected a lacuna.

If the king will leave promptly (975), he can avoid meeting Danaus on his way in. He has five lines and should exit to the same wing as the one from which Danaus enters, if direction has any value. Such an exit and entrance—virtually simultaneous, yet without either character's noticing the other—cannot be paralleled in Aeschylean drama.

983 What had been done should be taken of the recent assault of the Egyptians, though Danaus has had no dramatic occasion to hear of this, nor does he mention a report. Otherwise the phrase must refer, redundantly, to the earlier persecutions of the Egyptians, to which the Argives have already responded. Aeschylus simply effects a little economy in a situation where he can count on the audience to think of recent events. The rest of the sentence means that the Argives are bitter at the Egyptians' manner, friendly toward their newly recognized kin.

987 As a received suppliant, he would **burden the land** with pollution should Argos fail to protect him.

991 Wisdom: from the same stem as "modest" (710) and "modesty" (1012); with the latter word it frames this admonitory passage. This and the following lines on **time** have their irony *if* Danaus subsequently plots the murder of the Egyptians.

994 ff. Beg means "urge," even "command." Danaus

seems anxious that his daughters may somehow yet run into sexually troubled waters. Even with a corrupt text at 1001 f., the imagery of harvest, fruit, and animals, joined explicitly with Aphrodite (= **Venus** 1001), implies a fear not only for them but from them, a fear that beneath their rejection of men lies a sexual energy greater than they know. As usual, a certain abstract quality haunts the passage, so that we do not find "You are at the age which attracts men, at which, too, you naturally turn your eyes toward men—regardless of what you may say." Instead, the imagery and language echo earlier motifs and, by indirection, impute desirability and frailty to the girls. For example, **sleek comeliness** (1002) translates a word denoting sensual self-indulgence, which the Danaids themselves used of the sensual Egyptians at 832 ("insolence," though the corruption of the passage makes the exact sense uncertain). Such repetitions are deliberate in Aeschylus, so Danaus as much as suggests that the cousins share a sexual pathology, however different its expression.

1004 f. The passive construction of the English is neither so direct nor so insinuating as the Greek active: "Let us do nothing that would be a shame for ourselves, a pleasure for our enemies."

1013 ff. Blush echoes "bloom" (996) and "fruit" (997); **lest** = "unless"; **course** means "track" and so recalls the trek of Io (same word at 539).

1017–24 These lines are probably addressed to the male bodyguard (see note to 954), though Benardete and others think the maidservants are addressed. **Praising** is a masculine form in the Greek, and the word for **servants** is the one used at 985 for "male attendants" (the usual meaning). That they are addressed, however, does not mean that they respond in song, for lines 1021–22 more likely mean, in Johansen's translation, "Listen with sympathy to our song, men of the bodyguard." So the passage denotes a song of praise for the city, which its representatives are asked to accept. The last line (1024) is more precisely translated "Let us respect with [our] psalms." The **Erasinus** is a large river near Argos.

1025 ff. Celebration of rivers for their fructifying powers is a commonplace; here an untranslated epithet modifies rivers and means "of many children." Onians (p. 227) cites the scholiast on *Iliad* 23. 142 ff.: "the rivers are regarded as youth rearers because their liquid gives growth." If such praise is normal, it nonetheless sounds odd that these frigid girls should praise male rivers.

1031 ff. Contrast the significance of **Artemis** at 674 (note); here, as in the Homeric *Hymn to Aphrodite*, she is the virgin goddess of chastity, juxtaposed with Aphrodite, who as goddess of sexual love forces marriage. Cf. the interest of Artemis at *Ag* 135 (see note to *Ag* 131–38). The reading in the last line is disputed. Wilamowitz's emendation yields a play on "hateful Styx," as in Johansen's "may this prize involve death!" Benardete's text gives Aphrodite's prize and death to the suitors.

1035 ff. This countervoice, with its admonitory praise of **Aphrodite,** is the surest evidence from our text for a change of singer. Regardless of who may be speaking, it is hard to imagine the full chorus of the Danaids expressing these sentiments. **Song** is convincingly emended: "But careless not of Cypris this prudent swarm." For "swarm" cf. 30, 684. For **Cypris,** see the note on *Eum* 215.

1039 ff. Hesiod says that **Eros** (1043) and **Desire** are companions of Aphrodite (*Theogony* 201), a conventional way of citing the attributes of a divinity. The link between **Persuasion** and love is also a commonplace (Sappho calls Persuasion the daughter of Aphrodite); cf. note on *Ag* 385 and Sophocles, *Women of Trachis* 660–62. **Concord** is Harmonia, the name given to the daughter of Aphrodite and Ares.

1044 ff. Bitter winds is uncertain, but some form of this word, which echoes "breathing" of line 17, should be retained. As R. D. Murray, Jr., observes (p. 68), at line 17 "breathing" denotes the sexual caress of Zeus, while here it expresses not only fear for the storms of war but also, if it is spoken by the Danaids, a fear of sexual violence. The sense of the line must be modified, however, by a word omitted from the translation, i.e., "for fugitives," which should be taken closely with "bitter winds." **I fear before** may conceivably mean, if spoken by Danaus, "I am already fearful of bitter winds against fugitives." It is clearly difficult to attribute such a sentiment to the Argive bodyguard; it would be easier to give it to some of the Danaids or to Danaus himself, but this stanza has turned away from the theme of the preceding strophe (1035–43).

1048 f. Doomed means "fated," and a fuller version would run: "whatever is fated, may this come to pass." **Infinite** translates an emendation. I prefer Johansen's version: "one cannot go beyond the mighty will of Zeus which no one crosses."

1051 f. The sense is disputed. The thought may be turned into a wish: "May this marriage end (happily), as many marriages before." Or the lines might mean: "This marriage may end as so many others have before."

1053 ff. Not all editors assign these lines in the same fashion. Murray, e.g., gives 1056 to Chorus B (his pattern for the whole passage is 2:2:1:2:2:1). Benardete's attribution is the same as Smyth's and Johansen's. Page offers 2:2:1:3:1:1. All of which makes a nice tribute to the vagueness of the passage.

1060–62 The mean: the Greek adds "in speech." Cf. Hesiod, *Works and Days* 694:

> Observe the mean; the limit is best in all things.

For **limit** see on *Sev* 1 ("speak home"); it suggests both the "opportune" and the "timely."

Nothing excessive is a close variant on the Delphic admonition, "Nothing in excess."

1063 Here the distinct voices apparently unite. Such differences as they have expressed yield to a common wish for happiness, health, and reasonable prosperity.

1066–68 The tie to Zeus is more direct: "Zeus who released Io from ill, protected her with healing hand, with kind might curing her."

1069 The Greek text gives power to the feminists: "And may he award victory to the women!" (Smyth). Cf. 531.

The Persians

While Onesilus was busy with the siege of Amathus, news
was brought to Darius that Sardis had been taken and burnt
by the Athenians and Ionians, and that the prime mover in
the joint enterprise was Aristagoras of Miletus. The story
goes that when Darius learnt of the disaster, he did not give a
thought to the Ionians, knowing perfectly well that the punishment for their revolt would come; instead, the first thing
he did was to ask who the Athenians were, and then, on
being told, gave orders that his bow should be handed to
him. He took the bow, set an arrow on the string, shot it up
into the air and cried: "Grant, O god, that I may punish the
Athenians." Then he commanded one of his servants to re-
peat to him the words, "Master, remember the Athenians,"
three times, whenever he sat down to dinner. [Herodotus 5.
105; trans. de Selincourt]

FOR THE TOPICALITY OF THIS PLAY, which alone among the extant dramas does not belong to a trilogy, see Benardete's introduction. On the setting see the note to 140 ff. There is no
prologue; the choral anapests continue until line 65. The chorus is composed of old men appointed by Xerxes to be guard-
ians of the country.

1 Gone is ominous because, as in English, a secondary
meaning is "lost" (cf. 13, 59e, and 546c).
5 Persian wealth is reflected in **golden** four times in these
anapests (9c, 45, 54; cf. 77 and 159d). Herodotus (9. 80) describes the rich spoils left at Plataea after the Persian defeat.
12 Whines is more commonly rendered "is troubled."
16 I shall not comment extensively on the places and proper
names of the Persians. The interested reader should consult
Broadhead's commentary on these matters. See on 21 ff.
21 ff. Three passages (this one and 302 ff., 956 ff.) are
studded with the names of Persian and allied leaders. Some of

these can be identified with captains mentioned by Herodotus, but most of them are unknown. How well Aeschylus' audience would have known or remembered such foreign names cannot be determined, nor need we believe that Herodotus' account is absolutely accurate. For a tally and assessment see Broadhead's appendix (pp. 318 ff.). Inevitably, manuscript problems compound our uncertainties (e.g., **Agbatana** or Ekbatana at 16), and scholars have offered conflicting judgments on the linguistic authenticity of names not otherwise known. Finally, both here and at 958, lists are prefaced with "men like" and "men such as" (untranslated here but rendered "like" at 959). For example, **Artaphrenes** must have been well known as the Persian general who commanded at the Battle of Marathon, but Aeschylus does not make more of him than of any other name in the list. On balance, then, it looks as if Aeschylus was much more interested in the generic than the particular and in exaggerating Persian losses rather than in achieving accuracy in specific details.

24 The Greek word for **slaves** may not be quite so demeaning; perhaps "subjects."

35 ff. The Egyptian cities of **Memphis** and **Thebes** are named for their fame rather than for any military significance. Size ("countless," "many," "crowds") and effect ("fearful," "dreadful," and "awesome") are more the point than historical detail. In a negative way this view is supported by **Arsames** (37), who in Herodotus is a son of Darius but for Aeschylus is apparently just an exotic name.

41 ff. The **soft Lydians** became proverbial for their luxury. **Sardis** is the capital of this district in Asia Minor, and **Tmolus** is a famous mountain nearby. The **Mysians** (51) are their neighbors to the northwest. Note that no mention is made of the Ionian Greeks, who inhabited the coast of Asia Minor and nearby islands and who, as subjects of the Great King, had to fight for him against the Greeks of the homeland.

49a Though the imagery of the **yoke** is traditional, Aeschylus had a ready-made symbol for Persian autocracy in Xerxes' yoking of the Hellespont with a pontoon bridge (130, 722, 736). Here, as at 591 ff., the yoking refers to political subjection. Other extensions occur in the yoke of marriage

(135) and in the queen's dream (191–96). Cf. *Sev* 76, 471, and *PB* 462 f. In the *Persians* the moral is drawn at 747–50.

67–71 For the building of the bridge over the Hellespont (the modern Dardanelles) see Herodotus 7. 33 ff. When a storm destroys the first bridge, Xerxes orders the Hellespont to receive three hundred lashes and have a pair of fetters thrown in it. Hellespont means "sea of Helle" and is named for **Helle,** the daughter of **Athamas,** who fell into the sea here (cf. 872, and see Apollodorus 1. 9. 1).

72 Furious (cf. 718) is the Homeric epithet for the war god, Ares; it connotes rash impetuosity.

74 Wonderful modifies **herd,** i.e., "a marvelous sight."

77–80 As often in these lyrics, the English phrase (**gold his descent**) represents a compound adjective in the Greek. **Equal of god** (80), another example, is Homeric, but whereas in the *Iliad* it is a generic adjective, celebrating heroes, in the *Persians* it foreshadows the god-defying *hybris* of Xerxes (748–50). **Perseus,** the hero born to Danaë and Zeus, who appeared to Danaë as a shower of gold, is not mentioned here in the Greek, but the adjective would seem to allude to this golden shower. His son Perses was the eponymous founder of the Persian race (Apollodorus 2. 4. 5).

86 Even as early as Homer the gods are more or less equated in some passages with their functions; so **Ares** stands for war or battle. The Persians are **archers,** the Greeks **spearmen** (cf. 144 f.).

87–90 The Persian host is likened to a **great torrent** and to **unconquerable billows of ocean.** As Conacher notes (p. 151), "all these unconscious anticipations are later to be grimly and fully realized" when the Persian force is overwhelmed in the naval battle of Salamis. They are the victims of many such ironies; e.g., see their confident prediction of their divinely appointed fate in the next stanza.

93–101 These lines are called a mesode because they are independent of the metrical response defined by the strophe/antistrophe pattern of these lyrics. They have been transposed in the name of improved continuity and coherence, but a decent case can be made for either position. Whether it is placed after 92 or 114, the mesode marks an abrupt turn from the

contemplation of Persian power to an abstract theological per-
spective. Two traditional concepts, deception (*apatē*) and delusion (*atē*) merge into a virtual identity. **Deception** comes
from the god and leads to futile and deluded action by mortals. Agamemnon says to the assembled Greeks:

> Zeus son of Kronos has caught me fast in bitter futility
>   [*atē*].
> He is hard, who before this time promised me and
>   consented
> that I might sack strong-walled Ilion and sail homeward.
> Now he has devised a vile deception [*apatē*].
>   (*Iliad* 2. 111–14)

The two words are also linked at *Suppl* 110. For the imagery
of **nets** see *Ag* 35. The **it** (98) is actually *atē*, which leads man,
like a hunted animal, into the **nets.** That all of this happens **of
god** (i.e., at god's instigation) is natural to Greek thinking:

> From righteous deception God standeth not aloof.
>   (Aeschylus, Frag. 162; trans. Lloyd-Jones)

As for the mesode's proper place in the lyric, if it is retained
after 92, as in the manuscripts, the deception would seem to
be what the chorus expects the Greeks to suffer: "The contrast
is between mortals and the god. The Greeks—and other enemies—are merely mortals while Persians have the might of
god supporting their army. There is every reason for the Persian elders to feel supremely confident; no mere mortal could
ever escape the plans of god" (Scott, p. 265). On the other
hand, as Conacher notes (pp. 150–52), the chorus surely
doesn't feel "supremely confident." Even so, Conacher would
keep the traditional order.

116 It is characteristic of Aeschylean tragedy that the play
begins in dread, fear, and anxiety and just as characteristic that
the language draws attention to these emotions; cf. the queen's
words at 161 ff, 210, 603 ff., and the herald's at 391.

132 In softness weep represents a compound adjective, a
kind of conceptual oxymoron suggesting, in one word, both
soft Asiatic luxury and suffering. Cf. 543 and 548. These
compounds are as natural to Greek as to German, but they
must often be translated by phrases or clauses in English (e.g.,

at 103 and 104 we have "tower-destroying" and "knight-delighting").

140 ff. These lines are spoken by the coryphaeus. They are not literally **in** a **palace**, but some commentators would have us imagine that they are in some sort of hall. With some point, Broadhead asks why Aeschylus would have suggested a building, for which there is no particular dramatic need, unless he had a wall or stage building actually representing it. Broadhead suggests that the leader invites the chorus to sit down on the steps of the council chamber.

151 ff. The queen appears in "pomp and ceremony" (609, where Benardete omits "former," with which she contrasts her present mourning with the glory of her equipage at 151 ff.). She is in a chariot (609), probably has a number of attendants, and wears a splendid dress (156). Other chariot entries occur at *Ag* 783 and *Suppl* 234 (not certain) and in Euripides' *Electra* (988) and *Trojan Women* (567).

159 f. God: divinity hedges Darius and Xerxes more than most kings in Greek drama, at least until the news of Salamis arrives. Cf. 80, 637, 857 (all three contain compound adjectives unique to this play); Darius' prosperity remained intact (652–56, 710 f.), but Xerxes squanders his (827) by "sinning against the gods" (832).

159b Although *daimōn* is aptly translated **fortune** here, the word occurs so often of supernatural influence that the notion of divine, usually malevolent, influence is never far. Cf. 601 ("a god"), 724 f., 826 ("fortune"), 911 ("deity"), 920 ("a god"), and 953. See also on 353.

163 A variant on the familiar idea that **great wealth** leads to insatiable greed, which in turn destroys true **prosperity** (which is itself always more than material wealth). Cf. *Ag* 751 (note) and 1331; for the theme in the *Persians* see 249 ff., 826 f., and 841 f.

Gallop: one abstraction (wealth) ruins another (prosperity) by trampling and overturning, as if the one abstraction were a horse or charioteer running the other down.

164 Exalted refers to the prosperity that Darius, aided by divinity, produced.

169a Eye signifies both power and affection, but here the latter meaning predominates. Xerxes is the "palace-eye" (170), just as Orestes is the "eyes' light in this house" (*LB* 934).

177 That **dreams** are significant and prophetic is familiar from Homer. In the *Iliad* (2. 1–36) Zeus sends a deceptive dream to Agamemnon; in the *Odyssey* (19. 535 ff.) Penelope tells her dream to Odysseus and asks him to interpret it. Penelope's dream, like Clytaemestra's at *LB* 523 ff., is symbolically prophetic.

183 Of the three branches of the Greek people (Doric, Ionic, Aeolic), **Doric** is most commonly used, by metonymy, for "Greek."

185 Us now means "contemporary women."

197 The presence of Darius and the humiliation of Xerxes anticipate later events in the play.

200 Washing after an evil dream was customary; cf. Aristophanes, *Frogs* 1340 (where Aeschylus, a character in the play, mocks Euripidean dreams).

204 Phoebus is Apollo. Because the **eagle** is the bird of Zeus (*Ag* 114), the queen is terrified to see it fleeing and unnaturally cowering like a hare. Apparently the symbolism is no deeper than the inversion of power seen in the triumph of the smaller **falcon** (Greece) over the king of birds (Persia).

212 f. Athenian magistrates were subject to an audit after their year in office. Unlike the Athenian democrats, the king cannot be called **to account.**

219a Libations are liquid offerings, usually of milk or wine. She offers them to **Earth** because the dead Darius appeared in her dream; spirits of the dead must be placated. Cf. *LB* 538 ff.

231 This is the first of a series of questions that could hardly be imagined in a play that pretended to historical verisimilitude.

236 The line alludes, like 245 and 474 f., to the Athenian victory over Darius at Marathon in 490 B.C. Since this defeat contradicts the image of a blessed Darius, Aeschylus does not dwell on it.

241 The Athenian **silver** mines at Laurium provided the funds for building ships (Herodotus 7. 144).

243 There is less Athenian chauvinism in this play than might be expected. Cf. 23 f. The former Spartan king Demaratus, speaking to Xerxes, argues the Greek love of freedom in this fashion: "They are free—yes—but not entirely free; for they have a master, and that master is Law, which they fear more than your subjects fear you. Whatever this master commands, they do; and his command never varies: it is never to retreat in battle, however great the odds, but always to stand firm, and to conquer or die" (Herodotus 7. 104; trans. de Selincourt).

248 For the role of the herald, see on *Ag* 503. He addresses the land (cf. *Ag* 503), finally the elders (254), but says nothing to the queen, who does not speak until 289; cf. the silence of Clytaemestra at *Ag* 503 ff., who, if she is onstage, is completely ignored by the herald. Taplin (p. 87) argues that "the Queen's silence conveys both her aloofness and her even greater suffering." Perhaps; but the staging seems more conventional than naturalistic.

254 For the Greeks, all foreigners were **barbarians,** the earliest meaning being "people who don't speak Greek." It is odd, even apart from modern connotations of the word, to hear the herald speak of his own countrymen as barbarians.

255–96 Brief responsive choral lyrics are paired with the messenger's spoken iambic lines. The pairing is broken in the sixth set by the queen's response. See on *Ag* 1072.

The alliteration and assonance reflect the Greek. Cf. the verbal responsions (**unexpected**, 261 and 265).

273 The first mention of **Salamis,** the island off which the Greek fleet defeated the Persians.

285 See the passage from Herodotus (5. 105) that serves as the epigraph to this chapter.

288 Vain is deleted by some editors; if it is kept, the line must mean "made them wives in vain," i.e., unable to be wives. But **widowed** (rather than wives) seems the more obvious sense. Delete *vain.*

289a f. The queen self-consciously recognizes and explains her prolonged silence.

291 Cf. 93 (note) and *Sev* 719.

297–301 Since "seeing the light" is idiomatic for "being alive," both the English and the Greek (**lives to behold the light**) are pleonastic. Such fullness is in the epic manner. Since light is commonly metaphorical for salvation, as at 261, the queen's interruption is perhaps in a more personal vein than the praise at 152. Having suppressed a direct question about her son, she is so relieved that she breaks the very beginning of his narrative.

303 Silenia is said to be the name of a strip of Salamis' coast. Two other variations for Salamis are "Ajax' isle" (308: it was the home of the famous Homeric and Athenian hero) and "where doves do thrive" (310).

304 Satrap is the Persian term designating the governor of a province.

305 Lightly tumble may reflect Homeric imagery, e.g., "Epikles dropped / like a diver from the high bastion" (*Iliad* 12. 385 f.). The particular description of 316 f. is certainly Homeric, and **native-born** (306) is also Homeric.

314 Podlecki suggests a pun in **Matallos:** change one letter and we have Metallos ("metal"), which falls out neatly with Chrysa (= "golden"). **Chrysa** is a town near Troy, mentioned in book 1 of the *Iliad*.

315 Herodotus tells us that the Persian army was organized in multiples of ten (cf. "ten thousand" at 302). For Aeschylus the repeated use of large numbers augments the sense of calamity.

318 Magian refers to a tribe of the Medes; **Bactria** (cf. 307) was situated in what is now eastern Iran, Afghanistan, and southern Russia.

346 f. This imagery of the **beam of fortune** derives from Homer, who lets Zeus take out golden scales for weighing the fortunes of men and of battle. For this passage Sideras (p. 213) compares *Iliad* 16. 658, where Hector sees "the way of Zeus' / sacred balance." The doomed person or party finds its lot weighing more heavily than that of the favored party (in contrast to the tradition in Christian iconography), and in some passages (e.g., *Iliad* 8. 69 ff., 22. 209 ff.) what is explicitly weighed is the "death-spirit" (*kēr*: see on *Ag* 206). This spirit drags a man down and so seems at least a first cousin of the daimon who regularly "leaps heavily" (516 f.) on its victim. Here the scales are associated with an impersonal **fortune** (*tychē*), while at *Ag* 250 Justice tips the balance.

348 ff. The **goddess** is Athene. In fact, the city was taken and burned prior to the battle (Herodotus 8. 53). Broadhead notes that **unsacked** would recall the Delphic oracle that "The wooden wall alone will come through unsacked" (Herodotus 7. 141). This word, and the herald's evasive reply, would seem to compliment Themistocles, who had urged the Athenians to take to the wooden walls of their ships.

353 Avenger is the *alastōr* (see notes on *Suppl* 414 and *Ag* 1507 f.), a spirit of vengeance. **Wicked god** (= "harmful daimon") is probably a pleonastic alternative, used by the herald to name the unnamable. Like any Greek, he sees the hand of god in misfortune (cf. 373, 495 ff., 515).

355 Herodotus (8. 75) tells how Themistocles sent his slave Sicinnus to the Persian camp with a false report concerning the Greek plans.

362 The coordination of **guile** and **jealousy** is the usual Greek way of seeing divine purpose in human decision and action. For **jealousy** (= "envy") see *Ag* 904 and the note on 742–45, below.

The present report is much more dramatic than the preceding account of the disaster, which utilizes a catalogue form. There is little specifically Persian here and much that is calculated to raise Greek goose bumps. Cf. Herodotus 8. 83 ff.

367 Salamis lies close to the neighboring shore and so offers narrow passages in which Xerxes hoped to trap the escaping Greeks.

373 Humored pride means "confidently"; as in the next sentence, judgment is implicitly rather than explicitly passed. Cf. the similar observation at 454 f.

376 In battle, ancient ships rowed for maneuverability. The oars were attached by **thongs** to pegs to facilitate control and to save them from slipping overboard during the crashes of battle (see 408 ff for the ramming).

379 Who knew them represents a rather grand phrase; i.e., the Greek reads: "Every man at arms was a lord of weapons." Cf. 363 ff. for the baroque description of dawn; "steeds of day" (384) looks back to *Odyssey* 23. 246 ("Bright and Shining, the colts who carry Dawn"). This is the sort of writing the comic poets parodied.

393 Paean: a song of celebration, usually of victory and generally addressed to Apollo.

394 Trumpets flared: a striking synaesthesia, which draws attention to the morning sun striking the trumpets even as they sound the call to battle.

406 The **babel** echoes the "dissonance" (396) of the oars striking the water.

410 The **Phoenicians** were experienced sailors and provided the best ships in the Persian fleet.

427–28 Black eye of evening is apparently only a periphrastic expression for "night," although at *Sev* 390 the "night's eye" is the moon.

435 Here (and in 437 and 440) the image of the scales returns (cf. 346). My report, he says, has not yet told half the woe; what follows will double these in weight of grief.

447 This **island** was identified by the ancient historians as Psyttalia, which is now usually identified with Lipsokontali, at the southern end of the strait. Note the characteristic use of periphrasis (circumlocution) in 447–49.

449 Pan, a rural deity associated with wild animals and satyrs, had recently (Herodotus 6. 105) received a state cult in Athens. The uninhabited isle would naturally suit Pan.

456 Fenced in bronze: heavy-armed troops called hoplites.

465–67 Herodotus (8. 90) tells us that Xerxes watched the battle from a hill on the mainland. The tearing of **his robes** foreshadows the king's later appearance (1028; cf. 1060 and the queen's dream at 198 f.).

470 In fact the Persian host on land did not beat such a precipitate retreat, and, even after the king had returned home, a sufficient army remained to fight a major engagement at Plataea the next year.

474 ff. Xerxes invaded Greece to avenge his father's defeat and for that **vengeance** found retribution. The idea of revenge bringing retribution will be worked out fully in the *Oresteia*. The *Persians* is unique in that neither the divine nor the human avengers appear onstage. In the queen's view, Xerxes planned to avenge the Persian defeat at Marathon (in 490 B.C. and actually suffered by his father, Darius). Contrast her ignorance at 231 ff. **Requital** implies payment in turn and in kind, such as the Furies demand from Orestes (*Eum* 268).

482–501 Cf. Darius' comment on those "who now remain in Greece" (796 f.). Herodotus (8. 113) tells of an army of

300,000 left behind. This line might be more accurately rendered "began to perish." The herald now describes the trials that faced the army in its march north. **Phocis, Locria,** the **Malian Gulf,** and the river **Spercheios** are north of Boeotia; **Achaea** and **Thessaly** (487) mark the next districts, and so on north through Macedonia to the river Strymon in Thrace, whose waters, according to the herald, froze overnight (501). Herodotus does not confirm this premature freeze, which appears to be an Aeschylean invention for the sake of a theological point (496 ff.). Though the historian's account of the retreat is horrible enough, Aeschylus exaggerates the suffering still more.

484 Sidgwick takes **gasping emptily on air** as a "rather strained and bold expression for 'exhausted with hard efforts.'"

516–17 For the heavy weight of the daimon leaping down on the victim compare *Eum* 372–76. So at 911 the god "swooped" (or "stepped on" the Persians). As in English, misfortunes weigh on one (692 f.).

518 Bright (= "clear," "manifest") is transferred from **dreams** to **night.**

520 f. Poorly judged: see 225 f.; **as you counseled:** see 216 ff.

522 ff. The news of the disaster confirms what the dream ominously foretold. She will pray to placate the powers of the underworld. Libations (219) and cakes (of honey, meal, and oil) were the usual offerings.

527 Worthy . . . worthy plays by declension on the same words rendered "faithful followers" at 681. Cf. "burden's burdening" (683), "ships unshipped" (680, where Benardete takes a more careful course), and "all they made all woe" (282).

528–30 These lines lead us to expect the arrival of Xerxes, when in fact the queen returns before her son does. Explanations strain a little (e.g., the lines characterize the queen's concern for her son, or they maintain our interest in Xerxes' arrival). Taplin (p. 94) calls this technique "counterpreparation" (we are prepared for one course of action only to be presented with another). For example, Aeschylus gives Orestes a speech at *LB* 554 ff. that suggests possible receptions and his contingent plans, thereby leading the audience to expectations that the actual events frustrate. As Taplin says, in *LB* this technique heightens suspense and creates excitement. Here it is difficult to find dramatic gain comparable to that in *LB*. Taplin himself likes Nikitine's transposition of these lines to follow 852. The advantage in the change is great, but there is no accounting for how the lines might have got to their present place in the text. Simply to delete them is arbitrary.

531 Zeus is addressed in the vocative, as at *Ag* 355.

537 ff. The stanza describes the grief of the Persian widows. The language is striking for the combination of references to luxuriance and suffering. **Paean** (cf. 393) is not in the Greek.

548–57 The lament intensifies: brief sentences and phrases are punctuated with exclamations of grief (**alas, o woe**); anaphora (**Xerxes** is repeated three times; cf. repetition of "warships" three times in the next stanza) and parallel constructions (**Xerxes led . . . Warships led**) create a pounding staccato. Present loss is contrasted with the prosperity of Darius' reign. Their sense of loss does not make them uncritical of Xerxes (**heedless**).

558–67 The center of the antistrophe very nearly falls into incoherence as the grandeur of the destroyed fleet is remembered and lamented.

Lazuli-eyed: of the painted prows of the ships.

568–73 This and the following stanza dwell on the losses at sea; phrases evoking the horror of death at sea are mingled with imperatives and exclamations expressing their mourning.

570 Kychraean is named after Kychreus, son of Poseidon and Salamis.

578 The sea is **unstained** because it is used to wash away all impurity.

584–90 This reads more like a Greek view of what Persians might think than like authentic Persian sentiment. The subject of 584 (**They**) is not identified but is apparently not merely the Ionian Greeks. In the next stanza (591–97), however, their complaint that former subjects will now **bawl their liberty** smacks of a conservative Greek's thinking.

598 Taplin attaches great dramatic and symbolic significance to the contrast between this entry of the queen and her first entry (155). As we learn from 607–9, her first entry was accompanied "by pomp and ceremony" (signifying a chariot, attendants, and rich robes). Now she returns alone, without attendants, perhaps in a black costume more in keeping with sacrifice, carrying simple gifts to be offered to the dead king. Taplin comments (pp. 99 f.):

> The dramatic and moral explanation, which the Queen explicitly attaches to her different mode of entry, is her appreciation of the divine control over changes of fortune and prosperity (598–606). The material embodiment of her new insight is able to convey its ramifications in a way more direct and immediate than any amount of purely verbal moralizing. The Queen appreciates that material wealth is the mere outward manifestation of the prosperity which follows from divine favour, and that a thoughtless over-confidence in these externals leads to their destruction.

598–603 Evil means misfortune. Other nautical imagery will be found at 249 and 767. Here the metaphor of life's voyage shapes the figure. The evils recently announced make her fearful of still more harm.

605 Songs and chants often figured in medical treatment. Her premonition comes in songs that do not heal (**cureless**).

608 In the Greek a temporal adverb clearly marks a contrast with her previous appearance. See on 151 ff.

609a ff. When she divulged her dream, the chorus recommended that she pray and also try to appease the netherworld (220). Now she means to evoke Darius (619 ff.), an unexpected turn in the action. The elaborate description of the **milk, honey, water, wine, olives,** and wreaths (**plaited flowers**) is, as Broadhead observes, "typically Aeschylean and at the same time in harmony with the solemnity of the occasion." Purity was always important for proper sacrifice; hence **unblemished, resplendent** (clean), **maiden** (never before used, or not used for profane purposes).

620 Over these libations to the dead may be more intelligible if taken with the preceding sentence: "recite, with libation to the dead, your chants; summon Darius, daimon; and I shall send these sepulchral honors to the nether gods."

In adapting Greek necromancy to the stage, Aeschylus made his greatest deviation from normal practice when he gave the song to the chorus. Normally the person offering sacrifice would also summon the spirit, but that would leave the chorus, whose business it is to sing, with nothing to do.

627–32 Permission is sought from the rulers of the underworld. **Hermes** was known as the "conductor of spirits" (cf. *LB* 124), but Eitrem thinks he is here invoked simply as a king of the dead. **Earth** holds the dead and must free the spirits for passage (cf. *LB* 126–28, 399). Cf. 650, where Aedoneus (Hades) is called "conductor." In the Greek **A remedy knowing** is conditional: "if he knows a remedy for our trouble." So far, the reason for summoning Darius has not been made clear; cf. 788.

640–46 Podlecki follows L. R. Taylor in believing that the Persians actually did worship their kings as gods. Of course obeisance does not entail belief in the divinity of a king. At any rate, Aeschylus dramatizes such a belief, and his audience would have scorned them all the more for the thought. Cf. "god in wisdom," 654 f., and see the note on 159 f.

652–56 These stanzas are comparatively short, their sentences are short, and the incidence of repeated words is high. In addition, alliteration and assonance are intense. **Infatuate** harshly and obliquely looks at Xerxes (*atē* in the plural: see on 1007).

657 Hesychius tells us that the word rendered **Padshah** is Phrygian for "king." The exotic sartorial details hardly add to the solemnity of the chant.

665 Stygian gloom: the Styx is the most famous of the five rivers of the underworld.

680 How did Aeschylus stage the appearance of Darius? A mound four or five feet high would be sufficient to hide the actor before he climbed up. The tomb was probably not in the center of the orchestra, where it would have interfered with the dancing and would have been too dominant in the other scenes. Perhaps it was near the back edge of the acting area; this would give it a central but not obstructing position and would make access to it by the actor, who had earlier played the herald, easier. It does not seem unreasonable or particularly difficult for the actor to have used a subterranean passage to reach the tomb. Both the familiarity of necromantic rites and the tone of the scene suggest a degree of realism. See Taplin's discussion, pp. 116–19, and Arnott, pp. 57–59.

681 Darius has been slipped into the play, as it were, for there is neither need nor specific reason for his presence. The audience is prepared for this summoning, however, as early as the queen's first speech, where he is credited with exalting

Persian wealth. Her dream (177 ff.) is naturally associated with the underworld and so with the dead monarch, whose blessings the chorus urged her to seek (220 ff.). So when she returns, wishing to appease the powers below, she again thinks of the dead king as one who may aid them in propitiating the angry spirits among whom he resides. To this end she urges (619a) that the chorus "recall" (= "summon him up") his spirit. In the choral litany only vague reasons are offered for calling him forth (634 f., 663). And when he appears, he can tell them little of recent events, since, like the ghosts of the *Odyssey* (11. 492 ff.), he is ignorant of the immediate past. Far from assuaging grief, he is chiefly concerned to admonish and prophesy, and these moral judgments distinguish him completely from Teiresias, Odysseus' informant in the *Odyssey*. He is a potentate among the dead, fortunate in life and in death, a supreme contrast to his son Xerxes, who will appear in the final scene. Such contrasts, probably reinforced by their costuming, are characteristic of Aeschylus' dramaturgy.

684 f. For the dead the **plains** of the earth are their ceiling, so that stamping on the earth causes them to think that the sky is falling (hence **terrified I**). Unlike most commentators, Eitrem is willing to see some ghostly humor in Darius' terror and possibly some folk humor in 689–90 ("anybody can go to hell, but not many get a round-trip ticket"). Cf. on 838–42. **Potentate** he may be, but he must still be punctual (691 f.). So 698 f. (**lengthen not your tale**) is tragic idiom for "get on with it."

706 Happiness = "prosperity" (163), "wealth" (756).

718 For **furious** see on 72; it recurs in 752.

723 Bosphorus here = Hellespont (see on 67–71; for the name see *PB* 733–34). Herodotus (4. 83) tells us that Darius also bridged the channel.

724 Contrived it is repeated at 743 (note). As Sidgwick says, what the queen hints at, Darius then makes plain.

736 Herodotus tells us that the **bridge** was down when the army returned. If it was down, Aeschylus surely knew that.

739 ff. Since Darius is not himself a prophet, Aeschylus invents some oracles. Oracles and prophecy are very common, and are never depreciated, in Aeschylus; cf. 800, *Ag* 1100 ff., *LB* 297 ff., *PB* 700 ff. and 822 ff., and *Sev* 745 ff.

Here and in Darius' last speech (800–841) Xerxes becomes

a paradigm of moral error. He must be admonished (829 ff.), though it is a little late for him. This type of warning and exhortation, with its clear didactic aspect, is common in Greek tragedy.

740 The man who has lost his wits and done a stupid thing is often described as "struck" (cf. etymology of English "stupid"). The blow may precede and cause senseless action, or it may signify a deranged act. Cf. *Ag* 367 and the note to *Ag* 904–11. Here the mixed metaphor compresses elliptically the lightning of Zeus, the blasting of Xerxes, and the fulfillment of the oracle. Cf. Podlecki's translation: "Zeus hurled down against my son accomplishment of prophecies."

742–45 Cf. 362 (note) and 724. Note the double aspect of the action, divine and human, in which man's folly (Xerxes' ignorance and youthful rashness [= **pride**]) is abetted by the god. Fragments from two lost plays show both sides of this coin:

> God plants in men a cause whenever he wants to destroy completely a house. [Frag. 77; trans. Lloyd-Jones]

> Glory the child of labor is owed by the gods to the man who labors. [Frag. 175; my translation]

All this is summed up in the frequently cited line:

> God loves to help him who strives to help himself. [Frag. 223; trans. Lloyd-Jones]

Heraclitus (Frag. 250, Kirk and Raven) had a variant on this:

> Character is daimon (daimon is character).

The philosopher means that external compulsion, such as man customarily attributes to the supernatural, is just as well explained by looking within to our own motivation and action. **The spring of evil's found:** add "for all his friends."

747 The commentators note the lack of reference to Xerxes' scourging the Hellespont with chains (see Herodotus 7. 35). Rose notes "ancient scruples about bridging water" and suggests that the reason for such superstition may be that the spirits of the water would be angry because someone, in passing over them, put himself above the water and thus in a "position of magical superiority to the *daimones* of the water."

748 Neptune is the Roman name for Poseidon.

749–51 A gaggle of commonplaces: for **mortal though he was** see on 819c ff.; for **diseased his sense** see *PB* 251 and the note on *PB* 250–52. Although the Greek word for a man "who fights against god" (*theomachos*) does not occur until Euripides (see on *Bacchae* 45), the theme is present in such plays as the *Ajax* and *Hippolytus* and figures prominently in Aeschylus' *Seven* (see on 424 f.). Rebellion against god permeates the *Prometheus* and must have been central to the lost trilogy about Lycurgus, the Thracian king who opposed the worship of Dionysus (Apollodorus 3. 5. 1). In archaic literature, theomachy is found in Zeus's war with the Titans, with the Giants, and with Typhon. Homer knows the theme (*Iliad* 6. 128; 5. 407) and dramatizes it most spectacularly in Achilles' fight with the river god Scamander (*Iliad*, bk. 21). In our play the idea is made more striking by the numerous descriptions of Darius and Xerxes as "godlike." Cf. 822–32, where the last phrase, "sinning against the gods," returns to this theme.

751 Labored wealth: wealth got from labor.

752 Herodotus (7. 6) corroborates the queen's complaint that Xerxes was the victim of bad advice. Cf. *Sev* 599 ff.

759 The **their** is ambiguous: it has been taken to refer to (1) the evil advisers; (2) the Greeks; (3) Xerxes himself (the form is also used for the singular). The queen's speech suggests Xerxes, but what follows argues for the Greeks.

762 ff. That **honor** and **authority** to rule come from Zeus is certified by *Iliad* 2. 100–108 (cf. on *Ag* 44) and numerous other passages. In the following list of the rulers of Persia, Aeschylus' list is historically accurate after **Medus** (which may mean simply "a Mede") and his son. It was **Cyrus** (768) who extended Persian rule into Asia Minor (over the Lydians, Phrygians, and Ionia). His son Cambyses was a little mad and so is not given much praise here (773 f.; Benardete omitted a line here; other editors question **Artaphrenes** because he is not otherwise known as a Persian king). The conspiracy alluded to at 778–80 is described by Herodotus at 3. 84.

781 Cf. 245, 860 ff. Once again Darius' defeat at Marathon is ignored.

786–99 This section makes a pattern of iambic trimeters of the following form: 3:3:1:1:1:2:2. Cf. the more elaborate symmetry at *LB* 479 ff. (see note to 503 ff.).

787 On **harp** Broadhead observes: "The Chorus speaks as if they were somewhat bored by the King's excursion into Persian history, and with their vivacious questions bring him back to the realities of the moment."

792 In Herodotus 7. 49 Artabanus warns Xerxes that the sea and the land are allies of the Greeks.

796 ff. The herald has suggested that virtually the entire army has perished on its return (482 ff.). Now we hear Darius describe a large remaining force, which in fact fought the Battle of Plataea the next year. The apparent contradiction between the messenger's report and Darius' prophecy has agitated some commentators, but, after all, could the messenger say with effect: "Don't worry! Quite a large army remains in Greece under Mardonius. They will reclaim our losses." Aeschylus has magnified the earlier disaster and saved Plataea for Darius; perhaps his Athenian audience has been waiting for some news of the "payment" at Plataea (808).

804 Empty hopes directs us to a pervasive motif in Aeschylean tragedy; see on *PB* 250–52.

806 The **Asopus** river flows east from the village of Plataea, which lies on the slope of the Cithaeron range between Attica and Boeotia. The Boeotian plain, watered by the Asopus, is one of the richest in Greece.

809 ff. Pride is *hybris*; **godless** probably does not signify "atheist"—a very rare animal in the fifth century, as Rose points out—but describes the man who disregards the gods and their prerogatives. Herodotus (5. 102) suggests that the plundering of Greek sanctuaries by the Persians was in revenge for the Ionian sacking of the temple of Cybebe in Sardis.

813 f. For other examples of "doing and suffering" see on *Ag* 1560–66. Conceptually, this precept looks to *dikē* as an order of nature; metaphorically, it looks to the balance inherent in the scales of Zeus.

816 If **fount** is correct (the line is variously emended), compare 743 f. ("spring of evil") and *Sev* 586.

818 f. Real **sacrificial cakes** were offered by the queen (204, 524); now the same cakes, compounded of Persian blood, will be offered once more. It was the **Dorian,** i.e., Spartan, infantry that was given greatest credit for the victory at **Plataea.** For the dead at Plataea see Herodotus 3. 12. 1.

819c ff. Being mortal defines man by contrast with the immortal gods. The biological limit of mortality implies other boundaries, most notably the boundary imposed on man's power and ambition. Such limits may be symbolic and psychological, as we see from Agamemnon's caution (*Ag* 922 ff.). A typical censure falls on **thoughts too high** (we might compare "having the bighead," but the Greek denotes more ambition than vanity). The two categories, mortality and excessive ambition, are often connected (see, e.g., *Alcestis* 799 and Herodotus 7. 10, cited in the note on *Ag* 904–11). Disregard for personal limits manifests itself in the violence and **insolence** the Greeks called *hybris* (821). To describe the progress of *hybris*, the Greeks used biological metaphors: *hybris* is like a blossoming plant (cf. *Ag* 763–71) whose only fruit can be **doom** (= *atē*; see 1007); for the **harvest** cf. *Ag* 502. From line 824 on, Darius runs through the same argument in plainer language: the disaster in Greece becomes a paradigm that warns against **disdaining** (= "thoughts too high") present **fortune** (*daimōn*; see on 159b), and thus squandering real **prosperity** (= "happiness" at 708) for vain ambition. Being **overboastful** (828 and 831: the **over** [Greek *hyper*] occurs four times in this passage) is a symptom rather than the disease itself.

Zeus the **corrector** carries the same metaphor as in 212 f. (note); contrary to the queen's assumption, Xerxes' accounts can be audited.

833 ff. These instructions clearly anticipate what everyone has expected since the herald's news, the arrival of Xerxes. But they also anticipate the reunion of the queen and her son, which in fact does not take place. As Broadhead puts it: "Why raise an expectation that is not fulfilled? There is justice in the criticism, but it should be noted that Darius' description of Xerxes' condition at least does prepare the spectator for what he will presently see: it cushions the shock of a spectacle that otherwise might have been felt as grotesque or even bordering on the comic" (Introduction, p. xxxix). So some fault in dramatic construction may be granted: Aeschylus wanted a solitary, humiliated king who could enter into a responsive lyric lament (a kommos) with the chorus but without the necessary mitigation of the queen's consolation.

The actor who played the queen now changed to play Xerxes (some scholars suggest that Aeschylus himself played these roles). Such an allotment of parts, however, should probably not be accepted as the reason for her departure (cf. Flickinger, p. 175).

838–42 Darius' final lines change the key rather suddenly. Various explanations have been given: they offer consolation, or recommend resignation, or somehow reflect on the sorry character of the old men, or reflect the contempt of the dead king for his counselors. Eitrem sees a pun on **wealth** (*ploutos*) and the god of the dead (*Ploutōn*), but most critics reject any comedy in these solemnities.

847 Rose notes how natural it is for the Greek to speak of an abstract noun (**dishonor**) as enfolding the person.

850 The **try** embarrasses those who think that Aeschylus can do no dramatic wrong. The Greek, unless emended, says: "having taken adornments from the house, I shall try to meet my son." Housman emended the text to get: "I shall try to meet him on the way." Since Aeschylus clearly did not want her in the final scene, it is just as well not to savage the text for such small advantage.

853 ff. Perhaps because of the great threnody to come in the final scene, this stasimon, by contrast, looks back to the days of Persian glory and the majesty of Darius.

865–69 The **Halys** river was the old boundary between the kingdoms of Persia and Lydia. At 867 a catalogue of Persian conquests begins. The significance of **Achelous,** best known as a river in Aetolia, does not seem to have been explained.

870–79 Both is apparently to be taken with **and** [those] **who.** The **cities** are not specified. **Strait of Helle:** see on 67–71; the **Propontis** is the Sea of Marmara; the **Bosphor** is the strait on which modern Istanbul is situated, which separates the Propontis from the **Pontus,** i.e., the Black Sea.

880 ff. Headland has been interpreted as the Troad and as the whole of projecting Asia Minor. The first three islands do lie southward along the coast of modern Turkey, but the next five are closer to mainland Greece.

890 ff. The catalogue moves south from Lemnos, an island north of Lesbos, to Rhodes. Some poignancy may be the point of mentioning Salamis, an island said to have been founded by Teucer, brother of Ajax, and to have taken its name from the home island and scene of the recent disaster.

905 ff. The entry of Xerxes: the text tells us so little about the appearance and retinue of the king that directions for staging this scene vary immensely. Some commentators speak of attendants, royal robes, and a carriage to carry either the king or his luggage, while others see him as entering alone, unattended, in the rags of his royal splendor. The only evidence within the scene seems to be "remnants" at 1016, which ambiguously refers either to his army or his robes. Here I think we want to agree with Taplin that the whole tenor of the scene, as well as anticipations of it (e.g., 833 ff.), implies a completely humiliated figure, the very emblem of his nation's loss. Contrasted with the glory of the opening scenes, and particularly with the queen's first entrance, the ruined king would be both striking and moving. It is pathos, not spectacle, that is the theatrical goal here.

> Truly lamentation is a prop of suffering.
> (Aeschylus, Frag. 213; trans. Lloyd-Jones)

In the first scenes of the play, spectacle and apprehension; in the last scene, rags and grief. Lacking the music, gesture, dance, and a feeling for the ritual of Greek lamentation, we are particularly hard pressed to grasp the tone and feel of this scene. The cries of grief reflected in "alas" and "woe" are, as Else says ("Ritual and Drama"), but the bare bones of the Greek *thrēnos* ("lamentation," English "threnody"). In producing such a scene, the director of an English version should, then, be particularly attentive to the spirit of loss and grief that animates this devastated nation. Else notes the gradual intensification of the scene: it begins with recitative anapests, which accompany marching; proceeds to melic anapests, with an admixture of livelier, metrically more irregular, dochmiacs; then the lamentation proper begins at 931, as Xerxes and the chorus sing responsively in mixed lyric meters; finally, there is the stichomythia, beginning at 1002, where, as Else says (p. 77), "the tempo speeds up and there is a staccato responsion between the short lines, seldom longer than a dimeter."

911 Savagely swooped the deity: see on 516.

921 The lament is very stylized, leaning heavily on assonance, alliteration, parallelism (e.g., 936 and 943), anaphora, and the like to achieve intensity.

922 Stuffed up hell violently represents the popular notion that the dead are devoured by a monster (Rose).

935 Evil-practiced means "full of the harm we've known." **Evil** (*kakon*) in this translation usually denotes an objective condition ("harm" or "harmful") rather than a subjective attitude. See the note on "woe" at 1040 ff.

944–53 Ionian apparently stands for "Greek." The Persian fleet had a contingent from the Ionian islands and cities of Asia Minor. Podlecki wonders if the lines seek to mitigate Ionian involvement in the invasion. Although the interpretation of the passage is much disputed, the image of **reaping** a harvest of misfortune from the sea is Aeschylean (see the note to 819c ff.).

956–61 See the note to 21. **Pharandakas** and **Sousiscanes** were mentioned in the parodos (32 and 37). In the list at 967 ff. five of the warriors were mentioned previously.

963 Tyre was a leading port of Phoenicia, whose ships opened the battle (410).

980 Aristophanes mocks the "king's eye" at *Acharnians* 90 ff. Apparently these officers were inspectors general for the Great King.

991 Magic wheel is a colorful touch from popular superstition. The word literally signifies a bird, the wryneck, used in a curious piece of love magic: "the object of spinning round the wheel to which the wry-neck was tied was to bring near the loved one, the absent person for whom the other yearned; so wry-neck being symbolical of the yearning came to = desire" (Broadhead). We know this from Theocritus' second poem.

1000 f. The chorus alludes to the king's habit of traveling in a covered carriage, accompanied by a large honor guard. The meaning is: "I marvel that these followers do not accompany you." Some scholars have taken **moving tents** as evidence for the presence of a carriage (see on 905 ff.). Alternatively: "I see no followers around the moving tents (which I saw when you departed)."

1007 The **eye of doom** translates *atē*, here probably personified. It appears in "infatuate" at 653, and in the mesode (93–101) it is equated with "the deception of god." Cf. 1015, where "thou curse" reflects a compound that means "victimized by *atē*." See also on *Ag* 385 f.

1008 ff. The many references to **striking** must have been accompanied by gestures, the mimetic correlative for this common metaphor. Cf. on 740.

1016 For **remnants** see the note on 905 ff.

1020 He points to his empty quiver. If **remnants** refers to a few soldiers, then this line and what follows must point to the poor number left in his guard.

1028 He appears onstage as if, having just witnessed the battle, he has only moments before torn his garments in grief. This telescoping of time, so that only the essential actions matter, is common in Aeschylus. The physical problems of time and space are not the stuff of tragedy, as we see from the timing of beacons, herald, and king in the *Agamemnon*.

1040 ff. Xerxes becomes the leader of the chant (cf. 1048, 1050). The thrice-repeated **woe** (1041) reflects the jangling Greek: *kakan kakōn kakois.*

1052 ff. Here we have some suggestion of gesture and dance as the chorus mimes the breast-beating (1052 f.), hair-tearing (1055), shrill cry (1058), and rending of garments that characterized mourning in Greek antiquity. Cf. *Iliad* 18. 22–31.

1077 Xerxes and the chorus depart together. Though the reference to home (1069) has been taken by some as another piece of evidence for a represented palace, it does not require a visually present building. They depart by the side exits.

Nothing in this scene suggests a stage or the separation of Xerxes from the actors. Taplin seems right to argue that the scene would play more effectively if Xerxes joined the chorus in the orchestra.

Seven against Thebes

THE *Seven against Thebes* was the third play in a trilogy, following a *Laius* and an *Oedipus*. Although we know next to nothing about the content of these plays, general lines of action can be inferred from the *Seven* and other versions of the Theban cycle. Laius, king of Thebes, was warned by Apollo's oracle not to have children if he would save his city. Failing to obey this admonition, Laius got a child, Oedipus, whom his parents exposed on Mt. Cithaeron. Yet Oedipus was saved, grew up, and lived to kill his father Laius. Oedipus killed Laius in ignorance, and only later, after he had married his own mother (Jocasta), inherited the throne of Thebes, and gotten children by his mother, did he discover that he was a parricide. Subsequently Oedipus quarreled with his sons and cursed them (for possible motives see the note on 782–91). After the death of Oedipus the boys divided the rule, perhaps to share it in alternating periods, but Polyneices' exile became permanent. As the *Seven* opens, he has raised an army in Argos and returned to Thebes to take by force his share—or more—of the kingdom.

1–3 We don't know whether or not Aeschylus brought on a crowd of extras for this speech; if not, then we have another case of an address to the audience of the type noticed at *LB* 973. **Speak home** means "opportunely," as at 65. **Rudders** are actually at the stern, which is what he says; cf. 761 for the same phrase. This imagery of the "ship of state" is traditional and is extensively developed in this play; cf. 62 ff., 112, 207–10, 652, 691 f., 771, 854 ff.

4 ff. Defining the character of Eteocles has led to a variety of often contradictory assessments. These lines have been used as evidence for both atheism and pragmatism. The former will hardly stick; cf., e.g., 14, 35, 69, and 237 ff.

9 f. Since he wishes that Zeus may prove true to his name, some commentators agree with Rose's skeptical comment that we have here "pious rhetoric." No play by Aeschylus more self-consciously plays on names; see, e.g., 144, 405 (see the note on 399 f.), 439, 537, 578, 828. **Cadmus** is the founder of Thebes, whose citizens are therefore called Cadmaeans, as at 75. Cf. 134–42.

16 Earth is the mother of us all, but the descent is particularly significant for the Thebans, whose leading families are styled "the sown men" (see on 412) because they literally sprang from the earth. Cf. 69a.

21 Or: "Until this day god has favored us."

24 f. The **prophet,** never named, is Teiresias, who reads the omens by studying the habits of birds (cf. *Antigone* 1000 ff.). For **and fire** read "without fire."

36 In effect the line announces the messenger. For similar opportune arrivals see Sophocles, *Oedipus the King* 69–86, Euripides, *Phoenician Women* 690–96.

43 Seven is the traditional number. By taking an oath on the animal's blood they invoke the animal's fate on anyone who violates the oath. The greatest of animals, the bull, makes the strongest oath.

46 ff. The personification is Homeric:

> and Terror drove them, and Fear, and Hate whose wrath is relentless,
> she the sister and companion of murderous Ares.
>
> (*Iliad* 4. 440–41)

Enyo is a feminine counterpart to Ares, sometimes called his sister or mother. **Battle rout** is *phobos* (= "fear" at 121); cf. on 500.

50 Adrastus is the king of Argos.

53 More Homeric imagery: Hector tells Achilles that he has a "heart of iron" (*Iliad* 22. 357). Fire imagery is extremely common in the *Iliad*; for Aeschylus' use of it see 287, 389, 432 ff., 445 ff., 493 f., 511 ff. For **iron** see 730.

56 Two variations on the same idea make **casting lots** emphatic. Cf. 126 and the note on 377 f. What at first seems an innocent literary adaptation—in book 7 of the *Iliad* the heroes draw lots to see who will face Hector—becomes the key to the fate of Eteocles (see the note to 729–33).

64 Bellows . . . wave compares the alien army to the sea roaring over the land. Cf. *Oedipus the King* 24–26.

69 For **within** read "without." The messenger now exits.

69a ff. Eteocles prays to the powers of the world and the city (Ares, Athene, Poseidon, and Aphrodite will be mentioned shortly) for protection and, most surprisingly, to the **Curse,** here equated with the Fury (= **evil spirit;** cf. the equation at *Eum* 417). See on 640 f. and 699a. This must be a reference to his father's curse, but why does it come to his mind now? Perhaps the mention of lots (56) has reminded him of his father's enigmatic curse and its allotments (see on 649–55 and 729–33); perhaps the very last phrase (**no harm,** 69) recalls, at least subliminally, "Oedipus astray in his mind" (727), since both "harm" and "astray" translate the same stem (*blabē*, which is frequently linked with the ruining delusion known as *atē*). A Greek particle following the word for city makes it possible to translate "*at least* do not root out the city," with the implication, perhaps, that he is ready to accept his personal fate or even to sacrifice himself to save the city. While there isn't much doubt about the meaning of this particle, it seems a very small thing to hang an entire interpretation on. Sacrifice and self-sacrifice are not alien to Greek tragedy; the disagreement among critics turns on his conscious volition and his intention.

74–76 The first line is especially odd because, obviously, the invaders are Greeks and speak **a Greek tongue.** Line 74 (73 in the Oxford text) is an interpolation, as Dawe argues (*Collations*, pp. 180 f.). For the **slavish yoke** see *Pers* 49–50.

78 Does Eteocles leave, or does he remain present but silent through the parodos? What would he do, apart from fuming, during the lyric? Though he is mad enough at 181, it is hard to believe that he has been waiting his turn for one hundred lines. His motivation to leave is the business of defense; that he does not tell us so means only that we cannot count on the text for every cue. See the discussion at *Ag* 83.

79 Fearful strikes the key for the entire parodos. Women enter, terrified, near hysteria, shouting, calling on the gods, summoning the audience's imagination to the tumult of a city under siege. Many editions divide the choral role into individual voices, but there is little textual support for such division, either here or elsewhere. On the other hand, this chorus enters, not with the marching anapests found in the *Persians, Sup-*

pliants, and *Agamemnon*, but to agitated iambic and dochmiac rhythms; and, what is perhaps more significant, there is no lyric responsion until line 109, after which more coherence emerges. Lines 79–109 are more naturally suited to individual voices than many passages that are thus divided.

89a White was the traditional color for the Argives, perhaps because of a pun on Argos meaning "white" or "gleaming." In the *Phoenician Women* Polyneices speaks of the Theban "temples of the gods who ride white horses" (606), but I don't know where the present horses came from.

93 As in the *Suppliant Maidens*, **images of the Gods** offer a sacred place for safety.

101 f. Gifts accompany prayer and supplication; cf. *Oedipus the King* 911 ff.

104 With so many words for noise throughout this section, we should consider the possibility of offstage sound.

106–8 To found Thebes, Cadmus had to kill a dragon sacred to **Ares,** who demanded expiation. Subsquently Cadmus married Harmonia, daughter of Ares and Aphrodite. In the Homeric *Hymn to Ares* Ares is given a **golden helmet.**

109b ff. There is so much prayer in Greek tragedy that it is easily taken for granted; this prayer continues until line 150. Cf. 271 ff. Besides being more stylized than normal prayer and ritual, there is an element of self-consciousness, as, e.g., in 121, which would seem foreign to usual religious practice. The punning at 134 f. (see the note there) and 144 are similarly artful.

122 In **ringing,** Haldane (p. 37) identifies a metaphor from the sound of the "Hebraic harp (*kinnor*) . . . an instrument which, on account of its lugubrious tones, was used in mourning." If the reference is not so specific, there might be something in Tucker's comparison of the reins and bit binding a horse's mouth to the band attached to the mouthpiece of the flute and tied around the head of the flutist (frequently represented in vase paintings). Cf. the "axles screech" (205), where the axle is likened to the shrill syrinx, a pipe that gave a peculiar high, hissing sound; see also 463 (note) and *PB* 358. So bells (387) and trumpet (395) enliven the description of Tydeus, who hisses like a snake (381).

128–30 Lines 128–29 may also modify **Pallas** (Athene). In that case **save our city** should read "savior of our city," with a comma to follow.

130–31 Poseidon was worshiped with Athene in the Athenian Erechtheum; he may have had even closer ties with Thebes. His association with **horses** is variously explained; it is probably very old, going back to the nomadic invaders of Greece, who brought their horse god to find a fitting place in the Aegean. See Guthrie, pp. 95 ff.

134 f. The acropolis in Thebes was called the Cadmeia (**that bears your name**). There is punning in **Cadmus/care:** Tucker notes that the Greek word for "care" suggests both "concern" and a matrimonial tie, both of which are appropriate here; cf. the pun at *Ag* 702 (explained in the note to *Ag* 699–702).

140 Cypris is Aphrodite (see *Suppl* 1035); see note on 106–8.

144 Apollo Lykeios is etymologized to mean "Apollo the **wolf God**." See on *Ag* 1257 and Guthrie, pp. 82 ff. The **daughter of Leto** is Artemis, sister of Apollo and goddess of the hunt.

170 Cf. 74. Calling them **foreign-tongued** may simply be an exaggeration for "alien."

173–80 Since in prayer it is important to omit no one, the last category catches all the rest (**Spirits** = *daimones*). Reminding the god of prior service and sacrifice is usual in Greek prayer. Man owes the gods such gifts, and the gods owe him a return for them. Cf. 77 f. and the prayer of Chryses, *Iliad* 1. 36–42.

181–202 The misogyny is not specifically Aeschylean. Garton argues (p. 252): "He speaks like a misogynist, but you cannot investigate him as such; the poet makes him say this merely because two formative strands of action—namely, responsibility for defence in the rule, and shrill demoralising panic in the women—cross each other at that point."

197 Or in between is not a misprint but the excited bluster of a man who has lost his composure. Lines 191 f. ask us to believe that he has seen panic inspired by their hysteria. Modern film or theater may show such effects; Greek theater reports them and so appeals more to the imagination than to actual seeing.

203–44 This section has the following formal structure: the

chorus has three pairs of responsive lyrics, each pair a little
shorter than the last (in the Greek 4½ lines, 3½ lines, 2½ lines);
Eteocles responds to each lyric section with three lines of
spoken iambic trimeters. In the present translation, symmetry
is broken by Grene's decision to follow the manuscripts that
divide lines 217 ff. Cf. Dawson's version of these lines as a
continuous speech:

> *Eteocles*:
> Our walls—pray that these keep off enemy spears!
> Thus the gods will save us. Yet as for gods,
> gods of a captured town leave it, they say.

Cf. the epirrhematic form at 686–711.

203–7 If **rattle, rattle** seems silly, then it misleads us in the
search for the right tone. Horses' bits can be compared to
ships' **rudder oars** because Greek ships had two rudders.

213 The synaesthesia of **snowflakes crashed** may be derived from their shaken nerves or from

> the flung stones dropped to the ground
> like snowflakes . . .
> > (*Iliad* 12. 156 f.)

Also cf. *Iliad* 12. 278–87, where volleys of stones are compared to the snowflakes of a driving winter storm.

214 For **with force** read "with fear," and see on 46 f.

217 ff. See the note on 203–44. **Gods** do in fact **desert**
cities; cf. 307 and Euripides, *Trojan Women* 25–27, Herodotus 8. 41, and Vergil, *Aeneid* 2. 351. Welcker conjectured that
Sophocles in his *Laocoön* described the gods fleeing Troy,
carrying their own icons. **They say** indicates a proverb. Cf.
225–27.

223 f. Eteocles is not against calling on the gods (237–39),
but man must plan well if he expects divine help. Cf. on *Pers*
742–45.

225–27 Cf. Creon's more discursive homily on the same
theme in Sophocles' *Antigone* 672–76. **Obedience** is a variation on the persuasion motif.

244 Ares feeds on the dead, who are his proper sacrificial
victims. Cf. on *Eum* 302–5.

251 Blessed Band probably refers to gods of the city, as at
109b ff.

257 f. In touching the images as they speak of a captured

town the women inadvertently pray for just what they don't
want. So Eteocles has proof of how pernicious their excitement can be. Note his own care at lines 5 and 427 f. to depre-
cate any harmful influence his own talk of defeat may have.
Correct speech may successfully avert evil, just as incor-
rect speech, no matter what the intention, may bring harm.
Cf. *Ag* 1652 f. (note).

269 ff. The **paean** is a song of victory, sung immediately
before battle or just after. **Cry of sacrifice** = "cry of joy"
(*Ag* 586).

271–79 A comprehensive prayer promises sacrificial thank
offerings in return for divine protection. The spring **Dirce** is
the most famous of local springs (cf. 309), the **Ismenus** the
primary river. For worship of rivers see *Suppl* 1025 ff. Other
prayers at 419 ff., 481, 568, 627.

283–87 The plain sense of this speech, at the end of which
Eteocles exits, is that he will now go to post his own champions at each gate, so that rumor (= **messengers . . . words**)
may not catch the army unprepared. He will, that is, avoid
panic by taking immediate action. Since he says that he is going
to **post** them, then leaves and returns, with no more being
said of the posting, we naturally assume that he has accomplished this task. The trouble with all this is that, when the
messenger describes each of the Argive champions, Eteocles
responds (397 ff. and passim) by saying that he *will* (future
tense at 407) nominate his own champion to oppose each of
the Argives.

Our understanding of what happens is further complicated
by two aspects of the language: at 408 and again at 472 demonstrative pronouns, which can be taken to mean "*this* man
here," suggest a person (mute) on the stage; on the other hand,
in naming the champions, Eteocles uses a variety of tenses
(future, present, and past), some of which imply that the
posting has already been accomplished. The following interpretations and solutions have been offered:

1. Lines 283 ff. are inconsistent with what follows in the
central scene of the play; the contradiction, which some find
insignificant, is simply a dramatic lapse.

2. Lines 283 ff. are emended, deleted, or interpreted in such
a way as to bring them in line with a later posting of the

champions. Most efforts in this direction seem tendentious, but Taplin's emendation of "fetch" for **post** (284) is very easy.

3. Eteocles goes off and posts his warriors; the central scene is an elaborate and retrospective description of what has already been accomplished. This view is clearly difficult in light of the messenger's concluding questions and admonitions (e.g., 395 ff., 470, 596).

Because no interpretation seems to me clear of all problems, I have included in the following notes discussions of several passages crucial to our understanding, and I hope that the reader will be able to reach an independent judgment. My own view, however, is that Eteocles returns *leading* his six champions. As the messenger describes each of the opposing champions (375 ff., 423 ff., etc.) Eteocles dispatches his own man, chosen carefully to match the peculiar style, device, name, and vaunt of the Argive enemy as described by the messenger. There are, then, in the dramatic evolution of the scene, elements of chance, choice, and symmetry that conspire to implicate the two brothers in their ultimate confrontation. The audience will have the opportunity to observe armor and devices on the shields of the Theban champions, to follow and approve Eteocles' decisions, and to see, as well as feel, how he is drawn, by omens, luck, and his own intelligence, into fulfilling his father's curse. In connection with this interpretation see the notes on textual difficulties and problems of staging at 371, 377, 395 f., 398, 399 ff., 407, 470–73, 481, 506 ff., and 649–55.

288–368 The first stasimon is composed of three responsive pairs (288–304 and 305–21; 322–33 and 334–44; 345–56 and 357–67). Their fears are not completely allayed, but the tone, if pessimistic, is calmer.

290 f. With **neighbors** compare *Ag* 1002, where strength and sickness are neighbors. With **kindle** compare "burn" (287) and "afire" (389).

293–96 At *Iliad* 2. 308 ff. Odysseus tells of a snake who ate eight nestlings and their mother; cf. 504.

301 ff. The strophe ends with a prayer, as does the antistrophe (312–21).

311 Upholder, a traditional epithet, was understood to mean both "the god who sustains the land" as well as "the god who is lord of the land." **Tethys** is the wife of Ocean; their children are the rivers, fountains, and seas of the world. Since Ocean encircles the world, he makes a natural source for the living fluid of life.

322 In the remaining lyrics they imagine a city sacked. This commonplace, a species of ecphrasis (imagined description), has its roots in passages such as *Iliad* 6. 447 ff., where Hector imagines the fate of Troy, and 22. 66 ff., where Priam imagines how he will be killed and eaten by his own dogs. This particular topic becomes historical in Deianira's pity for the captive women (Sophocles, *Women of Trachis* 298–302) and is later elaborated into the dramatic substance of Euripides' *Trojan Women.*

326 Achaean contradicts the earlier emphasis on the foreign, non-Greek character of the invader.

329 Other equine imagery at 80, 203–7, 393–95, 461–64, 476.

343 f. At the beginning of chapter 12 of *The Red Badge of Courage* Stephen Crane describes how "War, the red animal, war, the blood-swollen god, would have bloated fill." His sentence is not so far from the style and tone of the present passage. Cf. the "blast of Ares" at 63.

346 Cf. the **net** over Troy at *Ag* 357 ff.

351 Grene's version of this line makes it a foreshadowing of the fratricide ahead; cf. 416. Another possible version: "In flight, families are violently separated." There are only three words in the Greek, and no verb; such concision is not only difficult to translate but makes one wonder about the pace and articulation of the singing.

353 Empty means that he has not yet found his share of the loot. This is another three-word sentence, with the connective offering a quadruple alliteration of the sound *k*: *kai kenos kenon kalei.*

356 The text is corrupt. In Grene's version the chorus momentarily pauses to ask, ironically, what may be expected from such plundering.

357–67 The transition probably depends on the familiar metaphor of the harvest of war (e.g., at *Suppl* 635 ff., 663 ff.). Shifting images of wasteful streaming dominate. The ambiguities (**man**/husband; **successful**/happy; **consummation**/ritual of marriage; **expectation**/hope) heighten the pathos by contrast.

368–75 These iambic lines, three for each announcement, are spoken by individuals rather than a half-chorus. The simultaneous entry of two characters is very rare; here the symmetrical entry of the messenger and Eteocles initiates a scene composed of paired speeches.

371 The sentence is odder in Greek: "he is speeding the rapid axles—of his legs" (Tucker's version; he notes that the surprise depends on the postponement of the final genitive, before which the sentence suggests that the messenger comes in a chariot. There is no textual evidence that Eteocles is attended, which may tell against his dispatching warriors from the stage in the following scene (see note to 283–87).

377 f. See the note on **lot** at 56. Eteocles will speak of the "dice of Ares" (415). Other echoes and variations occur at 424, 451, 457 f. See the note on 729. The city has seven gates, the Argives seven champions, Eteocles must post seven champions. **Tydeus** is the son of Oeneus and Periboea and the father of the Homeric hero Diomedes. Like Polyneices, the exiled Tydeus married a daughter of Adrastus, king of Argos (50 and 575). Adrastus promised to return both his sons-in-law to their lands. Polyneices' turn came first, so the two fight before Thebes (see Euripides, *Phoenician Women* 427 ff.). For a Homeric scene concerning these men and their sons see *Iliad* 4. 365 ff. For Tydeus see Apollodorus 1. 8. 5–6. The word for **thunders** was heard earlier at 85 ("rings") and at 350 ("cry bitterly").

379–82 The **prophet** is Amphiaraus, son of Oecles (= **Oecleides;** see on 569 ff.), who alone among the seven is not described as monstrous and unnatural. For descriptions of enraged warriors, Aeschylus could draw on numerous passages in the *Iliad*. For example, **enraged** is cognate with "lash out in fury" in Ares' complaint to Zeus:

> See now, the son of Tydeus, Diomedes the haughty,
> She [Athene] has egged on to lash out in fury against the
>   immortal gods.
>
> (*Iliad* 5. 881–83)

The Greek expected and found brutal bestiality in war. Even Patroclus becomes daimonically possessed (*Iliad* 16. 783–87), while his friend Achilles can say to the dying Hector:

> No more entreating of me, you dog, by knees or parents.
> I wish only that my spirit and fury would drive me
> to hack your meat away and eat it raw for the things that
> you have done to me.
>
> (*Iliad* 22. 345–48)

"Haughty" in Ares' whine (*Iliad* 5. 881), like "Overweening" at 391 and "arrogant" at 387, denotes "over-reaching" (the Greek *hyper-*; see the moralizing of Darius at *Pers* 819 ff. and the note there).

387–90 The description of armor is a commonplace in heroic poetry; cf. *Iliad* 18. 478–607 (the shield of Achilles) and 11. 32–40 (the shield of Agamemnon) and Hesiod's *Shield of Heracles* (139 ff.). Apparently the shield's arrogance consists of symbolically representing Tydeus as the grand moon among the paltry stars.

395 f. The future tense clearly implies that the posting has not yet been accomplished. If the six heroes have returned with him and are now onstage, unassigned to particular gates but ready to go, the problem may be solved.

398 Aeschylus has a habit of employing significant words repeatedly. **Fit to deserve our trust** translates a single adjective, which occurs again (as "trustworthy") at 449, 470, and 797 but is otherwise found only once in the extant plays (*Eum* 87). The connotations are commercial and legal, as in "bonded," "giving surety." Sansone (p. 35) thinks the messenger hints that Eteocles is the appropriate defender. Since in the next line Eteocles uses the first person ("I would not tremble before . . ."), Garvie thinks that for a moment the audience may have thought he was going to take this challenge personally (Garvie, "Simple Plots," p. 72).

399 ff. Eteocles is challenged by each successive report to find the right man to represent Thebes. This challenge entails a responsibility to speak suitably to the challenger's vaunt and to interpret the messenger's report in such a way that the omens will be good for Thebes. This process of reinterpretation is shown very deliberately in the present speech: I do not fear mere weaponry, and, as for the message on his shield, the moon must yield to night, in which case his sign will truly signify his fate. In **truly and most justly pregnant** occurs the first of several explorations of naming (439 [see on 424 ff.], 537, 578, 658, 670). The whole process of correct naming involves a magic control over the person or thing accurately identified. Connected with this superstition is the idea, also common in ancient literature, myth, and folktale, that the name truly signifies the nature of the thing (the Latin phrase for this belief, *nomen omen* ["name = omen"], concisely summarizes this aspect of the usage). In this particular scene, where the verbal articulation of men and manners preempts all action, that kind of power in the word finds a peculiarly suitable dramatic ground.

407 Here his language exactly responds (**nominate** = both "will set" at 396 and "shall range in combat" at 621) to the messenger's phrasing, which surely implies that he is going to assign the station now. Though such pronouns are not conclusive evidence, the fact that, in the Greek, Astacus is described as "*this* worthy son" has led some scholars to argue for his presence onstage.

412 When Cadmus came to the future site of Thebes, he killed a dragon guarding the place. Being advised by Athene, he sowed the dragon's teeth, and, from them, armed men sprang up. They fought one another, and the survivors of these **sown men** founded the leading families of the city. See Apollodorus 2. 4. 1. The dragon was sacred to Ares; since these sown men (*Spartoi*) came into the world fighting, and only five survived, Ares may be said to have **spared** them.

416 Justice (*dikē*) gets a lot of play (e.g., 405, 445, 584, 607) and comes up very emphatically at 646 and 663. **Blood of his blood** because, as a descendant of one born from the earth, Astacus has the natural right to defend his land, which Polyneices and company unnaturally attack.

424 ff. Capaneus is a native Argive. The Greek calls him *another* **giant,** thereby comparing him to the race of earthborn monsters who in primeval times fought the Olympian gods at Phlegra. As a blasphemous god-defier, he scorns even the anger of Zeus. A firebrand himself (432–34), he will be destroyed by the fire of Zeus:

> Just as he reached the cornice of the wall
> Zeus struck with lightning.
>   (*Phoenician Women* 1180 f.)

Eteocles turns Capaneus' threats (438 f.), the god whom he defies (443), and another man of fire (448) against him. The chorus will get its wish (454).

443 See on *Pers* 819c.

459a It is not certain that **Eteoclus** belonged to the epic tradition. If Aeschylus invented his name, he surely did so to match him as a double with Eteocles.

461 The two previous gates take their names from persons; **Neïs** probably means "lowest" and is on the west side of the city.

463 Tucker notes: "A muzzle of bronze attached to the bridle was perforated with pipes, forming a series like those of the *syrinx* or Pan's-pipe, through which the breathing or snorting of the horses created a kind of tuneless music *in terrorem*." Cf. 206 and *Suppl* 181.

470–73 The imperative in the present tense (**send;** cf. 596 and 650) has more point if Eteocles is actually dispatching the warriors as he matches them. But the first two lines in response complicate the issue. **I'll send** implies purpose and intention, while **he is gone** (a perfect or pluperfect, depending on the editor) reports an accomplished action. Many editors delete one or the other of these lines because they appear mutually contradictory. Grene's translation and spacing suggest a gesture of dismissal (?) and the departure of Megareus before he is named. Like Grene, some commentators assume that Eteocles has assigned the posts prior to bringing the six heroes onstage. Such an assumption makes the matching onstage so much verbal legerdemain, but it does account for the perfect tense here and at 448, where Grene changes "Polyphontes has been stationed" to "shall be stationed." If Eteocles decided prior to the messenger's report which of the champions was to be stationed at each gate, then the present scene represents, as Burnett (p. 348) says, "recognition, not decision." On this hypothesis Eteocles discovers the appropriateness of the pairings already made, and, more significantly, he has in ignorance cast himself to oppose his brother. Chance, then, not choice, has determined the course of the pairings—or is this "chance" fate? See Kitto, *Greek Tragedy*, p. 52. Other references to luck and fortune occur at 415, 419 f., 423, 427.

478 f. An alternative version: "or having taken two men and a city on his shield, he will adorn his father's house with spoils." Since Eteoclus has *one* man on his shield, the point is that Megareus will cap this by showing, on his own shield, himself vanquishing his foe.

481 Since **to you** is interpretative, it should not be used as evidence for Megareus' presence.

486 f. Dawson translates as "Zeus the Requiter" and sees in this epithet an anticipation of the later emphasis on property distribution.

489 The meaning of **Onca,** a uniquely Theban title for Athene, is unknown; it appears again at 501 and also, untranslated, at 149. Pausanias (9. 12. 2) took the title to prove the Phoenician provenance of Cadmus.

493 Typho (also spelled Typhon and Typhoeus) is the typical earthborn (523) dragon of Greek and Oriental myth. Hesiod (*Theogony* 820 ff.) describes him as a child of Earth and Tartarus, with a hundred snake-heads issuing from his shoulders and fire flashing from the eyes of these heads. In a last great contest Zeus overcomes Typho and casts him into the underworld. Hence Eteocles' capping at 510 ff. See the description at *PB* 353–74. Like the giants (425), Typho typifies defiance of the Olympian order.

494 Though they may seem forced to us, expressions like **sister of fire** are not so forced to the Greek ear. Cf. on *Ag* 495. A cousin to this sort of personification is "Justice, blood of his blood" (416), where the abstract quality Melanippus exemplifies is personified and made blood kin to him.

499 For **Bacchanal** see on *Eum* 24–26.

500 Excepting Amphiaraus (591 ff.), they all **boast:** e.g., 391, 426, 467 f., 480, 539, 551. **Panic** (*phobos*), if fully personified, would give the alternative version: "Even now Panic vaunts at the gate." *Phobos* is often rendered "fear" (see notes on 46 f. and 79). It is so frequent that the translator must look for variations, e.g., "murder" at 499, "blench" at 475, "force" at 214.

503 Violence is *hybris*, which at 406 is translated as "insolence."

506 ff. The present-perfect tense, **has been chosen,** conceals the problem. More literally: "was chosen." **At fortune's need** means "in the service of fortune." Hermes is called "lucky" (*tychōn*) and naturally comes to mind after "fortune" (*tychē*). See on *LB* 815–18.

515–20 Interpolation has been suspected at the conclusion of this speech. An undefeated Zeus would be a strong conclusion, but perhaps we should let Eteocles have his doubts. Three lines are omitted by Grene, which, though hardly vigorous, deserve a hearing, if only because the very last word in the speech continues the play on *tychē/tychōn* (see preceding note). Smyth translates: "Yet it is like that the mortal champions too should fare even as their gods; and so to Hyperbius, in accordance with his blazon, Zeus will prove a Savior, for that he is set upon his shield."

533 ff. In a riddling variation the name of Parthenopaeus (548) is postponed, too long for some editors, who would transpose 548–49b to follow 537, so that the name would follow immediately upon the clues. This transposition accords with Aeschylus' usual manner in such riddles. Parthenopaeus' mother was the Arcadian huntress Atalanta; his father was Melanion or Ares. The pun on his name also includes a more esoteric play on **savage** (*ōmon*) and **name** (*epōnymon*). **Grim regard** (538) means "having the aspect of a Gorgon," an oblique continuity with the monsters previously mentioned.

541 Hesiod makes the **Sphinx** the child of Echidna (or Chimaera) and Orthus (*Theogony* 326 f.). Like the Chimaera, she is an eclectic beast, with the face of a woman, the breast, feet, and tail of a lion, and the wings of a bird. See Apollodorus 3. 5. 8; *Oedipus the King* 1200–1201. At the command of Hera she devastated Thebes until Oedipus solved her riddle. That she **ate men raw** (*ōmositon*) continues the play on "savage" (preceding note).

554–58 The familiar fifth-century antithesis between words and deeds is implicit here (cf. 592 f.). The name **Actor** means "leader," and the motif is continued in **heedless tongue** (= "tongue without works"). Verrall suggests that **flow . . . gates . . . breed** is drawn from irrigation. Other agricultural metaphors at 589, 593 f., 600 f.

561 The "embossed" (542) beast—i.e., the beast on the shield—will take a **hammering.**

569 ff. Knowing that the expedition would fail and bring his death, the seer **Amphiaraus** did not want to join it. Adrastus bribed Amphiaraus' wife, Eriphyle, to persuade him to join them, and for this treachery the doomed hero instructed his sons to kill her. He fled in the general rout and was swallowed up by the earth (588 f.) when Zeus split his path with lightning. See Pindar, *Ninth Nemean*, and Apollodorus 3. 6. 8. His daimonic spirit maintained an oracle at Oropus in Attica, a site still worth visiting.

571–75 This abuse responds to Tydeus (382 f.). **Tydeus,** an Aetolian in exile, had murdered a kinsman. When he is called **a summoning herald of the Fury,** the audience can hardly fail to think of the curse of Oedipus. Thalmann (p. 117) interprets: "He has also been the instrument of the Erinys by furthering the quarrel within the Theban ruling house."

580–89 Since the speech condemns Polyneices, it is some evidence that justice is on Eteocles' side. No one onstage ever censures Eteocles, but we cannot be certain that he is altogether blameless in the quarrel that led to his brother's exile. See Euripides' *Phoenician Women* 504 ff. for a different picture.

584 f. Grene has emended this sentence. The Oxford texts yield: "What Justice will put an end to the maternal spring?" Dawson (p. 21), comparing 752–76, sees a latent reference to Oedipus' begetting of children on his own mother and his simultaneous violation of his father's land (586). Jocasta, his father's wife, is the land they both sowed (753). A variety of other metaphors related to sowing, the earth, and kinship can be linked to the imagery here.

588 f. For the allusion in **make fat this soil** see the note to 569 ff.

592 Variations on the contrast of **seeming** and **being** occur at *Ag* 788 f. and 839. Heinimann (p. 109) says that the present passage is the first such contrast in nonphilosophical Greek. Cf. "In speech seem to be a friend to all" (Theognis 63) and "Seeming is wrought over all things" (Xenophanes, Kirk and Raven No. 189).

600–602 Because of the lack of a connective and the contradition (**no fruit** yet a **harvest**), many editors condemn the second sentence (**The field of doom . . .**), even though the metaphor is Aeschylean (cf. *Pers* 821–23 and *Ag* 502). A single line in the Greek, it is probably an intrusive gloss, perhaps borrowed from another play of Aeschylus.

607 Or a just man is not an alternative to a **pious man** (Amphiaraus is both) but, rather, a second comparison, shifting from a nautical to a political context.

609a At *Iliad* 12. 37 the Argives are "beaten by the scourge of Zeus." Cf. *Ag* 642. Two different but related figures are combined in the present line: the goad or whip with which a god drives men in confusion and thereby subdues them; the lightning bolt of Zeus that manifests his will (*Pers* 740) and destroys (629b below and *Ag* 367). Cf. 689c. **Common** is proleptic, i.e., the **scourge** strikes them all, indiscriminately.

613 "There is perhaps a grim allusion to marching to death, or making the journey to Hades. After [receiving] extreme unction Rabelais remarked that they had 'greased his boots for the long journey'" (Tucker).

615–19 Eteocles knows of oracles from Apollo (= **Loxias**) foretelling the failure of the expedition. Amphiaraus knows them, too (knows that, not how, he will die), and it seems a little odd that we know nothing more of them.

627 The stems from *dikē*, as in **lawful**, have become more frequent (occurring in 599 ["honest"] and three times in 607–610), no doubt in order to build toward the antithetical claims of the brothers (646, 663 ff.).

629 Prosper echoes "success" (626) and is picked up by "fate" (633), all three words from the *tychē* ("fortune") stem (see notes at 470–73, 506 ff.). For Eteocles the "cursed luck" is that he will face his brother.

640 f. Ambiguities (**race** also = "family"; **fatherland** also = "father") involve Polyneices in the invocation of the Furies with which Oedipus cursed his sons (699 and 700). Seeing how violent he is, we may suppose that he intends to bring down the house with himself. **A very violent** not only calls attention to his name (cf. 578 and 821–31) but also uses a familiar Homeric periphrasis of the type "the strength of Heracles" (*Iliad* 2. 658).

649–55 Signs refers to the emblems on the shields. The

messenger, who exits at 652, seems neither excited nor concerned for Eteocles. If Eteocles has already assigned himself to the remaining gate, the messenger, very composed, euphemistically avoids reference to the fratricidal duel, which was fixed by fate or chance before Eteocles knew where the Argive heroes would be stationed. If Eteocles has not actually assigned himself but intends to take a post, his surprise (653 ff.) is strange: How can he not expect Polyneices to be the remaining champion? Perhaps Eteocles' memory is triggered by **steer** (652), which means "to own or manage a ship" (cf. 62 ff.) but also contains the stem for the word "lot": *nauklērein* ("to steer") and *klēros* ("lot"); see on 729–33 for the lot-oracle. The tone of 653–67 implies a sudden revelation or surprise, as if only now he sees the way things must be. Ironically, the steersman of the state and master of words finds in the steering (*nauklērein*) his lot (*klēros*) **fulfilled** (with 655 cf. 70). His use of the *tel*-stem twice (655 and 659) is another sign that he sees the fulfillment of his lot. (For the meaning of the *tel*-stem, see the note on *Ag* 972–74.)

663–73 As Hesiod says:

> Then Zeus married shining Themis, who gave birth to the Hours,
> to Good-Order, to Justice, and to flourishing Peace.
>
> (*Theogony* 901–2)

Cf. on *LB* 948 ff. Eteocles' insistence on his **right** (673) is reflected in five appearances of the *dikē* stem in 663–73. As the punning 670 shows, passion and theme are always at the command of style: "or else she would most justly be falsely named Justice."

675 f. Since heroic arming began with the **greaves** (armor for the part of the legs below the knees), we might assume that an attendant now brings armor, which Eteocles will put on during the subsequent dialogue. Because he departs to die in battle, most commentators agree that his exit would gain in dramatic power if he left in full battle gear (no previous passage in the play indicates whether or not he is already armed). Yet there is no subsequent reference to arming, and for this reason Taplin doubts that we see Eteocles arm. In his words: "in Greek tragedy all important stage action is given by the words, and is the object of full attention" (p. 159). That is to say, if Eteocles were arming, and if we assume that arming is an "important stage action," then we would expect a description of the arming to focus *full* attention on it (the sort of paradigm Taplin has in mind will be found at *PB* 52 ff., where the chaining of Prometheus is described in detail). Lacking any such description, Taplin cannot believe that the dramatic focus is divided between the actual topic of the dialogue and a visually compelling scene in which the hero puts on his armor, piece by piece. As he argues (p. 31), "If actions are to be significant, which means they must be given concentrated attention, then time and words must be spent on them." We are left with a protagonist who departs for battle unarmed (which Taplin himself, on p. 161, styles "a serious diminution in the dramatic power of Eteocles' fatal departure") or else we may, with Taplin, cut out lines 675 f. and assume that Eteocles has been wearing his battle gear throughout the play.

Changing the text in order to satisfy a deductive dramatic principle is at best suspect. We have already seen (note on *Pers* 151 ff.) that Aeschylus was capable of introducing major visual components without making any descriptive reference to them. It is well to remember other factors: our knowledge of early Greek theater is limited to seven extant plays; consequently, even a careful inductive approach cannot possibly inform us of the full range of dramatic staging. Aeschylus produced and directed his own plays, which means that in practice he could tell his own actors and chorus what to do. Certainly, then, he had every opportunity to present a double focus if he chose to do so. Taplin argues that such a double focus (here the argument between chorus and Eteocles about whether he should face his brother and, second, the actual process of putting on the armor) would create a "competing distraction"; that is, the force of the argument would be diminished by the *visual* presentation of his determination to face Polyneices. It will be apparent from various critical comments I have cited from time to time that not all readers share Taplin's demand (p. 31) for a "concentrated and single-purposed" scenic production. To take Taplin's own example, we may cite his comments (p. 159) on Rose's interpretation: "Rose (p. 217) . . . praises 'the contrast between Eteocles' matter-of-fact occupation with his equipment and the chorus's impassioned appeals.' But are Eteocles' *words* matter-of-fact, and could such powerful words be accompanied by action independent of them?" Clearly, for Taplin the manner of scenic representation entails a view of tone. Rose does not intend to depreciate the scene's power when he suggests a contrast in tone; passionate appeal is pitted against resolute action (Eteocles quietly arms), and we may suppose that Eteocles' iambics are just as "powerful" for Rose, even though the hero speaks them while arming.

677 ff. After this speech the chorus sings, while Eteocles speaks. Reversing their roles in the second scene (181 ff.), they urge restraint, while he is committed, though hardly in panic, to fatal action. Since Solmsen's article appeared, most commentators have described Eteocles as one possessed by a Fury (see on 699a). If so, he would seem to have little choice but to act, yet the chorus's argument is predicated on the belief that he may still avoid fighting Polyneices (679 f.). These two perspectives are not mutually exclusive: they may think that he has a choice when actually he has none. **Of brothers mutually shed** echoes 351 and 416; cf. 734 ff. All bloodshed brings **pollution,** but none stains so deeply as that of kindred blood.

683 ff. His responses reflect the values of archaic epic (shame, disgrace, fame). In **word of good** he may be punning on his own name (which means "true fame"). If he is manic, the Fury works in a very Homeric mode.

687–711 In the Greek text the pattern of the lines is 3:3:3:3:4:3:4:3.

688–89a Two compound adjectives, both unique to this passage but of a type much favored by the poets, are represented by **lust for battle** and **filling the heart.** They modify *atē* ("delusion," here translated by the adjective **frantic**). Together these words give the description a more formal and traditional than personal cast.

689c–92 **Drives** is often used of a chariot and horses; cf. the imagery at 609a and the note on "scourge." Unlike the preceding speech, everything here suggests that he has turned himself over to the gods. The captain is "sailing with the wind," having drawn as his lot (**share**) a **wave of hell** (literally, "of Cocytus," one of the rivers of the underworld). For the blaming of Apollo cf. *Oedipus the King* 1329 f.

699a Lyrics are sparing of definite articles and pronouns. The "my" in **my dry and tearless eyes** is interpretative. "Nor does it matter greatly how we take [this] line. Whose eyes are dry? Does the Curse haunt the dry eyes of Eteocles or haunt him with dry eyes? It does not matter, because at this point the line of distinction between the Curse and the mind of Eteocles is hard to draw, because the Curse is working on him and in him. At least it is certain that what the Curse says to Eteocles is also what Eteocles is saying to himself" (Winnington-Ingram, "*Septem*," p. 25).

700–705 For rites to cleanse the house of the Furies see *LB* 965 ff. Which gods are not specified, and Solmsen argues that we should distinguish between the operation of the Olympian and chthonic divinities. In his response, then, Eteocles may be saying that sacrifice to the Olympians will now accomplish nothing. On the other hand, his death, as an offering, more naturally directs us to the Furies.

705–9b Fawning is the same verb as "cringe" at 383. It is useless to play the dog. The next line is vague, perhaps corrupt, but Dawson interprets: "Cringe now, when death stands before you." **Veering change** denotes the wind, whether it changes seaward or toward the land. The sentence fuses images of changing winds, daimonic possession, and a seething sea. For wind and breathing in physiological imagery see on *Ag* 186 and cf. 54, 63, and 343, above.

711 Showing gives the sense, but the more vivid Greek says "nightmares, dividers of my father's heritage." See 729 ff. for the **nightmare. Heritage** is a commercial term meaning "property" or perhaps "accounts."

712 ff. As at 245 ff., the symmetrically paired speeches resolve into stichomythia. Like most protagonists in tragedy, having made his decision he cannot be persuaded to relent.

719 The *gifts of the gods* is a commonplace of poetry and popular morality. Cf. 626, *Odyssey* 18. 140 f., and this fragment of Solon:

> and what the gods give us for gifts no man can refuse.
> (Solon, Frag. 1, line 64, trans. Lattimore, p. 20)

Exit Eteocles.

720–91 This stasimon has been called the climax of the play and the trilogy. It looks back on the oracles given to Laius and Oedipus, on their folly and the cursed house, and ahead to the imminent fulfillment of the curse on the brothers. Nowhere in the *Seven* does the loss of the preceding plays of the trilogy so hamper our understanding as in this passage, where a number of allusions, e.g., to the dream (cf. 710 and the note to 729–33), evidently depend on a knowledge of the earlier plays. Most scholars agree that if we knew the reason(s) for Oedipus' curse on his sons (785 ff.), the phrasing of the curse, and the content of the dream, we would be in a better position to understand Eteocles' sudden and violent reaction to the messenger's description of his brother.

720–26 Both strophe and antistrophe begin with riddling, or at least periodic, sentences that postpone key words until the end of the fourth line. For the first stanza the word is **Fury** (724), which tells who the **Goddess** is; for the second stanza the word is **Steel** (730), which tells who the **stranger** is. These words occupy the same metrical positions in their respective stanzas, and the music may have stressed this responsion. They are related thematically, in that the agent of the Fury, herself the agent of the curse, is the Steel.

The Furies are **unlike all other Gods** both in appearance (see on *Eum* 183 f.) and in function. Whereas the Olympians are thoroughly anthropomorphic and embody various attributes of human culture, so that Ares = War, Aphrodite = Love, etc., the Furies embody the malicious hatred of another human being. With 724 cf.

> Doomed by my father and his avenging Furies.
> (*Oedipus at Colonus* 1434)

727 f. For **astray in his mind** see the note on 69a ff. **Strife** (*eris*) puns on Fury (*Erinys*).

729–33 The antistrophe contains, without preface, the dream alluded to at 710 f. We do not know who had the dream, nor do we know its exact content, and some critics treat the dream and curse as essentially the same, while others ignore the dream. Burnett, however, who considers them as distinct and complementary halves of a riddle that Eteocles solves during the course of the messenger's report, says (p. 359): "Evidently the Aeschylean Oedipus had cursed his sons by saying something like, 'May a bitter Ares guide you, as you portion out my property with iron-bearing hand!' His words plainly threatened a civil war that would be fought between the princes for the rule of Thebes. The Dream, however, had offered to its sleeper the phantasmagoric figure of a lawful mediator, one who would bring quarrels to an end with a drawing of lots. And this seemed to promise peace." During the messenger's speech Eteocles realizes that the lots (see on 56) are those cast for the gates, that the Scythian stranger is not a human mediator but Chalybian (i.e., Scythian) steel, and that dream and curse are two pieces of one fateful design entailing the death of both brothers. For Burnett, who believes that all the posts have been assigned prior to the paired speeches, Eteocles only late recognizes that his death is demanded by the Curse and his destiny; the tangible evidence for this fate is the fact that he himself assigned himself to the very gate his brother Polyneices drew by lot. So Eteocles knowingly sacrifices himself to appease the daimonic vengeance of his father and thereby saves his city and purges the house of its pollution.

Engelmann points out the Greek custom of bringing in arbitrators to settle civic disputes. Normally such men came from friendly Greek cities, and, if they arbitrated successfully, they were honored with crowns and public inscriptions. Herodotus offers some examples of such settlement (see 4. 161, where a man from Mantinea in Arcadia is called to Cyrene in Africa). Such methods of course aimed at peaceful settlement, which in the curse/dream Aeschylus ironically perverts, so that the settlement instead brings death by mutual slaughter. Manton's interpretation is different from the others but does not rule them out. He traces the language of the dream ("dividers," 711) and the antistrophe (**divider of possessions**, 729b) as well as other references (**allotment**, 729, and "divider," 945) to the Athenian law courts. In litigation concerning an estate, arbitrators ("divider" at 945 is the technical term) were appointed by the state; their rulings, e.g., on the portion of an inheritance due each party, were binding and could not be returned to court by the plaintiffs. Aeschylus seems to have drawn on both types of arbitration in order to create a complex metaphor applicable to the sons of Oedipus.

Land allotment is a simple noun in the Greek, the verbal form of which appears at 56 ("casting lots"). **Chalyb:** the Chalybian ironworkers lived on the north shore of the Black Sea (cf. *PB* 715). Cf. the report at 816 ff. ("hammered steel of Scythia").

738 Cf. the chorus's argument at 680–82. Eteocles saves his city, which is not to say that his primary purpose is to save the city, and by their mutual deaths the brothers appease the Curse and Fury. But do they, in spite of these gains for the public, leave a pollution on the land? As we have it, the end of the play does not really offer a satisfactory answer, unless we are ready to accept such anxieties as are expressed here for certain future fact.

742–49 "Trespasses" (**sin**) captures the Greek idea of overstepping boundaries, in this case the interdiction of Apollo. For **Navel-of-Earth** see on *Eum* 39 ff. The paradox for Laius, enforced by the action of the entire trilogy, is that a king may save his city only if he has no sons to succeed himself. In the epic cycle Eteocles and Polyneices had sons who, in the next generation, renewed their fathers' rivalry.

750–57 Euripides' Jocasta offers the familiar version of Laius' folly:

> But Laius, in his lust, and drunk besides,
> begot a child on me.
>> (*Phoenician Women* 21 f.)

Here, however, **loving** may be more erotic than the Greek will bear; perhaps "mastered by his own folly." See on 584 f. Lines 754 f. might also be translated:

> where he was nurtured
> and endured the bloody root.

Sophocles calls the womb "this field of double sowing" (*Oedipus the King* 1257). Harvest imagery also occurs at 618, 696, 718.

758–67 For the imagery of the ship at sea see on 1–3.

767–72 Settlement is a commercial term for exchange or

profit in a business transaction. See the note on "heritage" at
711 ("possessions" at 729b = "heritage" at 711). In the next
sentence Bücheler's emendation would continue this language
and give us: "Evils pass by the poor." For **prosperity** see
notes on *Ag* 928 and *Pers* 163. Cf. the imagery at *Suppl*
615–21 (note). Here the imagery of the preceding stanza returns in **compels jettisoning** (cf. *Ag* 1009 ff.).

773–78 On the honor Oedipus won for saving the city
from the Sphinx see *Oedipus the King* 33–39. The **Sphinx** is
here identified as the *kēr*, the daimon of death (see on *Ag* 206).

782–91 For the blinding of Oedipus see *Oedipus the King*
1268 ff., 1372 ff. The **maledictions** are the curses. The theme
of **tendance** was traditional and remains a primary theme in
the *Oedipus at Colonus*, but we do not know what specific
fault occurred in the Aeschylean version. In the epic poem
Thebaïs it was said that Polyneices put a golden cup which had
belonged to Laius on Oedipus' table, and "immediately he
was angry and cursed both sons" (i.e., they had violated his
interdiction of all things pertaining to Laius); or they gave
him a portion of food he had forbidden or a less honorable
portion than was his right (this is the explanation offered by
the scholiast on *Oedipus at Colonus* 1375); or he cursed the day
they were born (the word for "tendance" may refer to the
rearing of his sons). What for us is allusive and obscure must
have been clear to the Greek audience from Aeschylus' *Oedipus* play or from their knowledge of the epic poems on Thebes.
As Winnington-Ingram observes, references to wealth, here
in **possessions,** pervade this lyric. If Oedipus cursed his sons
for stinting his portion, a curse that condemned them to perish for their greed would have a nice point. As usual, the
Greek leaves the possessions unmodified by the possessive, so
his own is interpretative. With **nimble-footed** compare the
imagery at *Eum* 372–76 (note). At *Ajax* 837 the Furies "come
with long strides," and Teiresias speaks of the "deadly footed
curse" (*Oedipus the King* 418). Here, as at *LB* 651, **Fury** is the
last word in the Greek lyric.

792–802 The messenger's report is brief, perhaps because
the lengthy descriptions in the central scene are a kind of
battle report in their own right. Virtually every line of this

speech echoes at least one earlier passage in the play. For example, for **yoke of slavery** see 471; for **trustworthy** see 398.

800 Aeschylus has adapted an epithet meaning "born on the seventh" (Apollo's birthday) to seven-gated Thebes. Pythagoreans in the audience may have thought of their association of seven with the "opportune" (*kairos*), especially if they recalled that word from the first line of the play, where it is translated "speak home."

803–20 The lines in this section have been shuffled variously by the editors.

804 Twin might also be translated "sown in the same place," which directs us to the agricultural metaphors so frequent in the play. On the motif of shared blood see 416, 681, 940.

816–20 He refers to the guiding spirit (*daimōn*). With 819–19b cf. 729 ff., a nice example of thematic considerations overriding any interest in characterizing the speaker. With **down the wind** cf. 690 and 854.

821–31 Cf. the prayer at 109b. **Cry aloud** = "cry of sacrifice" at 269a. On **city's safety** see the note at 738 and cf. 844 f. With **childless** cf. the apparent contradiction at 902. The dramatists seem to have preferred to end the line of the Labdacids with the sons of Oedipus, even though the tradition gave both men sons (see the note to 742–49). See on *Antigone* 174. With **men of strife** cf. the naming at 578, 641, 658, and *Antigone* 110. The pun is on *Polyneikēs*, and *neikos* ("strife").

835–39a Haldane (p. 37) takes these lines to refer to the song at 720 ff., which turned out ill-omened because in something like the ecstatic frenzy of a **Bacchanal** they accurately predicted the brothers' death. On this interpretation 835 might be translated: "I raised the dirge for a tomb."

842 With **wanting in faith** cf. the "folly" of 750 and 802. The phrase means that Laius did not trust the oracles, which had told him not to have children.

844 f. These lines may reflect concern for the future or the present. Despite relief that the city is saved (804, 825), they may still feel some anxiety about any residual pollution or daimonic anger (680–82, 734–41), as well as some ambivalence that their own survival should have been at the price of Eteocles' life.

854–60 A metaphor from sailing likens the rhythm of the hands beating in mourning to the **speeding stroke** of oars. The ship will cross the Acheron (**through death's waters**) to Hades, visited by all save **Apollo** and the **sun.**

861–1078 From this point to the end of the play various passages, particularly 861–74 and 1005–78, have been condemned as interpolations from a later production. Most scholars agree (1) that the addition of Antigone and Ismene is the work of a later production, probably one subsequent to Sophocles' *Antigone*; (2) that in adding to and extending Aeschylus' play a conflation of at least two productions emerged, so that (3) Aeschylean and spurious lines are in some sections inextricably interwoven, and (4) much of what was added was from a writer who had mastered Aeschylus' style and thought.

Much of the argument against the authenticity of the final scene derives from an unwillingness to believe that Aeschylus ended the play by introducing the unresolved problem of the burial of Polyneices. The present conclusion not only leaves an open-ended plot but also, and perhaps more to the point, introduces characters and a theme that are never anticipated in the first three-fourths of the *Seven*.

862 Ismene and **Antigone** are the daughters of Oedipus; see the prologue of the *Antigone*. Nothing earlier in the play anticipates their appearance, but as members of the family they are proper to the lament. A dirge ends the *Persians*, shares space with argument at the end of the *Agamemnon*, and contributes to the kommos of the *Libation Bearers*.

868–70 If they do sing **before their song,** then it would seem reasonable to give the chorus 875–960, as the manuscripts do. On the other hand, that is a long time for the girls to stand idle, especially after this introduction. The **Hades' paean** is the victory song of Hades.

872 Those who find stylistic faults in this last scene naturally condemn this bloated phrase as un-Aeschylean.

875–960 The distribution of the parts in the manuscripts seems to have no value. Some editors attribute the two roles to semichoruses, others to the chorus and the two girls, others to a full chorus, with the semichoruses taking some sections. Putting aside the question of authenticity, it seems pointless to hold the girls as silent spectators for a hundred lines. If we are going to stage the scene with them entering at 861, then some portion of the lament should be theirs.

The lament is typical (see the end of the *Persians*) for its frequent repetitions, anaphora, parallelism, strong assonance and alliteration, and recapitulation of themes and motifs.

880 There are other references to the **ruin of the house** at 877, 882, 894, 914.

886 The **Curse** and the **Fury** also appear at 892, 896, 946, 954. The Fury came last at 791, following the curses ("savage maledictions") of 785 f.

888 The spearman normally holds his shield with his left hand, thus protecting his left side. Tucker suggests that these unnatural wounds may carry "an implied antithesis to the usual manner of reconciliation," i.e., with the right hands clasped.

890–93 Common echoes the motif of blood brothers (see 681) and is continued at 931 f. and 940. All these words underscore verbally the idea of "sameness." Allied to this motif is the idea of reciprocity, as in **answered;** cf. "reconciled" (884), which is echoed in "arbitrator" (909a) and "shared" (907).

902 If **descendants** refers to their sons, it contradicts "childless" at 826. Several editors are willing to accept something more vague, like Dawson's "their goods await followers."

907 f. Both **shared** and **possessions** keep us in touch with Oedipus' curse (788 f.), and **shared** (913 and 948 as well) is also one of the words for "drawing lots" (e.g., 56 and 691). Later allusions to the curse/prophecy occur at 913, 941, 945.

922 Here and elsewhere in this scene those who lament discriminate very little between the two dead warriors. Such an attitude, which disregards Polyneices' moral and civic failings, would be most natural to the girls. Cf. 924, 931, the neutral reference to **enmity** at 936, and 971–72.

941 f. Cf. 729 ff. The Chalybian would come from **over the sea.**

956 The personified **Destruction** (*atē*) has, in the Greek

fashion, left a monument at the gates where she achieved her
victory. At 688 f. the word *atē* occurs in "frantic lust for
battle," at 315 in "ruin," and as "doom" at 601 and 1003.

961–1004 with the exception of the refrains (977 ff.,
988 ff.), this section is composed of paired half-lines, with
each sister, or semichorus, taking up the lament for one of the
two brothers. Hence the repetitions and parallelism, which,
since it is occasionally broken, has been thought to have suffered a loss of one or more lines. The lines are sung and are
mostly in free iambics.

971 f. Loving does not seem satisfactory for the Greek
philos, which denotes the circle of intimacy defined by the
family and those dependent upon it. "When, however, the
tragic event occurs *within the sphere of the natural affections*—
when, for instance, a brother kills or is on the point of killing
his brother, or a son his father, or a mother her son, or a son
his mother, or something equally drastic is done—that is the
kind of event a poet must try for" (Aristotle, *Poetics*, chap. 14;
Hutton's translation, my italics).

989–92 As these lines stand, they look like a variant on
"suffering and learning" (*Ag* 176–78), but **lesson** more naturally refers to **Fury** and, taken with 991 (of Polyneices), may
mean "when you returned to the city you came to know the
Fury from (in) your passage."

1004 If we follow the Oxford texts in putting 1003 ("O
brothers . . .") after 1000, the question of burial coheres in the
climactic three lines leading to the herald. This last line then
calls their burial "a pain sleeping by their father"; the metaphor inevitably recalls the incestuous bed of Oedipus.

1005 ff. For the girls, all is forgiven; for the herald and the
state, vengeance pursues Polyneices to deny him the burial all
Greeks thought necessary if the dead were to have a peaceful
passage to the underworld. Denial of burial begins in extant
literature with Achilles' mutilation of Hector's body (*Iliad* 22.
395 ff.). Finally the gods require Achilles to give up the body
for burial. Sophocles incorporates this theme in both the *Ajax*
and the *Antigone*, and it is this last play (produced perhaps in
442) that is thought to have influenced the revision and interpolation at the end of the *Seven*. With the sentiments of the
herald cf. Creon's edict at *Antigone* 192 ff.

1006 Grene would apparently bring **counselors** onstage. It is easier and more likely to assume that the herald declares "the resolves and present pleasure *of* the counselors of the people."

1011 Young men die honorably in the front line of battle.

1015 Since *Iliad* 1. 4–5 it has been the fate of the unburied to be torn apart by **dogs** and birds of prey (1021). Cf. *Antigone* 207.

1018 Guilt connotes anything polluted and accursed, thus devoted to the world below, and not purified.

1026 The prominence of the **I** (in the Greek text it is the first word in lines 1026 and 1028) is very much in the manner of Sophocles' Antigone (cf., e.g., *Antigone* 31). Both characters base their arguments on claims of religion and kinship.

1031 ff. Perhaps she turns away in a monologue. I assume that 1034 means that Polyneices, in her view, would not require such a sacrifice of her.

1039 f. If we take 1039 literally, she plans a real burial, not the symbolic rite found in Sophocles. On the other hand, she cannot **carry** enough **earth** (no object for "carry" occurs in the Greek) to accomplish burial.

1044 Thebes seems to have become a democracy after the fall of eagles.

1047 The sentiment is like that at *Antigone* 455 ff., but this corrupt line is not much use for evidence.

1051 Contention (*Eris*) is a "demon" at *Ag* 1460; she has a long Homeric and Hesiodic pedigree.

1054 ff. Chanting in anapests, the chorus now divides and exits, a semichorus to either side. The atmosphere is anxious and hostile, with a lack of resolution hardly to be expected at the end of a trilogy.

1055 Fatal Furies equates the *Kēres* and the *Erinyes* (see on 777 and on *Ag* 206).

1060 This is in the spirit of Sophocles' Ismene, who fears not the people but Creon.

1071 f. The last sentence means that, while grief always unites a family, the city will sometimes have one view of justice, sometimes another.

Prometheus Bound

THIS PLAY IS PROBABLY the first in a trilogy. Titles of two other plays, *Prometheus Unbound* and *Prometheus the Fire-Bearer*, along with fragments of the former, suggest the outlines of the plot, at least until the freeing of Prometheus. In the second play, *Prometheus Unbound*, Prometheus remains bound to the rock, where, every third day, an eagle comes to feast on his liver. A chorus of Titans, now released from their prison in Tartarus, consoles him. Earth probably also appears, and Heracles certainly does. It would appear that this drama was also fairly static, with more monologue by Prometheus than decisive action, at least until Heracles kills the eagle and frees Prometheus. Of *Prometheus the Fire-Bearer* we know so little that it is still disputed whether it was the first or third play in the trilogy—if we have a trilogy. Those who think that it is the first play argue that the title inevitably suggests the theft of fire. We hear of this in *Prometheus Bound*, but there is little in our play that requires the theft as a preceding action, and it therefore seems likely that the *Fire-Bearer* was the final play and celebrated the reconciliation of Zeus and Prometheus and the founding of the torch race and festival honoring Prometheus at Athens. The title, then, would refer to these ceremonies rather than to the theft of fire. Conacher's discussion (pp. 98–119) treats the evidence in detail.

The pre-Aeschylean sources are Hesiod's *Works and Days* 42–105 and *Theogony* 507–616. An interesting interpretation for anthropologists and philosophers can be found in Plato's *Protagoras* 320c–323a. Cf. Euripides, *Suppliant Women* 201–15. Prometheus appears as a figure of burlesque in Aristophanes' *Birds* 1494–1552.

As Grene's introduction to his translation makes clear, this play has been controversial. Aeschylus had from the Hesiodic tradition a typical trickster hero, similar to the Scandinavian Loki. This character, already a serious figure in Hesiod, becomes in *Prometheus Bound* the archetypal rebel, "an eternal martyr, chained to a pillar, at the ends of the earth, condemned forever because he refuses to ask forgiveness" (Camus, *The Rebel*, p. 26 of the Vintage paperback edition). Unlike Loki, he is essentially identified with humanity, even though he is a god; not a little of his interest, in fact, stems from this ambiguous divine/human aspect. The controversy in recent times has derived not so much from the nature of Promethean symbolism as from the structure of the play and from the question of Aeschylean authorship. Grene notes its unpopularity with eighteenth-century critics; but more recent scholars, less tied to Aristotle and more sensitive to Aeschylean practice in the other extant dramas, have found it equally unworthy of the poet, not because it lacks unity—that topic is debated— but because its dramatic techniques differ in so many ways from those of the other plays. Other studies, most notably Griffith's, have extended the question of authenticity to meter, prosody, diction, and style, with the result that we are now much better placed to look objectively at *Prometheus Bound* not only in the context of Aeschylus' other plays but in that of the whole of fifth-century drama. The upshot of these studies offers a nice paradox, for this most popular and influential of Aeschylean plays seems now more than ever less likely to be the work of Aeschylus. There is no proof of this contention, and there probably never will be.

My notes tend to emphasize problematic elements, differences in dramatic technique, difficulties in staging, and other "negative" factors, all of which have little to do with the kind of reading that Grene, Camus, and a host of other modern interpretations offer. Since the two approaches differ in kind, they are not necessarily incompatible, and it may even be argued that some aspects of the play's uniqueness have contributed to its profound appeal for modern readers.

The scene is the eastern edge of the world, and several references to cliffs and heights (4, 15, 159a, etc.) have led some commentators to assume that a scaffolding was erected onstage to represent the "wintry cliff." Others, convinced that the play's imagery is meant to evoke a landscape more symbolic than real, are content with a post against which Prometheus is pinned (64 f.). In a play so symbolic, this seems the better idea. Might, Violence, Hephaestus, and Prometheus are present at the crag at the beginning; i.e., there is no indication that they walk on talking (cf. the beginning of Sophocles' *Philoctetes*). So they simply come on, take their places, and then begin the scene. Personified powers like Might and Violence are simply attributes of Zeus (*Theogony* 385–88), and their masks and costumes ought to be less human than those of Hephaestus, the god of the fire and forge, who was associated in Athenian cult with Prometheus. Prometheus accompanies them but remains silent until they leave. Dialogue in a prologue is not common (it occurs only in *Rhesus*, *Iphigenia in Aulis*, *Ajax*, *Antigone*, *Philoctetes*), and no play brings more characters and speaking parts on for the first scene.

The entire Greek text is in the usual poetic meters. The translator's decision to render some passages in prose does not reflect a comparable stylistic distinction in the original.

1 Several variations on the idea of **limit** will be found in the play. Cf. the "earth's end" (117), the limits to Io's wanderings (622 and 822), the limits of suffering (99c), the limits imposed by kinship, as in the case of Hephaestus and Oceanos, and especially in the term defined for Prometheus' suffering (186 and 1026), with its implicit limit on the power of Zeus (518). The "*Caucasus*" is not specified here and would be less remote for the Greek audience than desolate **Scythia.**

3 Since "**Father** of gods and men" is a traditional title for Zeus, some critics will not see irony in such language (Might is a nasty thug). Cf. 17, 40, 948, 1019. In the Greek word translated as **malefactor** the Athenian audience may have heard a (false) etymology, "he who works for the people."

5 That Prometheus stole **fire** and gave it to man is known from Hesiod (*Works and Days* 50 ff.). See 254 ff. As the god of fire, Hephaestus might be expected to denounce this theft most strongly, but he has only pity for the fallen Titan.

6 Sin (*hamartia*) means "error" or "mistake." Cf. the cognate verbal forms: "erred" at 262 and 263, "transgressed" at 269, "fault" at 578, and "in error" at 1039. Prometheus has struck at divine power, but he has not violated a moral or religious sanction. See on *Ag* 1194.

11 Sovereignty means "tyranny." Cf. 227 f., 309, 359a. Hatred of tyranny is a commonplace; tyranny is associated with *hybris*, malice, and irresponsibility (cf. 736 ff., Herodotus 3. 80, and Euripides' *Suppliants* 426 ff.).

12–17 Hephaestus' recognition of kinship with Prometheus points more to sympathy than to any close family tie. Cf. 39. They are related by common descent from Uranos (207), the great-grandfather of Hephaestus, the grandfather of Prometheus, and the simple difference in generations might have been sufficient to make them enemies, as we see from 201 ff. But Aeschylus clearly intends Prometheus to be an object of pity (35, 42, 66–68, 145–48, 240–44, etc.). Force (**constraint;** for the Greek *anagkē* see on 513 f.) subverts pity. See Vickers, pp. 70–76.

18 Hephaestus addresses Prometheus; for **Themis** see on 211.

26 He that shall cause it to cease is Heracles, an unconscious prophecy on Hephaestus' part, since he cannot imagine escape from these chains. Such allusions and anticipations are frequent: 99a ff., 169 f., 518 f., 871 f. (of Heracles).

28 Man-loving disposition repeats the phrase used at 11; cf. 123.

29 f. Power rather than justice is the issue, as the repeated references to **honors,** privileges (37, 82, 109), and various forms of physical coercion imply. Here **just** (*dikē*) may mean, euphemistically, "the usual or proper way."

34 That **new rule** is harsh may be more than a commonplace if, in the course of the trilogy, Zeus's severity was softened. Long (p. 234) points out how frequently forms for "new" occur: 97, 149 f., 235, 955–56. Cf. *Antigone* 154 ff.

39 Regard for **kinship** also motivates Oceanos (291). Later in the play the theme is varied with an account of the line of descent from Zeus to Heracles, who is destined to free Prometheus.

From line 39 through 81 the Greek text alternates one line (Hephaestus) with two lines (Might).

49 f. Even Zeus is not so **free** as Might imagines; see 514 ff. Cf. *Eum* 339 f. The gods are usually said to live a happy, painless life (the "Blessed Ones," 98), so Hephaestus' rejection of his own craft and his grief for Prometheus, like Prometheus' suffering, contradict a common distinction between man and god. In a similar way the theft of divine fire confuses the boundaries between the divine and human orders by transferring an immortal power to mortals.

54 Fetters are "the chain which connects the bit with the guiding rein" (Thomson). "Nail" at 3 and 618 also means "to break in (a horse)." More equestrian imagery at 61 ("nail"), 70, 74. Prometheus is treated like an animal ("yoked" at 109a). Cf. 1010 ff. Besides these shackles, a wedge is driven through his chest (64 f.). It would be a mistake to strive for realistic staging in this chaining of the god.

58 f. Like Odysseus, Sisyphus, and Autolycus, Prometheus has the reputation for being a trickster.

61 With **learn,** Might continues to mock the hero who has taught mankind survival (440 ff.). For "teaching" see 111, 196, 325, 376, 633.

71 Here and at 329a we seem to have allusions to the Delphic admonition "Nothing in excess." See on *Suppl* 1060–62.

75 f. For other titles of Zeus cf. 96 and 170. **Overseer** means "assessor of penalties."

81 Though the Greek translated here as **harness** is not a technical term for gear for an animal, in a general way it continues the imagery discussed at 54.

82–86 Play the insolent translates the verbal form of *hybris*. Anyone who insults or attacks another person is guilty of *hybris* in the latter's eyes. So Hesiod calls Typhon, the monstrous antagonist of Zeus, a *hybristēs* (one who commits *hybris*). Cf. Prometheus on Hermes at 970. The Greek word for **creatures of a day** gives us the English word "ephemeral." It also occurs at 253 (untranslated), 549, 947. The Greeks took Prometheus' name to mean **Forethought,** while that of his brother Epimetheus was taken to mean Afterthought. **Contrivance** translates *technē* (English "technical"), which is translated elsewhere as "craft" (46, 111, 256, 476, 496), the meaning that Might turns against him here, with a sneer.

87 ff. Useful studies of Greek tragedy have described Prometheus as represented onstage by a mute puppet. There is little persuasive evidence for this view, which apparently arose from questions about the chaining of the god and from the belief that the play has only two actors. On this view, the actor who played Hephaestus would speak Prometheus' part from offstage. Most recent critics believe that Prometheus is played by a third actor.

The position of this soliloquy is unique in Aeschylus; the other two that he wrote open the *Agamemnon* and the *Eumenides*. It is also unique in that the iambic speech switches to anapests at 93–100 and again at 120–27; there are also two lines in lyric meter (115 and 117), which should indicate song.

"Often in tragedy a character under stress of some strong emotion calls on the elements and declares that emotion to them, or calls them to witness what is happening" (Barrett on *Hippolytus* 601). For the apostrophe to **sun** and **earth** see Euripides' *Electra* 866–67, Sophocles' *Electra* 86–87, and cf. *Philoctetes* 936 ff.

93 Torture connotes insulting and outrageous treatment. Variants on this idea occur at 178 ("what I suffer"), 197 ("punished"), and 989 ("torture").

100–104 Prometheus knows both past (589 ff., 825 ff.) and future (702 ff., 771 ff.) but remains allusive and riddling for a time, only slowly revealing the power of his knowledge. Cf. his stalling at 520. The present allusions to **fate** and **destiny** are amplified at 511–18.

109b According to Hesiod's *Theogony* (561 ff.), Zeus withheld fire from man after Prometheus had tricked him into taking the lesser portion of man's sacrifice (Zeus chose the bones wrapped in fat). "But the noble son of Iapetus outwitted him and stole the far-seen gleam of unwearying fire in a hollow fennel stalk. And Zeus who thunders on high was stung in spirit, and his dear heart was angered when he saw amongst men the far-seen ray of fire" (trans. Evelyn-White, lines 565–69).

As for the **narthex stem,** Sikes and Willson explain (Introduction, p. xvi): "This plant . . . has a stalk, the pith of which, when lighted, will smoulder for some time. It was thus useful as a means of keeping fire alight in days when the kindling of it was a laborious process." ("Narthex" and "fennel" are two names for the same plant.)

115–27 In **sightless smell** the adjective has been transferred from person to scent. Apparently he does not see them until they speak.

Prometheus' description of the chorus, together with their remarks on their mode of arrival, poses problems of staging. Disagreement rests in part on how literally we should take the text or, to put it another way, on how much such descriptions as we have were intended to evoke imaginative response from the audience. Since it is difficult to find a dramatic function for an elaborately costumed chorus, some critics argue that the references to **strokes of wings** do not point to actual staging so much as they figuratively evoke the exotic origin and nature of the Oceanids. Others, seeing Aeschylean theater in more baroque terms, find not only elaborate costuming but a descent from cranes (thus satisfying the text's **chariot of wings,** 137). A second cause of disagreement enters here, for since we know so little of the fifth-century theater in any case and, more particularly, cannot be sure of the date for the *Prometheus Bound*, there is little way of knowing what facilities were available. If the play is Aeschylean, an elaborate staging, with one or more cranes transporting the chorus individually or as a group (?), seems very unlikely. More than that, the text clearly indicates that the chorus remains in its "chariot" through the parodos, until Prometheus invites them to "alight" (276), a request they explicitly assent to (281 f.). Archeologically, the simplest solution is to suppose that they enter on a wagon or cart. Such an entry is less grand than flying in on cranes, whether to the orchestra or to the top of the stage building, but it has the merit of being possible. A compromise between cranes and wagons would have them appear first on the top of the stage building; from here they would then descend, after the parodos (this is Pickard-Cambridge's view). If they are in a cart or on the roof, they cannot dance; for this reason Thomson suggests that they enter on foot, "pretending to fly in a dance." But this simplicity contradicts 276–82. Conacher (pp. 182–85) covers these problems in more detail.

127–28 The tie between **for fear** and **fear not** strikes me as implying smart timing, but Taplin (p. 251) argues, to the contrary, that they are there and have been present long enough to hear the announcement.

The chorus immediately begins its responsive lyrics, which are interspersed with Prometheus' anapests, a unique structure for a parodos in Aeschylus.

130 Rivalry lends support to the view that the chorus appears one by one.

131 Their **father** is Oceanos (140), their mother Tethys

(138). When Oceanos appears (285), he takes no notice of these daughters, nor they of him. Oceanos and Tethys are children of Earth and Sky (Uranos, 167) and so belong to the generation of the Titans, but they are not involved in the war of succession, perhaps because Oceanos is so closely identified with the waters circling the world (Hesiod, *Theogony* 787 ff.).

144 Paradox and contradiction characterize Prometheus throughout the play. The gods are always happy and blessed, but he is "wretched" (120). The condition of the gods naturally inspires **envy,** but his does not.

149 For the metaphor in **steersman** see *Sev* 62 and below, 515.

151–55 Brings to nothingness means "to make unseen," which naturally calls to mind the fate of the Titans, whom Zeus cast into **Tartarus**—probably a synonym for Hades—after he had defeated their rebellion.

158 ff. From Homer through tragedy, the laughter of one's enemies motivates grief and revenge. Cf. *LB* 222 and *Eum* 788 f.

168 ff. It is well known that a tyrant is never satisfied. So the alternative is in effect a leading question: "What **device of subtlety** will you use to take the rule from him?" It is not a trick this time, however, but secret knowledge that will provide the leverage.

171–78 Kronos deposed Uranos, Zeus deposed Kronos; in each case the youngest son had succeeded the old king, and in the early Greek view there was no intrinsic reason why this process should not continue. (See on 201 ff.) Hesiod can imagine Zeus falling before a son yet unborn, and so he tells how Zeus swallows Metis (Thought) before she can bear that son (*Theogony* 886 ff.).

180 ff. So the chorus does not respond with surprise to these threats, in which they may find more bitter exaggeration on a familiar theme than prophetic clarity. They are sympathetic but critical, realizing that Prometheus has freely taken the course of daring (cf. 236).

186 f. More imagery from sailing and the sea occurs at 745, 965, 1016. Cf. *Suppl* 806 f. (note).

194 f. To speak of eventual **amity and union** seems to contradict line 178. By the end of the trilogy Zeus may have abandoned the savage and personal justice (189b f.) of this new rule for a policy of reconciliation such as we find in Hesiod's *Theogony*. Theological critics like to talk about Zeus's evolution into the deity whose daughter will be Justice.

196 One reason the play has been called static is that so much of it is description of past and future. Here the chorus prompts the first major exposition.

201 ff. As told by Hesiod, the succession of rule (Uranos, Kronos, Zeus) passes in three generations from brutally repressive power to the more intelligent management of Zeus. **Kronos** (= Cronus) castrates his father Uranos and then swallows all his children until Rhea, his wife, tricks him by offering a stone in place of the baby, Zeus. Zeus, when he reaches manhood, frees his brothers and sisters (the Olympians) from the stomach of Kronos and then proceeds to wage a ten-year war for the throne of Kronos. In Hesiod's account the secret of victory is known by Earth, not Prometheus, and she gives it to Zeus (he frees three giants whose aid is instrumental in his ultimate triumph). So in Hesiod's version the intelligence and management of Zeus not only win the day but also bring a more benign rule to the world. Aeschylus has taken the motif of the secret—here simply that guile will triumph over force—and attributed it to Prometheus, who has it from Earth. Thus Zeus is in the debt of Prometheus, but, at the same time, Prometheus has turned his back on his own generation, the Titans, becoming a rebel without a party. Presumably he would have enjoyed the favor of Zeus had he not taken up the cause of mankind against the plan of Zeus (233 ff.).

204–10 Thomson, comparing 955 ff., says the point of **the fools** is that "Zeus will not reign for long." The contrast is between persuasion (**to win**) and guile, on the one hand, and arrogance and violence, on the other. No particular trick or specific knowledge is mentioned (213 f.), which has the effect of making knowledge itself the crucial weapon.

211 For **Themis** see *Eum* 2–4 and *Suppl* 359–64. According to Hesiod, Prometheus is the son of Clymene and Iapetus, both minor figures. In making Prometheus the son of Earth/Themis, Aeschylus enhances the prestige of his parentage and explains his visionary power, since Hesiod had already made

Earth a primeval prophetic power who "devises a guileful, harmful trick" (*Theogony* 160) against the oppressive Uranos.

216 The kind of wordplay managed by Grene in **conquerors to conquer** is extremely common in this play. Cf. "hastily . . . haste" (193 f.) and "God . . . Gods" (29), both of which are formed by the inflection and juxtaposition of the same verb and noun forms. Such play is very easy in Greek, and some readers have found it more facile than forceful in this play. The author probably saw this figure—it is called "polyptoton" by the rhetoricians—as a verbal analogue to the opposition and reciprocity in the play's themes. Zeus and Prometheus have more than a little in common, for all their differences. Other examples occur at 386 and 905 f.

217 Guile (*dolos*) is several times emphasized as the craft (*technē*) of Prometheus in the *Theogony* (e.g., 540, 547, 555), but the word occurs only here in the *PB*; see, however, 169a, 171, and 310. Perhaps its absence can be explained by its tainted associations with such devious tricksters as Hermes and Sisyphus, whereas Aeschylus wanted a more magnanimous, humanely motivated character.

223–24 For their fate see *Iliad* 8. 477–81 and *Theogony* 716 ff.

227 Fowler (*AJP*) takes the metaphors from medicine to be the dominating imagery of the play. See examples at 251, 379–82, 386, 580, 605 ff., 1070. She points out that Alcmaeon of Croton, a contemporary of Aeschylus', maintained that "the bond of health is the 'equal balance' of the powers, moist and dry, cold and hot, bitter and sweet, and the rest, while the 'supremacy' of one is the cause of disease" (trans. Kirk and Raven, Frag. 286). In a similar vein, the Pythagoreans defined health as "harmony." In Fowler's view this kind of medical theory is reflected in the *Prometheus Bound* through ideas of proportion, order, symmetry, and their opposites.

231–35 The assignment of **privileges** is derived from *Theogony* 73 f.; but **to blot the race** of mankind out is not Hesiodic, unless we can find it, allusively, in *Theogony* 551 f. and in the end of the silver age in *Works and Days* 138 f.

240–44 Pitiful sights and appeals to **pity** are not uncommon in tragedy—Aristotle could have found all the pity and fear he wanted in Aeschylus. See on 12–17. Here Prometheus' complaint culminates in an idea strange to archaic Greek literature, namely, that the spectacle of suffering **dishonors** the victor.

245 Iron-Minded and made of stone are derived from passages like *Iliad* 24. 205 and 16. 33–35.

250–52 Doom means "death." **Foreseeing** suggests "glancing at," "catching sight of," as if from some anxiety. Man did not cease to know that he was mortal; rather, he ceased working and thinking like one whose efforts are doomed to be ephemeral (the sense of "men" at 253). Man will strive only so long as he has **hope,** which is **blind** because he is ultimately doomed by his mortality. Hope is all that remains in Pandora's jar after all the evils have escaped into the world (*Works and Days* 96). Cf. the choral comment at 261. Aeschylus has a number of variations on "blind hopes": *Pers* 804, *Ag* 1668, *LB* 698.

265 f. The **foot outside of calamity** is related to metaphors from travel, since "keeping on the straight path" and "not stumbling" are common expressions for success.

268–70 For **transgressed** see on line 6. **I knew** signifies the voluntary character of the action. What does this "confession" mean? Gagarin (p. 134): "The *dikē* on Zeus' side is the result of Prometheus' theft of fire, which even he admits was an error." Sikes and Willson: "Prometheus is far from confessing himself in the wrong; he merely admits having transgressed the laws of conventional orthodoxy." Lattimore (*Poetry of Greek Tragedy*, p. 53): "Prometheus claimed omniscience, but it lapsed, or he acted mistakenly (*hamartia*) despite it. This is the agony of the intelligent *man*, his self-fury when his intelligence fails him." Verdenius cites Lesky's view that the emphasis carries a sarcastic reference to the point of view taken by Zeus, not an objective fault at all. Sarcasm certainly seems right for 265 ff., and it will be his chief weapon against Oceanos and Hermes. Bitterness we may allow him without jeopardizing the pity due him; but if he sneers and jeers, the audience may be less sympathetic. Cf. 300 ff., 332 ff., and his taunts at Hermes at 941 f. and 954 ff. Note that his tone does not alienate the chorus, which comes to sympathize, yet is not uncritical (180 ff.), and finally stays to suffer with him.

However we define this error, we cannot call it recantation or contrition and so hardly an admission of "sin," since all these would imply submission to the will of Zeus, which in fact we never find in the play. Perhaps he erred—if we need an objective mistake—only in guessing the quality (**such tortures**) of his certain suffering.

274 For the problems attached to **alight on earth** see the note on 115.

276–78 Thomson suggests that the metaphor is drawn from the flight of a bird or bee. Wandering is a prominent motif in the story of Io and one of the links between her and Prometheus; see 472 f., 564, 577, 623, 820.

281–84 See on 115. It is hard to believe, with Thomson, that these lines signify no more than leaving a raised central altar for the orchestra. Do the Oceanids leave the orchestra? Oceanos takes no notice of them, nor does Prometheus, in the following scene. If, as Pickard-Cambridge suggests, they descend from the roof of the stage building, they may linger backstage long enough for the interview to pass. But we should take account of Taplin's complaint that such unmotivated exits and unnoticed (re)entries are extremely rare. Taplin puts the right sort of question: What is the dramatic purpose of taking the chorus off? If they remain, why are they unnoticed? This last is a particularly pointed question, since Aeschylean characters have a way of speaking to the chorus even before addressing other characters onstage.

285 ff. Both in his first speech and in his last (395 ff.) Oceanos calls our attention to the bird that carries him. While he may have mimed a flying entrance, the language certainly encourages us to think that here Aeschylus may have used a crane. If Oceanos is hoisted onto the stage, the entrance would be both spectacular and consistent with the "four-legged bird" (395 f.) he glories in. Thomson speaks of a "wooden object on wheels," but that tempts one to think of a hobby horse and the dangers of unintended burlesque. Cf. the way Athene announces her own arrival at *Eum* 397 ff.

292 For Oceanos see on 131. As for his **kinship,** in Hesiod's genealogy Oceanos is both uncle (as brother of Iapetus) and grandfather (as father of Clymene) to Prometheus. Cf. 12–17 and 39.

300 In his article on the play (*CP* 35:22–38) Grene describes this speech as "pure sarcasm." Prometheus is certainly ambivalent about company, at once desiring sympathy and yet, from shame, fearing derision.

303 Iron-mother because the region was famous for its ironworking. Cf. 715.

304 Self-established means "natural." For Oceanos to **leave the stream** named after him means that he must differentiate himself from his natural function as the boundary of the world and source of all water. Cf. *Iliad* 20. 5 ff.

310 Cleverness translates a word from Hesiod (*Theogony* 511), but **Know yourself** is one of the two famous admonitions of the Delphic Apollo (cf. on 71).

319a. Old and commonplace is a strange attitude toward the past for any Aeschylean character, and Griffith (p. 219) takes the meaning here as characteristic of later, sophistic attitudes. Griffith (p. 196) also marks the contrast at 339a between words and deeds (cf. 1080) as more at home in the second half of the century. He compares *Alcestis* 339 for the earliest expression of what was to become a conventional contrast, but he also notes *Sev* 849, where the contrast is at least implicit. Cf. the note on *Sev* 554–58.

In urging that Prometheus yield to misfortune Oceanos anticipates a line of characters who serve as foils, from Ismene (*Antigone*) and Tecmessa (*Ajax*) to the temporizing Cadmus (*Bacchae*).

325–33 There is a nice irony in taking Oceanos for **schoolmaster** (see on 61). **Kick against the pricks** is proverbial; see *Ag* 1624 and cf. 597, below. For the metaphor in **auditing accounts** see on *Pers* 212 f. There is a pedantic smugness in this passage that might well invite a tart, sarcastic reply, though Sikes and Willson describe Prometheus as speaking "courteously, if somewhat wearily" (they find no irony until 343). Yet **shared and dared in everything** is not literally true, and unless we emend the line, as several editors have, we must assume that a tone of irony or sarcasm explains the untruth.

347–50 The *tychē* stem (**unlucky . . . fortunes;** cf. 107) appears three times in the four lines, very emphatic for the foreknowing Titan. Cf. on 377. **Atlas,** Prometheus' brother, also described at 425 ff., gave his name to the Atlas Mountains of northern Africa:

> [he] has discovered
> all the depths of the sea, and himself sustains the towering
> columns which bracket earth and sky and hold them
>   together.

(*Odyssey* I. 52–54)

Cf. Hesiod, *Theogony* 517–20, who makes Atlas support the heavens but not the earth as well.

355–74 Pitying **Typho** is no mean feat. At *Theogony* 820 ff. this dragon battles Zeus—this follows the defeat of the Titans—in an encounter that clinches Zeus's victory over the forces of darkness. In describing Typho, Hesiod says that

> from his shoulders
> there grew a hundred snake heads,
>   those of a dreaded dragon,
> and the heads licked with dark tongues,
>   and from the eyes on
> the inhuman heads fire glittered
>   from under the eyelids:
> from all his heads fire flared
>   from his eyes' glancing;
> and inside each one of these horrible heads
>   there were many voices
> that threw out every sort of horrible sound.
>   (*Theogony* 824–30; trans. Lattimore)

Cf. *Sev* 493–94. Typho comes from the east (**in caves Cilician**) to be buried in defeat under Mt. **Aetna** in Sicily. Volcanic mountains are typically the site of buried dragons, whose fiery breath provides the kind of furnace required by **the smith Hephaestus.** The known dates for the eruption of Aetna, 479/8 and 423, do not help much in dating the play.

376 For **reassure** prefer "save."

377 f. Grene's translation may suggest false New Testament associations, e.g., with Mark 10:38. The verb **drain** denotes pumping out the bilge water from the hold of a ship, and its object is *tychē* ("fortune").

379–82 Oceanos' reply intimates that he can persuade Zeus to relent from his anger. Zeus and persuasion have already been mentioned together in 33 f., 173 f., 189, 335. Prometheus' reply argues that medicine will work only when the circumstances (**in season**) are propitious. Cf. 505 and 522.

383 Tell me = "teach me." See on 61. There must be at least gentle mockery in asking the helpless Titan for advice on personal safety. By 393, however, Oceanos is whistling a different tune to the same words.

390 Doings is, more concretely, "lament."

394 Three imperatives make a very curt, imperious line.

395 Oceanos is easily persuaded. What has the scene accomplished? Several scholars have found so little dramatic point, so much bluster and nastiness, that they have condemned it as an interpolation. For a more sympathetic evaluation see Conacher, p. 45.

398 Oceanos leaves, and his daughters now sing the first stasimon, a lament for the suffering Titan. If they have been offstage, they must enter before beginning the song, which does not have an anapestic prelude.

403–5 Laws = "customs" at 149a. Cf. the complaint at *Eum* 778–80.

410 Fall = "Honor"; i.e., they lament the lost honor. His **brethren,** the Titans, tried for greater honor for themselves, whereas Prometheus honored man.

414–20 No Greeks are mentioned. **Colchis** is to the east of the Black Sea; **Scythia** to the north; **Lake Maeotis** is the Sea of Azov; **Arabia** has been emended, but it is hard to say how exact Aeschylus' geography was.

425–30 The **one God** is Atlas; see on 347–50. **Alas,** in 428, is a misprint for Atlas.

437 Normally, actors exit before the stasimon. Prometheus cannot, and the stage convention was apparently so strong that the poet felt obliged to let the character comment on his silence.

Perhaps because of "A man's pride shall bring him low" and other such admonitions, we are inclined to see **pride** as the only, or at least the prime, cause of the fall of Greek tragic protagonists. Usually there is more to it. The same word here translated "pride" is "luxury" at 466 and "delight" at *Ag* 1447. These translations bring out the connotations of a wanton delight in excessive pleasure. Since Prometheus can hardly be described as "luxuriating" in his chains, he would seem to mock his own incapacity. When this word next appears, in the taunt at 971 ff., Hermes says "You will find your present lot too *soft*," at which Prometheus repeats the word (this time the verb) twice, wishing his enemies might enjoy such softness.

Prometheus is obviously proud of what he has done for mankind, but his fault lies in offending and impairing the honor and privilege of Zeus, not in any personal attitude toward his "error" or even toward Zeus. **Stubbornness** is another of those qualities shared by Zeus and Prometheus. Hermes charges "obstinacy" (1013), and the chorus assents (1037). The same stem is beneath "pride of heart" (909a), and apparently Might (79) would accept stubbornness as natural to himself and to Zeus.

443 The present passage would seem a good place, had the poet wanted one, to explain the ultimate reason for Prometheus' good will toward men, i.e., why he would risk alienating the regard of his own kind to aid mankind, who could not repay him. The tradition made Prometheus the father of Deucalion, the Greek Noah.

446 For the comparison to a **dream** see *Ag* 82. The entire speech is pragmatic and materialistic. Cf. Protagoras' speech on the same theme in Plato, *Protagoras* 320d–322d.

461 Memory is the **Muses' mother** (*Theogony* 53 ff.).

472–75 Why should they say that he is **astray and bewildered** after such a recital? Cf. 277. With **bad doctor** cf. 379 ff. **Cannot find** echoes "discovered" (466 and 470; cf. 501 f.) and "devised" (97). **Drugs** = "cure" at 251; cf. 607.

476–77 Resources suggests, in the Greek, "passage" and "way out" (59c). Cf. his "set mortals on the road to" at 496. Such ironies are very frequent.

483 ff. Various kinds of divination are listed, some of which we can illustrate from tragedy. For a **true dream** see *LB* 523 ff. **Ominous cries** are chance or accidental remarks, such as we find at *Sev* 257 (note). **Omens of the highway** are significant chance encounters (*LB* 837). An omen from the flight of **birds** will be found at *Ag* 108 ff. **Smoothness of the vitals . . . gall and lobe** refers to reading signs from the entrails of animals. **Burned thighs** refers to observing the process of sacrifice, such as we find at *Antigone* 1006–12, a

passage that follows one that speaks of unhappy omens drawn
from avian manners. **Flaming signs of the sky** would refer
to observing heavenly bodies, but this phrase may suggest
divination from fire, since "of the sky" is interpretative.

In the last chapter of *Greek Popular Religion*, "Seers and
Oracles," Nilsson discusses Greek attitudes toward such
matters.

505 Expediency translates *kairos*, the same word translated as "season" at 522, thereby defining this section by a
kind of ring composition. *Kairos* suggests timeliness, opportunity, propitious circumstances. Why is the chorus so
sanguine?

511 ff. For **Fate** (*moira*) see on *Ag* 129. It is probably personified. The present passage is much discussed because here
alone among the extant plays Zeus is made subordinate to another power in the universe. Cf. *Suppl* 524 ff. and especially
590–99. The tradition seems to me ambiguous, sometimes
treating Fate as an impersonal power apart from, and perhaps
superior to, Zeus, sometimes making Zeus the supreme power
in the world. For some scholars the theology expressed here is
so foreign to Aeschylus' thinking elsewhere that they are willing to invoke it as evidence that the play is not by Aeschylus;
others contend that the playwright has a perfect right to express different views in different plays. It has also been argued
that Prometheus' view need not be taken as the poet's, and
some would say that Prometheus may, after all, be wrong. The
former view is undeniable, but the latter seems a little suspect,
since Zeus will shortly send Hermes to demand knowledge of
Zeus's fate. The conceptual limitation of fate can be seen clearly
from the fact that, when Zeus knows what danger threatens
him, he will be able to circumvent fate and necessity.

513 f. The master of all crafts has no way to escape the
physical restraint (= **necessity**) of his bondage. Necessity
is another of those words that express reciprocal relations
between Zeus and Prometheus; cf. 16 ("constraint"), 72
("forced"), 105 ("necessity"), and 1052 ("compulsive"). See
the note on *Ag* 217.

516 Hesiod makes the **Fates** daughters of Zeus and Themis
(*Theogony* 904), but he also calls them daughters of Night
(*Theogony* 217); cf. *Eum* 321 and 960 ff. They are **triple-
formed** because they are represented as three old women,

Clotho, Lachesis, and Atropos. For the **Furies** see on *Ag* 59. Hesiod's subordination of the Fates to Zeus (as his daughters) is the usual way of looking at their relationship, but since they are here joined with the Furies it seems likely that the poet thinks of them, as at *Eum* 960 ff., as children of Night and sisters of the Furies. Or, like Agamemnon at *Iliad* 19. 86–88, he may consider the Furies the agents of the Fates and the natural agents of his vengeance. As Agamemnon offends Achilles and pays for that offense, so Zeus may, if he cannot extort Prometheus' secret from him, pay for his philandering by getting a son stronger than himself. Zeus, neither omniscient nor omnipotent, is subject to physical and biological necessity. If he mates with Thetis, he will get a son stronger than himself. Then like Kronos and Uranos before him, he will inevitably yield the rule of the world to the stronger (cf. 954–59).

525 ff. The second stasimon. Though they sympathize with Prometheus, they do not reject or denigrate the rule of Zeus. Sacrifice, like modest speech (534), is a token of respect.

533 ff. Quenchless means that his flow cannot be stopped. With **sin in word** cf. 182, 313, and 932. **Melt away** suggests a metaphor from engraving on wax.

537–46 Cheerful hopes echoes 252. **Your mind was yours** obliquely reflects on Zeus's "private laws" (403): both act without regard for the opinion or feeling of others. **Regarded** (= "revered") is properly said of man's worship of the gods. For excess (**too high**) as a motif see 182, 321, 329, and the note to 71.

547–53 Man cannot return the Titan's favor. The phrase is a variation on "grace without grace" (*LB* 43). Cf. Prometheus' irony at 985. For **creatures of a day** see on 82–86; with **dreamlike** cf. 446. **Ordered law** translates *harmonia*; the metaphor may be from medicine (see on 227) or music.

557 ff. The wedding song was sung first when the bride and groom bathed, again when they went to the ceremony, and finally before the wedding chamber (**couching**). A scholiast reports that **Hesione** was a daughter of Oceanos; so **your own** may be "our own." The mother's name is not known.

561 Io is an example of the argument of the second strophe. She is the helpless plaything and victim of the gods, unable to protect herself, much less return kindness to god or man. The question in 548 f.—"What succor in creatures of a day?"—ambiguously anticipates her, for it may also mean "What succor is there for creatures of a day?"

Io describes herself as "cow-horned" (588 and 675). In Greek art she is represented both as a heifer and as a horned girl. For us such a figure can hardly escape the ludicrous, but the Greek spectator, familiar with the legend and the representations of it in paintings, may have found this mad victim of Zeus's lechery more pathetic than grotesque. See Aristotle's *Poetics*, chap. 14, on spectacle and the "portentous." Such metamorphoses are not uncommon in Greek myth; cf., e.g., *Bacchae* 1330–31, where Dionysus tells Cadmus that he will be changed into a serpent.

After four lines in anapests, the remainder of Io's song is in iambic and dochmiac rhythms, the latter especially suited to wild, excited speech. Her dance—and we know nothing of the choreography—may have been spectacular. The long monologues that follow seem a tame sequel. Taplin (p. 266) observes: "Elsewhere in Aeschylus when actors sing it is always in lyric dialogue with the chorus."

For the story of Io see *Suppl* 291 ff. and the notes there.

566–70 Gadfly may be literal, as 676 suggests, or figurative, since the word here is also used metaphorically of a sting, frenzy, or passion. Apollodorus (2. 1. 2) says that **Argos** was called the "all-seeing" because he had eyes all over his body. At Zeus's command Hermes killed Argos, whom Hera had set to guard the girl. Cf. "Argos, a son of Earth, whom Hermes slew" (*Suppl* 305). For a continuing persecution, Hera sent the gadfly. As far as we know, Aeschylus invented the idea that the gadfly is the **ghost of Argos.**

575 This is the shepherd's pipe or panpipe, made of reeds, which she still remembers from the playing of the herdsman Argos.

577–79 Wandering, fault (see on 6), and **yoke** all link her to Prometheus. The fault, of course, is not hers but Zeus's.

582–83 For the wish cf. *Suppl* 779a–82 and note.

585 Much wandering wanderings represents *polyplanoi planai*. Cf. 578. For the motif see on 276.

589–92 Unlike Io, who sings her frenzy, Prometheus is given spoken iambic trimeters. The chorus has no part until

631. **Inachus** is the major river of the Argolid as well as the father of Io. Cf. Ovid, *Metamorphoses* 1. 583 ff., for another version of Io's rape.

595 Verdenius (p. 464) suggests that **exactly** points to an etymological pun on Inachus' name (*Inachos* and *achos*, "grief").

596–97 The **disease** refers to her madness, to the love of Zeus which caused it, and to the gadfly, which in **pricking with goads** is likened to a rider or charioteer.

601 The **jealous plots** are Hera's.

605 ff. Her request precedes knowledge of who he is. Once again delaying, he answers her earlier question (593 f.) first, and thus begins a digression. Cf. 621 ff.

609a–640 As usual, the Greek—iambics now—appears more patterned than the English: 4:2:7(1):2:7(1):4:5.

612 Blessing refers to Prometheus as a *useful* benefactor. The same Greek root is present in "services" (224), "gift" (253), and "blessing" (501). Long, in his notes on this play, speaks of a theme of "lost labor," e.g., in "labor uselessly" (43) and "trouble to no purpose" (344).

623–24 Know and **endure** make a variant on "wisdom through suffering" (*Ag* 176–78).

631–34 The coryphaeus interrupts to correct a potential chronological inversion. Some anticlimax would be inevitable if Prometheus were to forecast future suffering before Io has told of her past. It is striking to establish an apparent direction only to have another agent change it so self-consciously. On the other hand, such false starts and retardations characterize the entire play.

637 For **ill fortune** see the note on 347–50. The sentiment is aesthetic, i.e., more about the function of drama than about their need to know.

643 Storm echoes "tortured" (562) and thus provides another imagistic parallel between Io and Prometheus. See on 745. With **sent by God** cf. 596.

652 A marshy area near Argos, **Lerna** is best known as the home of the hydra killed by Heracles.

658 f. Pytho is the home of Apollo's oracle at Delphi. Apollo is a riddling god, which is perhaps a satisfactory translation of Loxias (670). **Dodona** is the site of the oracle of Zeus in Thesprotia (see 830 f.).

661 Vague and ambiguous oracles are a familiar motif in

Greek tragedy; cf. Sophocles' *Women of Trachis* 169–72 and Euripides' *Suppliants* 138. When Inachus finally has a clear word, this oracle, like those regarding Oedipus and others, threatens the family if the child is not sacrificed.

672 Bit recalls the binding of Prometheus (see on 54) and the "bondage" of 562. **Compelled** is the verbal form of "necessity" (514–15). Thus Zeus is a rider compelling and subduing a rebellious animal. Cf. the "god-sent scourge" at 684.

674 Often the metamorphosis is said to be a result of Hera's suspicion, or her discovery, that Zeus is pursuing Io. Cf. 704 and 900. Here it is the suffering of Io rather than the rivalry of the gods that has the primary focus.

689a–95 Despite some textual uncertainty here, the chorus's reaction is clearly marked by pain, horror, and visual revulsion. Much in the language of the play calls attention to vision and spectacle. Prometheus is a pitiful sight that hurts the eye (69, 120, 145–56); he is ashamed of himself as spectacle (248, 300 ff.); he has given sight to man (445) and made man blind to foreseeing (250), though he could not make the Titans "glance" at his advice (218). Io is shaken by the sight of him (561 f.), is driven in fear by the eyes of Argos (568–71), and is haunted by "visions" in the night (646).

694 Alas, Alas in Greek is *iō*, *iō*, homophonic with Io's name. Cf. the punning on names at *Ag* 1082 (note), *Suppl* 777 (note), and Ajax 430–32.

700–735 Prometheus and Io are also bound thematically by their mutual endurance of the persecution of Zeus: Prometheus is immobilized and isolated, while Io must roam the furthest reaches of the world, where she will encounter dangerous tribes and places. Still, there are limits (see on line 1) to their suffering (706). The geographic and ethnographic references in the following narrative defy intelligible order, unless a kind of general movement from northeast to southwest may be called an order. The Greeks placed the **Scythians** in the vast region north and east of the Black Sea (713); the **Chalybes** (cf. *Sev* 728) are usually situated on the southeastern coast of the Black Sea, but here they are apparently to the north of it; the river **Insolence** (the *hybris* stem; see on 82) is unknown and probably the poet's invention. Verdenius (p. 466) suggests that, rather than being a proper name, "insolence" is a riddling pun on the river Borysthenes (the Dnieper), with the name interpreted to mean "pouncing upon its prey." Since the **Cimmerian isthmus** (729 f.) and **the channel of Maeotis** normally refer to the Straits of Kerch and the Sea of Azov, it follows that the peoples and places preceding ought to be, on the poet's map, northeast of the Black Sea. The **Caucasus** is of course east. The **Amazons** are usually south of that sea, as is the **Thermodon** river. **Salmydessos** has been transposed from the western (Thracian) shore; it is the **stepmother of ships** because of its treacherous shoals and the savage scavenging of its wild inhabitants. All this confusion leads to a crossing at the Crimean Bosporus (whereas in the *Suppliants* [542 ff.] Io gives the name to the Thracian Bosporus, where the Black Sea debouches into the Sea of Marmara at modern Istanbul). It is yet another aberration from Greek geography to reckon the Crimean Bosporus as the boundary between Asia and Europe (cf. 791).

745 More imagery from wintry storms occurs at 562, (where "tortured" = "storm-driven" at 839), 643, 1016.

752–54 He is a god and so cannot die (cf. 1052). **Power** = "tyranny." On the fall of Zeus see notes at 171–78 and 511 ff. Some commentators point out that 753–54 contradict 258–60, but too much should not be made of this, since the contradiction seems a function of Prometheus' reluctant and gradual disclosure of the future.

764 Marriage that shall hurt him: for Hesiod the wife in this marriage is Metis (Wisdom); for Aeschylus and most later writers she is Thetis, daughter of Nereus. Warned by Themis (Apollodorus 3. 13. 5) or Prometheus, Zeus gives Thetis to Peleus, and they become the parents of Achilles, the hero of Homer's *Iliad*. In a number of Greek myths, e.g., the stories of Perseus, Oedipus, and Jason, a father or substitute for the father learns from an oracle that a son or grandson, if born, will threaten him. As in the case of Zeus, it is possible to alter this fate by forestalling the birth or destroying the child. Zeus is more successful than his mortal counterparts.

769 Downfall translates the same word discussed in the note on 347–50, *tychē*, which is often rendered "chance" or "luck."

772 What is not yet revealed is that Io's **descendant** will

also be a son of Zeus on both sides, from Io and, more immediately, from Alcmene, another mortal victim of Zeus's lust.
See on 848 ff. and 871.

778 Long suggests that the lines allude to the Delphic habit
of asking for alternative questions. As he observes, the coy offer of **one of two,** with the chorus asking for the leftovers, is
a transparent device to include in the play all that the poet
wishes to include.

785–818 Though Bolton offers a map of Io's route, the
number of mythical references in this catalogue makes geo-
graphical accuracy less natural than in the preceding recital.
An exotic travelogue, and not any relevance to Io, is clearly
the poet's aim.

790 For the metaphor see on *Eum* 273–75.

791 Channel: another reference to the Cimmerian Bosporus, i.e., the Crimea (cf. 730–35).

794–801 Later writers seem to favor the far west for the
Gorgons (799) and Graeae (= **the children of Phorcys**), but
in the *Tenth Pythian* Pindar puts these antagonists of Perseus in
the neighborhood of the Hyperboreans. Hesiod speaks of two
Graeae, grey and old from birth. They are said to share a
single tooth and a single eye. Medusa, whose head was cut off
by Perseus, is the best known of the three Gorgons; her gruesome aspect could turn a man to stone. See Apollodorus 2. 4. 2.
Dodds (*The Greeks and the Irrational*, p. 162) suggests that the
swan-formed maidens (our **hags** is interpretative) have "a
good parallel in the 'swan-maidens' of Central Asiatic belief,
who live in the dark and have eyes of lead."

803–8 The **vultures** are the griffins, "the hook nosed."
They appear to be traditional enemies of the **Arimaspians.**
"Aristeas of Prokonnesos says in his poem that these griffins
fight for gold with the Arimaspians, away beyond the north
of Thrace, and the gold they guard grows out of the earth; the
Arimaspians are born one-eyed, but the griffins are wild
monsters like lions with wings and the beak of an eagle"
(Pausanias 1. 24. 6). **Pluto's river** (= "Wealth's river") is unknown and may be invented for the gold.

809b–11 The **fountain of the sun** ought to be in the east,
but some commentators take fountain to stand for the flood
of the ocean, which, since it circles, could be in the west. In

Greek literature **Aethiopian** refers to any region far to the south. Apparently Io circles to the south of Egypt and proceeds north along the Nile to the delta (**the triangular land of the Nile**). The **Bibline,** i.e., papyrus, hills are unknown.

819 "The bitter humour of this line is very pathetic" (Sikes and Willson).

828–32 He omits the journey from Argos to northwest Greece. The **Molossi** and **Thesprotians** are tribes within the larger district of Epirus. **Dodona,** the most famous oracle of Zeus (cf. 659), is located inland on the continent opposite the island of Corfu, the ancient Corcyra. There divination was practiced by listening to the rustling of the leaves of the oak tree; hence **talking oaks.**

837–41 The **gulf of Rhea** is the Adriatic, known as the **Ionian Sea** in antiquity. Rhea is the consort of Kronos and mother of Zeus; there seems to be no known reason for her association with the Adriatic. The etymology connecting Io's name with the Ionians, a major branch of the Greek people, is false.

847 Canobus is also mentioned at *Suppl* 311.

848–52 Epaphos means "the one touched." See on *Suppl* 16–18. The **touching** at once brings back her sanity and begets Epaphos. Perhaps in **with a hand that brings no fear** there is a touch of ambiguous and cynical humor; the adjective would usually be translated "with a fearless hand."

R. D. Murray's summary of the Io motif and its significance for the trilogy illustrates the generosity of modern criticism:

> The release of Io from her woes is to provide the initial indication of the increasing wisdom of Zeus and the concomitant sowing of the seeds of compassion for humanity (848–52). The glory of her offspring Epaphus (850–2) is to be supplemented by the foundation of the royal Argive line (869); finally and climactically, her descendant Heracles is to free Prometheus (871–3) and his act marks the coming of age of the divine wisdom and the synthesis of Promethean knowledge and humanitarianism with the effective Jovian power. Thus Io the persecuted becomes Io the glorious mother of national benefactors; her suffering is rewarded abundantly. The trilogy is a paian in honor of the Greek

mind, but above all an affirmation of the dignity of man and wise majesty of God, qualities attained through the perfecting course of evolution. Zeus the tyrant and Prometheus the forethinker coalesce in a compound slowly effected by the catalyst of *pathei mathos*. [*The Motif of Io in Aeschylus' " Suppliants,"* pp. 47 f.]

(*Pathei mathos* = "learning through suffering.")

855–70 Here we have the subject not only of Aeschylus' *Suppliants* but, in the allusions to the death of the Egyptians, of the two lost plays of that trilogy. The suppliant women from Egypt were given sanctuary in Argos but subsequently had to accept their Egyptian cousins and pursuers as husbands (perhaps because the Argives lost a battle in which the girls were the stake). On their wedding night forty-nine of the fifty descendants of Io murdered their bridegrooms, only one, Hypermnestra, sparing her new husband (866–67). From Hypermnestra, then, descends the line of Argive kings.

859 ff. Cf. the simile at *Suppl* 223 f. No specific **god** is intended. When, contrary to expectation and probability, the stronger party—in this case the Egyptian cousins—is frustrated or destroyed, the Greek habit is to see such an aberration as the result of divine intervention. The speaker does not know which god acted but assumes—to explain the improbable—that some god must have taken a hand. This way of offering vague after-the-fact explanations is both moralistic and rationalizing.

864 f. Prometheus cannot resist an aside as he reflects that love will be the undoing of Zeus.

871 The man renowned is Heracles, son of Zeus and Alcmene; appropriately, the descent from Io to Heracles is on the female side. In his later account Apollodorus (1. 7. 1) summarizes as follows:

> Prometheus moulded men out of water and earth and gave them also fire, which, unknown to Zeus, he had hidden in a stalk of fennel. But when Zeus learned of it, he ordered Hephaestus to nail his body to Mount Caucasus, which is the Scythian mountain. On it Prometheus was nailed and kept bound for many years. Every day an eagle swooped on him and devoured the lobes of his liver, which grew by night. That was the penalty that Prometheus paid for the theft of

fire until Heracles afterwards released him, as we shall show in dealing with Heracles.

Cf. the note on 1019–29.

873 For **Themis** and her powers of prophecy see on 211.

878 Eleleu: the meaning of this cry is uncertain. Elsewhere it is a war cry, and Sikes and Willson translate "On, on!" Her mad convulsions have again seized her; the lines are anapestic.

879–87 The Greek is more terse and excited. For example, in 880 **steel** and **tempered** are interpretative. **Fireless** may mean "untempered," or "cold," or "without fever"; the first meaning is most naturally paired with a steel point, the second looks at the quality of Zeus's love, and the third, a medical sense, makes a violent paradox after **burning me up. Knocks** also means "kicks," and Silk points out how the image of a "horse and chariot out of control" continues until **frenzy** (also meaning "storm wind"), where "the chariot turns surreally into a ship in distress" (Silk, p. 238). While the imagery describes her wild, uncontrolled frenzy, the lines conclude with characteristic self-consciousness in **hateful mischief** (*atē*); cf. Orestes' madness at *LB* 1021 ff.

887 Io exits.

888–909 The third stasimon. In myth many a Greek girl was raped by Zeus or one of his friends. See Euripides' *Ion* 10 and the stories of Alceme, Semele, and Danaë in any handbook. In this brief lyric the chorus expresses its fear of such divine affection.

The **wise man** may have been Pittacus of Mytilene (circa 650–570), a contemporary of Solon. The proverb hardly applies to Io or to most of the girls raped, for few **aspired** to a divine marriage, and virtually all suffered from the liaison.

896 Omit **to share it with the kings.**

905 f. A double set of Greek privatives in a single line yields this stylized verse, something like "unwarlike war, fruitful fruitlessness." Because the Greek negates with a privative (comparable to the English prefixes un- and in-), assonance and alliteration are ready at hand in such naturally antithetic, paradoxical lines, which English associates with the euphuistic style:

> *apolemos hode g' ho polemos, apora porimos*
> no war this war, unfruitful (making) fruitful

Fruitful has a root meaning "passage" or "way" and is thus connected with Io's literal wanderings and figuratively with Prometheus' "resources" (see the note on 476–77).

907–9 Grene seems to have emended the text, substituting **anger** for "plan." Smyth translates: "I do not see how I could escape the designs of Zeus."

909a f. For **pride** see on 437. **Humble** implies both a change of temper, in contrast to pride, as well as a change in station: he will be "brought low."

912 Although the father's curse is a typical motif in such stories (e.g., *Sev* 70, 653–55, and Euripides, *Hippolytus* 887–90), there is no other mention of **Kronos' curse** in this play or, apparently, in other versions of the story.

920–27 The athletic Greeks liked metaphors from wrestling. So "master" at *Ag* 172 indicates a victory in three falls. Cf. *Eum* 589 and Sophocles, *Philoctetes* 431. Aeschylus has in mind the contention of Zeus and Poseidon for the hand of Thetis. With 924 ff. cf. Pindar, where Themis foretold

> how it was destined for this sea-goddess to bring to birth
>   a lord
> stronger than his father, to wield in his hand a shaft heavier
>   than the thunderbolt
> or the weariless trident, if she lay with Zeus or his brothers.
>   (*Eighth Isthmian* 36–38; trans. Lattimore)

Whereas Aeschylus apparently views **Poseidon** as the ally of Zeus against his progeny, Pindar entertains the possibility that either may win. The child of Thetis would surpass in power those primary symbols of the father's power: for Zeus the lightning bolt, for Poseidon the **trident.** This last weapon is a **curse** (or "plague," a common word for "disease," as at 596) because of its ability to devastate. Such language verges on cliché at 977 f.

928 f. Another variation on learning from experience; cf. 981 f.

929a Wishes: The chorus cannot quite believe that Prometheus' predictions are more than wishful thinking.

931 Worse, i.e., harder to bear, harder on the neck; for the yoking metaphor see on 672.

936 Farnell (*Cults*, 2:499) calls **Adrasteia** "a sort of twin sister of Nemesis." The chorus means that Prometheus should have regard for divine indignation, which, being a god himself, he finds less than forbidding. See the note to *Ag* 904–11 for a similar concern. In Euripides' *Rhesus* (342 f.) the chorus prays:

> Adrasteia, Zeus's
> daughter! Keep bad luck from my mouth.

941 ff. Enter Hermes, the usual messenger of Zeus, although he is seldom the nasty minion we find here. In Hermes' speech Thomson notes a variety of echoes from the prologue, e.g., in **subtle-spirit** (= "for all your cleverness" at 61), **sinned** (cf. 6), **creatures of a day** (83), **Father** (3, 18). Normal Greek dramatic practice would bring Hermes on after the last song. His late entry is one more occasion for surprise.

955 f. Young = "new" (943, 961; cf. on 34).

958 The **two tyrants** are Uranos and Kronos.

964 Prometheus' **obstinacy** is discussed in the note to 437.

970 Several modern editors assume a lost verse, belonging to Prometheus, before 970. Here **insolence** is *hybris*, and it is supposed that in the lost line Prometheus insults Hermes so vigorously that he then offers a line of explanation. In Grene's version Prometheus refers to the insolent mockery of Hermes.

971 On **soft** see the note on 437 (there "pride").

975 f. Prometheus is a *theomachos*, one who battles against god. See the notes on *Pers* 749–51 and *Sev* 424 ff.

979a–80 This is perhaps the only line in Aeschylus shared by two speakers, a phenomenon found in the later plays of Sophocles, e.g., *Oedipus the King* 626–29. The technical term for this is *antilabē*. It is probably better to drop the first **Alas** and divide the single line thus:

> *Prometheus:* Alas! *Hermes:* Zeus does not know that word.

981 Time is frequently the catalyst for commonplaces; cf. *Ag* 983, *Eum* 286. Pindar (Frag. 33, Snell) speaks of "Time the lord who triumphs over all the blessed gods."

994 "About the feathers which the Scythians say fill the air, and make it impossible to traverse, or even to see, the more northerly parts of the continent—I think myself that it must be always snowing in these northerly regions, though less, of course, in summer than in the winter. Anyone who has seen heavy snow at close quarters will know what I mean—it is very like feathers" (Herodotus 4. 31).

1001 As Hermes' comment at 980 suggests, there is throughout this dialogue a good deal of wordplay. Here **senseless** retorts to **foolish** in line 1000; cf. 971–73, 977–78.

1002 This figure is a variation on one found at *Iliad* 16. 33–35, where Patroclus calls Achilles "pitiless," too hard to have had natural parents:

> but it was the grey sea that bore you
> and the towering rocks, so sheer the heart in you is turned
> from us.

So the Nurse rebukes Phaedra:

> But this you shall know, though to my reasoning
> you are more dumbly obstinate than the sea;
> (Euripides, *Hippolytus* 303–4)

1004–6 In prayer the hands were extended with palms upward. For **womanish** see the note at *Ag* 10 f. on sexual antagonism.

1010 For the imagery see the note on 54.

1016 See on 745.

1018–29 Prometheus will be buried beneath the earth, then raised to have his **liver** daily eaten by an **eagle** and daily renewed to be eaten again. Apollodorus 2. 5. 11 (trans. Frazer) is relevant to the following lines: "And having crossed to the opposite mainland he [Heracles] shot on the Caucasus the eagle, offspring of Echidna and Typhon, that was devouring the liver of Prometheus, and he released Prometheus, after choosing for himself the bond of olive, and to Zeus he presented Chiron, who, though immortal, consented to die in his stead." (Frazer [1:228–29] explains the "bond of olive" as "the crown of olive which Hercules brought from the land of the Hyperboreans and instituted as the badge of victory in the

Olympic games." The crown or garland thus became a memorial of the chains of Prometheus.) Most commentators have
assumed that Chiron (the good centaur accidentally wounded
by Heracles' arrow) died in the place of Prometheus, thus
fulfilling Hermes' prophecy at 1026 ff. Aeschylus does not
specifically mention Chiron or, of course, the name of Heracles. Hermes probably thinks these terms most unlikely to be
fulfilled, even if they are the actual terms of Zeus and not
merely an imagined end. So we have another unconscious
prophecy (cf. 58–59). There is also unconscious irony in **end**
(1026; cf. 186, 259, 285, 829). If Apollodorus is following
Aeschylus, then this allusion would be clarified in subsequent
plays of the trilogy. Possibly Zeus did demand that someone
assume Prometheus' suffering perpetually, even banishment
to the underworld. As a god, Prometheus cannot die, but
Zeus might have required that he either give up his immor-
tality voluntarily or find **some god** who would do as much
for him, a stipulation Zeus did not expect to be met. Cf.
Lloyd-Jones (*Justice of Zeus*, p. 96): "It is as though Zeus had
passed upon his enemy a sentence of death which the immor-
tality of Prometheus made it impossible to carry out, so that
Zeus was obliged to adopt the nearest possible equivalent."

1036–39 Several earlier motifs gather here: **out of season**
(see on 379–82); **obstinacy** (cf. 1034, 1013, 437); **wise good
counsel** (cf. "subtle-spirit," 944); **Hearken to him,** i.e., "be
persuaded" (e.g., at 379 f.); **error** (see on line 6).

1041 f. No disgrace: this is not the usual Greek view, nor
was it Prometheus' at 91 ff. His defiance, as Sikes and Willson
note, has outstripped humiliation and shame.

1043 ff. These lines foreshadow the cataclysm described as
presently happening at 1080 ff. We know next to nothing of
what special effects Aeschylus may have used. One function
of this passage may be to prepare the audience to imagine the
"staggering earth" of the final lines. Another function reminds us of Io: **convulsing** (1046) echoes "spasm" at 879; the
storm imagery looks back to 882 ff., 839, 745.

1053–55 Madness is a common motif in Greek literature,
from Homer's raging warriors to the sick protagonists in Euripides. A few instances in Sophocles: *Ajax* 50 ff., 217, 611;

Women of Trachis 999; *Oedipus the King* 1300. Sometimes the metaphor is purely medical, sometimes the madness is actual, or it may suggest, as here, the agent "struck out of his wits."

1062 Roar, regularly of the bellowing of cattle, is yet another word calculated to evoke Io's bovine wretchedness; so too "bellows" at 1082.

1063–70 It is a little surprising to find the chorus so vehemently for Prometheus after their last speech, which urges moderation and conciliation. They came to sympathize and have stayed to suffer, and this response clearly indicates how the author expected the spectacle and narratives of Prometheus and Io to affect the audience. As Hermes speaks, they move toward Prometheus, huddling around the god as he utters his final defiance. See on 1080.

The **disease** metaphor (1070) takes an unexpected turn with its application to **treachery,** which has not been an issue to this point.

1071 ff. Hermes gives a hunting metaphor (**trapped by ruin; net of ruin**) a new turn by stressing the self-conscious choice made by the chorus to join Prometheus in his suffering. Cf. 100 ff. **Ruin** is *atē* (in both 1072 and 1078), with connotations of intellectual blindness (see on *Pers* 93–101). **Fortune:** see on 347–50.

1079 Exit Hermes.

1080 The line in Greek explicitly contrasts words and deeds (cf. 339a). The storm imagery of this passage is in the present tense and descriptive of an upheaval foreshadowed by references to Prometheus' fall to Tartarus (1018 ff.). What actually happened? Some scholars suppose a realistic descent: "I conceive that a wooden frame-work, rudely suggesting a rock, was propped up at the outer extremity of the orchestra. At the moment of the catastrophe the supports were removed and the structure allowed to collapse into the declivity" (Flickinger, p. 228). This takes "in very truth" (1080) literally, but we have no external evidence for such staging, nor is it easy to imagine how Flickinger's staging could live up to the vivid and powerful description of these last lines. If, on the other hand, there is no illusion of cataclysm, the audience must imagine the actor (and chorus?) swept off, all the while seeing them remaining in the orchestra. Neither view has found general favor, and to some extent our requirements for spectacle here will probably be determined by, or at least should be compatible with, the earlier staging of the choral entry and of Oceanos' entry and exit.

1090 f. Cf. his invocation at 89 ff. (**Holy mother mine** = "earth," 90; **Sky** = "bright light," 89).

BIBLIOGRAPHY

THIS BIBLIOGRAPHY of writers cited in this commentary is divided into four parts: (1) translations of Greek writers other than Aeschylus; (2) translations of the fragments of Aeschylus and other Greek writers; (3) Greek texts, commentaries, and translations of one or more of the plays of Aeschylus; and (4) articles, monographs, commentaries, and other texts that I have cited in my notes.

Translations of Works by Greek Authors Other Than Aeschylus

Apollodorus. *The Library*. Greek text, with English translation by James G. Frazer. 2 vols. Loeb Classical Library. Cambridge, Mass.: Harvard University Press; London: William Heinemann, 1921. Reprinted 1963.

Aristophanes. *Plays*. Translated by Patric Dickinson. 2 vols. London: Oxford University Press, 1970.

Aristotle. *Aristotle's "Poetics."* Translated, with an introduction and notes, by James Hutton. New York: Norton, 1982.

Empedocles. *See* Translations of Fragments

Heraclitus. *See* Translations of Fragments

Herodotus. *The Histories*. Translated by Aubrey de Selincourt. Revised, with an introduction and notes, by A. R. Burn. Harmondsworth, Eng.: Penguin Books, 1972.

———. *Herodotus*. Translated by A. D. Godley. Loeb Classical Library. 4 vols. Cambridge, Mass.: Harvard University Press; London: William Heinemann, 1936. Reprinted 1954.

Hesiod. *Hesiod, The Homeric Hymns, and Homerica*. Edited and translated by Hugh G. Evelyn-White. Loeb Classical Library. Cambridge, Mass.: Harvard University Press; London: William Heinemann, 1936. Reprinted 1954.

———. *The Works and Days, Theogony, The Shield of Heracles*. Translated by Richmond Lattimore. Ann Arbor: University of Michigan Press, 1959.

Homer. *The Iliad*. Translated by Richmond Lattimore. Chicago: University of Chicago Press, 1951.

——. *The Odyssey*. Translated by Richmond Lattimore. New York: Harper & Row, 1967.

Homeric Hymns. *See* Hesiod

Pausanias. *Guide to Greece*. Translated by Peter Levi. 2 vols. Harmondsworth, Eng.: Penguin Books, 1971.

Pindar. *The Odes of Pindar*. Translated by Richmond Lattimore. Chicago: University of Chicago Press, 1947.

Plato. *The Laws*. Translated by R. G. Bury. Loeb Classical Library. 2 vols. London: William Heinemann; New York: G. P. Putnam, 1926.

——. *The Republic*. Translated by Desmond Lee. 2d ed. Harmondsworth, Eng.: Penguin Books, 1974.

Solon. *Greek Lyrics*. Translated by Richmond Lattimore. Chicago: University of Chicago Press, 1955.

Theognis. *Elegy and Iambus: Greek Elegiac and Iambic Poets from Callinus to Crates*. Edited and translated by J. M. Edmonds. 2 vols. Loeb Classical Library. London: William Heinemann; New York: G. P. Putnam's Sons, 1931.

Translations of the Fragments

Aeschylus. *Aeschylus*. Translated by Herbert Weir Smyth. Loeb Classical Library. 2 vols. Volume 2, with an appendix containing the more considerable fragments published since 1930 and a new text of frag. 50, edited by Hugh Lloyd-Jones. London: William Heinemann; Cambridge, Mass.: Harvard University Press, 1971.

Empedocles. *The Presocratic Philosophers*. G. S. Kirk and J. E. Raven. Cambridge, Eng.: Cambridge University Press, 1957.

Heraclitus. Ibid.

Xenophanes. Ibid.

Greek Texts, Commentaries, and Translations of the Plays of Aeschylus

Editions of the Plays in Greek

Murray, Gilbert, ed. *Septem Quae Supersunt Tragoediae*. Oxford: Clarendon Press, 1955.

Page, Denys, ed. *Septem Quae Supersunt Tragoediae.* Oxford: Clarendon Press, 1972.

Wilamowitz-Moellendorff, Ulrich von, ed. *Aeschyli Tragoediae.* Berlin: Weidmann, 1914.

Commentaries and Translations

All Seven Plays

Rose, Herbert Jennings. *A Commentary on the Surviving Plays of Aeschylus.* 2 vols. Amsterdam: Noord-Hollandsche Uitgevers Maatschappij, 1957, 1958.

Smyth, Herbert Weir. *Aeschylus.* Edited and translated by H. W. Smyth. 2 vols. Volume 2 with an appendix containing the more considerable fragments, edited and translated by Hugh Lloyd-Jones. Loeb Classical Library. Cambridge, Mass.: Harvard University Press; London: William Heinemann, 1957.

The *Oresteia*

Thomson, George. *The "Oresteia" of Aeschylus.* Greek text, with an introduction and commentary incorporating the notes of Walter Headlam. 2d ed. 2 vols. Amsterdam: Hakkert, 1966.

Agamemnon

Denniston, John Dewar, and Page, Denys. *Agamemnon.* Greek text, edited, with commentary. Oxford: Clarendon Press, 1957.

Fraenkel, Eduard. *Agamemnon.* With introduction, translation, and commentary. 3 vols. Oxford: Oxford University Press, 1950.

Lloyd-Jones, Hugh. *Agamemnon.* Translated, with commentary. Prentice-Hall Greek Drama Series. Englewood Cliffs, N.J.: Prentice-Hall, 1970.

The Libation Bearers

Lloyd-Jones, Hugh. *The Libation Bearers.* Translated, with commentary. Prentice-Hall Greek Drama Series. Englewood Cliffs, N.J.: Prentice-Hall, 1970.

The Eumenides

Lloyd-Jones, Hugh. *The Eumenides*. Translated, with commentary. Prentice-Hall Greek Drama Series. Englewood Cliffs, N.J.: Prentice-Hall, 1970.

Sidgwick, A. *The Eumenides*. Greek text, with introduction and notes. Oxford: Clarendon Press, 1927.

The Suppliant Maidens

Johansen, H. Friis. *The Suppliants*. Volume 1, Greek text and translation. Copenhagen: Gyldendals Forlag, 1970.

Tucker, T. G. *The "Supplices" of Aeschylus*. Edited, with commentary. London: Macmillan, 1889.

The Persians

Broadhead, H. D. *The "Persae" of Aeschylus*. Greek text, edited, with introduction, critical notes, and commentary. Cambridge, Eng.: Cambridge University Press, 1960.

Podlecki, Anthony J. *The Persians*. Translated, with commentary. Prentice-Hall Greek Drama Series. Englewood Cliffs, N.J.: Prentice-Hall, 1970.

Sidgwick, A. *Persae*. Greek text, with introduction and notes. Oxford: Clarendon Press, 1903.

Seven against Thebes

Dawson, Christopher M. *The Seven against Thebes*. Translated, with commentary. Prentice-Hall Greek Drama Series. Englewood Cliffs, N.J.: Prentice-Hall, 1970.

Tucker, T. G. *The "Seven against Thebes" of Aeschylus*. Greek text, edited, with commentary. Cambridge, Eng.: Cambridge University Press, 1908.

Verrall, A. W., and Bayfield, M. A. *The "Seven against Thebes" of Aeschylus*. Greek text, with introduction and notes. London: Macmillan, 1901.

Prometheus Bound

Sikes, E. E., and Willson, St. J. B. W. *Prometheus Vinctus*. Edited, with commentary. London: Macmillan, 1906.

Thomson, George. *The Prometheus Bound*. Edited, with commentary. Cambridge, Eng.: Cambridge University Press, 1932.

General Bibliography

Abel, D. Herbert. "Genealogies of Ethical Concepts." *Transactions of the American Philological Association* [*TAPA*] 74 (1943): 92–101.

Arnott, Peter. *Greek Scenic Conventions in the Fifth Century B.C.* Oxford: Clarendon Press, 1962.

Bain, David. "Audience Address in Greek Tragedy." *Classical Quarterly* n.s. 25 (1975): 13–25.

———. *Actors and Audiences: A Study of Asides and Related Conventions in Greek Drama.* Oxford: The University Press, 1977.

Barrett, W. S., ed. *"Hippolytus," by Euripides.* Oxford: Clarendon Press, 1964.

Becker, Otfrid. *Das Bild des Weges.* Hermes Einzelschriften no. 4. Berlin: Weidmann, 1937.

Bergson, Henri. "Laughter." Pp. 61–190 in *Comedy.* Edited and introduced by Wylie Sypher. New York: Doubleday/Anchor, 1956.

Bolton, James D. P. *Aristeas of Proconnesus.* Oxford: Clarendon Press, 1962.

Borthwick, E. K. "A 'Femme Fatale' in Asclepiades." *Classical Review* 17 (1967): 250–54.

Burkert, Walter. *Griechische Religion der archaischen und klassischen Epoche.* Stuttgart: W. Kohlhammer, 1977.

Burnett, Anne P. "Curse and Dream in Aeschylus' *Septem.*" *Greek, Roman and Byzantine Studies* 14 (1973): 343–68.

Burton, R. W. B. *The Chorus in Sophocles' Tragedies.* Oxford: Clarendon Press, 1980.

Caldwell, R. S. "The Psychology of Aeschylus' *Supplices.*" *Arethusa* 7 (1974): 45–70.

Clinton, Kevin. "Apollo, Pan, and Zeus, Avengers of Vultures: *Agamemnon* 55–59." *American Journal of Philology* 94 (1973): 282–88.

Conacher, D. J. "Aeschylus' *Persae*: A Literary Commentary." Pp. 143–68 in *Serta Turyniana,* edited by John L. Heller. Urbana: University of Illinois Press, 1974.

———. *Aeschylus' "Prometheus Bound": A Literary Commentary.* Toronto: University of Toronto Press, 1980.

Dale, A. M. "The Chorus in the Action of Greek Tragedy." Pp. 210–20 in *Collected Papers of A. M. Dale,* edited by T. B. L. Webster and E. G. Turner. London: Cambridge University Press, 1969.

Daremberg, Charles Victor, and Saglio, Edmond, eds. *Dictionnaire des antiquités grecques et romaines d'après les textes et les monuments.* 5 vols. in 9. Paris: Hachette, 1877–1919.

Dawe, R. D. "Inconsistency of Plot and Character in Aeschylus." *Proceedings of the Cambridge Philological Society* n.s. 9 (1963): 21–62.

———. *The Collation and Investigation of Manuscripts of Aeschylus.* Cambridge: The University Press, 1964.

Dietrich, B. C. *Death, Fate and the Gods.* London: Athlone Press, 1967.

Dodds, E. R. *The Greeks and the Irrational.* Sather Classical Lectures. Berkeley: University of California Press, 1951.

———. "Notes on the *Oresteia.*" *Classical Quarterly* n.s. 3 (1953): 11–21.

Dover, K. J. "The Political Aspect of Aeschylus' *Eumenides.*" *Journal of Hellenic Studies* 77 (1957): 230–37.

Doyle, Richard E. "Ὄλβος, Κότος, Ὕβρις, and Ἄτη from Hesiod to Aeschylus." *Traditio* 26 (1970): 283–303.

Eitrem, S. "Necromancy in the *Persae* of Aeschylus." *Symbolae Osloenses* 6 (1928): 1–16.

Else, Gerald F. *The Origin and Early Form of Greek Tragedy.* Martin Classical Lectures no. 20. Cambridge, Mass.: Harvard University Press, 1965.

———. "Ritual and Drama in Aischyleian Tragedy." Pp. 70–87 in *Illinois Classical Studies* no. 2 (1977).

Engelmann, Helmut. "Der Schiedsrichter aus der Fremde." *Rheinisches Museum* 110 (1967): 97–102.

Farnell, Lewis Richard. *The Cults of the Greek States.* 5 vols. Chicago: Aegean Press, 1971. (Reprint of the edition of 1896–1909.)

Flickinger, Roy D. *The Greek Theater and Its Drama.* 4th ed. Chicago: University of Chicago Press, 1968.

Fontenrose, Joseph. *Python: A Study of the Delphic Myth and Its Origins.* Berkeley: University of California Press, 1959.

Fowler, B. Hughes. "Aeschylus' Imagery." *Classica et Mediaevalia* 28 (1971): 1–74.

———. "The Imagery of the *Prometheus Bound.*" *American Journal of Philology* 78 (1957): 173–84.

———. "The Imagery of the *Seven against Thebes.*" *Symbolae Osloenses* 45 (1970): 24–37.

Gagarin, Michael. *Aeschylean Drama*. Berkeley: University of California Press, 1976.

Garton, Charles. "Characterization in Greek Tragedy." *Journal of Hellenic Studies* 77 (1957): 247–54.

Garvie, A. F. "Aeschylus' Simple Plots." Pp. 63–86 in *Dio-nysiaca: Nine Studies in Greek Poetry Presented to Denys Page on His Seventieth Birthday*. Edited by R. D. Dawe, J. Diggle, and P. E. Easterling. Cambridge: Cambridge Faculty Library, 1978.

———. *Aeschylus' "Supplices": Play and Trilogy*. London: Cambridge University Press, 1969.

Goheen, Robert F. "Aspects of Dramatic Symbolism: Three Studies in the *Oresteia*." *American Journal of Philology* 76 (1955): 113–37.

Golden, Leon. "The Character of Eteocles and the Meaning of the *Septem*." *Classical Philology* 59 (1964): 79–89.

Goodell, Thomas D. "Structural Variety in Attic Tragedy." *Transactions of the American Philological Association* [*TAPA*] 41 (1910): 71–98.

Gould, John. "Dramatic Character and 'Human Intelligibility' in Greek Tragedy." *Proceedings of the Cambridge Philological Society* n.s. 24 (1978): 43–67.

Grene, David. "*Prometheus Bound*." *Classical Philology* 35 (1940): 22–38.

Griffith Mark. *The Authenticity of the "Prometheus Bound."* Cambridge and New York: Cambridge University Press, 1977.

Guépin, J.-P. *The Tragic Paradox: Myth and Ritual in Greek Tragedy*. Amsterdam: Hakkert, 1968.

Guthrie, W. K. C. *The Greeks and Their Gods*. Boston: Beacon Press, 1951.

Haldane, J. A. "Musical Themes and Imagery in Aeschylus." *Journal of Hellenic Studies* 85 (1965): 33–41.

Hammond, N. G. L. "The Conditions of Dramatic Production to the Death of Aeschylus." *Greek, Roman and Byzantine Studies* 13 (1972): 387–450.

Harrison, Jane. *Prolegomena to the Study of Greek Religion*. 3d ed. New York: Meridian Books, 1955. (Reprint of Cambridge University Press edition of 1922.)

————. *Themis*. Cambridge, Eng.: Cambridge University Press, 1912.

Headlam, Walter. *See* Thomson, George, *The Oresteia*.

Heilman, Robert B. *Tragedy and Melodrama: Versions of Experience*. Seattle: University of Washington Press, 1968.

Heinimann, Felix. *Nomos und Physis*. Basel: Friedrich Reinhardt Verlags, 1945.

Herington, C. J. "The Influence of Old Comedy on Aeschylus' Later Trilogies." *Transactions of the American Philological Association* [*TAPA*] 94 (1963): 113–23.

Housman, A. E. "Fragment of a Greek Tragedy." *Cornhill Magazine* n.s. 10 (1901): 443.

Italie, G. *Index Aeschyleus*. 2d ed., edited by S. L. Radt. Leiden: Brill, 1964.

Jens, W. "Strukturgesetze der frühen griechischen Tragödie." *Studium Generale* 8 (1955): 246–53.

Jones, John. *On Aristotle and Greek Tragedy*. New York: Oxford University Press, 1962.

Kamerbeek, J. C. "On the Concept of ΘΕΟΜΑΧΟΣ in Relation with Greek Tragedy." *Mnemosyne* 4th ser. 1 (1948): 271–83.

Kirkwood, Gordon M. "Eteocles Oiakostrophos." *Phoenix* 23 (1969): 9–25.

Kitto, H. D. F. *Form and Meaning in Drama: A Study of Six Greek Plays and of "Hamlet."* New York: Barnes & Noble, 1960.

————. *Greek Tragedy*. London: Methuen, 1939; New York: Anchor Press edition, 1954.

Knox, Bernard M. W. "Aeschylus and the Third Actor." *American Journal of Philology* 93 (1972): 104–24.

————. "The Lion in the House (*Agamemnon* 717–36)." *Classical Philology* 47 (1952): 12–25.

Koniaris, G. L., and Tyrrell, W. B. "An Obscene Word in Aeschylus." *American Journal of Philology* 101 (1980): 42–46.

Kranz, Walther. *Stasimon*. Berlin: Weidmann, 1933.

Lattimore, Richmond. "Aeschylus on the Defeat of Xerxes." Pp. 82–93 in *Classical Studies in Honor of W. A. Oldfather*. Urbana: University of Illinois Press, 1943.

————. *The Poetry of Greek Tragedy*. Baltimore: Johns Hopkins University Press, 1958.

———. *Story Patterns in Greek Tragedy*. Ann Arbor: University of Michigan Press, 1964.

Lebeck, Ann. "The First Stasimon of Aeschylus' *Choephori*: Myth and Mirror Image." *Classical Philology* 62 (1967): 182–85.

———. *The "Oresteia": A Study in Language and Structure*. Cambridge, Mass.: Harvard University Press; London: Oxford University Press, 1971.

Lesky, Albin. "Der Kommos der *Choephoren*." *Sitzungsberichte der österreichischen Akademie der Wissenschaft in Wien, philosophische-historische Klasse* 221, pt. 3 (1943): 3–130.

Liddell, Henry George, and Scott, Robert. *A Greek-English Lexicon*. 9th ed. Revised and augmented by Henry Stuart Jones and Roderick McKenzie. Oxford: Clarendon Press, 1940.

Lloyd-Jones, Hugh. "Zeus in Aeschylus." *Journal of Hellenic Studies* 76 (1956): 55–67.

———. "The End of the *Seven against Thebes*." *Classical Quarterly* n.s. 9 (1959): 80–114.

———. "The *Supplices* of Aeschylus: The New Date and the Old Problem." *L'Antiquité Classique* 33 (1964): 356–74.

———. *The Justice of Zeus*. Sather Classical Lectures no. 41. Berkeley and Los Angeles: University of California Press, 1971.

Long, Herbert S. "Notes on Aeschylus' *Prometheus Bound*." *Proceedings of the American Philosophical Society* 102 (1958): 229–80.

McCall, Marsh. "The Secondary Choruses in Aeschylus' *Supplices*." *California Studies in Classical Antiquity* 9 (1977): 117–31.

MacDowell, D. M. *The Law in Classical Athens*. Ithaca: Cornell University Press, 1978.

Manton, G. R. "The Second Stasimon of the *Seven against Thebes*." *Bulletin of the Institute of Classical Studies, The University of London* 8 (1961): 77–84.

Maxwell-Stuart, P. G. "The Appearance of Aeschylus' Erinyes." *Greece and Rome* 20 (1973): 81–84.

Murray, R. D., Jr. *The Motif of Io in Aeschylus' "Suppliants."* Princeton: Princeton University Press, 1958.

Nilsson, Martin Persson. *A History of Greek Religion*. 2d ed.

Translated by F. J. Fielden. Oxford: Clarendon Press, 1925. (I have cited the Norton Library reprint, New York, 1964.)

———. *Greek Popular Religion*. New York: Columbia University Press, 1940.

———. *Greek Piety*. Translated by Herbert Jennings Rose. London: Oxford University Press, 1948. (I have cited the Norton Library reprint, New York, 1969.)

Onians, R. B. *The Origins of European Thought about the Body, the Mind, the Soul, the World, Time and Fate*. Cambridge, Eng.: University Press, 1951. (I have cited the Arno Press reprint, New York, 1973.)

Parke, H. W. *Festivals of the Athenians*. London: Thames & Hudson, 1977.

Peradotto, John J. "Some Patterns of Nature Imagery in the *Oresteia*." *American Journal of Philology* 85 (1964): 378–93.

———. "The Omen of the Eagles and the ἦθος of Agamemnon." *Phoenix* 23 (1969): 237–63.

Petrounias, Evangelos. *Funktion und Thematik der Bilder bei Aischylos*. Hypomnemata no. 48. Göttingen: Vandenhoeck & Ruprecht, 1976.

Pickard-Cambridge, Arthur. *The Theatre of Dionysus in Athens*. Oxford: Clarendon Press, 1946.

———. *Dithyramb, Tragedy, and Comedy*. 2d ed., revised by T. B. L. Webster. Oxford: Clarendon Press, 1962.

———. *The Dramatic Festivals of Athens*. 2d ed., revised by John Gould and D. M. Lewis. London: Oxford University Press, 1968.

Podlecki, Anthony. *The Political Background of Aeschylean Tragedy*. Ann Arbor: University of Michigan Press, 1966.

———. "Reciprocity in *Prometheus Bound*." *Greek, Roman and Byzantine Studies* 10 (1969): 287–92.

Rohde, Erwin. *Psyche*. Translated by W. B. Hillis. New York: Harcourt, Brace, 1925.

Rosenmeyer, Thomas. *The Masks of Tragedy*. Berkeley: University of California Press, 1961.

Rösler, W. *Reflexe vorsokratischen Denkens bei Aischylos*. Beiträge zur klassischen Philologie no. 37. Meisenheim am Glan: Anton Hain, 1970.

Sansone, David. *Aeschylean Metaphors for Intellectual Activity*. Wiesbaden: Franz Steiner, 1975.

Schweizer-Keller, Regala. *Vom Umgang des Aischylos mit der Sprache*. Aarau: Sauerländer, 1972.

Scott, William C. "The Mesode at *Persae* 93–100." *Greek, Roman and Byzantine Studies* 9 (1968): 259–60.

———. "Lines for Clytemnestra (*Agamemnon* 489–501)." *Transactions of the American Philological Association* [*TAPA*] 108 (1978): 259–70.

Sideras, Alexander. *Aeschylus Homericus*. Hypomnemata no. 31. Göttingen: Vandenhoeck & Ruprecht, 1971.

Silk, M. S. *Interaction in Poetic Imagery*. London and New York: Cambridge University Press, 1974.

Smith, Ole. "Some Observations on the Structure of Imagery in Aeschylus." *Classica et Mediaevalia* 26 (1965): 10–72.

Smith, Peter. *On the Hymn to Zeus in Aeschylus' "Agamemnon."* American Classical Studies no. 5. Ann Arbor, 1980.

Smyth, H. W. *Aeschylean Tragedy*. Berkeley: University of California Press, 1924.

Snell, Bruno, ed. *Pindari Carmina cum Fragmentis*. 2d ed. Leipzig: Teubner, 1955.

Solmsen, Friedrich. "The Erinys in Aischylos' *Septem*." *Transactions of the American Philological Association* [*TAPA*] 68 (1947): 197–211.

Stanford, W. B. *Greek Metaphor*. Oxford: Basil Blackwell, 1936.

———. *Ambiguity in Greek Literature*. Oxford, Basil Blackwell, 1939.

———. *Aeschylus in His Style*. Dublin: The University Press, 1942.

Taplin, Oliver. *The Stagecraft of Aeschylus*. Oxford: Clarendon Press, 1977.

Tarkow, T. A. "The Dilemma of Pelasgus and the Nautical Imagery of Aeschylus' *Suppliants*." *Classica et Mediaevalia* 31 (1970): 1–13.

Tarrant, D. "Greek Metaphors of Light." *Classical Quarterly* n.s. 10 (1960): 181–87.

Thalman, W. G. *Dramatic Art in Aeschylus' "Seven against Thebes."* New Haven: Yale University Press, 1978.

Verdenius, W. J. "Notes on the *Prometheus Bound*." Pp. 451–70 in *Miscellanea Tragica in Honorem J. C. Kamerbeek*. Edited by J. C. Bremer et al. Amsterdam: Hakkert, 1976.

Vickers, Brian. *Towards Greek Tragedy*. London: Longmans, 1973.

Wartelle, André. *Bibiliographie historique et critique d'Eschyle*. Paris: Société d'édition Les Belles Lettres, 1978.

Webster, T. B. L., and Trendall, A. D. *Illustrations of Greek Drama*. London: Phaidon, 1971.

Whallon, William. *Problem and Spectacle: Studies in the "Oresteia."* Heidelberg: C. Winter, 1980.

Wilamowitz-Moellendorff, U. von. *Aischylos: Interpretationen*. Berlin: Weidmann, 1914.

Winnington-Ingram, R. P. "*Choephori* 691–9 (687–95)." *Classical Review* 60 (1946): 58–60.

———. "Clytemnestra and the Vote of Athena." *Journal of Hellenic Studies* 68 (1948): 130–47.

———. "Aeschylus, *Agamemnon* 1343–1371." *Classical Quarterly* n.s. 4 (1954): 23–30.

———. "The Danaid Trilogy of Aeschylus." *Journal of Hellenic Studies* 81 (1961): 141–52.

———. "Zeus in the *Persae*." *Journal of Hellenic Studies* 93 (1973): 162–68.

———. "Notes on the *Agamemnon* of Aeschylus." *Bulletin of the Institute of Classical Studies, The University of London* 21 (1974): 3–19.

———. "The Delphic Temple in Greek Tragedy." Pp. 483–500 in *Miscellanea Tragica in Honorem J. C. Kamerbeek*. Edited by J. C. Bremer et al. Amsterdam: Hakkert, 1976.

———. "*Septem contra Thebas*." *Yale Classical Studies* 25 (1977):1–46.

Zeitlin, Froma I. "The Motif of the Corrupted Sacrifice in Aeschylus' *Oresteia*." *Transactions of the American Philological Association* [*TAPA*] 96 (1965): 463–508.

———. "Postscript to Sacrificial Imagery in the *Oresteia*." *Transactions of the American Philological Association* 97 [*TAPA*] (1966): 645–53.

SUBJECT INDEX

THIS INDEX is selective rather than complete. It is keyed to notes in the commentary where definitions, examples, problems, further references, and longer discussions will be found. Separate indexes, also selective, are provided for common proper names and for the Greek words discussed.

INDEX OF PROPER NAMES